Continental
Humanist
Poetics

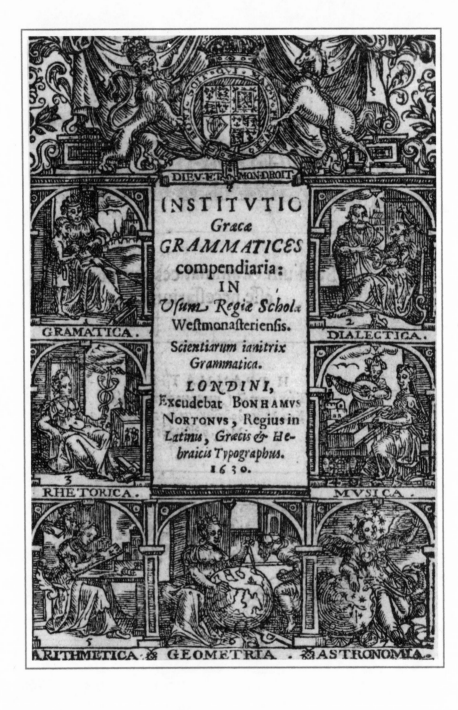

DIEV·ET·MON·DROIT

INSTITVTIO
Graecae
GRAMMATICES
compendiaria:
IN
Vsum Regiae Scholae
Westmonasteriensis.

Scientiarum ianitrix
Grammatica.

LONDINI,
Excudebat BONHAMVS
NORTONVS, Regius in
Latinis, Graecis & He-
braicis Typographus.
1630.

GRAMATICA.

DIALECTICA.

RHETORICA.

MVSICA.

ARITHMETICA. GEOMETRIA. ASTRONOMIA.

Continental
Humanist Poetics

STUDIES IN ERASMUS, CASTIGLIONE,

MARGUERITE DE NAVARRE,

RABELAIS, AND

CERVANTES

ARTHUR F. KINNEY

THE UNIVERSITY OF MASSACHUSETTS PRESS

AMHERST

Copyright © 1989 by The University of Massachusetts Press
All rights reserved
Printed in the United States of America
Designed by Barbara Werden
Set in Linotron Garamond No. 3 at G&S Typesetters, Inc.
Printed by Thomson-Shore and bound by John Dekker & Sons.

Library of Congress Cataloging-in-Publication Data

Kinney, Arthur F., 1933–
Continental humanist poetics : studies in Erasmus, Castiglione,
Marguerite de Navarre, Rabelais, and Cervantes / Arthur F. Kinney.
p.   cm.
Bibliography: p.
Includes index.
ISBN 0–87023–665–2
1. European literature—Renaissance, 1450–1600—History and
criticism.   2. European literature—17th century—History and
criticism.   3. Humanism in literature.   I. Title.
PN721.K5   1989
809'.894—dc19   88–24992
                                   CIP

British Library Cataloguing in Publication data is available.

This publication has been supported by the National Endowment for the
Humanities, a federal agency which supports the study of such fields as
history, literature, and language.

Frontispiece: Mason M.5. Used with permission of the Curators of
the Bodleian Library

FOR THE EDITORS AND STAFF OF

English Literary Renaissance,

PAST AND PRESENT

ALSO BY ARTHUR F. KINNEY

Titled Elizabethans: A Directory of State and Church Officers in
England, Scotland, and Wales, 1558–1603

Elizabethan Backgrounds: Historical Documents in the
Age of Elizabeth I

Markets of Bawdrie: The Dramatic Criticism of Stephen Gosson

Rogues, Vagabonds, and Sturdy Beggars

H. R.'s *Mythomystes*

Rhetoric and Poetic in Thomas More's *Utopia*

John Skelton: The Priest as Poet

Humanist Poetics: Thought, Rhetoric, and Fiction in
Sixteenth-Century England

Essential Articles for the Study of Sir Philip Sidney
(editor)

Sidney in Retrospect: Selections from *English Literary Renaissance*
(editor)

Nicholas Hilliard's *The Art of Limning*
(with Linda Bradley Salamon)

Sir Philip Sidney: 1576 and the Making of a Legend
(with Dominic Baker-Smith and Jan Van Dorsten)

Renaissance Historicism: Selections from *English Literary Renaissance*
(editor with Dan S. Collins)

Men are moved not by things but by the views which
they take of them.

EPICTETUS

Now before we use, either to write, or speak eloquently, we
must dedicate our myndes wholy, to followe the most wise and
learned men and seeke to fashion as wel their speache and
gesturing, as their witte or endyting. The which when we
earnestly mynd to doe, we can not but in time appere
somewhat like them. . . . By companying with the wise,
a man shall learne wisedome.

THOMAS WILSON
The Arte of Rhetorique

CONTENTS

PREFACE

MICHEL FOUCAULT writes in *Les mots et les choses,* translated as *The Order of Things: An Archaeology of the Human Sciences,* that "The fundamental codes of a culture—those governing its language, its schemas of perception, its exchanges, its techniques, its values, the hierarchy of its practices—establish for every man, from the very first, the empirical orders with which he will be dealing and within which he will be at home." Nowhere is this truer than in the codes—antique, Neoplatonic, Reformist Christian—that characterize the European Renaissance. Throughout the decade and more during which I was researching and writing *Humanist Poetics: Thought, Rhetoric, and Fiction in Sixteenth-Century England,* I was increasingly aware of how closely English humanist poetics was allied to its Continental roots, how the humanist movement was almost from the start a consciously international movement, and how much practitioners of English thought, rhetoric, and fiction owed to their Continental forebears and contemporaries. *Continental Humanist Poetics* seems, therefore, to be the natural and necessary counterpart to my earlier study.

At the same time that the powerfully sweeping "archaeologies" established by Foucault help to locate the various forces in a culture that collocate to establish an identifiable *episteme,* he is also quick to point out, as he does in *The Archaeology of Knowledge,* the *breaks* in history that prevent any linear tracing of events, any study of progress or development in a unilateral way; he speaks of the "discontinuity, rupture, threshold, limit, series, and transformation" that characterize his and other current studies of history. For Foucault, who here expands the term *document* to include all material objects, no single object—his keenest example is the book—has a single, final unity. All are subject to shift and change, to disassemblage and reassemblage, to continuous atomization and fragmentation, recombination and fusion. To illustrate his sense of sharp breaks in history (as we can best recover them from our own limited and necessarily prejudiced viewpoints) and his sense of the culture in flux, he cites one of my examples here, Cervantes' *Don Quijote.* Like nearly everyone else, he views the *Quijote* (as I will not) as an example of rupture.

> *Don Quixote* is the first modern work of literature, because in it we see the cruel
> reason of identities and differences make endless sport of signs and similitudes;

xi

because in it language breaks off its old kinship with things and enters into that lonely sovereignty from which it will reappear, in its separated state, only as literature; because it marks the point where resemblance enters an age which is, from the point of view of resemblance, one of madness and imagination. Once similitude and signs are sundered from each other, two experiences can be established and two characters appear face to face. The madman, understood not as one who is sick but as an established and maintained deviant, as an indispensable cultural function, has become, in Western experience, the man of primitive resemblances. This character, as he is depicted in the novels or plays of the Baroque age, and as he was gradually institutionalized right up to the advent of nineteenth-century psychiatry, is the man who is *alienated* in *analogy*. He is the disordered player of the Same and the Other. He takes things for what they are not, and people one for another; he cuts his friends and recognizes complete strangers; he thinks he is unmasking when, in fact, he is putting on a mask. He inverts all values and all proportions, because he is constantly under the impression that he is deciphering signs: for him, the crown makes the king. In the cultural perception of the madman that prevailed up to the end of the eighteenth century, he is Different only in so far as he is unaware of Difference; he sees nothing but resemblances and signs of resemblances everywhere; for him all signs resemble one another, and all resemblances have the value of signs. At the other end of the cultural area, but brought close by symmetry, the poet is he who, beneath the named, constantly expected differences, rediscovers the buried kinships between things, their scattered resemblances. Beneath the established signs, and in spite of them, he hears another, deeper, discourse, which recalls the time when words glittered in the universal resemblance of things; in the language of the poet, the Sovereignty of the Same, so difficult to express, eclipses the distinction existing between signs.

Here our best modern historian of madness and civilization displays his own cultural bias both in his concern with semiotics and (like that of current Marxist critics) with master narratives (and dominant ideologies that marginalize those who are not easily contained otherwise). Cervantes was concerned with deviance, with madness and its relationship to the imagination and poetry, and with *significatio*—or what his character takes to be significant signs because they interpret the landscape and his adventures so as to help him make sense of them (as men have done at least since the beginning of recorded history). But the Don is not, in the end, marginalized; rather, he becomes the central concern of those around him, and he influences them far more than they influence him. If we look at Cervantes' grand novel in connection with its own time instead of ours—in connection both with its filiation with the tradition of antique and humanist poetics from which it sprang and its affiliations with post-Armada Spain, to use Freudian terms made popular by Edward W. Said— then we shall see quite a different work. *El Ingenioso Hidalgo* (with its play on *genius* and *ingenious*) draws heavily on the humanist concern with imitation, the humanist form of dialectic, and the humanist *technē* of paradoxy introduced by Erasmus in the *Encomium Moriae,* to which *Don Quijote* is frequently indebted (and not just in scenes with Sancho Panza). We can say—and I think we ought to say—that Cervantes' masterpiece, for all its energy and individuality, is the outgrowth and, in many ways, the culmination of a humanist poetics that had characterized the best creative work of the Continental Renaissance for a century. This is not to argue that *Don Quijote* does not sustain and in some instances introduce characteristics that will become central to the later development of the Western novel; but it does not break so sharply with its past nor its present, as Foucault would have it. And without claiming a single line of unbroken and steady development in the poetics brought about by humanism—its fits and starts are mirrored in my choosing individual texts rather than tracing a gradual growth—I think the *Quijote* is best seen, most *transparently* witnessed, when we look at Cervantes' resources and what he did with them.

Humanist Poetics argued that the humanist concerns with the dignity and educability of man were promulgated through a rhetorically based poetic that stemmed directly from the ideas and examples in the antique texts the humanists recovered and made their central study. Surely no recovered text, any more than a recovered age for Foucault, is necessarily fixed and stable. But in the high age of rhetoric and, I think, of poetic, some clear masters—Erasmus, Rabelais, and Cervantes among them—saw a way to use such texts to fashion a humanist poetics that even at its most paradoxical and equivocating could help them explore, test, and validate the ideals and beliefs of humanism. In time the idealistic concerns of humanism would seem increasingly less valid to a humanist poetics concerned more and more with equivalent multiplicity of meaning and with the complicity of the reader, but in the age in which it flourished it provided extraordinary, and extraordinarily significant, works of literature that reveal for us many of the attitudes not only of Renaissance civilization but of the antique civilization as they rediscovered it. *Continental Humanist Poetics* attempts to study the Renaissance humanist movement through five key texts by five major writers that will help us not only to understand their culture as they saw it (insofar as we are able to ascertain that) but further to understand how their rhetorical and poetic art gave form and substance to a new and vital form of art. Moving out of antique epic and romance, they also founded what we know as the novel.

As with my earlier study, I am indebted to many foundations and colleagues for help and guidance—for direction and admonition—along the way. I first tested my ideas on Erasmus, Castiglione, and Rabelais in a course of public lectures at Oxford University during Trinity term 1977, and many who heard me—among them D. H. Craig, Nicholas Jose, David Norbrook, and Henry Woudhuysen—have been helpful and encouraging. I have been aided immeasurably by two year-long Senior Fellowships from the National Endowment for the Humanities, by two Huntington Library Senior Fellowships, by a Folger Library Fellowship, by a Fulbright-Hays Research Fellowship, by grants-in-aid from the American Philosophical Society, and by a University Research Award and paid and unpaid leaves from the University of Massachusetts at Amherst. Much of my initial study was done in Europe, particularly at the Bodleian Library, the British Library, and the libraries of the University of Cambridge, the University of Liverpool, the University of Leiden, and The Hague; it was continued and completed using the libraries of Harvard, Yale, and Cornell Universities and the University of Massachusetts, Amherst.

A study that has taken so much of my attention for so long a time has also involved the attention—whether they wished it or not—of many of my colleagues and students, and I have tried to make particular cases of indebtedness clear in my citations and comments. But I have been informed by so many on so many occasions that I can no longer recall them all or even when a specific idea first came to mind; I do remember, however, the decisive aid of Stanley Fish, Jackson Cope, and A. Leigh De Neef at the outset and of A. J. Krailsheimer and Ann L. Mackenzie near the end. Over the years, *Continental Humanist Poetics* has been the subject of individual lectures at the following institutions: Amherst College; University of Arizona at Tucson; Brandeis University; Brown University; University of California at Irvine and Santa Barbara; Duke University; Emory University; University of Florida at Gainesville; University of Maryland; University of New Mexico; University of North Carolina at Chapel Hill and Greensboro; University of Nottingham; Rice University; Smith College; University of South Carolina; University of Texas at Austin and El Paso; Tulane University; and Vanderbilt University; and I am indebted to the administrations and to the audiences at each of them. The editors and staff of *English Literary Renaissance,* to whom this book is dedicated, have excused me from responsibilities for three prolonged absences, and I offer this to them, if only in partial recompense. Previous versions of parts of this book, in different form, have appeared elsewhere, and I am grateful to the editors of *ELH* and of the publications of the UCLA Center for Medieval and Renaissance Studies for allowing me to reuse them here. I have also reworked and incorporated passages from *Humanist Poetics* where it seemed appropriate and useful, in part to suggest a kind of seamlessness between that work and this one.

Finally, I wish to acknowledge the help of Warren D. Anderson, as always my companion and mentor, my editors Richard Martin, Barbara Palmer, and Pam Wilkinson, and the designer Barbara Werden, Edward Curran, Derek Alwes, whose reliable proofreading came at a critical time, and Eugene D. Hill for help with the Index.

A NOTE ON THE TEXTS

A CONTEXTUAL and developmental study such as the present one needs to strike some sort of balance between the texts used by the writers under discussion and texts accessible to present-day readers. Wherever possible, therefore, I have made citations and references to the first editions of the sixteenth and early seventeenth centuries (including the earliest English translations) so as to capture insofar as possible the humanist community that wrote and read them.

With few exceptions, Loeb translations of classical texts have been used; specific translators and editions are given in the notes.

Continental
Humanist
Poetics

ONE

Poema rhetoricum et rhetor poeticus: The Forming of a Continental Humanist Poetics

"PERHAPS THE MOST CHAR-
ACTERISTIC FEATURE OF THE
SIXTEENTH CENTURY IS ITS BOUND-
LESS ENTHUSIASM," A. J.
KRAILSHEIMER WRITES; "NEITHER IN
THOUGHT NOR DEED DID MEN (OR WOMEN)
do things by halves."[1] The Continental Renaissance that he is describing—at once boldly searching, dramatically self-conscious, endlessly energetic—now seems to us almost legendary in its many stunning accomplishments. Yet persistently at the center of such activity, of such achievements, is what Krailsheimer calls "a prodigious appetite for learning" (p. 21). The contagious desire of men and women to study classical texts, many of them freshly discovered, and the urgent desire to know and apply antique thought to their own culture—the New Learning—is apparent wherever we turn, in Quattrocento and Cinquecento Italy, in France, in Germany, the Low Countries, and Spain. Their drive to study—for personal advancement, for service to a civilization they reinvigorated and were reshaping, for its own sake—seems insatiable. Even so untutored and so unlikely a person as the young Thomas Platter, as indelibly limned by Lucien Febvre, is a revealing pointer for his age.

> One day, when he was eighteen, Thomas Platter came to Sélestat. He could barely read. He went to the famous school of Johannes Sapidus. With a heroic effort he tried to clear the heavy layer of cobwebs from his brain. He carried on single combat with the Latin grammar of Donatus. Soon he was employed as a teacher, half tutor, half valet, to the two sons of a bourgeois family. During the day he served his masters. At night, he studied alone, fighting sleep by putting cold water or raw turnips or pebbles in his mouth to put his teeth on edge so that he would wake immediately should he doze off. In this way he taught himself

Latin, Greek, and a bit of Hebrew. His entire fortune consisted of a single gold coin which he spent without regret on a Hebrew Bible to be devoured in silence. But he had to earn his living and the duties of a private tutor did not please him. In Basle he became a rope-maker. At about the same time and in the same place the great and courageous Sebastion Castellion, who proclaimed the coming reign of toleration to Calvin's face, was earning his living by pulling out of the river Birse the logs which the rushing current carried down from the mountains on days of high water. In his spare time, Castellion translated the Bible.

Platter, under the direction of a coarse and brutal master rope-maker, learned the trade. At night, he rose secretly and lighted a sputtering candle. By its uncertain light, and with the help of a Latin trot, he learned to read Homer in Greek. In the morning, he returned to his ropes. The strange workman did not pass unnoticed in Basle. One day the poor manual worker, Platter, engaged in his trade at Saint Peter's Square where he was helping to make a thick rope, was stopped in his work by none other than Beatus Rhenanus, the great Alsatian Humanist. He too was a simple man, one of those open and hard-working good giants of the early Renaissance. And, on another day, at the same spot, another man could be seen, a shrunken little fellow, almost lost in his great coat, Mister Desiderius Erasmus in person, the greatest, the prince, the king of Humanists. Like Rhenanus, he too offered Platter a more comfortable way of earning his living, a position as tutor. Platter refused. Like Zwingli, to mention only one example, Platter had a touching respect for manual labor. A little later another strange scene took place in Basle. Oporinus, the great printer, had also come to Platter and had obtained from him the promise that each day for an hour Platter would teach him Hebrew. Platter came to keep his promise. But in the agreed-upon place he found not Oporinus alone, but twenty people, learned men, pastors, magistrates, doctors, and even a Frenchman rich enough to have a silk cape and his own servant. The poor rope-maker was intimidated by this gathering and wanted to flee. Oporinus persuaded him to remain, to sit, to teach. And from then on, every evening he could be seen in that room, seated near the warmth of the pottery stove in his leather workman's apron, his hands covered with calluses and sometimes bloody from his work, with his coarse, unkempt, bearded peasant's face, doing his best to teach those who gathered to learn what he knew: Hebrew.

Caught up himself by such staunch and costly dedication, Febvre continues:

Nor was this a unique case. The times abounded in men like that, wholly possessed by an epic thirst for learning. Toward 1471 we find Jean Standonck walking from Gouda to Paris (a distance of 400 miles) in the hope of getting a scholarship to one of those convents where the students suffered constantly from cold, dirt, and hunger. The canons regular of Sainte-Geneviève took him in as a servant. During the day he worked in the kitchen and at night he learned. As he was sometimes too poor to buy a candle, he found that if he climbed the bell tower at night he could read by the rays of the moon, gratis. And in the same way later, Guillaume Postel, the great orientalist of mid-century, was a servant at the Collège de Navarre and taught himself Greek and Hebrew at night. Still later we find Peter Ramus the valet of a rich student who, likewise, spent his nights in study and prepared, one by one, all the examinations so that he became, finally, director of the Collège de Presles.

Others, from more comfortable backgrounds, were formally schooled with a similar vigor. Febvre cites "Henry de Mesmes, at thirteen, studying at the Collège de Toulouse, [who] got up every day at four, and having said his prayers, went to class at five, his books under one arm, a candle and lapboard under the other. Course followed course, from five until ten without a break. Then there was lunch, followed by recreational reading of Sophocles or Aristophanes or Euripides, perhaps a bit of Demosthenes, Cicero, Virgil, or Horace. At one, classes began again until five. The hour before dinner was spent going over the work of the day. At six there was dinner and another recreational reading period, reading Greek or Latin. Such was the life of youth bereft of tenderness or special handling; such was the thirst for learning in a harsh age," [2] a thirst made central by Rabelais and even transcendent by Erasmus in two major works of Continental humanist fiction that seek to comprehend just such an age.

Still, the cause of this enormous excitement is not far to seek, for it was generated, time and again, by the antique texts that such men studied, in luxury or hardship, which assured them repeatedly of the dignity of human nature, the potentiality of man, even his *perfectibility*. Such resplendent praise of man has countless classical roots, of course—the myth of Prometheus and the second chorus of the *Antigone* of Sophocles are only two of these better known—but the heightened sense of man and of his capacities owes much of its instigating force to Florentine philosophy as well. The Continental humanists' fundamental premise concerning the inherent dignity of man developed by Plotinus and later Greek philosophers, along with their notions of natural law and the solidarity of mankind, is the basis of the influential work of Marsilio Ficino. His syncretic and synergistic thinking sought out in the ideal Forms of

Plato a basis for the ideality of man himself. "Turning his back on the Aristotelian logic of the [medieval] Schools," Krailsheimer sums,

> Ficino sought to reconcile religion and philosophy, that is Christian and pagan, through a kind of mysticism in which Plato himself was not really distinguished from Plotinus, Proclus or even the pseudo-Dionysius, who has exercised an extraordinary influence on Christian mystics through the ages. All the emphasis is on synthesis, on the oneness of the vision and the truth. The curious cosmology of the *Timaeus* and above all the *Symposium*'s teaching on love were of enormous importance through the next century because of Ficino's translations, commentaries and his grand synthesis in the *Theologia Platonica*.
>
> [*Continental Renaissance*, p. 24]

In this massive work of 1482, Ficino insists on man's capacities derived from the human mind and its fundamental affinity with God. The soul, he writes, tends to know all of truth and to attain all goodness; it tries to become all things, *including* God. But even though the soul is not actually able to attain the Godhead, Ficino claims, its glory is its diversity; if God alone actually *remains* all things, man's soul tends to *become* all things (*Theologia Platonica* 14.2−5).

The earliest important English humanists, William Grocyn and John Colet, studied the works of Ficino; Colet corresponded with him;[3] and Thomas More translated the life of Ficino's protégé Pico della Mirandola from the original biography by Pico's nephew. And it is Pico who extends still further Ficino's ideas into a memorable fable that must have lingered in the minds of many of the first generations of Continental and English humanists. It is presented in the prolegomenon to Pico's *Oration* of 1486, the undelivered speech he had prepared to defend his 900 theses, which he claimed contained all that was known and written—in antiquity and since—on man and the universe. Paul Oskar Kristeller sums Pico's fable this way:

> When the creation of the whole universe had been completed, the Creator decided to add a being capable of meditating on the reasons of the world, loving its beauty, and admiring its greatness. Thus He understood the creation of man. All gifts had by then been distributed among the other creatures. . . . Hence, the Creator decided that the being for which nothing had been left as its peculiar property might in turn have a share of all the gifts that had first been assigned singly to the various other beings. Man, therefore, has no clearly determined essence or nature. He is neither celestial nor earthly, neither mortal nor immortal. On the contrary, he may become all of this through his own will. The Creator

gave him the germs of every sort of life. Depending on whatever potentiality he develops, he may become a plant, an animal, a celestial being, an angel, or he may even be unified with God Himself. Man therefore possesses all possibilities within himself. It is his task to overcome the lower forms of life and to elevate himself toward God.[4]

This incredible vision—it is nothing less than Jacob's ladder of ascending and descending angels, with man displacing the inhabitants of Heaven—is likewise a root cause of the humanists' exuberance and optimism.

But there was also another, more practical Plato to whom Italian humanists turned only a decade or two later. We must not forget Plato's meditative trilogy on government, the *Republic,* the *Statesman,* and the *Laws,* and their concern with good rulers, with education, with the cultivation of virtue rather than war, and with proper leadership to guarantee a stable society. And Pico's ideas concerning the nature of man were considerably furthered and modified by the Aristotelian Pietro Pomponazzi in his *Tractatus de immortalitate animae,* his treatise on the soul's immortality, of 1516. Whereas the Platonists of Florence had taught that the goal of human life is ascension toward contemplation and God, Pomponazzi argues that this goal is attainable only in a future life; it follows, then, that during his mortal life man should concentrate on earthly affairs and behavior. His focus should be the daily routine of this life as propaedeutic, his thought and behavior as proleptic. In this way, the dignity of man would be maintained and man's earthbound life invested with greater intrinsic value. Man should not depend on any hopes or fears for the future, according to Pomponazzi, but should instead concentrate on an ethical life where virtue is its own reward, vice its own punishment (14).[5]

Such *embracing* of classical writers, however, such *familiarity* with them, actually began a century and a half earlier with Petrarch's discovery in 1333 of Cicero's *Pro Archia poeta* in Liège and, twelve years later, a manuscript of Cicero's *Epistulae ad Atticum* and *Ad Quintum fratrem* and the *Ad Brutum* (6–18) in Verona. Although these were only the first in a remarkable series of rediscovered Greek and Roman texts, discoveries that would continue through Salutati (1331–1406), who found Cicero's *Epistolae ad familiares,* and his protégé Poggio Bracciolini (1380–1459), who unearthed Quintilian's *Institutio Oratoria* and many other key works, Petrarch nevertheless remains today, as he did for the humanists, the epitome of the humanist scholar and student. In a letter to Luca da Penna, the papal secretary, in early 1374, he notes that from his very childhood, when other boys were yawning their way through Prosper or Aesop, he fell in love with Cicero either by instinct or through the urging of his father.[6] In an earlier letter of 1359 to Boccaccio he describes the life of an exemplary humanist.

> Virgilio, Orazio, Tito Livio, Cicerone non una volta, ma mille lessi e rilessi, ne già correndo, ma a piè fermo, e tutte in essi adoperando le forze dell'ingegno mio. Gustai la mattina il cibo che digerii nella sera: mangiai fanciullo per ruminare da vecchio; e tanto con loro mi addomesticai, talmente mi passarono, non dico nella memoria, ma nel sangue e nelle midolle, e coll'ingegno mio siffattamente si furono immedesimate, che quantunque mi stessi dal rileggerli infin ch'io viva, sempre mi rimarrebbero profondamente nell'anima impressi.

I have read and reread Virgil, Horace, Livy, Cicero, not once but a thousand times, not hastily but in repose, and I have pondered them with all the powers of my mind. I ate in the morning what I would digest in the evening; I swallowed as a boy what I would ruminate upon as a man. These writings I have so thoroughly absorbed and fixed, not only in my memory but in my very marrow, these have become so much a part of myself, that even though I should never read them again they would cling in my spirit, deep-rooted in its inmost recesses.[7]

Indeed, Petrarch had come in time to witness Cicero as a living presence.

> E molto parve a me che ne prendesse diletto e avesse caro di meco rimanersi Cicerone in quel luogo, ove dieci giorni passammo tranquilli e sereni. Chè fuor d'Italia non v'ha luogo per me di più riposato soggiorno. E questo è proprio della virtù e dello studio: cessar la noia della moltitudine, appagare il desiderio della vita solitaria, e procacciare ai seguaci loro in mezzo alle turbe una perfetta tranquillità, o tra la selve deserte mille nobili cure ed una comitiva di personaggi illustrissimi. Era il mio compagno da innumerabili e preclarissimi uomini circondato; chè dei greci tacendomi, v'eran de'nostri Bruto, Attico, Erennio dai doni di Tullio stesso resi famosi. V'era fra tutti dottissimo Varrone, col quale ei si piaceva vagar discorrendo l'Accademica villa. Cotta v'era, e Velleio, e Lucilio Balbo, che con lui sottilmente della natura degli Dei andavano disputando. Con Nigidio e con Cratippo gli arcani della natura, e l'origine, e l'essenza del mondo investigava. Trattava con Q. Cicerone suo fratello della divinazione e delle leggi: col figliuol suo, non ancora pervertito, trattava degli Offici, e dell'onesto e dell'utile con lui ragionando insegnava come fra loro l'uno e l'altro non sempre si convengano. Con Sulpicio, con Antonio, con Crasso luminari di eloquenza parlava de'segreti dell'arte oratoria. Del venerando vecchio Catone il censore

mostrava ad esempio la lodata vecchiezza. Lucio Torquato, Marco Catone Uti-
cense, e Marco Pisone acutamente con lui disputavano intorno al fine del bene.
Con Ortensio oratore nelle lodi della filosofia, con Epicuro nel vituperio della
voluttà s'intrateneva, e con Lelio e con Scipione della vera amicizia, e della
migliore repubblica determinava la natura e la forme. E v'eran pure, per non
entrare nell'infinito, misti ai Romani cittadini i Re stranieri, che in cause capitali
con orazioni al tutto divine Cicerone difese. E, di quello toccando che precisa-
mente al libro tuo si riferisce, eran con lui Milone difeso, Laterense preso di mira,
Silla scusato, e Pompeo obbietto delle sue lodi.

Cicero and I spent ten tranquil, leisurely days together; and I think he enjoyed
his stay and liked my company. I can breathe here, as I can nowhere else outside
of Italy. Virtuous purpose has a great merit; it can banish the desire for solitude
and afford an escape from boring company. It can bring an unwonted peace amid
the city's hordes, and in the vacant groves it can assemble a crowd of illustrious
companions and noble thoughts. Cicero was accompanied by many eminent,
superior men. Not to mention the Greeks, there were Brutus, Atticus, and
Herennius, whom Cicero has made famous. There was that most learned of all
men, Varro, with whom Cicero liked to stroll in the academic groves. There
were Cotta, Velleius, and Lucilius Balba, with whom Cicero made keen examinations of the nature of the gods. There were Nigidius and Cratippus, with
whom he sought out the secrets of nature, the origin, and the essence of the
world. There was his brother, Quintus Cicero, with whom he discussed divination and law. And his son Marcus Cicero, who had not yet turned to the bad.
With him he dealt with the Offices, and what is the discordance between the
useful and the good. There were those very eloquent men, Sulpitius, Crassus,
and Antonius, with whom he explored the secrets of oratory. And old Cato the
Censor, whose honorable old age he proposed as an example. With Lucius
Torquatus, Marcus Cato of Utica, and Marcus Piso he disputed learnedly on the
aims of the good life. The orator Hortensius was there, and Epicurus; against the
first he advanced the claims of his philosophy, against the second the condemnation of pleasure. With Laelius and Scipio he defined true friendship and the
proper form of the republic. And not to prolong this endlessly, foreign kings
mingled there with Roman citizens, and with them Cicero expounded his views
on matters of the highest moment, with truly divine utterances. And, my
friend, to touch on the subject matter of your own book, Milo was defended,
Lateranus reprehended, Sulla excused, and Pompey praised.

[12.8; 3:149–50; pp. 109–10.]

This letter of 1 April 1352 to Lapo de Castiglionchio, a Florentine professor of law, shows Petrarch's saturation in the classical and rhetorical treatises of his predecessor, whose works he wishes, like their author, to *possess*. Extraordinary as this letter seems to us now, it must not have seemed quite so unusual to those humanists of the Cinquecento whose energy and industry produced numerous translations of classical works: texts of Cicero's *Letters* and treatises (1536–37), Plato's *Lysis* and Xenophon's *Memorabilia* (1551), Demetrius's *De Elocutione* (1562), Cicero's *Philippics* (1563), Aesop (1564), Catullus, Horace, and Terence; and commentaries on Aristotle's *Rhetoric* (1548), *Poetics* (1560), *Politics* (1576), and *Nicomachean Ethics* (1584) and on Cicero's *Orator* (1552), *De Oratore* (1587), and *Tusculan Disputations;* and a splendid folio edition of Livy (1555). Nor was Italy an isolated case. In France, for instance, Guillaume Budé translated into Latin three treatises of Plutarch (1502–5); Jean Calvin's earliest work was a commentary on Seneca's *De Clementia* (1532); Jacques Amyot translated Heliodorus (1547) with an important theoretical preface, *Daphnis and Chloe* (1559), and Plutarch's *Lives* and *Moralia;* Denys Lambin (Dionysius Lambinus) translated into Latin Aristotle's *Ethics* (1558) and *Politics* (1567), Horace (1561), Lucretius (1564), and the whole of Cicero (1566); Louis Le Roy translated Demosthenes' *Olynthiacs* and *Philippics,* Plato's *Timaeus, Phaedo, Symposium,* and *Republic,* Aristotle's *Politics,* and some treatises of Isocrates and Xenophon; the printer Robert Estienne published the *editiones princpes* of Eusebius (1544–46), Dionysius of Halicarnassus (1546–47), Dio Cassius (1548), and Appian (1551); and his son Henri produced before his death fifty-eight Latin and seventy-four Greek authors as well as the great Stephanus edition of Plato (1578) and the *Thesaurus Graecae Linguae* (1572). In Spain, where activity was considerably less, Nuñez de Guzman produced editions of Seneca (1536) and of Pliny's *Natural History,* and Sepúlveda translated Aristotle's *Politics* into Latin (1548). At the same time, various rhetorical handbooks were appearing throughout Europe, such as the collections of *facetiae* recently compiled by Barbara C. Bowen.[8]

Such studies were encouraged by new schools, which also flourished under the Continental humanists. Ficino's Academy in Florence, which began in 1462, and the later Filelleni (Philhellenes) in Venice encouraged many others in Italy and in France. By 1530 Budé persuaded François I to found his *Lecteurs royaux* (later the Collège de France) in Latin, Greek, Hebrew, and mathematics, incurring the anger of the Sorbonne, threatened in their long hegemony over the University of Paris. Similar trilingual colleges were founded elsewhere at about the same time, such as Corpus Christi College at Oxford, and Busleiden's college at Louvain. By 1600 such schools flourished nearly everywhere, realizing through a humanist curriculum centered on grammar, rhetoric, and logic a new civilization derived from deep study of the cultural past. Such establishments encouraged some of the best Continental humanist fiction, too: Following the patronage of Catherine de Médicis (descended from a Florentine family), Marguerite de Navarre formed her own circle of learning, which is used as a setting for her *Heptaméron*, and, if we are to take Castiglione seriously, a courtly academy also flourished at Urbino. Together such formal and informal institutions realized man's wide-reaching capabilities just as the antique Seneca had:

> Non sunt di fastidiosi, non invidi; admittunt et ascendentibus manum porrigunt. Miraris hominem ad deos ire? Deus ad homines venit, immo quod est propius, in homines venit; nulla sine deo mens bona est. Semina in corporibus humanis divina dispersa sunt, quae si bonus cultor excipit, simlia origini prodeunt et paria iis, ex quibus orta sunt, surgunt; si malus, non aliter quam humus sterilis ac palustris necat ac deinde creat purgamenta pro frugibus.

> The gods are not disdainful or envious; they open the door to you; they lend a hand as you climb. Do you marvel that man goes to the gods? God comes to men; nay, he comes nearer,—he comes into men. No mind that has not God, is good. Divine seeds are scattered throughout our mortal bodies; if a good husbandman receives them, they spring up in the likeness of their source and of a parity with those from which they came. If, however, the husbandman be bad, like a barren or marshy soil, he kills the seeds, and causes tares to grow up instead of wheat.[9]

Continental humanists took Seneca's words as prescriptive. In emulating classical civilization, they saw themselves *cultivating* the present, teachers turned husbandmen. By learning the past, such humanists—as well as writers of humanist fiction—learned about themselves, about fashioning themselves and their society into a civilization as glorious as those of ancient Greece and Rome.

Thus reinforced by freshly discovered texts and swiftly expanding numbers of schools, Continental humanists like their English counterparts formulated a plan of lessons centered on the trivium of the *ars disserendi,* or the arts of speaking correctly, speaking well, and arguing well. Together such verbal studies would lead men toward individual perfection while also training them to be ideal citizens through reasoning by Aristotelian *pisteis* (modes of persuasion) as epitomized in the treatises of Cicero and the rhetorical handbook of Quintilian. Once again Petrarch served as a model; "O della romana eloquenza padre e signore," he writes to Cicero himself from Avignon on 19 December 1345, "a te non io solo ma tutti immortali grazie rendiamo noi che ad irrigare i nostri prati dalla fonte tua deriviamo la acque"; "O great father of Roman eloquence, I thank you, as do all who [bedeck themselves with the flowers of the Latin language]. It is from your fount that we draw the waters that bathe our fields" (*Lettere* 24.4; 5 : 142–43; p. 208). Cicero remained central to the standard curriculum throughout the Quattrocento and the Cinquecento in Europe precisely because in both his works and his life he embodied the *rhetor* as philosopher, the man of both precept and practice, the effective speaker and therefore the effective citizen (and lawmaker). Isocrates—the later John Milton's "Old Man Eloquent"—had urged oratory as the basic means of civilized human life (*Against the Sophists* 14) and the management of the state (*Antidosis* 187), and Cicero himself sets out the symbiotic relationship between philosophy and rhetoric, especially as the essential components of education, in the *Orator* (4.15) and again in the image of the two rivers of philosophy and rhetoric which ought to flow together in his *De Oratore,* his portrait of the ideal orator (3.19). Earlier in the *De Oratore,* in Book 1, he has also linked the two, since philosophy supplies substance and rhetoric form; in setting forth the relationship, he also proposes the exemplary humanist curriculum as the Continental Renaissance received it.

> Educenda deinde dictio est ex hac domestica exercitatione et umbratili medium in agmen, in pulverem, in clamorem, in castra, atque in aciem forensem; subeundus usus omnium, et periclitandae vires ingenii; et illa commentatio inclusa in veritatis lucem proferenda est. Legendi etiam poetae, cognoscenda historia, omnium bonarum artium scriptores ac doctores et legendi, et pervolutandi, et exercitationis causa laudandi, interpretandi, corrigendi, vituperandi, refellendi; disputandumque de omni re in contrarias partes, et, quidquid erit in quaque re, quod probabile, videri possit, eliciendum atque dicendum; perdiscendum ius civile, cognoscendae leges, percipienda omnis antiquitas, senatoria consuetudo, disciplina reipublicae, iura sociorum, foedera, pactiones, causa imperii cognoscenda est: libandus est etiam ex omni genere urbanitatis facetiarum quidam lepos; quo, tanquam sale, perspergatur omnis oratio.

> Then at last must our Oratory be conducted out of this sheltered training-ground at home, right into action, into the dust and uproar, into the camp and the fighting-line of public debate; she must face putting everything to the proof and test the strength of her talent, and her secluded preparation must be brought

forth into the daylight of reality. We must also read the poets, acquaint ourselves with histories, study and peruse the masters and authors in every excellent art, and by way of practice praise, expound, emend, criticize and confute them; we must argue every question on both sides, and bring out on every topic whatever points can be deemed plausible; besides this we must become learned in the common law and familiar with the statutes, and must contemplate all the olden time, and investigate the ways of the senate, political philosophy, the rights of allies, the treatises and conventions, and the policy of empire; and lastly we have to cull, from all the forms of pleasantry, a certain charm of humour, with which to give a sprinkle of salt, as it were, to all of our discourse.[10]

Learning and life were thus indivisible, and both were centered on the *power* and *utility* of language. Even Strabo, in Book 1 of his *Geography,* describes poetry as "a kind of elementary philosophy, which introduces us early to life, and gives us pleasurable instruction in reference to character, emotion, action."[11]

The New Learning of the Continental humanists thus emphasized the study of rhetoric as the keystone of their curriculum, an emphasis that would lead naturally, swiftly, and with surprising effectiveness to a particularly humanist poetics to be utilized and transformed throughout the sixteenth century, from the work of Erasmus to that of Cervantes, into a humanist fiction that is the source of fictional practice even today. Such a curriculum, beginning with Latin grammar and syntax, moved quickly (and nearly permanently) into a study of rhetoric, of declamations or orations and of disputations or *controversiae,* as the chief means of exploring issues, defining subjects and positions, and determining action; in time it would also serve the writers of Continental humanist fiction as the basic formulation for exercising the imagination and determining belief. Plato summarizes the major parts of the oration as the Renaissance received it in his treatise on rhetoric and love, the *Phaedrus* (266D–267A), but it is Cicero, as we might expect, who remained the primary authority. His summary will serve our understanding too.

Cumque esset omnis oratoris vis ac facultas in quinque partes distributa; ut deberet reperire primum, quid diceret; deinde inventa non solum ordine, sed etiam momento quodam atque iudicio dispensare atque componere; tum ea denique vestire atque ornare oratione; post memoria saepire; ad extremum agere cum dignitate ac venustate: etiam illa cognoram, et acceperam, antequam de re diceremus, initio conciliandos eorum esse animos, qui audirent; deinde rem demonstrandam; postea controversiam constituendam; tum id, quod nos intenderemus, confirmandum; post, quae contra dicerentur, refellenda; extrema autem oratione, ea, quae pro nobis essent, amplificanda, et augenda; quaeque essent pro adversariis, infirmanda atque frangenda.

And, since all the activity and ability of an orator falls into five divisions, I learned that he must first hit upon what to say; then manage and marshal his discoveries, not merely in orderly fashion, but with a discriminating eye for the exact weight as it were of each argument; next go on to array them in the adornments of style; after that keep them guarded in his memory; and in the end deliver them with effect and charm; I had also been taught that, before speaking on the issue, we must first secure the goodwill of our audience; that next we must state our case; afterwards define the dispute; then establish our own allegations; subsequently disprove those of the other side; and in our peroration expand and reinforce all that was in our favour, while we weakened and demolished whatever went to support our opponents. [*De Oratore* 1.31.142−43]

We shall see these traditional parts of the declamation—*exordium, propositio, partitio, confirmatio, refutatio, conclusio,* and *peroratio*—as the entire basis for Erasmus's mockery throughout the *Encomium Moriae* as well as the more serious means for proposal and persuasion by the members of the symposia in the fictions of Castiglione and Marguerite de Navarre, Rabelais and Cervantes. Rhetoric, that is, is also made indivisible from poetic.

But learning was more than a matter of definition and rule; both in conceptualization and in schoolroom practice, it was based on *imitatio,* the use of models of speech as models of behavior. To teach is to exemplify. The reasons for such a sense of in-struction are given succinctly in the *Epistolae* of Pliny. He tells Fuscus,

Quaeris, quem ad modum in secessu, quo iamdiu frueris, putem te studere oportere. Utile in primis, et multi praecipiunt, vel ex Graeco in Latinum, vel ex Latino vertere in Graecum; quo genere exercitationis proprietas splendorque verborum, copia figurarum, vis explicandi, praeterea imitatione optimorum similia inveniendi facultas paratur; simul, quae legentem fefellissent, transferentem fugere non possunt. Intellegentia ex hoc et iudicium adquiritur.

Nihil offuerit, quae legeris hactenus, ut rem argumentumque teneas, quasi aemulum scribere lectisque conferre ac sedulo pensitare, quid tu, quid ille commodius. Magna gratulatio, si non nulla tu, magnus pudor, si cuncta ille melius.

Licebit interdum et notissima eligere et certare cum electis. Audax haec, non tamen improba, quia secreta contentio; quamquam multos videmus eius modi certamina sibi cum multa laude sumpsisse, quosque subsequi satis habebant, dum non desperant, antecessisse.

You desire my sentiments concerning the method of study you should pursue, in that retirement which you have long enjoyed. It is a very advantageous practice (and what many recommend) to translate either from Greek into Latin, or from Latin into Greek. By this sort of exercise one acquires noble and proper expressions, variety of figures, and a forcible turn of exposition. Besides, to imitate the most approved authors, gives one aptitude to invent after their manner, and at the same time, things which you might have overlooked in reading cannot escape you in translating: and this method will open your understanding and improve your judgment.

It may not be amiss when you have read only so much of an author at once, as to carry in your head his subject and argument, to turn, as it were, his rival, and write something on the same topic; then compare your performance and his, and minutely examine in what points either you or he most happily succeeded. It will be a matter of very pleasing congratulation to yourself, if you shall find that in some things you have the advantage of him, as it will be a great mortification if he should rise above you in all. [7.9] [12]

This unresolved sense of imitatio—or even of speaking well—as emulation and rivalry is at the very heart of Cervantes' *Don Quijote,* but it is also there, if somewhat more distantly, in Marguerite's *Heptaméron* and in Rabelais's great sprawling untitled fiction. Imitatio, moreover, need not be limited to a single prototype. As Pliny himself writes to Arrianus somewhat earlier, he learned to write best by combining Demosthenes, Calvus, and Cicero (1.2). [13]

The act of imitatio, then, seems from nearly the beginning to be a matter not merely of *copying* but of improving, combining, transforming, and hence *creating.* And what is inherent not merely in Pliny's acknowledgment but doubtless in the practice of imitatio generally among the ancients becomes an openly proclaimed *poetic* in Cicero. At one point, he is talking about the painter Zeuxis of Heraclea, who was considered in his time the best of all artists but who painted, Cicero tells us, by selecting many models so as to create an ideal that is at best a composite of what is before him. This, says Cicero, is the way all forms of art—including rhetoric—should proceed.

Quod quoniam nobis quoque voluntatis accidit ut artem dicendi per-
scriberemus, non unum aliquod proposuimus exemplum cuius omnes partes,
quocumque essent in genere, exprimendae nobis necessarie viderentur; sed,
omnibus unum in locum coactis scriptoribus, quod quisque commodissime
praecipere videbatur excerpsimus et ex variis ingeniis excellentissima quaeque
libavimus. Ex eis enim qui nomine et memoria digni sunt nec nihil optime nec
omnia praeclarissime quisquam dicere nobis videbatur. Quapropter stultitia visa
est aut a bene inventis alicuius recedere si quo in vitio eius offenderemur, aut ad
vitia eius quoque accedere cuius aliquo bene praecepto duceremur. Quodsi in
ceteris quoque studiis a multis eligere homines commodissimum quoque quam
sese uni alicui certe vellent addicere, minus in arrogantiam offenderent, non
tanto opere in vitiis perseverarent, aliquanto levius ex inscientia laborarent. Ac
si par in nobis huius artis atque in illo picturae scientia fuisset, fortasse magic
hoc in suo genere opus nostrum, quam ille in sua pictura nobilis eniteret. Ex
maiore enim copia nobis quam illi fuit exemplorum eligendi potestas.

In a similar fashion when the inclination arose in my mind to write a text-
book of rhetoric, I did not set before myself some one model which I thought
necessary to reproduce in all details, of whatever sort they might be, but after
collecting all the works on the subject I excerpted what seemed the most suitable
precepts from each, and so culled the flower of many minds. For each of the
writers who are worthy of fame and reputation seemed to say something better
than anyone else, but not to attain pre-eminence in all points. It seemed folly,
therefore, either to refuse to follow the good ideas of any author, merely because I
was offended by some fault in his work, or to follow the mistakes of a writer who
had attracted me by some correct precept. And it is also true of other pursuits
that if men would choose the most appropriate contributions from many sources
rather than devote themselves unreservedly to one leader only, they would offend
less by arrogance, they would not be so obstinate in wrong courses, and would
suffer somewhat less from ignorance. And if my knowledge of the art of rhetoric
had equalled his knowledge of painting, perhaps this work of mine might be
more famous in its class than he is in painting. For I had a larger number of
models to choose from than he had.[14]

We even have testimony to this widespread sense of imitatio from the fifth-
century writer Macrobius who in the Praefatio to his *Saturnalia,* a book of
instructions for the education of his son, sets forth just this poetic in an analogy
taken up widely by the later humanists.

apes enim quodam modo debemus imitari, quae vagantur et flores carpunt, deinde, quidquid attulere, disponunt ac per favos diuidunt et sucum varium in unum saporem mixtura quadam et proprietate spiritus sui mutant. nos quoque, quidquid diversa lectione quaesiuimus, committemus stilo, ut in ordinem eodem digerent coalescat. nam et in animo melius distincta seruantur et ipsa distinctio non sine quodam fermento, quo conditur universitas, in unius saporis usum varia libamenta confundit, ut, etiam siquid apparuerit unde sumptum sit, aliud tamen esse quam unde sumptum noscetur appareat: quod in corpore nostro videmus sine ulla opera nostra facere naturam:

We ought in some sort to imitate the bees; and just as they, in their wanderings to and fro, sip the flowers, then arrange their spoil and distribute it among the combs, and transform the various juices to a single flavor by in some way mixing with them a property of their own being, so I too shall put into writing all that I have acquired in the varied course of my reading, to reduce it thereby to order and to give it coherence. For not only does arrangement help the memory, but the actual process of arrangement, accompanied by a kind of mental fermentation which serves to season the whole, blends the diverse extracts to make a single flavor; with the result that, even if the sources are evident, what we get in the end is still something clearly different from those known sources.

Macrobius goes on to make further analogies with eating food (and digesting food of the mind), preparing unguents, or singing in a choir (5–8).[15] Such assimilations of models result in a process that *changes* them, that produces *something new*. It is this new product, new work of art, that the artist thus *creates*, a work in which the sources have become so absorbed, or digested, as to have receded from sight so that only the newly created composite remains. In *Il Libro del Cortegiano,* Bembo will argue that this transformation will lead to nothing short of mystical experience; Oisille, in *L'Heptaméron,* will argue that such acts of imitatio, when properly conceived, will lead to a reformation of the soul and spirit; and Don Quijote, in his mad composite of Roldán and Amadís de Gaula will create a new sense of knight-errantry which, however foolish or mad, nevertheless will become *effective* just because of its newness, its strangeness, its divergence. Indeed, the sense of creativity through imitatio that the Quattrocento and Cinquecento inherited from their classical past was itself transformed by the modifying—the intervening, diverging—poetic redefined by Petrarch. It comes, not unexpectedly, in a letter to Boccaccio written from Pavia on 28 October 1366.

lo pongo in sull'avviso doversi imitare per modo che l'opera somigli l'archetipo, ma non sia con esse una cosa: ne lodevole somiglianza esser quella ch'è dall'originale al ritratto, il quale quanto a quello è più identico, tanto maggiore all'arista la lode procaccia: ma si quella che è dal figlio al padre, nei quali quantunque grandissima sia la diversità delle membra, quel tipo e quella che dicon aria i pittori, e che dal volto e massimamente dagli occhi traspare, producono somiglianza siffatta, che visto il figlio, ci torna issofatto il padre alla memoria; se tu per singulo ne ragguagli le parti, l'uno dall'altro è totalmente diverso: ma v'è fra loro un non so che di comune, che dice l'uno fatto sullo stampo dell'altro.

A proper imitator should take care that what he writes resembles the original without reproducing it. The resemblance should not be that of a portrait to the sitter—in that case the closer the likeness is the better—but it should be the resemblance of a son to his father. Therein is often a great divergence in particular features, but there is a certain suggestion, what our painters call an "air," most noticeable in the face and eyes, which makes the resemblance. As soon as we see the son, he recalls the father to us, although if we should measure every feature we should find them all different. But there is a mysterious something there that has this power.

[*Lettere* 23.19; 5:90; pp. 198–99]

The successful art of imitatio is not simply the newly created composite that diverges successfully from particular features of its source(s) but one in which the audience may see the residual traces of the original, which has been the initial impulse or model. The *significatio,* that is, now lies precisely in charting *what* the divergence is (and, consequently, why and how). Folly's tumbling catalogue (which mixes but does not hide its sources), Panurge's speeches, and Don Quijote's actions will all creatively teach us when we recognize *what* is being *transformed:* The *divergence* itself points to the essential meaning. This may at first seem retrogressive, but it is the natural, perhaps the necessary and sole legacy for a culture that is digging back into the antique texts for new self-identification. Such a humanist poetics of creative imitatio based in divergence from resources cherishes and preserves *both* the old text *and the new.*

"The imitations of the classics became, in a word, the basis of literary creation," J. E. Spingarn sums, but it also became more: "this imitation became a dogma of literary criticism" in the Cinquecento. He goes on to report that

Vida, for example, affirms that the poet must imitate classical literature, for only by such imitation is perfection attainable in modern poetry. In fact, this notion is carried to such an extreme that the highest originality becomes for Vida merely the ingenious translation of passages from the classic poets:—

> Haud minor est adeo virtus, si te audit Apollo,
> Inventa Argivûm in patriam convertere vocem,
> Quam si tute aliquid intactum inveneris ante.

Muzio, echoing Horace, urges the poet to study the classics by day and by night; and Scaliger . . . makes all literary creation depend ultimately on judicious imitation: "Nemo est qui non aliquid de Echo." [*History*, p. 131]

Technē (Latin *artes*) for such imitation were advocated by Marco Girolamo Vida's Aristotelian *De arte poetica* in his sense of imitative harmony of parts; by Pietro Bembo's interest in the effect of different sounds, in which he was followed by Lodovico Dolce and others; and by Giangiorgio Trissino's systematic researches on vernacular language as well as the rhetorical treatises of Bartolomeo Cavalcanti (1565), Lionardi (1554), and Bernardino Partenio (1560) and the more practical handbooks of Fanucci (1533), Equicola (1541), and Ruscelli (1559). But the chief means of expression, of imitatio, especially in orations, remained the *topoi* or commonplaces, sources of received ideas and expressions that could be used in various combinations and aggregates. Throughout his *Rhetoric,* Aristotle had conceived of "invention" as a conscious choice of alternatives from a fixed stock, and in subsequent ages *places* became the conceptual means of "locating" or "discovering" varying definitions or statements that could be used for evidence, illustration, or decoration—and could sometimes be recognized from their origins, so that the newly applied use would carry a secondary meaning as well. Plutarch directs writers and speakers to make their own collections of such expressions as others collect tools for farming (*Moralia* 8B); he is followed by Vida in Italy and by Juan Luis Vives in Spain, who urges students to keep at hand a notebook to jot down festive, elegant, or thoughtful things heard or read (*Exercitatio Linguae Latinae* 172). Such conventional expressions, then, are meant to tie new humanist work into long-established traditions inherited from ancient Greece and Rome at the same time that through rearrangement they set such works free.

Understanding now this building process as a way of thinking, "inventing," and creating, in which the building of topoi is in miniature similar to the larger building of a long tradition of works allying classical and humanist efforts, we can understand too why *copia* is so important a part of a humanist poetics for fiction. Indeed, "The whole essence of oratory is to embellish in some fashion all, or, at any rate, most of the ideas," Cicero teaches us in the *Orator;* "nec quicquam est aliud dicere nisi aut omnis aut certe plerasque aliqua specie illuminare sententias" (136).[16] Here he comments at length on such integrated (and vital) ornaments of style.

> Quibus sic abundabit, ut verbum ex ore nullum nisi aut elegans aut grave exeat, ex omnique genere frequentissimae tralationes erunt, quod eae propter similitudinem transferunt animos et referunt ac movent huc et illuc, qui motus cogitationis celeriter agitatus per se ipse delectat. Et reliqua ex collocatione verborum quae sumuntur quasi lumina magnum afferunt ornatum orationi. Sunt enim similia illis quae in amplo ornatu scaenae aut fori appellantur insignia, non quia sola ornent sed quod excellant. Eadem ratio est horum quae sunt orationis lumina et quodam modo insignia: cum aut duplicantur iteranturque verba aut leviter commutata ponuntur, aut ab eodem verbo ducitur saepius oratio aut in idem conicitur aut utrumque, aut adiungitur idem iteratum aut idem ad extremum refetur, aut continenter unum verbum non in eadem sententia ponitur, aut cum similiter vel cadunt verba vel desinunt, aut cum sunt contrariis relata contraria, aut cum gradatim sursum versus reditur, aut cum demptis coniunctionibus dissolute plura dicuntur, aut cum aliquid praetereuntes cur id faciamus ostendimus, aut cum corrigimus nosmet ipsos quasi reprehendentes, aut si est aliqua exclamatio vel admirationis vel questionis, aut cum eiusdem nominis casus saepius commutantur.

These will be so plentiful that no word will fall from the orator's lips that is not well chosen or impressive; there will be metaphors of all sorts in great abundance, because these figures by virtue of the comparison involved transport the mind and bring it back, and move it hither and thither; and this rapid stimulation of thought in itself produces pleasure. The other ornaments derived from combinations of words lend great brilliance to an oration. They are like those objects which in the embellishment of a stage or of a forum are called "ornaments," not because they are the only ornament, but because they stand out from the others. It is the same way with the embellishments and, as it were, the ornaments, of style; words are redoubled and repeated, or repeated with a slight change, or several successive phrases begin with the same words or end with the same, or have both figures, or the same word is repeated at the beginning of a clause or at the end, or a word is used immediately in a different sense, or words are used with similar case endings or other similar terminations; or contrasting ideas are put in juxtaposition (antithesis), or the sentence rises and falls in steps (climax); or many clauses are strung together loosely without conjunctions; or sometimes we omit something and give our reason for so doing: or we correct ourselves with a quasi-reproof; or make some exclamation of surprise or complaint; or use the same word repeatedly in different cases.

He continues by moving from purely grammatical and syntactical technē to technē of the mind, of conceptualization.

Sic igitur dicet ille quem expetimus, ut verset saepe multis modis eadem et una in re haereat in eademque commoretur sententia; saepe etiam ut extenuet aliquid, saepe ut irrideat; ut declinet a propositio deflectatque sententiam; ut proponat quid dicturus sit; ut, cum transegerit iam aliquid, definiat; ut se ipse revocet; ut quod dixit iteret; ut argumentum ratione concludat; ut interrogando urgeat; ut rursus quasi ad interrogata sibi ipse respondeat; ut contra ac dicat accipi et sentiri velit; ut addubitet ecquid potius aut quo modo dicat; ut dividat in partis; ut aliquid relinquat ac neglegat; ut ante praemuniat; ut in eo ipso, in quo reprehendatur, culpam in adversarium conferat; ut saepe cum eis qui audiunt, nonnunquam etiam cum adversario quasi deliberet; ut hominum sermones moresque describat; ut muta quaedam loquentia inducat; ut ab eo quod agitur avertat animos; ut saepe in hilaritatem risumve convertat; ut ante occupet quod videat opponi; ut comparet similitudines; ut utatur exemplis; ut aliud alii tribuens dispertiat; ut interpellatorem coerceat; ut aliquid reticere se dicat; ut denuntiet quid caveant; ut liberius quid audeat; ut irascatur etiam, ut obiurget aliquando; ut deprecetur, ut supplicet, ut medeatur; ut a propositio declinet aliquantum; ut optet, ut exsecretur; ut fiat eis apud quos dicet familiaris. Atque alias etiam dicendi quasi virtutes sequetur: brevitatem, si res petet; saepe etiam rem dicendo subiciet oculis; saepe supra feret quam fieri possit; significatio saepe erit maior quam oratio; saepe hilaritas, saepe vitae naturarumque imitatio. Hoc in genere—nam quasi silvam vides—omnis eluceat oportet eloquentiae magnitudo.

Let us be content merely to point out the subject. The orator, then, whom we are trying to discover, will make frequent use of the following figures: he will treat the same subject in many ways, sticking to the same idea and lingering over the same thought; he will often speak slightingly of something or ridicule it; he will turn from the subject and divert the thought; he will announce what he is about to discuss and sum up when concluding a topic; he will bring himself back to the subject; he will repeat what he has said; he will use a syllogism; he will urge his point by asking questions and will reply to himself as if to questions; he will say something, but desire to have it understood in the opposite sense; he will express doubt whether or how to mention some point; he will divide the subject into parts; will omit or disregard some topic; he will prepare the way for what is to come; he will transfer to his opponent the blame for the very act with which he is charged; he will seem to consult the audience, and sometimes even with the opponent; he will portray the talk and ways of men; he will make mute objects speak; he will divert the attention of the audience from the point at issue; he will frequently provoke merriment and laughter; he will reply to some point which he sees is likely to be brought up; he will use similes and examples; he will divide a sentence, giving part to a description of one person, part to another; he will put down interrupters; he will claim to be suppressing something; he will warn the audience to be on their guard; he will take the liberty to speak somewhat boldly; he will even fly into a passion and protest violently; he will plead and entreat and soothe the audience; he will digress briefly; he will pray and curse; he will put himself on terms of intimacy with his audience. Moreover he will aim at other desirable virtues, so to speak, of style: brevity, if the case demands; often also by his statement of the case he will make the scene live before our eyes; he will often exaggerate a statement above what could actually occur; his language will often have a significance deeper than his actual words; there will be passages in a lighter vein, and a portrayal of life and manners. In the employment of resources like these—you see what a mass of material is available—all the brilliance of style should be employed. [134–39]

Such statements seem to execute their own rules; but Erasmus will use such a sense of copia—or varying a single theme—as the primary technē in the *Encomium Moriae,* both mocking and reasserting humanist principles of speech and thought; Rabelais, in his endless exuberance, will use copia as his central means to conceal and reveal meaning, just as it will disguise and disclose the classical resources—the original texts—on which his various scenes and characters continually draw.

In the Greek and Roman cultures, where language was the chief means of governance and livelihood and where literary expression had significant value, we can understand the extraordinary power and value inherited in words. But the same sense of the power and excitement of language is also a distinctive, controlling feature of the Continental Renaissance, where the rediscovery of ancient texts—of ancient *writings*—revived the ways of older civilizations and provided the Renaissance with poetic works of stunning strength and beauty. Yet, like imitatio, the sense of copia changed even as the ancients practiced it, expanding the basis for humanist poetics in the sixteenth century. Quintilian, whose *Institutio Oratoria* was a redaction for teachers of the oratorical works of Cicero originally meant for governors and lawyers, notes that by varying expression the writer can *shape* meaning and even *control* responses. One of Quintilian's strongest examples comes at the outset of his discussion in *Oratoria 8.*

Prima est igitur amplificandi vel minuendi species in ipso rei nomine: ut cum eum, qui sit caesus, *occisum,* eum, qui sit improbus, *latronem,* contraque eum, qui pulsavit, *attigisse,* qui vulneravit, *laesisse* dicimus. Utriusque pariter exemplum est pro M. Caelio: *Si vidua libere, proterva petulanter, dives effuse, libidinosa meretricio more viveret, adulterum ego putarem, si qui hanc paulo liberius salutasset?* Nam et impudicam *meretricem* vocavit, et eum, cui longus cum illa fuerat usus, *liberius salutasse.* Hoc genus increscit ac fit manifestius, si ampliora verba cum ipsis nominibus, pro quibus ea posituri sumus, conferantur: ut Cicero in Verrem, *Non enim furem sed ereptorem, non adulterum sed expugnatorem pudicitiae, non sacrilegum sed hostem sacrorum religionu que, non sicarium sed crudelissimum carnificem civium sociorumque in vestrum iudicium adduximus.* Illo enim modo ut sit multum, hoc etiam plus ut sit efficitur. Quattuor tamen maxime generibus video constare amplificationem, incremento, comparatione, ratiocinatione, congerie.

The first method of *amplification* or *attenuation* is to be found in the actual word employed to describe a thing. For example, we may say that a man who was *beaten* was *murdered,* or that a *dishonest* fellow is a *robber,* or, on the other hand, we may say that one who *struck* another merely *touched* him, and that one who *wounded* another merely *hurt* him. The following passage from the *Pro Caelio,* provides examples of both: "If a widow lives freely, if being by nature bold she throws restraint to the winds, makes wealth an excuse for luxury, and strong passions for playing the harlot, would this be a reason for my regarding a man who was somewhat free in his method of saluting her to be an adulterer?" For here he calls an immodest woman a harlot, and says that one who had long been her lover saluted her with a certain freedom. This sort of *amplification* may be strengthened and made more striking by pointing the comparison between words of stronger meaning and those for which we propose to substitute them, as Cicero does in denouncing Verres: "I have brought before you, judges, not a thief, but a plunderer; not an adulterer, but a ravisher; not a mere committer of sacrilege, but the enemy of all religious observance and all holy things; not an assassin, but a bloodthirsty butcher who has slain our fellow-citizens and our allies. In this passage the first epithets are bad enough, but are rendered still worse by those which follow. I consider, however, that there are four principal methods of *amplification: augmentation, comparison, reasoning* and *accumulation.*

[8.4.1–3][17]

He continues by illustrating each of them in turn (8.4.4–29). Such *flexibility* of language allows *manipulation* of language exercising reason and imagination alike: On one hand, we see the wordplay of Erasmus as a natural consequence; on the other hand, we can see Castiglione's eloquence as equally natural. In both instances, this moves humanist writing (and humanist poetics) toward fiction, and this is something of which Quintilian is also aware. Orators, he argues, may turn with equal ease to the facts of history or the fictions of poets (12.4.1–2). *Making* can thus become, quite literally, *making up.*

Rhetorical orations as acts of persuasion (and, as we have seen, even of poetic creation) were further extended by the study of disputations—of debates—in which speakers would be asked to take one side or the other or, in time, *both* sides to demonstrate their skills at language and presentation. Elasticity of language arises from the possible elasticity of interpretation—perhaps even of truth—wherever *texts* are concerned: "In showing that the same arguments can be used on both sides of a question, and that the same text can be interpreted in different ways," Victoria Kahn writes "these authors also address themselves to the contrary interpretations that their own texts are capable of eliciting."[18] Speeches and texts were seen, therefore, not so much as attempts to recapitulate events or to establish true accounts but as *hypotheses, propositions* urged upon the audience. Such instability allows even more. Arguments of this kind, Kahn continues, may "call our attention to the fact that within the realm of rhetoric (that is, of language) every figure is 'potentially reversible' [the phrase is Jonathan Culler's[19]]: each can be read as serious or ironic [as in the fictions of Erasmus and Cervantes], as simply contradictory or profoundly paradoxical [as in the work of Marguerite de Navarre and Castiglione], as undecidable or the occasion for a decision [as in the long untitled work of Rabelais]. The humanist emphasis on the act of reading can itself be interpreted *in utramque partem* as conducive to action or as a substitute for action" (p. 22).

Models and materials for such disputations were found in fragments of *controversiae* recorded by the elder Seneca, Seneca Rhetor, just as his *suasoriae* served both ancient Greek and Renaissance European schoolrooms as models for orations. Here, two actual conflicting Roman laws were posed and the student required to argue either side.

A girl who has been raped may choose either marriage to her ravisher without a dowry or his death. On a single night a man rapes two girls. One demands his death, the other marriage. Speeches for and against the man. [*Controversiae* 1.3]

A man disinherits his son; the disinherited son goes to a prostitute and acknowledges a son by her. He falls ill and sends for his father; when the father arrives, he entrusts his son to the old man and dies. After his death the father adopts the boy. He is accused of insanity by his other son. [2.4]

James J. Murphy traces such problems as those found in Seneca Rhetor back to the invention of rhetoric itself around 476 B.C. by Corax, a resident of Syracuse in Sicily, who sued his pupil Tisias when the student attempted to leave without paying the fee for his lessons. Murphy summarizes the arguments on both sides:

> CORAX: You must pay me if you win the case, because that would prove the worth of my lessons. If you lose the case you must pay me also, for the court will force you to do so. In either case you pay.
>
> TISIAS: I will pay nothing, because if I lose the case it would prove that your instruction was worthless. If I win, however, the court will absolve me from paying. In either case I will not pay.

"Tradition holds," Murphy comments wryly, "that the court postponed decision indefinitely." [20]

Such dialectical means of arriving at interpretations or judgments can be seen, of course, in the dialogues of Socrates, but there too we are always alerted to situations in which discovery or truth rests on supposition and reason: There are no indisputable "facts" and no single "certainty" but only the probability of truth through a series of linked syllogisms. Such "certainties" are at best likely *hypotheses*—like many fictions. In education so grounded in logomachy, or contention, the skill to be learned is antilogy, the ability to argue either side of any issue with equal skill, conviction, and success. In his *Rhetoric*, Aristotle suggests using two kinds of proof (*pisteis*), artificial (*entechnos*) and inartificial (*atechnos*) (1.2.2−11, 14−18; 1.15.1−33). The first kind involves *ēthos*, or the character the speaker assigns (or fabricates) for himself; *pathos*, or the role he assigns (or creates) for his audience; and *logos*, or a stylized speech resulting from the use of colors of language. Inartificial proofs are those which may be found but which are always open to the speaker's interpretation: laws, contracts, witnesses, tortures, and oaths. In the instance of laws, Aristotle tells us, we may find that the law is against us. Then we will appeal to universal law, or to ambiguity in the law, or to a conflicting law. If we find the law is for us, however, we will argue that a law disregarded might just as well not have been made (1.13). As for witnesses, they may be ancient (such as the writings of poets) or contemporary. If, however, we can call on neither, we can argue that probabilities are more trustworthy; if we have witnesses, we can argue that probabilities are only speculative (1.15). In the case of contracts, we can argue for those that support us that relations between men would be impossible if such obligations were impaired; if they are against us, we can argue that they are contrary to equity or to some other law, that they are ambiguous, or that they were obtained by coercion or fraud (1.15). Such matters for debate rotate around three axes of concern: *an sit* (did it happen?), *quid sit* (how do we define what happened?), and *quale sit* (how do we interpret an act?); but we can quickly see, from Aristotle's teaching, that arguments are *created* to *persuade* the audience to certain interpretations, beliefs, or ends rather than to establish truth, and that such creating comes perilously close—as we shall see in the later chapters of this book—to fiction making.

In the *Ad Herennium,* the popular humanist schoolbook by the Pseudo-Cicero, such principles as Aristotle established are codified at considerable length around conjectural, legal, and juridical issues. Here is an example of each:

> Coniecturalis est cum de facto controversia est, hoc modo: Aiax in silva, postquam resciit quae fecisset per insaniam, gladio incubuit. Ulixes intervenit, occisum conspicatur, corpore telum cruentum educit. Teucer intervenit, fratrem occisum, inimicum fratris cum gladio cruento videt. Capitis arcessit. Hic coniectura verum quaeritur. De facto erit controversia; ex eo constitutio causae coniecturalis nominatur.
>
> Legitima est constitutio cum in scripto aut e scripto aliquid controversiae nascitur. Ea dividitur in partes sex: scriptum et sententiam, contrarias leges, ambiguum, definitionem, translationem, ratiocinationem.
>
> Ex scripto et sententia controversia nascitur cum videtur scriptoris voluntas cum scripto ipso dissentire, hoc modo: si lex sit quae iubeat eos qui propter tempestatem navem reliquerint omnia perdere, eorum navem ceteraque esse, si navis conservata sit, qui remanserunt in navi. Magnitudine tempestatis omnes perterriti navem reliquerunt, in scapham conscenderunt—praeter unum aegrotum; is propter morbum exire et fugere non potuit. Casu et fortuitu navis in portum incolumis delata est; illam aegrotus possedit. Navem petit ille cuius fuerat. Haec constitutio legitima est ex scripto et sententia. . . .
>
> Iuridicalis constitutio est cum factum convenit, sed iure an iniuria factum sit

quaeritur. Eius constitutionis partes duae sunt, quarum una absoluta, altera adsumptiva nominatur.

Absoluta est cum id ipsum quod factum est, ut aliud nihil foris adsumatur, recte factum esse dicemus, eiusmodi: Mimus quidam nominatim Accium poetam compellavit in scaena. Cum eo Accius iniuriarum agit. Hic nihil aliud defendit nisi licere nominari eum cuius nomine scripta dentur agenda.

The Issue is Conjectural when the controversy concerns a question of fact, as follows: In the forest Ajax, after realizing what in his madness he had done, fell on his sword. Ulysses appears, perceives that Ajax is dead, draws the bloody weapon from the corpse. Teucer appears, sees his brother dead, and his brother's enemy with bloody sword in hand. He accuses Ulysses of a capital crime. Here the truth is sought by conjecture. The controversy will concern the fact. And that is why the Issue in the cause is called Conjectural.

The Issue is Legal when some controversy turns upon the letter of a text or arises from an implication therein. A Legal Issue is divided into six subtypes: Letter and Spirit, Conflicting Laws, Ambiguity, Definition, Transference, and Reasoning from Analogy.

A controversy from Letter and Spirit arises when the framer's intention appears to be at variance with the letter of the text, as follows: Suppose a law which decrees that whoever have abandoned their ship in a storm shall lose all rights of title, and that their ship, if saved, and cargo as well, belong to those who have remained on board. Terrified by the storm's violence, all deserted the ship and took to the boat—all except one sick man who, on account of his illness, could not leave the ship and escape. By sheer chance the ship was driven safely to harbour. The invalid has come into possession of the ship, and the former owner claims it. Here is a Legal Issue based on Letter and Spirit. . . .

An Issue is Juridical when there is agreement on the act, but the right or wrong of the act is in question. Of this Issue there are two subtypes, one called Absolute, the other Assumptive.

It is an Absolute Issue when we contend that the act in and of itself, without our drawing on any extraneous considerations, was right. For example, a certain mime abused the poet Accius by name on the stage. Accius sues him on the ground of [wrongful behavior]. The player makes no defence except to maintain that it was permissible to name a person under whose name dramatic works were given to be performed on the stage. [1.11.18–19; 14.24][21]

It may astonish us now, but it is surely clear from such lessons and the daily drills that resulted that students of Continental humanists were asked again and again to *construct narrative situations* which, though cast in the *forms* of declamations and disputations, nevertheless established situations that were like stories, situations that were *probable* and *persuasive*. That is, they were persuasive *because* they were probable, and probable because they were persuasive; and they were both because they upheld a characteristic common to both conditions—that of verisimilitude. It may clarify matters to recall that the Greek word for probability is *eikos,* which means resemblance or appearance; it stops just short of our word *image.* The Continental humanist writers of fiction understood this, too, as we shall see in Erasmus's imaging of Folly and Rabelais's of giants.

The centrality of disputation to humanist education also points to something else: that narrative is grounded in dialectic or *conflict.* "Rhetoric produced individuals predisposed to approach any subject by taking a side, because they were not formally trained to do anything else," Walter J. Ong writes of the Tudor humanists especially; "any side, perhaps, but some side certainly." [22] The establishing of situations—what will become fictions in the hands of Marguerite and Cervantes—thus implies oppositions, whether or not they are stated; and it further implies the need for adjudication. Humanist poetics, then, rhetorically conceived, is always aimed at an audience and is incomplete without one; it demands interpretations that lie, ultimately, beyond the presentation of probability, of *eikos.* Such an art is essentially triangular, playing off its oppositions against the interpreting, adjudicating audience, which may choose one interpretation over another, may reject both, or may attempt to mediate between them. To help in such judging, the audiences at disputations, like the readers of texts, needed to hold up the argument against what experience had taught them; and it is only an extension of this awareness that caused most humanist education to test theory with practice, precept with travel. The Grand Tour inaugurated by Tudor humanists in England who completed their education with travel throughout the Continent was, on the Continent, a matter of travel generally. Here events and observations would help to clarify and define probability too; and such an understanding is essential for understanding Rabelais's fiction, where crucial ties between proper education and wise and eloquent citizenship in Books 1 and 2 give way, in the later books, to the need to find instruction in foreign and increasingly fabulous territories of the human mind and spirit. It is fundamental too to *Don Quijote,* where the very fictions of knight-errantry are tested by their utility through La Mancha, Barataria, and beyond. Yet in such an environment, where the testing of ideas and the testing of language are always vital challenges, we can also see the roots of the enthusiasm that marks the age of humanist poetics, much as it marked the earlier ages of Periclean Athens and Augustan Rome. For humanist poetics is characterized not only by its tensile commitment to the humanist beliefs in the dignity and educability of man but by its rhetorical energy. Early on, Pliny sees this:

> Debet enim orator erigi, attolli, interdum etiam effervescere, efferri ac saepe accedere ad praeceps. Nam plerumque altis et excelsis adiacent abrupta; tutius per plana, sed humilius et depressius iter; frequentior currentibus quam reptantibus lapsus, sed his non labentibus nulla, illis non nulla laus, etiamsi labantur. Nam ut quasdam artes ita eloquentiam nihil magis quam ancipitia commendant.

> For the true orator should be bold and elevated, and sometimes even flame out and be hurried away with all the warmth and violence of passion, in short, he should frequently soar to great, and even dangerous heights. For precipices are generally near whatever is towering and exalted, whereas the plain affords a safer, but for that reason a more humble and inglorious path; they that run are more likely to stumble than they that creep; but the latter gain no honour by not slipping, while the former even fall with glory. It is with eloquence as with some other arts; she is never more pleasing than when she hazards most. [*Letters* 9.26]

"The truth is that the poet is a very near kinsman of the orator, rather more heavily fettered as regards rhythm, but with ampler freedom in his choice of words, while in the use of many sorts of ornament he is his ally and almost his counterpart," Cicero writes in *De Oratore;* "Est enim finitimus oratori poeta, numeris astrictior paulo, verborum autem licentia liberior, multis vero ornandi generibus socius, ac paene par" (1.16.70). In the Renaissance, Erasmus for one is joyous over such a blurring of boundaries, as he comments in a letter to Andrew Ammonius on 21 December 1513: "me vehementer delectat poema rhetoricum et rhetor poeticus, ut et in oratione soluta carmen agnoscas et in carmine rhetoricam phrasin"; "What especially delights me is a rhetorical poem and a poetical oration, in which you can see the poetry in the prose and the rhetorical expression in the poetry."[23] A significant part of the excitement of humanism is the excitement fostered by humanist poetics.

Yet the extraordinary force of such a union could also be a dangerous one, as the humanists well knew. Within the narrative and poetic power of persuasion also lay the power to deceive; making up could also be making false. This was, after all, Plato's chief objection to rhetoric in the *Phaedrus*. As Socrates sums near the close of that dialogue, he who is to be a competent rhetorician need have nothing at all to do, they say, with truth in considering things which are just or good, or men who are so, whether by nature or by education. For in the courts, they say, nobody cares for truth about these matters, but for that which is convincing; and that is probability, so that he who is to be an artist in speech must fix his attention upon probability. For sometimes one must not even tell what was actually done, if it was not likely to be done, but what was probable, whether in accusation or defence; and in brief, a speaker must always aim at probability, paying no attention to truth; for this method, if pursued throughout the whole speech, provides us with the entire art.[24]

Socrates anticipates Cicero's Antonius when he tells Crassus how he wins his law cases in his portrait of the ideal orator:

Ego enim cum ad causam sum aggressus atque omnia cogitando quoad facere potui persecutus, cum et argumenta causae et eos locos quibus animi iudicum concilientur et ilios quibus permoventur vidi atque cognovi, tum constituo quid habeat causa quaeque boni, quid mali; nulla enim fere potest res in dicendi disceptationem aut controversiam vocari quae non habeat utrumque, sed quantum habeat id refert; mea autem ratio in dicendo haec esse solet, ut boni quod habeat id amplectar, exornem, exaggerem, ibi commorer, ibi habitem, ibi haeream, a malo autem vitioque causae ita recedam non ut me id fugere appareat sed ut totum bono illo ornando et augendo dissimulatum obruatur; et, si causa est in argumentis, firmissima quaeque maxime tueor, sive plura sunt sive aliquod unum; sin autem in conciliatione aut in permotione causa est, ad eam me potissimum partem quae maxime movere animos hominum potest confero. Summa denique huius generis haec est, ut si in refellendo adversario firmior esse oratio quam in confirmandis nostris rebus potest, omnia in illum tela conferam, sin nostra probari facilius quam illa redargui possunt, abducere animos a contraria defensione et ad nostram coner deducere.

For my part when I am launched on a case and have to the best of my ability passed all the facts under consideration, having discerned and ascertained the arguments that belong to the case and also the topics calculated to win the favour of the court and those adapted to arouse its emotions, I then decide what are the good and what the bad points in the case of each of the parties, as it is almost impossible for any matter to be brought under discussion or dispute which does not contain both—the thing that matters is *how much* of them it contains; but my own method in a speech usually is to take the good points of my case and elaborate these, embellishing and enlarging and lingering and dwelling on and sticking to them, while any bad part or weakness in my case I leave on one side, not in such a manner as to give the appearance of running away from it but so as to disguise it and entirely cover it up by embellishing and amplifying the good point referred to; and if the case is one that turns on arguments, I maintain all the strongest among them in the fullest measure, whether they are several or only one, or if it is a matter of winning favour or arousing feeling, I concentrate particularly on the part of the case that is most capable of influencing men's minds. In short, the chief thing in a case of this kind is, if my speech can be stronger in refuting our opponent than in proving our own points, for me to concentrate all my shafts upon him, but if on the contrary, our points can be more easily proved than his can be refuted, to aim at drawing off their attention from our opponent's defence and directing it to our own.

[*De Oratore* 2.72.291–93].

Combative or contestatory rhetoric, that is—the rhetoric used in law courts—established narratives and narrative conflicts by using precisely the means rhetoric contributed to poetry, including *prosopographia;* the impersonation (or re-creation) of a historical individual; *prosopopoeia,* the creation (or feigning) of a fictive person; and *topographia,* the description (or creation) of places, as well as *ēthos* and *pathos.* We can see, then, why the Greek word for persuasion, *psychagogia,* could also be translated as "enchantment of the soul." Kathy Eden, in a compelling study of the close relationship of legal rhetoric and fictive poetic, traces this confusion back to Gorgias.

Defending poetry in the interests of his fictitious client, Helen, Gorgias concentrates on its psychagogic power. Poetry, he insists, exercises an irresistible force on the human soul. In particular, it eradicates fear (*phobon pausai*), while it increases pity (*eleon exauxēnai*). It mitigates pain (*lupē*), while it gives pleasure (*hēdonē, chara*). By so manipulating the emotions (*pathēmata*), poetry not only moves an audience to sympathize with the good and bad fortunes of another, it even persuades its listeners, through its deceptions (*doxēs apatēmata*), to pursue a particular course of action. Helen was persuaded in this way and therefore, Gorgias argues against the background of contemporary legal theory, her actions were involuntary (*akōn*) rather than voluntary (*hekōn*) and, consequently, not culpable.[25]

The necessity of prosecution and defense in courtrooms led to the practice (and the teaching) of eristics, of winning in whatever way possible; to the sophistry identified with Gorgias and Protagoras, in which the worse part could be made to *appear* the better or the better worse; and to skepticism, which, as developed by Sextus Empiricus, could show, largely through disjunctive propositions, the impossibility of proving *anything* even when induction, deduction, or syllogisms were employed. In his crucial *Outlines of Pyrrhonism*, Sextus even parodies the disjunctive proposition:

> Some argue also as follows: If Socrates was born, Socrates became either when Socrates existed not or when Socrates already existed; but if he shall be said to have become when he already existed, he will have become twice; and if when he did not exist, Socrates was both existent and non-existent at the same time—existent through having become, non-existent by hypothesis. And if Socrates died, he died either when he lived or when he died. Now he did not die when he lived, since he would have been at once both alive and dead; nor yet when he died, since he would have been dead twice. Therefore Socrates did not die. And by applying this argument in turn to each of the things said to become or perish it is possible to abolish becoming and perishing.[26]

In *Against the Professors* he notes even more caustically that in any set of contradictory speeches there must be the advocacy of injustice and untruth (2.46–47).

Of course Cicero recognized such inherent problems as the humanists did after him. At the outset of his *Rhetorici libri duo* (*De Inventione*), he acknowledges that eloquence without wisdom is dangerous (1.i.1). His solution is twofold. He insists that the philosopher and orator be joined, that the rhetorician be a wise man—the *vir bonus* which Quintilian is at great pains to stress chorically in the *Institutiones Oratoriae* and to describe at some length in Book 12 as one who respects public opinion (12.1.12), advocates noble policies (12.1.15, 25), and studies philosophy and logic (12.2.4), history, religion, and law (12.2.27; 3.1), and one who is characterized by fortitude (12.1.17), integrity (12.1.16), honor (12.1.24), virtue (12.1.31), and a sense of duty (12.1.29). We have already seen that the humanists are equally insistent on the joining of philosophy and rhetoric, of wisdom and poetry. Cicero's second solution, one equally important to the humanists, is service to the state—the precepts of humanist thought, advocating the dignity, educability, and even perfectibility of man depended on his ability to serve the state as well as himself. A third solution is inherent too in Cicero's framing his question to himself at the beginning of the *De Inventione* as wisdom versus eloquence, as a *debate*. He practices the art of triangulation: By putting two sides of the argument one against the other, he will assume also the third position of judge. His debate, then, autobiographical or propositional (that is, feigned, fictional, exemplary), is in itself incomplete *without* a judge or audience; it lacks closure. The debate relies instead on the wisdom and reason of those who judge it both in determining the best outcome and in *acting* on that judgment. The debate is a set of precepts that must be put into practice, just as the humanists will insistently advocate with their lessons, with their propositions, and with *their (necessary) fictions.*

Cicero's several attempts to define and promote rhetoric are all taken up by the humanists in the sixteenth century as a basis for their rhetorical *poetics.* But Cicero addresses only the qualifications of the rhetor (or poet) and the ends he serves. He says much about technē but nothing here about the *basis* for technē. Plato, however, attends to just such matters and where we might expect him to: in the *Sophist,* a middle or late dialogue where he is attempting to preserve for language a reliable purpose and means. Here an Elean Stranger informs Theaetetus (in the presence of Theodorus and Socrates) of two fundamental kinds of art, icastic and fantastic. Both kinds of art are what the Stranger calls productive rather than acquisitive (219A–C), for they are not acquired from things already existing but bring into being something new. Thus both permit fiction. But these two kinds of art, according to Plato, are different in process and thereby identifiably distinct in their results. Icastic or "likeness-making" art occurs "whenever anyone produces the imitation by following the proportions of the original in length, breadth, and depth, and giving, besides, the appropriate colours to each part" (235D)—when the artist records simply, without an intervenient imagination. Fantastic art, on the other hand, either creates that which does not exist or gives a disproportionate, faulty representation of the object being imitated; it "produces appearance," Plato says, "but not likeness" (236C). Icastic art copies the original precisely. Fantastic art is exemplified by

> those who produce some large work of sculpture or painting. For if they reproduced the true proportions of beautiful forms, the upper parts, you know, would seem smaller and the lower parts larger than they ought, because we see the former from a distance, the latter from near at hand. . . . So the artists abandon the truth and give their figures not the actual proportions but those which seem to be beautiful . . . but which would not even be likely to resemble that which it claims to be like, if a person were able to see such large works adequately. [235E–236B][27]

Representation, re-presentation, is the end of both forms of art, but the means are radically opposed. Icastic art conveys by reproducing an object; fantastic art re-creates the appearance only, because it must allow for a subjective, or displaced, perspective on the part of the viewer. It compensates and accommodates the viewer, persuading him to accept the fantastic as the icastic, to accept what *seems* to be for what is *known* to be. Plato's terms, already a nascent poetics because his examples are drawn from painting and sculpture, are meant to divide truth from sophistry in his own sophistic age; at the same time, however, they argue that the appearance of truth, and the sense of the truth, may be truer than the truth icastically reproduced but skewed by its representation or by the perspective of the audience. The essence of art, Plato is arguing, when it means to be representative, is in the way the imitation of the object or situation is conceived, executed, and received.

This is, of course, exactly the issue Aristotle makes central to his own *Poetics*. The term is considerably broader for him, however. In the useful arts, he says, imitation is that which is distinct from natural properties and that which men add to perfect or extend the usefulness of those arts. In the fine arts, though, such as poetry and drama, imitation intervenes rather than extends, because it must employ its own specialized media. Because of this intervention, the artist cannot—given the limits and necessities of his formal means—re-create the original; his work must forever be like Plato's fantastic art because it will compensate in its reproduction for both those means and the audience. The artist accommodates this situation by working with probability—as rhetoricians had long since done—which is suitably conveyed by the materials of his art. Consequently, a likely impossibility for Aristotle is preferable to an unconvincing possibility (an insight that is central to Cervantes and to *Don Quijote,* as we shall see). In a seminal essay on Aristotle and imitation, Richard McKeon commented some time ago on just what this means for the painter and the poet.

> The man who sits for his portrait assumes a posture which is determined by the laws of gravitation, by the anatomy of the human body, and the peculiarities of his habits; the painter must justify the line he chooses not in terms of physics or anatomy, but in terms of the composition which appears in the colors and lines on his canvas. A man performs an action as a consequence of his character, his heritage, his fate, or his past actions; the poet represents that action as necessary in his medium, which is words, by developing the man's character, by expressing his thoughts and those of men about him, by narrating incidents. For Aristotle,

consequently, imitation may be said to be, in the fine arts, the presentation of an aspect of things in a matter other than its natural matter, rendered inevitable by reasons other than its natural reasons; in the useful arts it is the realization of a function in another matter or under other circumstances than those which are natural. It is no contradiction, consequently, that the artist should imitate natural things, and that he should none the less imitate them "either as they were or are, or as they are said or thought to be or to have been, or as they ought to be" [1460a10–13]. Art imitates nature; the form joined to matter in the physical world is the same form that is expressed in the matter of the art. Art does not abstract universal forms as science does, but imitates the forms of individual things.[28]

In imitating individuals effectively, though, later Roman writers turned to the copying of what "ought to be"—an ideal concept which Aristotle draws from the model rather than, as with Plato, from an idea within the artist's mind—as we have seen in Cicero's remarks in the *De Inventione* (2.2.4–5; cf. *Brutus* 68 and *De optimo genere oratorum* 14), as well as in Quintilian (10.2.4) and his student Pliny (*Epistula* 1.2); Seneca's analogy of this process to the bee making honey (*Epistulae Morales* 74.3–5) was, as we have seen, transmitted to Continental Renaissance humanists through the *Saturnalia* of Macrobius.

Just as Roman writers extended the imitatio of a single model into a composite series of models, so they also extended the sense of an original source into a previous work or text. Here the desire was for a *pattern* which, as we have noted, fresh works might try to copy or imitate rather precisely or, on the other hand, obviously diverge from so as to signal meaning more openly and more precisely. The fullest treatment of this is in the *Epistula* 65 of Seneca, where he sees it as a "fifth cause," and it bears quoting at some length because it leads, as we shall repeatedly acknowledge, to the primary premise of Continental humanist poetics.

Omnis ars naturae imitatio est. Itaque quod de universo dicebam, ad haec transfero, quae ab homine facienda sunt. Statua et materiam habuit, quae pateretur artificem, et artificem, qui materiae daret faciem. Ergo in statua materia aes fuit, cause opifex. Eadem condicio rerum omnium est; ex eo constant, quod fit, et ex eo, quod facit. Stoicis placet unam causam esse, id, quod facit. Aristoteles putat causam tribus modis dici: "Prima," inquit, "causa est ipsa materia, sine qua nihil potest effici; secunda opifex. Tertia est forma, quae unicuique operi inponitur tanquam statuae"; nam hanc Aristoteles idos vocat. "Quarta quoque," inquit, "hic accedit, propositum totius operis." Quid sit hoc, aperiam. Aes prima statuae causa est. Numquam enim facta esset, nisi fuisset id, ex quo funderetur ducereturve. Secunda causa artifex est. Non potuisset enim aes illud in habitum statuae figurari, nisi accessissent peritae manus. Tertia causa est forma. Neque enim statua ista doryphoros aut diadumenos vocaretur, nisi haec illi esset impressa facies. Quarta causa est faciendi propositum. Nam nisi hoc fuiseet, facta non esset. Quid est propositum? Quod invitavit artificem, quod ille secutus fecit; vel pecunia est haec, si venditurus fabricavit, vel gloria, si laboravit in nomen, vel religio, si donum templo paravit. Ergo et haec causa est, propter quam fit; an non putas inter causas facti operis esse numerandum, quo remoto factum non esset?

His quintum Plato adicit exemplar, quam ipse idean vocat; hoc est enim, ad quod respiciens artifex id, quod destinabat, effecit. Nihil autem ad rem pertinet, utrum foris habeat exemplar, ad quod referat oculos, an intus, quod ibi ipse concepit et posuit. Haec exemplaria rerum omnium deus intra se habet numerosque universorum, quae agenda sunt, et modos mente complexus est; plenus his figuris est, quas Plato ideas appellat, immortales, immutabiles, infatigabiles. Itaque homines quidem pereunt, ipsa autem humanitas, ad quam homo effingitur, permanet, et hominibus laborantibus, intereuntibus illa nihil patitur. Quinque ergo causae sunt, ut Plato dicit: id ex quo, id a quo, id in quo, id ad quod, id propter quod. Novissime id quod ex his est. Tamquam in statua, quia de hac loqui coepimus, id ex quo aes est, id a quo artifex est, id in quo forma est, quae raptatur illi, id ad quod exemplar est, quod imitatur is, qui facit, id propter quod facientis propositum est, id quod ex istis est, ipsa statua est. Haec omnia mundus quoque, ut ait Plato, habet. Facientem: hic deus est. Ex quo fit: haec materia est. Formam: haec est habitus et ordo mundi, quem videmus. Exemplar, scilicet, ad quod deus hanc magnitudinem operis pulcherrmi fecit. Propositum, propter quod fecit. Quaeris, quod sit propositum deo? Bonitas. Ita certe Plato ait: "Quae deo faciendi mundum fuit causa? Bonus est; bono nulla cuiusquam boni invidia est. Fecit itaque quam optimum potuit." Fer ergo, iudex, sententiam et pronuntia, quis tibi videatur verissimum dicere, non quis verissimum dicat. Id enim tam supra nos est quam ipsa veritas.

All art is but imitation of nature; therefore, let me apply these statements of general principles to the things which have to be made by man. A statue, for example, has afforded matter which was to undergo treatment at the hands of the artist, and has had an artist who was to give form to the matter. Hence, in the case of the statue, the material was bronze, the cause was the workman. And so it goes with all things,—they consist of that which is made, and of the maker. The Stoics believe in one cause only,—the maker; but Aristotle thinks that the word "cause" can be used in three ways: "The first cause," he says, "is the actual matter, without which nothing can be created. The second is the workman. The third is the form, which is impressed upon every work, —a statue, for example." This last is what Aristotle calls the *idos*. "There is, too," says he, "a fourth, —the purpose of the work as a whole." Now I shall show you what this last means. Bronze is the "first cause" of the statue, for it could never have been made unless there had been something from which it could be cast and moulded. The "second cause" is the artist; for without the skilled hands of a workman that bronze could not have been shaped to the outlines of the statue. The "third cause" is the form, inasmuch as our statue could never be called The Lance-Bearer or The Boy Binding his Hair, had not this special shape been stamped upon it. The "fourth cause" is the purpose of the work. For if this purpose had not existed, the statue would not have been made. Now what is this purpose? It is that which attracted the artist, which he followed when he made the statue. It may have been money, if he has made it for sale; or renown, if he has worked for reputation; or religion, if he has wrought it as a gift for a temple. Therefore this also is a cause contributing towards the making of the statue: or do you think we should avoid including, among the causes of a thing which has been made, that element without which the thing in question would not have been made?

To these four Plato adds a fifth cause, —the pattern which he himself calls the "idea"; for it is this that the artist gazed upon when he created the work which he had decided to carry out. Now it makes no difference whether he has his pattern outside himself, that he may direct his glance to it, or within himself, conceived and placed there by himself. God has within himself these patterns of all things, and his mind comprehends the harmonies and the measures of the whole totality of things which are to be carried out; he is filled with these shapes which Plato calls the "ideas," —imperishable, unchangeable, not subject to decay. And therefore, though men die, humanity itself, or the idea of man, according to which man is moulded, lasts on, and though men toil and perish, it suffers no change. Accordingly, there are five causes, as Plato says: the material, the agent, the make-up, the model, and the end in view. Last comes the result of all these. Just as in the case of the statue, —to go back to the figure with which we began, —the material is the bronze, the agent is the artist, the make-up is the form which is to be adapted to the material, the model is the pattern imitated by the agent, the end in view is the purpose in the maker's mind, and, finally, the result of all these is the statue itself. The universe also, in Plato's opinion, possesses all these elements. The agent is God; the source, matter; the form, the shape and the arrangement of the visible world. The pattern is doubtless the model according to which God has made this great and most beautiful creation.

The purpose is his object in so doing. Do you ask what God's purpose is? It is goodness, Plato, at any rate, says: "What was God's reason for creating the world? God is good, and no good person is grudging of anything that is good. Therefore, God made it the best world possible." Hand down your opinion, then, O judge; state who seems to you to say what is truest, and not who says what is absolutely true. For to do that is as far beyond our ken as truth itself. [3–11].[29]

The need so decisively pronounced here is the need to pass beyond the four causes of the Aristotelian *Organon,* the causes which, as limned in the *Prior Analytics,* were susceptible to the fallacious arguments detailed in the *Rhetoric* and potential grounds for sophistry and eristics. It is a need *for a model.* This is not just the method of imitatio as a means of instruction but, rather, a *received statement, a stable guide against which or within which new signs and meanings can be located.* This *fifth* cause, what we might call the *Senecan original,* anchors humanist writing in received antique traditions, antique texts, and antique ideas about the dignity and the educability of man and so takes the means, or technē, of rhetoric and poetic past any danger of sophistry. This is not at all surprising, of course, given the centrality of the exemplar to the humanist process of cultivation, of education. But, as Wesley Trimpi has recently commented, by placing the fifth cause between the formal and final causes Seneca opens up the possibilities of creation while preventing the possibilities of incoherence or chaos.[30] The range this allows is enormous. It admits as resources for imitatio, and as sources of meaning for humanist fiction, Platonic treatises, Lucian satires, even Hellenic and Alexandrian romances, such as that of Heliodorus. Indeed, much of the fun (as well as the significance) of Don Quijote's imitatio of Amadís de Gaula or Roldán rests on just this sense of poetics, just this poetic tradition.

A humanist poetics grounded in a composed narrative conflict thus finds its means in the imitatio of composite models and one or more patterns derived from one or more texts; it also depends on a third imitation, the use of images, which guarantees constructed specificity and likelihood; indeed, as Plato's *Timaeus* implies, there is a striking analogy between the Greek *ho eikōn,* the image, and *to eikos,* probability, that, as Eden notes, is "an affiliation well preserved in the English *to be like* and *to be likely*" (*Poetic and Legal Fiction,* p. 69). The image works with noteworthy effectiveness for Plato—in the *Symposium,* say, or at the close of the *Republic*—because it is a concrete realization of a pattern or form it imitates. But for Aristotle, whose *Poetics* argues instead for *representative* types of action (*spoudaioteron*) rather than *singular, unique* types of action (*ta kath' hekaston*), the image is often too limiting; he elevates *eikon* to mean something like metaphor (*Rhetoric* 3.2.11–13). It is, in fact, because of the *specialized* use of the *eikon* for him that poets fail worst when they fail and succeed best when they succeed (*Rhetoric* 3.2.14; *Poetics* 1413a10–11). Aristotle is therefore more comfortable with the use of an example (*paradeigma;* Latin *evidentia*) as an alternative argument, which he finds more probative and more persuasive than even the enthymeme or demonstration (*Rhetoric* 2.20). By the time of Cicero, however, Aristotle's chief ground of probability for narrative was slowly giving way to verisimilitude, which Cicero advocates in the *De Inventione*.

> Probabilis erit narratio, si in ea videbuntur inesse ea quae solent apparere in veritate; si personarum dignitates servabuntur; si causae factorum exstabunt; si fuisse facultates faciendi videbuntur; si tempus idoneum, si spatii satis, si locus opportunus ad eandem rem qua de re narrabitur fuisse ostendetur; si res et ad eorum qui agent naturam et ad vulgi morem et ad eorum qui audient opinionem accommodabitur. Ac veri quidem similis ex his rationibus esse poterit.

> The narrative will be plausible if it seems to embody characteristics which are accustomed to appear in real life; if the proper qualities of the character are maintained, if reasons for their actions are plain, if there seems to have been ability to do the deed, if it can be shown that the time was opportune, the space sufficient and the place suitable for the events about to be narrated; if the story fits in with the nature of the actors in it, the habits of ordinary people and the beliefs of the audience. Verisimilitude can be secured by following these principles. [1.21.29]

Quintilian, as we might expect, enlarges on this point, applying verisimilitude to person, to place, and even to *mood*.

> Quas φαντασίας Graeci vocant, nos sane visiones appellemus, per quas imagines rerum absentium ita repraesentantur animo, ut eas cernere oculis ac praesentes habere videamur. Has quiquis bene conceperit, is erit in adfectibus potentissimus. Hunc quidam dicunt, εὐρχνασωγος, qui sibi res, voces, actus secundum verum optime finget; quod quidem nobis volentibus facile continget. Nisi vero inter otia animorum et spes inanes et velut somnia quaedam vigilantium ita nos hae de quibus loquor imagines prosequuntur, ut peregrinari, navigare, proeliari, populos alloqui, divitiarum, quas non habemus, usum videamur disponere, nec cogitare sed facere: hoc animi vitium ad utilitatem non

transferemus? At hominem occisum queror; non omnia, quae in re praesenti accidisse credibile est, in oculis habebo? non percussor ille subitus erumpet? non expavescet circumventus? exclamabit vel rogabit vel fugiet? non ferientem, non concidentem videbo? non animo sanguis et pallor et gemitus extremus, denique exspirantis hiatus insidet?

There are certain experiences which the Greeks call φαντασίαι, and the Romans *visions*, whereby things absent are presented to our imagination with such extreme vividness that they seem actually to be before our very eyes. It is the man who is really sensitive to such impressions who will have the greatest power over the emotions. Some writers describe the possessor of this power of vivid imagination, whereby things, words and actions are presented in the most realistic manner, by the Greek word εὐρχνασωγος; and it is a power which all may readily acquire if they will. When the mind is unoccupied or is absorbed by fantastic hopes or daydreams, we are haunted by these visions of which I am speaking to such an extent that we imagine that we are travelling abroad, crossing the sea, fighting, addressing the people, or enjoying the use of wealth that we do not actually possess, and seem to ourselves not to be dreaming but acting. Surely, then it may be possible to turn this form of hallucination to some profit. I am complaining that a man has been murdered. Shall I not bring before my eyes all the circumstances which it is reasonable to imagine must have occurred in such a connexion? Shall I not see the assassin burst suddenly from his hiding-place, the victim tremble, cry for help, beg for mercy, or turn to run? Shall I not see the fatal blow delivered and the stricken body fall? Will not the blood, the deathly pallor, the groan of agony, the death-rattle, be indelibly impressed upon my mind? [*Institutio Oratoria* 6.2.29–31]

Such imaginative uses of images as imitatio led Longinus to extend the argument so that they might also awaken wonder and transport the audience to a state of amazement, and Augustine would in time Christianize such *evidentia* by arguing that Christ is God's imitatio of Himself rendered comprehensible to man (*De Anima* 15.2.20) and that, in turn, man should imitate Christ (*De Trinitate* 8.5.7). This idea Rabelais will pursue through Pantagruel and Erasmus will turn upside down (like the image of the Silenus box) in his portrayal of Folly.

Such concerns as we have been reviewing were precisely those that fix the attention of literary critics in the Quattrocento and the Cinquecento. "It is now generally accepted that the Quattrocento humanists were decisively influenced both by Aristotle's *Ethics* and by Cicero's rhetorical works," Victoria Kahn writes. "But it is important to recognize that the influence of these works was itself determined by the humanist conflation of rhetoric and poetics. Whereas in the works of these classical authors literature was seen as separate from or a propaedeutic to the acquisition of rhetorical skills, in the Renaissance the two were often combined and literature was conceived of in Horatian and rhetorical terms as having its own persuasive and formative powers" (*Rhetoric*, p. 37). Thus Marco Girolamo Vida's *De arte poetica* (1527) combines a Horatian discussion of the training of the poet and a defense of poetry in Book 1 with rhetorical treatises on invention and disposition in Book 2 and elocution in Book 3; Bernardino Daniello's *Poetica* (1536) expands Horace around the same three rhetorical concerns; and even Antonio Sebastiano Minturno's *De Poeta* (1559) combines Horace and Aristotle's *Poetics* with rhetorical writings of Cicero and Quintilian. In the Quattrocento, Salutati had urged in *De Nobilitate legum et medicinae* the practice of disputations, or *controversiae*, as practical means to sharpen the mind, inspire further learning, and engender practical results in the life of the student; in the Cinquecento Girolamo Fracastoro, in the *Navagero*, was urging the same:

> cum duae partes sint in homine, voluntas & intellectus, & voluntatis prudentia sit finis, intellectus finis cognitio & intellectio, si poeta imitetur & naturalia, non tantum personas, videbitur quidem omnem finem & omne institutum adimplesse, in imitatione quidem personarum prudentiam faciendo, in illa vero, quae est naturalium & similium, faciendo cognitionem: imitabitur enim & in hoc perfectiones, & excellentias rerum.

> since there are two parts in man, the will and the intellect, and since the end of the will is prudence and the end of the intellect is knowledge and understanding, if the poet imitates natural things and not only persons (for characters) he will have accomplished his whole end and his whole purpose: by serving prudence through the imitation of characters, knowledge through the imitation of natural things; for he will, in the latter case, be imitating the perfection and excellence inherent in natural things. [*Opera Omnia*, 1555 ed., fol. 157B–C][31]

Finally, imitatio is taken up, at its fundamental level, by Julius Caesar Scaliger in his *Poetices libri septem* of 1561. Bernard Weinberg summarizes Scaliger most conveniently.

> Poetry is conceived of, in Scaliger's system, primarily as language. As language, it must enter into two distinct relationships: (1) with the things which

are signified by the words employed and (2) with the audience for whom the signification is intended; thus:

Things ← Words → Men

These relationships will be present in all the linguistic arts and sciences—logic, rhetoric, and history—and hence poetry will be like all of the rest in certain respects. In all of them words are related to things through the process of imitation; that is, the word represents or imitates the thing just as the thing (in true Platonic fashion) represents or imitates the Ideal or the Idea of the thing in nature. Thus the word is constantly called the "image" or "imitation" of the thing: "imagines rerum" (p. 347), "aut imitatio rei, aut species" (p. 18), "rei effigies atque imago" (p. 175). In all these arts, secondly, the end is some kind of persuasion: "unus enim idemque omnium finis, persuasio" (p. 2). Poetry will differ from the others in two respects: in the use of verse and in the imitation of fictional rather than true objects (pp. 3, 5).

But such imitation through language has an end beyond itself, in the audience, which is the final arbiter of meaning and significance: "Nulla igitur imitatio propter se. nempe ars omnis extra se prospectat quod alicui conducibile sit"; "There is thus no imitation for its own sake, for it goes without saying that every art looks beyond itself toward somebody's advantage."[32]

In fact, with the rediscovery of Aristotle's *Poetics* in the Cinquecento, *mimesis* reconceived as imitatio became, as we might suspect, the chief critical concern of the Continental Renaissance. Daniello argues that the poet, unlike the historian, can mingle fiction with fact in his imitations because he is held not to what is or was but rather to what ought to be. Francisco Robortelli, in his massive *Aristotelis de arte poetica explicationes* (1548), likewise argues that the poet can add invented material in imitating reality and cites Xenophon's portrait of Cyrus and Cicero's of the ideal orator as classical pedigrees; moreover, he adds, poets can invent matters that transcend nature so long as they can be logically inferred from what we know in nature. There is even room in the epic, he admits, for the marvelous. Fracastoro similarly argues that the poet, in depicting the simple and essential truth of things, should not simply reproduce it but clothe it in beauty—beauty that is formal, ethical, and aesthetic, keeping only to decorum, which is for him suggested by the Idea the poet wishes to portray. Torquato Tasso, in his *Discorsi dell'Arte Poetica e del Poema Eroico,* tries to seek some balance between the claims of Christian and allegorical truth and poetic license and adornment; the naked truth, he claims, should be enhanced by novelty and surprise that will increase the sense of wonder: "Longinus," Krailsheimer notes, "was being added to Horace and Aristotle" (*Continental Renaissance*, p. 40). Minturno agrees: In adding that the function of poetry is not merely to please and instruct but to move, he seeks too in poetry for *admiratio*. This finally became canonized (and codified) near the close of the century with the *Della poetica* of Francesco Patrizi (1586), popularly known as the *Deca ammirabile*. There are, for Patrizi, two sorts of the marvelous: One is a quality of the poem itself, springing from the divine enthusiasm of the poet, which properly combines the credible and the incredible and so makes the work admirable (*mirabile*); the other is the effect produced in the audience, the extrinsic end of poetry (*la maraviglia*). Although all audiences are not alike, the poet should strive for this effect. According to Patrizi,

> non ogni poesia, ogni ingegno fara marauigliare, [ma saranno elleno] secondo la distinzione sopradetta de soggetti, e degli vditori, piu agli vni ch'agli altri marauigliose, Ma doura il poeta però sempre come di proprio vfficio suo e come a proprio fine, studiare di fare mirabile ogni soggetto ch'egli prenda per le mani, comunque la si prendano i leggitori, che non tutti son vguali.

> not every poem will cause every mind to marvel, but they will be more marvelous to some than to others according to the aforementioned distinctions of subjects and of listeners. But nevertheless the poet must always, as his proper function and as his proper end, strive to make marvelous every subject that he takes into his hands, no matter how the readers, who are not all alike, may take it.[33]

The understanding of imitatio in the Cinquecento, then, made striking progress, moving from a sense of imitating the classics through a sense of adding fiction to an increasing interest in the marvelous, in admiratio. We shall find the same progression in the development of humanist fiction, too, from the wordplay of Erasmus, which is always contained in its literary predecessors, through the use of fiction to illuminate history in Castiglione and Marguerite to the admission of the marvelous in the fiction of Rabelais and Cervantes.

Although Italy was considerably more advanced in these matters, there was also an increasing interest in literary theory in sixteenth-century France and Spain. Here too the practice of imitatio was seen as the basis of poetics. Joachim du Bellay, in his *Défense et illustration de la langue française* (1549), claims that French poetry can hope to attain perfection only by imitating the classics; though the true poet is born, only education in the classics will keep his talent from being useless. Six years later, Jacques Pelletier du Mans in his *Art Poétique* argues (not unlike Tasso) that the poet's responsibility is to imitate old things by adding to them something new, something beautiful, and something novel. Pierre de Ronsard invokes the fundamental principle of imitatio both in his *Abbregé de l'art poëtique françois* and in the 1572 preface to his incomplete epic, *La Franciade;* though he urges the use of images that are inspiring (since he sees the end of poetry as moral edification), he rules out images that are fantastic, unnatural, marvelous. But the sense of moral imagery is strongest in the work of Vauquelin de la Fresnaye, who, unlike Ronsard and Bellay, prefers scriptural themes for poetry; indeed, he notes, had the Greeks been Christian they too would have sung of the life and death of Christ—

> Si les Grecs, comme vous, Chrestiens eussent escrit,
> Ils eussent les hauts faits chanté de Iesus Christ, . . .
> Hé! quel plasir seroit-ce à cette heure de voir
> Nos poëtes Chrestiens, les façons recevoir
> Du tragique ancien? Et voir à nos mistères
> Les Payens asservis sous les loix salutaires
> De nos Saints et Martyrs? et du vieux testament
> Voir une tragedie extraite proprement?
>
> [*Art poëtique* 3.845; cf.1.901]

—a position fostered by Marguerite de Navarre and even hinted at in the fiction of Rabelais. During this same period there were only two writers on poetics of note in Spain: The poet Fernando de Herrera argues in his *Anotaciones* on the works of Garcilaso (1580) that poetic composition is largely concerned with artifice and contrivance and proceeds to identify and define numerous rhetorical figures; Alonso López Pinciano, in his *Philosophía antigua poética* (1596), a commentary on Aristotle, treats *mimesis* as imitatio, verisimilitude, and admiratio. Much more interesting, however, is the less learned work of Juan Huarte, the Galenic *Examen de ingenios para las ciencias* (1575), in which he argues that eloquence is the union of memory and imagination; wisdom, he says, is displayed in copious ornament and polish.

Drawing on their humanist texts and resources, then, as well as on the poetry and fiction of the sixteenth century, Continental literary critics of the period continued to fashion and refashion a poetics that was essentially humanist in its orientation—humanist in its concern with the dignity and potentiality of human nature and humanist in its development of the poetics directly inherited from classical works on poetics and rhetoric. Central to this understanding was not only Aristotelian mimesis but Ciceronian verisimilitude:

Humanist poetics was seen as drawing on the rhetorical narratives and conflicts found in the earliest *suasoriae* and *controversiae* modified only (and irregularly) by admitting a sense of wonder that would transport the poet and the reader beyond historically verifiable circumstances. For the humanists, poetics was *never* a matter of aesthetic enjoyment alone but always an instructive activity that made reading exploratory, an activity in which the reader, responding dialectically to the text, found closure to that text only in his own judgment or interpretation. In his recent study of Renaissance imitation, Thomas M. Greene distinguishes four kinds of imitation in the sixteenth century, which he calls reproductive (emulative), eclectic (composite), heuristic, and dialectical. The last of these was, by far, the most prominent among the humanists; for Greene, such imitation reveals "the vulnerability of the subtext"—that is, the Senecan original it imitates and from which it diverges to establish meaning— "while exposing itself to the subtext's potential aggression"; here, he finds, "the text is the locus of a struggle between two rhetorical or semiotic systems."[34] Such a struggle, however, may end in irresolution in which meanings may be infinite. That conception too has antique roots that go back at least as far as the *Phaedrus*. Near the close of that dialogue, Socrates tell Phaedrus that serious discourse about justice and similar topics "is far nobler, when one employs the dialectic method and plants and sows in a fitting soul intelligent words which are able to help themselves and him who planted them, which are not fruitless, but yield seed from which there spring up in other minds other words capable of continuing the process for ever, and which make their possessor happy, to the farthest possible limit of human happiness" (276E–277A).

Part of the joy of reading humanist fiction now, as it must have been for its earliest readers, is the infectious way it invites us to participate and the multiple meanings it allows us to discover for ourselves. Nowhere is this more evident than in Erasmus's *Encomium Moriae,* but with the introduction of the marvelous it continues throughout the sixteenth century. When the number of such meanings diminishes, when verisimilitude grows so dense that a sense of constricting circumstances takes over the narrative and robs it of its conspiratorial quality, the realistic novel that we associate with the eighteenth century emerges. But in the roots of that form, in the humanist poetics of the sixteenth century, it is initially otherwise, and in the studies that follow we shall examine how this collusive poetics, and the novel that eventuates from it, comes into being in the tradition of key texts of our own inherited past.

TWO

Sancte Socrates, ora pro nobis: Erasmus, the *Encomium*

Moriae, and the Poetics of Wordplay

 CONTINENTAL HUMANIST
POETICS BEGINS, IN BOTH ITS
PHILOLOGICAL AND ITS CREATIVE FIC-
TIVE TRADITIONS, WITH THE PIO-
NEERING ACCOMPLISHMENTS OF DESIDERIUS
ERASMUS, THE PERIPATETIC SCHOLAR. "OUT-
side Italy," A. J. Krailsheimer notes, "Erasmus is unquestionably the point of
departure from which almost everything else stems."[1] Even within Italy, the
birthplace of humanism, he was soon (and singularly) praised by Aretino.
"There is no one to compare with him," Aretino writes in one of his letters, "for
he was a strong fountain of speech, a broad river of intellect, and an immense
sea of literature; therefore his stature is such as to defy description."[2] He is the
West's chief humanist at the dawn of humanism, the father of Continental
humanist poetics. And the work of Erasmus best known to us now, the *Encomium Moriae,* which Johan Huizinga once called "the perfect work of art,"[3] is
what we might expect to herald the age of humanist poetics: a classical speech
of praise which, defending indefensible folly, demonstrates the power of humanist oratory and the skill and ingenuity available to the humanist rhetorician
while everywhere displaying in the passionate and irreducible commitment
despite the ludic surface its serious aim to defend humanist learning and
reason. "Its fascination," Kathleen Williams reminds us, is also "the fascination of Erasmus' mind: subtle, penetrating, imaginative."[4]

This first major work of Continental humanist poetics was also the first to
reach England in those generations that immediately followed: Sidney in his
Defence of Poesie saw that in the *Encomium Moriae* Erasmus "had an other foundation then the superficiall part would promise" and so honored its wit,[5] and
nearly a century later the young Milton found the *Encomium* in everyone's hands
at Cambridge: "Et cuique jam in manibus est ingeniosissimum illud Moriae

46

encomium non infimi Scriptoris opis."[6] We might speculate that the carnival atmosphere that at the beginning of Erasmus's fiction and the contagious and joyful energy and play of Folly in her subsequent self-praise could have led most amused humanists of the Continental Renaissance to receive *Encomium Moriae* as the supreme act of folly, as the theologians and monks exemplified by Martin Dorp did, but in the end few were misled by Folly in this way. Erasmus "neuer shewed more arte, nor witte, in any the grauest boke he wrote, than in this his praise of Folie," Thomas Chaloner remarks in his preface to the first English translation (1549), although he was well aware that the reader "maie chaunce to see his own image more liuely described [there] than in any peincted table" (sigs. A3v, A2v). As one of the early Tudor humanists, Chaloner was less concerned with the open satire on scholasticism and Church teachings and practices than with the ingenuity of Erasmus's premise and the deft imagination of his execution. "Folie in al poincts is not (as I take it) so straunge vnto vs, but that hir name maie well be abidden, as long as will we or nill we, she will be sure to beare a stroke in most of our dooyngs" (sig. A2). Chaloner extends Erasmus's text considerably so as to make clear in his translation Erasmus's humor and meaning in the original Latin; he sees—as Sidney and Milton do— that the *Encomium Moriae* is an Aphthonian fable, defined by his countryman, the Tudor Richard Rainolde in his *Foundacion of Rhetorike* (1563) as "a forged tale, cōtaining in it by the colour of a lie, a matter of truthe" (sig. A2v).

Their ready appreciation stems from an education all Continental humanists shared: "Better unborn than untaught," as one of the more popular Erasmian adages reads. The sources of the *Encomium Moriae* can be traced to Erasmus's early education by the Brethren of the Common Life at Deventer where the young boy found himself "swept onwards towards the New Learning by a hidden and overpowering instinct: *occulta naturae vi rapiebar ad bonas literas.*"[7] The Brethren, who "exerted their crowning activities in the seclusion of the schoolroom and the silence of the writing cell,"[8] instilled in Erasmus the love of ancient texts, both pagan and patristic, that led to a lifetime of labor: his grand, astonishing editions of Plautus, Terence, Cicero, Quintius Curtius, Suetonius, Pliny the Elder, Livy, and Lucian; his translations of Galen, Xenophon, Plutarch, and Demosthenes; his new texts of Jerome, Cyprian, Hilary, Ambrose, Augustine, and the uncompleted Origen; and his translations of the Greek New Testament into reliable Latin. The Brethren led Erasmus, too, to classical satires such as those recorded in later editions of the *Encomium Moriae* as additional remarks, the *parerga:* Seneca's *Apocolocyntosis,* which applies elevated classical allusions to the paltry facts of the present, and

Synesius's *De Laudibus Calvitii*, which uses formal oratory for trivial subjects.[9] Likewise imbued with the Brethren's *Devotio Moderna*, Erasmus seems particularly indebted to two earlier writers associated with his order. From Thomas à Kempis he borrows the idea of a layman's manual mapping the road to a religious life of pietistic simplicity and strength: The *Imitatio Christi* (1441; Englished 1503) is a clear prototype of Erasmus's *Enchiridion Militis Christiani* (also 1503) as well as a source for the humble fool in the later passages of the *Encomium Moriae*.[10] Another resource was Nicholas of Cusa, who also studied with the Brethren; from Nicholas's 1450 dialogue *The Idiot* and from his treatise on "learned ignorance," *De Docta Ignorantia* (1440), Erasmus took the idea that foolish ignorance is the highest wisdom, since it leads to the intuitive discovery of what lies beyond the perpetually receding limits of normal human knowledge, arriving finally at a personal realization of God. As Nicholas's fool renounces customary human learning so as to withdraw from the world and approach God, so in the *Encomium Moriae* Folly recedes from us, coming at the end of her declamation to her own fuller appreciation of the holy fool that is Christ.

From first to last, then, Erasmus (like Thomas and Nicholas) practices a conflation of the secular and the sacred that distinguishes the syncretism of sources common to Continental humanist poetics and to writers of humanist fiction. Thus Erasmus's earliest work, the *De Contemptu Mundi* (1488–89?), has more citations to the classics than to the Scriptures despite its subject, and one of his last writings, the late colloquium "The Godly Feast" (1522), leads to the most famous Erasmian syncretism of them all: *Sancte Socrates, ora pro nobis;* "Saint Socrates, pray for us."[11] Such thoughts, unique to us, are by no means unique to him. Wherever Erasmus lived in his early years—at Deventer, at the austere monastery at Steyn, with the bishop of Cambrai, at the severely regulated Collège de Montaigu in Paris—and wherever he found his humanist friends and so later settled, briefly, to write, hastily, *tumultuarie*—in Paris or Rome, Louvain or London, Basle or Freiburg, Oxford or Cambridge—his letters (like schoolroom exercises)[12] and writings (resembling declamations and disputations) are just such a vast array of composing sources. His strength is the strength of humanist thinkers, discovering and renewing texts of an antique past through inclusion and imitatio that is at once composite and creative.

From first to last too, Erasmus was a declared student of humanist rhetoric. In 1507 he writes William Warham that he has translated two plays by Euripides, *Hecuba* and *Iphigenia*, not for their poetry but for "argumentorum densitate quasique declamatoria quadam suadendi ac dissuadendi facultate

parentem Euripidem magis refert"; "the closeness of his [Euripides'] arguments and a sort of declamatory power of persuading and dissuading." [13] Another letter, to Ammonius on 21 December 1513, shows his interest in oratory
emerging as a theory of poetics, as we have seen: "Mihi semper placuit carmen
quod a prosa, sed optima non longe recederet. . . . ita me vehementer delectat
poema rhetoricum et rhetor poeticus, vt et in oratione soluta carmen agnoscas
et in carmine rhetoricam phrasin"; "Personally I have always liked verse that
was not far removed from prose (albeit prose of the first order). . . . I gain
peculiarly intense pleasure from an oratorical poem, in the verses of which the
oratorical style can be detected, or from a poetical orator in whose prose we can
see and appreciate poetry." [14]

But for him this was not new either. His first published work is an epitome
of Valla's *Elegantiae*, a study of rhetoric, eloquence, and persuasion that arranges Valla's words in alphabetical order like a dictionary. Erasmus's subsequent *De Ratione Studii* (*Right Method of Instruction*), written to design a curriculum for Colet at St. Paul's School, London (1511), urges that students learn
ways to "adorn" orations and "attend to the niceties of exposition,—the exordium, the transition, the peroration": *ab exordio ad narrationem, a narratione ad
divisionem, a divisione ad argumentationem, a propositione ad propositionem, a ratione
ad rationem, ab argumentatione ad epilogum aut perorationem.* [15] To this end, he
provides other aids for students (as well as for the mature rhetor) in the *Adagia*
(1509), a collection of proverbial wisdom of the ancients meant to illustrate and
persuade (for what could be truer than what everybody has said?), and in *De
Copia* (1512), a handbook providing exemplary means of variation and embellishment. In *De Conscribendis Epistolis* (*On Composing Letters*, written 1498,
published 1501), Erasmus also applies oratory to writing epistles, classifying
letters as deliberative, epideictic, and judicial (chaps. 31 and 32), and inserting
his own declamation on matrimony, both persuasive and dissuasive, as a kind of
minidisputation. [16] Such precepts and practices are likewise illustrated by his
own writing in a periodic Latin style built by repetitions of words, antitheses of
ideas, and clauses of increasing length offset through a skilled employment of
ellipsis, asyndeton, and anacoluthon: Erasmus learned always to rely on a
careful reader by showing rather than telling. "Ut non satis est soli bonitas, nisi
accedat & cultor idoneus, & semina: Ita non sufficit ingenii felicitas, nisi
accedat doctor & institutor egregius, & pracepta idonea," he comments in the
Parabolae of 1515; "Good soil is not enough without the proper husbandman
and the right seed; and gifts of intellect do not suffice unless there is an excellent
instructor to teach the proper principles." [17]

The *Encomium Moriae*—published with two titles, not one: *Morias enkomion; Stultitiae laus*—pulls together all of Erasmus's interests in one great act of humanist fiction that is at once deeply philosophic and, with its surface levity, an apparent *jeu d'esprit*. Allegedly drafted in London in seven days of 1509 when Erasmus was forty-three, revised and augmented for publication in Paris in 1511 when he was forty-five, it makes obvious use of humanist purpose, thought, and rhetoric as well as a standard technique of classical declamation, irony. *Stultitia loquitur:* Folly speaks, not wisdom, we learn at the beginning: she—not he—stands analogously in Sebastian Brant's pulpit in the *Narrenschiff* of 1494,[18] but like her predecessor she hopes through humanist eloquence to become *sophie,* to become not foolish but wise.

> Lubitum est enim paulisper apud vos Sophistam agere, non quidem hujus generis quod hodie nugas quasdam anxias inculcat pueris, ac plusquam muliebrem rixandi pertinaciam tradit, sed veteres illos imitabor, qui quo infamem Sophorum appellationem vitarent, *Sophistae* vocari maluerunt. Horum studium erat, Deorum ac fortium virorum laudes encomiis calebrare. Encomium igitur audietis, non Herculis, neque Solonis, sed meum ipsius, hoc est, STULTITIAE.

> I purpose a season to become a *Sophiste,* mistake me not I praie you, as if I saied Sophistrer, suche as now a daies driue into childers heads, certaine tangled trifuls, with more than womens stubbournesse and skoldyng in their disputacions. But I meane the other, who to the ende they myght shonne that presumptuous name of *Sophi* or wysemen, did rather take vpon them to be called *Sophistes:* Whose study and profession it was, to aduaunce, and set foorth in theyr writyngs the praises bothe of the Godds, and of men also, suche as were famous and worthies here in earth. Ye shall heare therfore the praise set foorth, not of *Hercules.* nor yet of *Solon,* but rather of myne owne selfe, That is to saie of Folie.[19]

This emblem passage contains within it Folly's complex prosopopoeia. She evidently plans to speak in the respected tradition of the best ancient authors, although they disclaimed the name of wise man for that of *rhetor,* which Folly's syntax makes antonymous.[20] Alternatively, she will be straightforward with us—"Mihi porro semper gratissimum fuit οτλιαν επι γλυδτζνεχθι dicere" (*LB* 4:408A); "it hath euer best lyked me to speake streight what so euer laie on my tongues ende" (sig. A2v)—unlike those orators whose public character was merely a role for the end of persuasion and despite being a woman, which for her day figured fickleness, ignorance, and temptation.[21]

Folly's intentions and behavior are therefore divorced from the start. No one

should expect her, she says, "ut juxta vulgarium istorum Rhetorum con-
suetudinem, me ipsam finitione explicem porro ut dividam, multo minus";
"[in] these common Sophisters and Rhetoriciens maner, [to] go about to shew
by diffinicion what I am, and muche lesse vse any diuision" (*LB* 4 : 408A; sig.
A2v). Yet that is precisely what she does. She presents a classical declamation in
the five parts that Cicero and Quintilian teach. The partitioning of her argument and its component issues is clear; and she lectures *about* her audience
while lecturing *to* them. Folly's speech is thus from the start both wise and
foolish; it is learned in its allusions but absurd in its quotations, wrenched as
they are from their context;[22] and in both ways her speech is a deliberate parody
of the sort that Erasmus—whom Roger Ascham calls "the honor of learning of
all oure time" in *The Scholemaster* (1570; sig. G3)—had earlier hired himself
out to compose for Philip of Burgundy.[23] Although Folly denies speaking in
any traditional oratorical form, that is precisely her method, as Hoyt Hudson
and Walter Kaiser have long since shown us;[24] and whatever she says, rational or
not, will bear our close attending.

"Soli simplices ac veridici sunt," continues Folly in the *confirmatio.*

Quid autem veritate laudatius? Quamquam enim Alcibiadeum apud Platonem
proverbium, veritatem vino pueritiaeque tribuit, tamen omnis ea laus mihi
peculiariter debetur, vel Euripide teste, cujus exstat illud celebre de nobis
dictum, μωρὰ γὰρ μωρὸς λέγει. Fatuus quidquid habit in pectore, id & vultu
prae se fert, & oratione promit. At sapientum sunt duae, illae linguae, ut idem
meminit Euripides, quarum altera verum dicunt, altera, quae pro tempore
judicarint opportuna. Horum est nigrum in candida vertere, & eodem ex ore
frigidum pariter & calidum efflare, longeque aliud conditum habere in pectore,
aliud sermone fingere. Porro in tanta felicitate, tamen hoc nomine Principes
mihi videntur infelicissimi, quod deest, a quo verum audiant, & assentatores pro
amicis habere coguntur.

Yea, [fools] haue a meruailous propretee, in that they onely are plainsaiers, and
southspeakers. And what is more laudable (at least as outwardely ye commende
it) than plainesse of speche? For although *Alcibiades* prouerbe in *Plato ascribeth
trouth to children and dronkennes,* yet maie all the praise therof be chiefly appended
to me, as *Euripides* can well testifie, who wrote thus: *A foole speaketh like a foole (id
est) plainely.* For what soeuer he hath in his thought, that sheweth he also in his
continuaunce, and expresseth it in his talke. Wheras these wisemen are thei,
that ar *double tounged,* as the aforesaied *Euripides* telleth vs, with the one of whiche
they speake the trueth, with the other, thyngs mete for the tyme and audience.

Theyr propretee it is to chaunge blacke into white, and out of one mouthe to blow bothe hote and colde: and thynke vnhappeliest in their herts, whan they speake smotheliest with their toungs. How be it me seemth that princs, how euer the haboundant felicitee theyr estate is wont to dase meane folks eies, maie yet as to this respecte be counted right miserable, because they want, of whom to here the trouthe, and are faine therefore to take flattrers for their friends.

[LB 4:437E–438A; sigs. G2v–G3]

The true antitype of Minerva, Folly addresses us in a choplogic that displays that "trembling equipoise between jest and earnest," the *coincidentia oppositorum* J. A. K. Thomson has defined as irony.[25] Folly's style has its pedigree in the ancient syntactic rush of *volubilitas,* but she has stolen our language in the process and left us without any scraps; and the rapid transitions she makes from wit to satire to ecstasy force us into a similar Protean set of responses.[26]

The title mirrors this factual dissembling. The genitive *Moriae* is syntactically ambiguous; it may mean that Folly is doing the praising or it may mean that Folly is being praised. *Encomium Moriae,* first drafted at Thomas More's house at the Old Barge, Bucklersbury, can likewise be doubly translated as *The Praise of Folly* or *In Praise of More.* Raising all these possibilities for his *"small Declamation"* (sig. A2v) in a prefatory letter to *"disputant"* More (sig. A4), Erasmus refuses to choose among them. *"Deinde suspicabar hunc ingenii nostri lusum tibi praecipue probatum iri,"* he continues, allowing *ingenii* to mean *wisdom* or *foolery*—the same deliberate ambiguity More will use in *Utopia*—and adds,

> *propterea quod soleas hujus generis jocis, hoc est, ni fallor, nec usquequaque insulsis, impendio delectari, & omnino in communi mortalium vita Democritum quemdam agere. Quamquam tu quidem, ut pro singulari quadam ingenii tui perspicacitate, longe lateque a vulgo dissentire soles, ita pro incredibili morum sua vitate facilitatque cum omnibus omnium horarum hominem agere, & potes & gaudes.*

> I conceiv'd this exercise of wit, would not be least approv'd by you, inasmuch as you are wont to be delighted with such kind of mirth, that is to say, neither unlearned, if I am not mistaken, nor altogether insipid, and in the whole course of your life have play'd the part of a Democritus. And though, such is the excellence of your Iudgement, that 'twas ever contrary to that of the peoples, yet such is your incredible affability, and sweetness of temper that you both can, and delight to carry your self to all men, a man of all hours.

[LB 4:401–2; sig. A2v]

This portrait of More is one of an intellectual recluse—and *because of* his *"excellence of . . . Iudgement"*—yet one who nevertheless associates with those common people from whom his wisdom might estrange him. Thus, in a letter written directly to his reader rather than to More (for it tells More nothing he does not already know), More himself is made, at a second level of fiction, into the foolishly wise Folly, as the implicit equation of the punning title advocates.[27]

Customarily, critics have called upon this prefatory letter as a second perspective that can be used to interpret the declamation that follows, since it recalls the occasion of Erasmus's tiresome journey on horseback from Italy, the incubation of the *Encomium*, Erasmus's awareness of classical precedents, and his self-defense against his sarcasm and personal invective. The endeavor, Erasmus contends, is "*quem nec ista placare possunt, is saltem illud meminerit, pulcrum esse a stultitia vituperari, quam cum loquentem fecerimus, decoro personae serviendum fuit*" (*LB* 4:403–4); is "*rather to make mirth, than bite*," to deal with "*things, rather ridiculous, than dishonest*" (sig. A4). But such remarks, given the satire on the Church that they introduce, show us clearly that the letter is a parody of the dedicatory epistle, foreshadowing the parody of an epideictic declamation: "*stultitiam laudavimus, sed non omnino stulte*" (*LB* 4:403–4); "*I haue prais'd Folly, but not altogether foolishly*" (sig. A3v), Erasmus writes in his letter to More. The similarly maieutic Folly says precisely the same thing, and chorically. As if to guarantee that we shall in time share this joke, Erasmus concludes his epistle by remarking that any errors must be blamed on Folly, who is a notoriously unreliable speaker—a perfect complement to Folly's own insistent admonition that her speech has been transcribed for us by an unreliable amanuensis so that she too is blameless if there are errors in the record.[28]

Such a defense of the *Encomium* is, at its operational level, Folly so rhetorically manipulating subject and audience that words and meanings are unmoored, as we are. Her style is what Richard Sylvester has called "an anti-style" ("Problem of Unity," p. 131), arguably necessary in an age of eristics; and when we turn to the text we see that Folly's presentation is initially arranged in so impeccable a classical order[29] that it not only supplies us with our first clues for understanding but also reiterates and thereby salvages the rhetorical form in which it is couched. For the first Platonic Form, the first Senecan original that Erasmus means to imply in this exemplary work of humanist poetics, is the standard Aphthonian *encomium*—as the title insists—taught to later Tudor readers by Rainolde's *Foundacion of Rhetoricke* (sigs. K4–K4v).

Folly begins her self-praise with a brief biography. Her parents, she tells us unequivocally, are Plutus, god of riches, and a nymph named Youth; she is beautifully rich because she is richly beautiful—a clearly satiric comment. She was conceived out of wedlock, moreover, when her father was inebriated (*LB* 4:410A; sig. A4), on the Fortunate Isles (*LB* 4:410B; sig. A4v).[30] This is obvious joking, but it is also a little puzzling when we consider that wealth and beauty make her susceptible to drunkenness. Folly repeatedly sees materialism as evil (as we do), a foolishness she herself cannot abide. What she implies, then, is not that she is Riches or Youth, but that she is the singular product of both: and it is the riches *of* youth, which she redefines as instinctual pleasure and beauty, that she calls again and again the basis of a wisdom *misjudged* to be folly. She defines herself further by identifying her chief companions as Madness and Oblivion, again outrageous on the face of it (*LB* 4:410A–B, 412D; sigs. A4v, B2).[31] But by the close of her oration, we will realize that this is seriously meant, for wisdom resides only in states of madness and oblivion, both suggesting self-delusion from the wickedness and pain of the world.

The premise of Folly's character, like the title, is paradoxical. So is the execution of the argument where the worse continually appears the better part: *hoc est hominem esse;* at the heart of Folly's argument is the issue of semantics—or the very root of sophistical rhetoric. So for Folly, drawing on classical myth and contemporary proverbs for authority, a father's foolish love for his squint-eyed son provides family unity (*LB* 4:420A; sig. C4v); foolish youths can be seen as carefree men rather than experienced hypocrites; drunkenness can be a necessary sedative; blindness can make marriage possible; cities and empires are preserved by flattery; and self-love can lead to contentment and that in turn to generosity: for how can we love our neighbors as ourselves if, first, we do not love—that is, respect—ourselves?[32] And how, then, do we maintain art?

> Nisi adsit dextra haec Philautia. . . . Tolle hoc vitae condimentum & protinus frigebit cum sua actione Orator, nulli placebit cum suis numeris Musicus, explodetur cum sua gesticulatione Histrio, ridebitur una suis cum Musis Poëta, sordebit cum arte Pictor. . . . Ut ne dicam interim, nullum egregium facinus adiri, nisi meo impulsu, nullas egregias artes, nisi me auctore fuisse repertas.

> Take awaie this saulce of *Selflikyng* [Philautia], which is euin the verie relesse [release] of mans life and doyngs, and by and by ye shal see the *Oratour* cold in his mattier, the *Musicien* mislyked withall his discant, the *Plaier* hissed out of the place, the *Poete* and his muses taught to skorne, the *Peincter* and his art naught set by. [*LB* 4:421E–F, 422C; sig. D2v]

In sum, "I recke not much, to passe ouer vntouched," as Chaloner puts it, "now no maner arte, or noble deede was euer attempted, nor any arte or science inuented, other than of whiche I might fully be holden first author" (sig. D3).

This brief catalogue of putative folly redefined as wisdom is an accurate if miniature representation of the larger anthology that is Folly's *confirmatio*—and most of her oration. It is a joyful act of wordplay that Erasmus calls elsewhere an *argumentum fictum*.[33] She herself provides an initial index to it with her citation of the Socratic Silenus.

> Principio constat res omnes humanas, velut Alcibiadis Silenos, binas habere facies nimium inter sese dissimiles. Adeo ut quod prima, ut ajunt, fronte mors est, si interius inspicias, vita sit: contra quod vita, mors: quod formosum, deforme: quod opulentum, id pauperrimum: quod infame, gloriosum: quod doctum, indoctum: quod robustum, imbecille: quod generosum, ignobile; quod laetum, triste: quod prosperum, adversum: quod amicum, inimicum: quod salutare, noxium: breviter, omnia repente versa reperies, si Silenum aperueris.

> For fyrst it is not vnknowen, how all humaine thyngs lyke the *Silenes or duble images of Alcibiades,* haue two faces much vnlyke and dissemblable, that what outwardly seemed death, yet lokyng within ye shulde fynde it lyfe: and on the other side what semed life, to be death: what fayre, to be foule: what riche, beggerly: what cunnyng, rude: what stronge, feable: what noble, vile: what gladsome, sadde: what happie, vnlucky: what friendly, vnfriendly: what healthsome, noysome. Briefely the Silene ones beyng vndone and disclosed, ye shall fynde all thyngs tourned into a new semblance. [*LB* 4:428A–B; sig. E3][34]

As an emblem of myriad potentiality, though, we must also sense its darker and more serious purposes; the Silenus schemes man as *sub specie moriae.* Thus Folly realizes the possibilities of her own persona in this symbol of doubleness; in rhetorical terms, she has transformed the apparent declamation of praise, the *encomium,* into a disputation between what is said and its very opposite, a *disputatio.*[35] So perceiving, we can only marvel at Folly's attempt—or Erasmus's—to master such possibilities and dangers of rhetorical sophistry and convert them creatively, *fictively,* through an analogy and metaphor into a usable humanist poetics. Continental humanist fiction begins here.

Recognizing Folly's customary dichotomizing, moreover, allows us to locate and chart our own responses more carefully. Sometimes we agree with Folly, and she seems to agree with us; other times, she is outrageous, and she attacks us: *"qui se sapientiae studio dediderunt"*; "this kynd of men, that are bookisshe" are thereby "peuisshe" (*LB* 4:423C; sig. D4v). But Folly is also strangely limited. Her only possible strategy, we soon learn, is from one extreme to the other, from witnessing to life as we would have her if she were

wisdom and reporting actual life as folly. Thus her apparent joke, to find folly
in wisdom or wisdom in folly as Erasmus claims in his letter to More, is in fact
her one insistent point.[36] Beneath the inviting wordplay Folly is severely
circumscribed. The only complication is that, in love with rhetoric yet a bit
fearful of its backfiring, she assumes *both* the role of defendant and that of
respondent so as to assure herself of victory in her own argument.

Her oration, continuing this basic tactic, realizes the continuing value of
the Silenic disputation as a *poetic form*. Having recovered her own Senecan
original, she now becomes more indulgent in developing her paradoxical
themes—for, in love with the disputation, she seems limited to doublets—in
the notions of wisdom in madness and life in oblivion. Her observations,
deliberately nonbookish, are experiential; in this too she cannot help addressing a basic concern of humanism.

Principio si rerum usu constat prudentia, in utrum magis competet ejus cog-
nominis honos, in sapientem, qui partim ob pudorem, partim ob animi timidi-
tatem nihil aggreditur, auin stultum, quem necque pudor quo vacat, necque
periculum, quod non perpendit, ab ulla ne deterret? Sapiens ad libros Veterum
consugit, atque hinc meras vocum argutias ediscit. Stultus adeundis cominus-
que periclitandis rebus, veram, ni fallor, prudentiam colligit. Id quod vidisse
videtur Homerus, etiam si caecus, cum ait ρεχθὲν δέ τε νήπιος ἔγνω. Sunt
enim duo praecipua ad cognitionem rerum parandam obstacula, pudor, qui
fumum offundit animo, & metus, qui ostenso periculo, dehortatur ab adeundis
facinoribus. At his magnifice liberat Stultitia. Pauci mortales intelligunt ad
quam multas alias quoque commoditates conducat, numquam pudescere, &
nihil non audere.

And fyrst of all, if *Prudence* consisteth in longe practise and experience of thyngs,
vnto whether of these maie the honour of that name better square? Either to this
wyseman, who partly for shame, and partly for dastardnesse of herte, attempteth
nothyng, or els that foole, whom neither shame, beyng shameles, nor perill,
beyng reckeles, maie feare from prouyng any thyng. A wyseman reports hym
selfe to his bokes, and there learneth naught but mere triflyng distinctions of
woords. A foole in ieopardyng, and goyng presently where thyngs are to be
knowne, gathereth (vnles I am deceiued) the perfect true prudence. Whiche
Homer seemeth, notwithstandyng his blindnesse to haue seen, whan he saied
thus, *A foole knoweth the thyng, that is ones dooen.* For there be two stronge lettes
againste such knowlage of thyngs to be gathered, that is to saie, shame and
dreade: shame, that casts a mist before mens mynds: and dreade, that shewyng

the perilles, discounsaileth men from ventryng any enterprises. But I Folie maie, and am wonte to wype those lettes cleane awaie. Yea, few men consider, how many ways els it auaileth to blousshe at nothyng, and dare dooe euery thung.

[*LB* 4:417C–418A; sigs. E2v–E3]

Men hang onto life; "lothe they are to die yet" (sig. F2). "So that how lesse cause they haue, why they shoulde lyue, yet so muche leefer is life vnto theim, not that they fele any combraunce of the same" (sig. F2); "ut ne tum quidem libeat vitam relinquere cum exacto Parcarum stamine, ipsa jam dudum eos relinquit vita, quoque minus sit causae, cur in vita manere debeant, hoc magis juvet vivere, tantum abest, ut ullo vitae taedio tangantur" (*LB* 4:431C). Folly's gift is her lesson teaching us the value of—the inability to ignore or avoid—experiential learning. But this is also inescapably the occasion for human folly too.

> Fucis assidue vultum oblinere, nusquam a speculo discedere, [infirmae pubis silvam vellere,] vietas ac putres ostentare mammas, tremuloque gannitu languentem sollicitare cupidinem, potitare, misceri puellarum choris, litterulas amatorias scribere.
>
> [Old women, for example] still daube theyr lither chekes with peintyng, neuer goe from the glasses, shew out theyr flaggie and pendant dugges, prouoke theyr stale nature with hote restoratiues, sitte vp at bankettes, daunce galierds, write loueletters, &c. [*LB* 4:432B–433A; sig. F2v]

Man's insight can be a delusion; his hope, his despair; his pride, his ridiculousness.

In the second half of her oration Folly therefore logically devotes her attention to a series of mordacious illustrations at the urging of "these eluishe *Sophistrers*" (sig. F3), illustrations of foolish humanists who put living before learning, in which we would agree with her.

> Est, inquiunt, homini peculiariter addita disciplinarum cognito, quarum adminiculis id quod natura diminutum est, ingenio penset.
>
> *The knowlage* (saie they) *of disciplines is peculierly geuin to man, throughe helpe wherof, what he lacketh by nature, he maie supplie with his witte and learnyng.*
>
> [*LB* 4:433C; sig. F3]

They and not Folly are the true agents of excess; "nihil ultra sortem sapere velle"; "nothing can be more foolisshe than wisedome out of place" (*LB* 4:429C; sig. E4). She scoffs at the neoteric applications of grammar, logic, and rhetoric, of law and science (cf. *LB* 4:457A ff.; sig. K3v ff.).[37] The golden world had no need for them, she claims, anticipating Castiglione's Bembo and Cervantes' Don Quijote; only the iron age has turned to science and superstition.

> Atque in hoc ipso genere, quo quisque indoctior, audacior, incogitantiorque, hoc pluris fit etiam apud torquatos istos Principes.

> Yea and commenly the rasher, the vncunnynger, and lesse circumspect the vndertaker of any of those vsuall sciences is, the more yet is he regarded & allowed euen amonges great men also. [*LB* 4:434B–D; sig. F4]

Such men are broken, spurred, girded, hampered, whipped, laden, bound, and imprisoned with their own foolish desires (*LB* 4:435D–436A; sigs. F4v–G1). The passage anticipates a sterner diatribe which, encomium made invective, defense turned prosecution, assaults nearly all the secular seven liberal arts (*LB* 4:457A ff.; sig. K3v ff.) and sacred practices and rituals—all leveled to indulgences in both senses of that word—of the Holy Catholic Church (*LB* 4:481B ff.; sig. O3v ff.).[38] In abruptly dismissing *"Stoickes Syllogismes"* (*Stoicis enthymematis*), for "some familiar exemple" (*LB* 4:436C; sig. G1v), she prefers Grillus to Ulysses "for all his deep witte" (*LB* 4:436B; sig. G1), because wit leads only to suffering and chance. In her penchant for pushing to extremes so as to clarify true wisdom and true folly, Folly invites from us a moderation divorced from either alternative of her spiraling sophistry—we would not eliminate the education derived from experience, yet not all experience is equally educational—and so aligns the *effects* of her oration with a stunningly *usable* poetic. Her art, like the art of those who will follow her, is one of methexis, where the audience is invited (and even required) to join into the fiction, into *fiction making.*

The other continuing metaphor that Folly uses to complement and extend indefinitely that of the Silenus is the *topos* that Ernst Curtius has found in her declamation turned disputation, first employed by Lucian, that "all the world is a stage" (*totus mundus agit histrionem*).[39] It is the second leitmotif of her work. It appears first just after her discussion of the Silenus.

> Si quis histrionibus in scena fabulam agentibus personas detrahere conetur, ac spectatoribus veras nativasque facies ostendere, nonne is fabulam omnem perverterit, dignusque habentur, quem omnes e theatro velut lymphatum saxis ejiciant? . . . Porro mortalium vita omnis quid aliud est, quam fabula quaepiam, in qua alii aliis obtecti personis procedunt, aguntque suas quisque

partes, donec choragus educat e proscenio? . . . . Haud equidem inficias inverim, modo fateantur illi vicissim hoc esse, vitae fabulam agere.

If one at a solemne stage plaie, woulde take vpon hym to plucke of the plaiers garmentes, whiles they were saiyng theyr partes, and so disciphre vnto the lokers on, the true and natiue faces of eche of the plaiers, shoulde he not (trow ye) marre all the mattier? . . . All this life of mortall men, what is it els, but a certaine kynde of stage plaie? whereas men come foorthe disguised one in one arraie, an other in an other, eche plaiyng his parte, till at least the maker of the plaie, or bokebearer causeth theim to auoyde the skaffolde. . . . to dissemble, or erre so, is the right plaiyng of the pageants of this life.

> [*LB* 4:428B–C, 428C, 429D; sigs. E3–E3v, E3v, E4].

This accumulation of references suggests the ever-present immanence of folly by suggesting the impermanence of human action. Later Folly returns to this same metaphor.

Neque perperam sensit Argivus ille, qui hactenus insaniebat, ut totos dies solus desideret in theatro, ridens, plaudens, gaudens, quod crederet illic miras agi tragoedias, cum nihil omnino ageretur, cum in caeteris vitae officiis probe sese gereret, *jucundus amicis, comis in uxorem, posset qui ignoscere servis, Et signo laesa non insaniere lagena.*

(Lykewyse *Argiuus,* he whom *Horace* writeth of, iudged not muche amysse. Who this farsooth raued, that whole daies togethers he woulde sitte alone in the *Theatre* (a place where the commen plaies were plaied) laughyng, and clappyng his handes, and reioysyng muche to hym selfe, because hym seemed verily that some excellent *Tragedies* were in plaiyng there, wheras in deede he sawe nothyng at all. Whan yet for all that as to other respects, he behaued hym selfe wysely enough, beyng welbeloued of his friends, gentill to his wyfe, and easie to his seruants, without fallyng in any rage with theim, whan he founde a backe faulset set in his wyne vessell. Now whan his kinsfolkes procurement, geuyng hym medecines therfore, had healed his disease, and restored hym to his former wittes, marke ye, how he fell out with theim, in blamyng their thanklesse and double diligence. *Ye haue slaine, and not saued me, ô my friendes (quod he) in wrestyng my pleasure from me in this sort, and by force bereuyng me suche a most delectable errour of my mynde.* [*LB* 4:440A–B; sig. G4v]

This Grecian's act of looking at an empty stage was not madness but the sane choice of a distinguishing perspective.[40] But when we realize this, we take not the view of the man in the theater applauding the empty stage because it remains empty, or the view of his family that he is altogether mad, but a third view that can reconcile both. We see his distraction as a poetic alternative to mundane reality. We judge the man as both sane *and* mad. Again, when pressed by Folly to dismiss a stag hunt as coarse butchery,[41] we find it contains three independent commonplaces: the joy of sport, the beauty of the hunt, *and* the cruelty of slaying. Likewise, when we are confronted by Folly's over-simplification of national traits for England, Scotland, France, Italy, Turkey, Spain, and Germany (*LB* 4:448A–449A; sig. I2), we see at once the basis for them—they require us openly to moderate her excessive and reductive claims. The *Encomium Moriae* consistently asks us, then, to endorse not the double perspective of inside–outside (as with the Silenus) or defendant–respondent (as with Folly's disputation) but the third view of a judge. Methexis is demanded of us. Any other reaction would mislead and betray us; would render us functionless before Folly's satire, drawing Erasmus (both the real-life martyr and the actual author) into the fictive frame of reference; and finally blur all boundaries on which we normally rely for meaning in fiction and ask us to establish a moderating position of our own.

> Hic rursum adfines sunt ii, qui sibi stultam quidem, sed tamen jucundam persuasionem induerunt, futurum, ut si ligneum, aut pictum aliquem Polyphemum Christophorum adspexerint, eo die non sint perituri, aut qui sculptam Barbaram praescriptis verbis salutarit, sit incolumis praelio rediturus, aut si quis Erasmum certis diebus, certis cereolis, certisque preculis convenerit, brevi sit dives evasurus.

> Than againe next neyghbours to [those who tell old wives' tales], are suche as haue a foolisshe, but yet a pleasant perswasion to theim selues, that what daie thei see a woodden or a peincted image of the geant saincte *Christopher*, no mischaunce shall betide theim. Or if thei grete the grauen image of saincte *Barbara*, with some praier prescribed for that vse, they can not but retourne hurtelesse from the warres. Or if vpon the sondaies they woorship saincte *Erasmus*, with certaine tapers and *Paternosters*, thei shall in short space become riche men. [*LB* 4:443A–D; sig. H3]

Here we must condemn the practice but not its needs or motive; we can contemn the medals but not the saints they demean. The same requirement is levied when Folly condemns herself; simultaneously, Erasmus condemns this work for More. "Illud autem lepidissmum," she mocks, "cum mutuis epistolis, carminibus, encomiis sese vicissim laudant, stulti stultos, indoctos indocti"; "This is the best sporte of all, to see theim present eche other with *epistles, with verses, and with mattiers of prose,* sent from fooles, to fooles: and from asses, to asses" (*LB* 4 : 460C; sigs. L2v–L3).[42] The encomium—both encomia—have point as well as sport, but we must redefine the attack to see why; to say simply that this is both true and untrue (that is, paradoxical) is no longer sufficient. Confronted with such a tumbling perspective, with such apparently crumbling logic, and yet with such apparently surefooted rhetoric—for Erasmus is never anacoluthic—we are forced to remain stubbornly independent in our inter-pretation. Our own reason—the need for a logic, the preservation of a rheto-ric—is clearly at stake. So we develop a third view, a view that like the many roles we play in a single life depends on the judge, the occasion, and the context. Meaning is potentially multifold.[43]

Even in this observation, Folly precedes us. She encodes such variety by generalizing on the motif of the world as a theater, acknowledging that "per-petua quadam ebrietate, mentem gaudiis, delitiis, tripudiis, expleo"; "through a continuall drunkennesse (as it were) I replenishe your *mynds,* with more ioie, delite, and pleasure" (*LB* 4 : 452B; sig. I4v; my italics). It is in these terms that "this humaine life is nought but a certaine great plaie of Folie"; "*vitam hu-manum nihil aliud quam Stultitiae ludicrum esse*" (sig. Q3). Rosalie Colie has also pointed to this fundamental characteristic of the rhetorical *Encomium Moriae.* Folly "undercuts and undermines her whole argument herself," Colie claims, "to leave each reader alone with the unpleasant realization that Folly has been consistent to the last. . . . she has abandoned the reader to make his own decisions about value." For

> We know of Folly . . . Only what Folly herself tells us. . . . Her discourse is all
> of folly: her encomium is a *self*-praise. [Thus] readers are constantly off balance,
> aware only of the infinite progression, or regression, implied in Folly's simplest
> observation on folly. . . . A formal aspect of the end of the encomium . . . is
> that it has no formal ending. The discourse stops, certainly, but in such a way as
> to stimulate further thought in the reader, even further speculation—Folly cuts
> off her own discourse, but not discourse in general. . . . One might risk the
> further play, to suggest that paradox denies ends to assert the importance
> of means.[44]

Folly's ambiguity, Richard Sylvester adds, "which is her essence, results di-rectly from her awareness not merely that the world is irrational, but also that, if the world is ever to be made amenable to rationality, it must accommodate its irrationality by consciously and ironically indulging it" ("Problem of Unity," p. 132). In making the declamation-turned-disputation a work that is essentially *triangular,* Folly has opened up rhetoric to multiple perspectives without necessarily resorting to sophistry.[45] This is why at her conclusion she even embraces Erasmus into her speech and so removes him from outside it, even condemns him as the basis for her portrait of the scholar, so that the authority for judging her declamation-turned-disputation must come from us. Folly's main point, then, is that all of us compound wisdom and folly, are rational and irrational, need enlightenment and self-delusion. Humanism consists in a reverence for humanity such that each act as well as each actor on the stage of life has irrevocable worth; and humanist poetics becomes distinguished here not for its telling but for its inquiring, testing, and mediating powers.

Such continuing participatory revision is, in fact, required of us as readers. We must, as Erasmus was so in the habit of doing, *translate* the text. The job is not an easy one, for Folly's clues for interpretation seem so scattered, so extreme, and so problematic that to choose one or two or even three of them would only seem to make us foolish by ignoring so many more than we entertain. A more stable—and a more reliable—method for reading the *Encomium Moriae* is to compare it with its models or Senecan originals. The first of these (and the one most readily apparent) is Lucian; Folly's skill at fabrication and facility at language have strong affinities to the Greek rhetor of Samosata, whose dialogues Erasmus began translating with Thomas More in 1505 when both men were studying Greek. Indeed, Erasmus's description of Lucian in one of his letters seems more relevant to us now as Erasmus's best self-portrait than it does as a portrait of his model satirist.[46] "The same sentiments—forming the basis of Erasmus's humanist poetics of wordplay—are also to be found in the Greek epitaph on the title page of the Aldine edition of Lucian's *Opera* (1503): "These are the works of Lucian, who knew that folly is of ancient birth, and that what seems wise to some men appears ridiculous to others; there is no common judgment in men, but what you admire others will laugh at."[47]

It is this infectious Lucianic spirit—revealed in the startling but simple grounds of his fictions, the exuberance of his style, the extended exaggerations of his situational satires, and the inventiveness of his prosopopoeias—that in the *Icaromenippus* gives to Erasmus the chief metaphor for the *Encomium Moriae.* Here, on a flight to the moon, Menippus witnesses the world as a theater of fools.

> In one place there were banquets and weddings, elsewhere there were sessions of court and assemblies; in a different direction a man was offering sacrifice, and close at hand another was mourning a death. Whenever I looked at the country of the Getae I saw them fighting; whenever I transferred my gaze to the Scythians,

they could be seen roving about on their wagons; and when I turned my eyes aside slightly, I beheld the Egyptians working the land. The Phoenicians were on trading-ventures, the Cilicians were engaged in piracy, the Spartans were whipping themselves and the Athenians were attending court. As all these things were going on at the same time, you can imagine what a hodge-podge it looked. It is as if one should put on the stage a company of singers, or I should say a number of companies, and then should order each singer to abandon harmony and sing a tune of his own; with each one full of emulation and carrying his own tune and striving to outdo his neighbor in loudness of voice, what, in the name of Heaven, do you suppose the song would be like? . . . Well, my friend, such is the part that all earth's singers play and such is the discord that makes up the life of men. Not only do they sing different tunes, but they are unlike in costume and move at cross-purposes in the dance and agree in nothing until the manager drives each of them off the stage, saying that he has no further use for him. After that, however, they are all quiet alike, no longer singing that unrhythmical medley of theirs. But there in the play-house itself, full of variety and shifting spectacles, everything that took place was truly laughable.[48]

The metaphor of the world as stage and men and women as merely players is given an additional development by Zeus before a council of the gods at the close of the *Icaromenippus*. "There is a class of men which made its appearance in the world not long ago," Zeus announces in a tone reminiscent of Erasmus's Folly, and they are

> lazy, disputatious, vainglorious, quick-tempered, gluttonous, doltish, addle-pated, full of effrontery and to use the language of Homer, "a useless load to the soil" (*Iliad* 18:104). Well, these people, dividing themselves into schools and inventing various word-mazes, have called themselves Stoics, Academics, Epicureans, Peripatetics and other things much more laughable than these. Then, cloaking themselves in the high-sounding name of Virtue, elevating their eyebrows, wrinkling up their foreheads and letting their beards grow long, they go about hiding loathsome habits under a false garb, very like actors in tragedy; for if you take away from the latter their masks and their gold-embroidered robes, nothing is left but a comical little creature hired for the show at seven drachmas.
>
> [P. 317]

Such creatures are the Sileni of Lucian.

This definition of man as a comic creature whose pride leads to extravagant role playing is also taken over by the popular drama, poetry, and ceremony of the fifteenth and sixteenth centuries, such as the Fasching and carnival in

Germany and the Low Countries and the *société joyeux* in France where a Prince of Fools or Mother Folly presents satires organized as *sotties*, roll calls of fools, and *sermons joyeux*. "In its simplest form," Clarence H. Miller informs us concerning the *sottie*, "two or three fools met and exchanged nonsense with each other. The costume was the fool's cap with ass's ears and the fool's scepter; Mother Folly herself appears in many of them. The principal theme was that everyone from the highest to the lowest obeys the lordship of Folly. The motto of the *société joyeuse* at Dijon was 'The number of fools is infinite,'"[49] a motto adopted by Folly herself in the *Encomium Moriae*. In Rome, where Erasmus stayed between 1508 and 1509, he also saw such satiric attacks in the lampoons, epigrams, and bits of doggerel hung on the ancient, mutilated statue in the piazza Navona that had been unearthed and put up in 1501 and given the name Pasquino. Such "pasquinades," Margaret Mann Phillips records,[50] only increased Erasmus's recognition of universal folly.

Later Lucianic works by Erasmus are similar in form and subject to the *Encomium Moriae*. The hilarious dialogue of *Julius Exclusus* (*Julius Locked Out*, published 1517), for instance, between the newly dead Pope Julius II who demands admittance to Paradise and Saint Peter who refuses to permit him to enter the pearly gates, satirizes some of the same Church practices as the *Encomium Moriae* and, like the *Encomium*, relies for much of its humor on our awareness of unintended irony on the part of Julius. The dead pope, "all belches and the smell of drunkenness and booze,"[51] is accompanied by a crowd of followers who cheer him from the periphery of the dialogue, much as Folly's audience applauds her at the edges of the *Encomium*. The *Julius*, moreover, like the *Encomium*, is built on a dialectic, juxtaposing the blessed humble fisherman inside the walls of Heaven and the damned vulgar prelate without. Another dialogue, the *Ciceronianus* (1517), is even more complex in its development of a Lucianic poetics. Like the *Encomium*, it is composed of three movements: In the first, we learn of the Ciceronian fool Nosoponus who is starving himself in order to concentrate exclusively, day and night, on imitating Cicero. So that he may write using only words and rhythms once used by his master in rhetoric, Nosoponus has read and dreamed of nothing but Cicero for seven years, and he has compiled three vast dictionaries—one of words, one of phrases, and one of rhythmical patterns (parodying grammar, logic, and rhetoric)—which have become too hefty to be useful. Now, composing a sentence each evening, Nosoponus longs to complete a work that is verifiably Ciceronian. In the second movement, his friends, led by the counselor Philoponus, pretend to share his illness so as to encourage him to change his way of life. They advance a number of arguments to prevent excessive Ciceronianism: They note that Cicero teaches the rhetorician to take many models rather than a single one; they point out that Cicero's occasions for writing can never be duplicated by Nosoponus, who must write from his own needs in his own voice; and, finally, they argue that pure Ciceronianism cannot accommodate Christian thought and vocabulary. When these arguments fail, the friends change their tactics and, in the third section, ask Nosoponus who, of all classical and contemporary writers, he would acknowledge to be a successful Ciceronian. They mean to prove to him that no one needs to imitate so slavishly to be an effective writer—that imitatio too is governed by moderation. The catalogue that follows permits Erasmus a chance to categorize most of his contemporaries, some of whom took offense. As with the *Julius,* the point is the excessiveness of the pravity. Here dismay at the limitations of humanism—and even of misology—leads to Erasmian persiflage.

In several works of humanist poetics, then, Erasmus insists on a poetics deliberately Lucianic in its combination of wit and wisdom, *dulce* alongside *utile.* Thomas Wilson, noting the usefulness of this combination in *The Arte of Rhetorique* (1553), may have Erasmus's works in mind rather than Lucian's when he notes that such wit and wordplay provide the most successful instruction.

> And that is the reason, that menne commonly tary the ende of a merie plaie, and cannot abide the halfe hearyng of a sower checkyng Sermon. Therefore, euen these auncient preachers, must now and then plaie the fooles in the pulpite, to serue the tickle eares of their fleetyng audience, or els thei are like some tymes to preache to the bare walles, for though their spirite bee apte, and our will prone, yet our fleshe is so heauie, and humours so ouerwhelm vs, that wee cannot without refreshyng, long abide to heare any one thyng. [Sig. a2v]

Yet what Wilson reveals is that Lucianic poetics is more concerned with manner than with philosophic statement, such as we might expect from the Erasmus who writes to Martin Dorp that the *Encomium* is a jesting version of the more serious pilgrimage of his *Enchiridion* (EE 2 : 93). As a consequence, we long for more inclusive patterns in the *Encomium Moriae.* Teased by Folly's continual hints at following the form of a declamation, we are asked by her to construct a larger rhetorical meaning, one that is familiar and so instructive, and thereby locate an annealing cognitive unity for what seem, even on rereading, to be fragmented bits and pieces of witty (and even sophistic) oratory. Not unexpectedly, this has been the chief task of commentators then and now. One of the most satisfying modern readings of the *Encomium* is Wayne A. Rebhorn's account of the reflexive and interlocking episodes: Folly undergoes, he tells us, a general "metamorphosis from ironist to satirist to Christian mystic,"[52] a series of transformations in which her initial rueful separation from the real ways of men leads to a willing acceptance, in the end, of the way of God. Her final "vision of Christian folly," Rebhorn continues, transcends "the illusory hope of the first section and the horrifying 'reality' of the second. Note that Folly no longer claims man's worship, for Christian folly clearly means worship of God. . . . Folly defines what she calls the doctrine of Christ and what else-where Erasmus labeled the 'Philosophia Christi,' insisting that it involves mildness, tolerance, charity, and most significantly, contempt for the life of this world" (p. 471). Rebhorn, that is, sees the triadic *Encomium* as a more serious variant of the *Julius*. Clarence H. Miller supplies a clue to yet another sort of unity by establishing the medieval "estates" of morality plays and tracts as the model for the *dispositio* of the second section of the *Encomium*.[53]

But what we work out so carefully the humanists, accustomed to imitatio and to the resources of rhetoric and dialectic, must have seen almost intuitively. The triangular presentation, for instance, by which we are asked to take every statement as a possible hypothesis, was nowhere better known among the humanists than in the dialogues of Plato, whose own trust in human reason and judgment is an important foundation of humanist philosophy. The use of the Silenus takes on a more pronounced significance when we see in it allusions to the *Symposium* in the *Encomium Moriae*. Like Plato's dialogue on love, Erasmus's *Encomium* begins with a search for a suitable topic for panegyric, continues with several voices making their own additions to a various and accretive encomium, moves from earthly vicissitudes of human love to the more satisfying wholeness of the intellectual love of God, and ends with praise for the highest forms of folly as love. Read against the *Symposium*, the *Encomium* renews the form of classical dialectic; just as significantly, it follows the curve of Plato's presenta-tion. Erasmus's final witty comment is that no man yet has achieved what Folly achieves in experiencing mystical ecstasy as the highest form of pleasure, an experience she shares through the *Symposium* with the historical Socrates.

The *Symposium*, we know, was not only fundamental to the thought of Continental humanists; it was a particular favorite of Ficino, Pico, and Colet (who came to represent Plato to Erasmus).[54] But in turning to Plato at a critical juncture in her argument—at the definition of love as the common distinctive frenzy of poets, prophets, and lovers (*LB* 4:439B; sig. G4)—Folly also alludes to Plato's *Phaedrus*.[55] This later dialogue, which focuses as Folly does on the twin concerns of rhetoric and love, or the necessary coordinates of form and substance, even more closely resembles—and so helps to explain—the *Encomium Moriae*. The titular character Phaedrus, like the titular Folly, has an extraordinary attraction to rhetoric (242A),[56] and his encounter with Socrates (after hearing a speech by Lysias, which he takes with him so as to memorize it exactly) leads to a dialogue that is, thematically, identical to the *Encomium Moriae*. In aligning poor judgment with poor rhetoric—a classical belief that becomes a basis for the New Learning of the Continental humanists—Socrates warns Phaedrus "of those whose opinions are at variance with facts and who are deceived" (262B; 521–23/75–76): Like Folly, the youthful Phaedrus cannot tell the bad from the good because he relies on appearances. Rather, as Socrates has told his friend and student earlier, "in reality the greatest of blessings come to us through madness, when it is sent as a gift of the gods" (244A; 465/46). The *Phaedrus* deals with the definition of love, as the *Encomium* deals centrally with the nature and power of love, as the force which can cement human society but also transcend society and lead to mystical unity with God. Congruent with the *Encomium,* the *Phaedrus* pursues this line of thought in a tripartite dialectic whose resemblance to Folly's oration show on her part an imitation of the classics that astonishes us with its frequency. Plato's dialogue, like Erasmus's, opens with an unusual concern paid to describing the setting for the discussion, in this instance a plane tree on the banks of the Ilissus River outside Athens, as uncustomary a place for Socrates (as he acknowledges) as Folly claims the pulpit is for her. The first stage of Plato's dialogue, comparable to Folly's amusing and ironic catalogue of commonplace fools and foolish behavior, is Lysias's foolish and nearly incoherent speech, an encomium on love that Phaedrus has tucked under his toga but has not yet memorized, as the good rhetorician should. When he reads it to Socrates and to us, we find that this encomium is, like Folly's, inextricably wise and foolish because it too is scattered in its presentation and jumbled in its thought. "Such are the exhibitions of the power of Love," Lysias pronounces:

> he makes the unsuccessful lovers think that things are grievous which cause no pain to others, and he compels the successful to praise what ought not to give pleasure; therefore those whom they love are more to be pitied than envied. But if you yield to me, I shall consort with you, not with a view to present pleasure only, but to future advantage also, not being overcome by passion but in full control of myself, and not taking up violent enmity because of small matters, but slowly gathering little anger when the transgressions are great, forgiving involuntary wrongs and trying to prevent intentional ones; for these are the

proofs of a friendship that will endure for a long time. But if you have a notion that friendship cannot be firm unless one is in love, you should bear in mind that in that case we should not have great affection for sons or for fathers and mothers, nor should we possess faithful friends who have been gained not through passion but through associations of a different kind. [233C–D; 431–33/29–30]

Moreover, Lysias adds, lovers "themselves confess that they are insane, rather than in their right mind, and that they know they are foolish, but cannot control themselves; and so, how could they, when they have come to their senses, think those acts were good which they determined upon when in such a condition?" (231D; 427/27). In the second section of the *Phaedrus,* in which Socrates provides an alternative panegyric by way of parodic correction, his attack on foolish lovers is sufficiently stern to provide a startling contrast in tone.

A lover is not only harmful to his beloved but extremely disagreeable to live with as well. The old proverb says, "birds of a feather flock together"; that is, I suppose, equality of age leads them to similar pleasures and through similarity begets friendship; and yet even they grow tired of each other's society. Now compulsion of every kind is said to be oppressive to every one, and the lover not only is unlike his beloved, but he exercises the strongest compulsion. . . . And while he is in love he is harmful and disagreeable, but when his love has ceased he is thereafter false to him whom he formerly hardly induced to endure his wearisome companionship through the hope of future benefits by making promises with many prayers and oaths. . . . He runs away from these things, and the former lover is compelled to become a defaulter. The shell has fallen with the other side up; and he changes his part and runs away; and the other is forced to run after him in anger and with imprecations, who did not know at the start that he ought never to have accepted a lover who was necessarily without reason, but rather a reasonable non-lover; for otherwise he would have to surrender himself to one who was faithless, irritable, jealous, and disagreeable, harmful to his property, harmful to his physical condition, and most harmful by far to the cultivation of his soul. [240C–241C; 453–57/40–41]

The same sharp break in Folly's genial presentation also introduces the second part of her encomium in a passage we have already seen in part:

Sed multo etiam suavius, si quis animadvertat anus, longo jam senio mortuas, adeoque cadaverosos, ut ab inferis redisse videri possint, tamen illud semper in ore habere, φωϑάγαθτν adhuc catullire, atque, Graeci dicere solent, χαπρδυ &

magna mercede conductum aliquem Phaonem inducere, fucis assidue vultum oblinere, nusquam a speculo discedere, infimae pubis silvam vellere, vietas ac putres ostentare mammas, tremuloque gannitu languentem sollicitare, cupidinem, potitare, misceri puellarum choris, litterulas amatorias scribere. Ridentur haec ab omnibus, tamquam uti sunt, stultissima: at ipsae sibi placent, & in summis interim versantur delitiis, totasque sese melle perungunt, meo videlicet beneficio felices. Porro quibus haec deridicula videntur, illud secum expendant velim, utrum satius ducant hujusmodi stultitia vitam plane mellitam exigere, an trabem, ut ajunt, suspendio quaerere. Porro quod haec vulgo putantur infamiae obnoxia, istud nihil ad stultos meos, qui malum hoc aut non sentiunt, aut si quid sentiunt, facile negligunt. Si faxum in caput incidat, id vere malum sit.

But this is nothyng, in comparison of the pleasant spectacle, whiche ye maie haue at many of these oldwomen, who beyng neuer so muche palled with longe age, yea and so carcaslyke, as if they had lately come from deathes Court, will euer yet haue this prouerbe in their mouthes (*life* is *life*) still plaie the wantons, and still by tuppyng. Or at lest hyre some younge *Phaon* for mede to dooe the thyng, still daube theyr lither chekes with paintyng, neuer goe from the glasse, shew out theyr flaggie and pendant dugges, prouoke stale nature with hote restoritiues, sitte vp at banketts, daunce galierds, write loueletters, &c. These thynges are mocked commenly, for the greattest folies (without question) that maie be. But yet dooe these my oldguries not a little lyke theim selues herein, takyng it for a singuler and onely delight, as if they swamme vp to the chinnes in a sea of hony, wherin who but I doeth vphold them? and yet these deinty wisemen for all theyr scornefulnes, I woulde they shoulde no more but perpend thus with them selues, whither it be better through such folie to lede a sugred life, or elles standyng euer vppon narow poyncts of wysedome, to seke (as a man woulde saie) an halter to hange withall? [*LB* 4:432A–433A; sig. F2]

The remainder of the middle section of the *Phaedrus* is given over to the marvelous myth of the soul as a charioteer with two horses, one representing spirit and one appetite, with the pain and cruelty of appetite discussed first in terms of the various social classes of man (248); the directness of the portrayal finds its counterpart in Folly's shrill attack on the estates of man. Socrates' myth concludes, in the third section of the *Phaedrus,* with a realization of the intellectual and mystical love of God, which subdues the part of the soul containing the seeds of vice, setting forth only virtue. Out of gratitude Socrates ends his speech with a prayer (256–57). Folly, in her turn, concludes in mystical ecstasy and with an invitation to partake of Holy Communion, a merging of love with the divine. In thus duplicating in broad outline one of the central Socratic panegyrics for the humanists in writing his own encomium on love, Erasmus reiterates the close relationship between *bonae litterae* and *sacrae litterae* that is at the heart of his humanist thinking.[57]

Yet, despite the triadic arrangement of Plato's dialogue, the *Phaedrus* ends not on the note of a higher love but on lessons Socrates provides for Phaedrus in practical rhetoric. The instruction at first seems distracting and irrelevant, but to conclude this misses the point. The opening speech by the sophist Lysias, like Socrates' opening speech in a style that clearly is meant to imitate the sophist Isocrates, both corrected by the final speech on higher love, suggests that false rhetoric relies on appearances, true rhetoric on Platonic Forms. Bad rhetoric is itself betrayed by "likeness to truth" (273D), and it is this—which has led Lysias, Phaedrus, and Folly (at the first) astray—that Socrates is at some pains to prevent when he teaches his young pupil about definition (265A–B), places (270C–D), and propriety (275) so that he in turn may teach others. For

> serious discourse . . . is far nobler, when one employs the dialectic method and plants and sows in a fitting soul intelligent words which are able to help themselves and him who planted them, which are not fruitless, but yield seed from which there spring up in other minds other words capable of continuing the process for ever, and which make their possessor happy, to the farthest possible limit of human happiness. [276E–277A; 569–71/99]

We recall that Folly tells us at the outset that she will play the sophist with us while presuming to be one of the *sophie* or wise men (sig. A1v); in the course of the *Encomium,* she too is transformed into the wise woman she hopes to become because of her discovery of Christian love. The *Encomium Moriae* not only saves Folly; it also redeems rhetoric.[58]

But it is characteristic of Erasmian literary works that they draw not only on Greek philosophers but on Roman ones too. W. David Kay has also recently shown us in some detail how the *Encomium* draws on Cicero's *De Senectute* by deliberately drawing Folly in one reversed detail after another to be the antitype of Cato.[59] The Ciceronian encomium on old age thus is jokingly used to undermine Folly's anxious insistence on youth (cf. *De Senectute* 6.17) and turn her praise into dispraise. Cicero's pointed remark that he considers an attack on old age such as Folly gives us (*LB* 4:432B–433A; sig. F2v) a sign of *insipientes,* foolish persons (5.14), is also meant to help us chart our way through the *Encomium Moriae* by holding it up to a Senecan original. The same practice is true in her willful denial or misconstruction of Cicero's *De Amicitia* (especially 6.20, 22). Kay further comments that

> Folly's argument becomes even more amusing if one recognizes the particular discussion of human nature she is distorting. Erasmus never has her identify the "philosophers" she is attacking, but Folly's allusion would seem to be Cicero's *De Officiis*, on which Erasmus had written a commentary a few years previously. In language similar to Folly's, Cicero argues the contrary view that "knowledge of truth" is the category of moral goodness which "touches human nature most closely": "For we are all attracted and drawn to a zeal for learning and knowing; and we think it glorious to excel therein, while we count it base and immoral to fall into error, to wander from the truth, to be ignorant, to be led astray" (I.vi.18). Cicero repeats this statement later in his discussion of "propriety" (*decorum*), where he observes that humans are endowed with two characters: a universal character, "arising from the fact of our being all alike endowed with reason and with that superiority which lifts us above the brute," and a particular character, dependent on our individual temperament and personality (I.xxx.107). Both our particular and our universal natures must be followed if we are to act properly: "For it is of no avail to fight against one's own nature [i.e., one's temperament] or to aim at what is impossible of attainment. From this fact the nature of that propriety defined above comes into still clearer light, inasmuch as nothing is proper that 'goes against the grain' [*invitâ Minervâ*] as the saying is—that is, if it is in direct opposition to one's natural genius" (I.xxxi.110). The irony of Folly's position that ignorance and error are natural and that "nothing can be called unhappy if it fulfills its own nature" should now be clear. Both here and in her discussion of women, she perverts the Ciceronian principle that one must act in accordance with nature from its original application to one's "particular character" or temperament and turns it into a brazen argument against Cicero's fundamental assumption—that man is distinguished from the beasts by his reason. Attempts to counter such "logic" are doomed to exasperation; one can only laughingly deny her premise, just as she implicitly denies Cicero's. [P. 258]

Erasmus's use of imitatio as fundamental to his humanist poetics could not be signaled more clearly.

Erasmian poetics stems, then, from classical philosophy—and also from classical rhetoric. If, as we note, Folly's misuse of ideas corrupts classical ideas, then her misuse of words can corrupt the Word; the chief delight we experience in the *Encomium Moriae* is sensing how through imitatio Erasmus parodies humanist rhetoric through Folly's sophistry, the better to preserve it at the end. The original text behind this dimension of Erasmus's creative achievement is Cicero's *Paradoxa Stoicorum*, his parody of the Stoics. A favorite text of many humanists, it was eventually Englished by T. N. (Thomas Newton) under Elizabeth I. These brief lampoons treat such central Stoic beliefs as the idea that virtue is the sole good and the sole requisite for happiness, that all good deeds are equally meritorious, and that folly is insanity and slavery, the last perhaps recalling the *Paradoxa* most readily to the minds of Erasmus's readers, as it may have suggested itself to Erasmus, writing his *Encomium* so swiftly at the home of *morus*, or More. *"Herein shalt thou haue a taste of those kinds of Exercises, which I customably vse, whensoeuer I transpose and bringe those Positiue Groundes and Argumentes, which in Scholes be tearmed Thetica, vnto this our Rhetoricall kinde of Pleading and Oratorie,"* Cicero says in the homely 1577 translation; "cum ea quae dicuntur in scholis θετικῶς ad nostrum hoc oratorium transfero dicendi genus."[60] For Cicero, Stoic thought led automatically to sophistry.

> Animadverti, Brute saepe Catonem avunculum tuum cum in senatu sententiam diceret locos graves ex philosophia tractare abhorrentes ab hoc usu forensi et publico, sed dicendo consequi tamen ut illa etiam populo probabilia viderentur. . . . Sed nihil est tam incredibile quod non dicendo fiat probabile, nihil tam horridum tam incultum quod non splendescat oratione et tanquam excolatur
>
> *Sundrie times (freende Brutus) haue I marked thine vncle Cato, that whensoeuer hee vttered his minde in ye Senate, he entreated of waighty matters taken out of Philosophie, much dyffering from the ludicial and publique vse, whiche we vse in our cōmō Pleading. But yet notwithstādinge, he preuayled so much by Oratorious perswasion, that his wordes seemed vnto the people probable and allowable. . . . But there is nothinge so incredible, but by artificiall handelynge maye bee made probable: nothinge so rugged and rustye, but by Eloquence maye bee poolyshed (and as it were glitteringly burnished).*
>
> [Proem 1–3; sigs. M4–M4v; M5]

Some of these paradoxes relate directly to the Erasmian *Encomium*, either in theme—"Nemo potest non beatissimus esse qui est totus aptus ex sese quique in se uno sua ponit omnia"; "That man cannot bee but moste happye, whose Mynde is wholye setled and accustomed to Vertue, and which putteth and reposeth all thinges in himselfe alone" (17; sig. N4v)—or in perspective and technique:

> Auri navem evertat gubernator an paleae, in re aliquantulum, in gubernatoris inscitia nihil interest. Lapsa est libido in muliere ignota: dolor ad pauciores

pertinet quam si petulans fuisset in aliqua generosa ac nobili virgine, peccavit vero nihilominus, si quidem est peccare tamquam transire lineas, quod cum feceris culpa commissa est. . . . "Nihilne igitur interest" (nam hoc dicet aliquis) "patrem quis enecet an servum?" Nuda ista si ponas, iudicari qualia sint non facile possunt: patrem vita privare si per se scelus est, Saguntini qui parentes suos liberos emori quam servos vivere maluerunt parricidae fuerunt.

A Pylote or chiefe Mariner whych negligently drowneth a Shippe, whether the same be fraughted with Gold, or with Chaffe, is asmuch to bee reprehended & disallowed, for the one, as for the other. For although there be some oddes and difference in the worth & value of the thinges, yet his Ignoraunce and vnskilfulnesse is all one. If a man through inordinate Lust, do deflour a woman that is vnknowen, and of pore estate and Degree, the griefe of that villayny doth not (in deede) appertayne to so manye, as if hee had lasciuously constuprated a noble Damoysel, descended of some honorable House, and Pedagrewe. But the offence was of it selfe neuer a whit ye lesse. . . . "What? is there no difference (wyll some say) whether a man kyll his owne Father, or els some cōmon Seruant? If you meane these two comparisons barelye and simplye, it is harde to bee iudged of what sort they bee. For if it be of it selfe & simplie, an horrible offence, for one to kil his Father: then the *Saguntines* (who had leyfer their Parentes should dye being free and vnvāquished, then to lyue in seruitide and slauerye) were Parricides." [20, 24; sigs. N6v, N8v]

By wrenching one of a pair of terms out of context (such as responsibility for a worthless cargo as well as for one that is valuable) while dwelling on the serious term (responsibility), Cicero supplies Folly with a basic technique for ludic exposure.

We lack in Cicero only the formality of the full-dress encomium—or *mock* encomium, as in Glaucon's mock praise of injustice in Plato's *Republic*—but for that Erasmus may well have turned to the early mock encomium of Pseudo-Polycrates, thought in Erasmus's time to be by the sophist Gorgias. A good part of Pseudo-Polycrates' joke, as with Erasmus's, is in the subject he chooses to praise, Helen of Troy. Here is part of his elaborate declamation of praise, which, coming earlier in the rhetorical tradition, in many ways anticipates the *Encomium Moriae.*

For either by the disposition of fortune and the ratification of the gods and the determination of necessity she did what she did, or by violence confounded, or by persuasion dumbfounded, or to Love surrendered. If, however, it was against her will, the culpable should not be exculpated. For it is impossible to forestall divine disposals by human proposals. It is a law of nature that the stronger is not subordinated to the weaker, but the weaker is subjugated and dominated by the stronger; the stronger is the leader, while the weaker is the entreater. Divinity surpasses humanity in might, in sight, and in all else. Therefore, if on fortune and the deity we must visit condemnation, the infamy of Helen should find no confirmation.

But if by violence she was defeated and unlawfully she was treated and to her injustice was meted, clearly her violater as a terrifier was importunate, while she, translated and violated, was unfortunate. Therefore, the barbarian who verbally, legally, actually attempted the barbarous attempt, should meet with verbal accusation, verbal reprobation, and actual condemnation. For Helen, who was violated, and from her fatherland separated, and from her friends segregated, should justly meet with commiseration rather than with defamation. For he was the victor and she was the victim. It is just, therefore, to sympathize with the latter and anathematize the former. . . .

By this discourse I have freed a woman from evil reputation; I have kept the promise which I made in the beginning [to confute the detractors of Helen]; I have essayed to dispose of the injustice of defamation and the folly of allegation; I have prayed to compose a lucubration for Helen's adulation and my own delectation.[61]

Here too the subject is the praise of a foolish (and culpable) woman in a jangling rhetoric as self-conscious as Folly's, but far less successful. The master stylist among the sophists, Isocrates, was not pleased, or so he says mockingly, and he too set out to write his own *Helen.* But his encomium is also a joke. Not only does he turn from the places of praise to his own line of defense, but his long digression on Theseus (18–30), like Folly's on the Schoolmen and the Church, undermines any mastery of form:

> There are some who are much pleased with themselves if, after setting up an absurd and self-contradictory subject, they succeed in discussing it in tolerable fashion. . . . It is their "philosophy" applied to eristic disputations that effectively produces this result; for these rhetoricians care nothing at all for either private or public affairs, but take most pleasure in these discourses which are of no practical service in any particular. [6]

"What sensible man would undertake to praise misfortunes?" (10), he asks; and he could as easily be referring to Folly herself as to the Pseudo-Polycrates.

Thomas Wilson discusses such mockery under the term "Dissembling" in his *Arte of Rhetorique:*

> It is a pleasaunt dissembling, when we speake one thing merelye, and thynke an other earnestlye, or elles when we prayse that which otherwise deserueth dis-prayse, to the shaming of those that are taken not to be most honest. . . . For praysinge the vnworthye, I remember once that our worthie *Latimer* did set out the deuyll for his diligence wonderfullie, and preferred him for that purpose before all the Bishoppes in England. [Sig. V3]

The staunchly Protestant Wilson is taken with Latimer, but Erasmus found many similar companions among his humanist contemporaries. Daniel Heinsius wrote a mock encomium on the louse (*Laus Pediculi*), Philipp Melanchthon on the ant (*Laus Formicae*), Bilibaldi Pirckheimer on the gout (*Laus* or *Apologia Podagrae*), Caelio Calcagnino on the flea (*Pulicis Encomium*), M. Antonius Majoragio on mud (*Luti Encomium*), Joannes Passerati on the ass (*Encomium Asini*), James Dousa on shade (*In Laudem Umbrae*), Justus Lipsius on the elephant (*Laus Elephantis*), Franciscus Scribanius on the fly (*Muscae ex Continua Comparatione cum Principe Encomium*), Erycius Puteanus on the egg (*Ovi Encomium*): German, Dutch, Italian, and French scholars all joined in the game of humanist wit and wordplay.[62] Next to these, Folly's general movement from sheer folly (we cannot agree with what she says) to sheer unfolly (we must agree) to paradoxical folly (where we agree and disagree, as in the need for human illusion) seems grounded in much more serious paradoxy: Folly calls on the authority of wise men but then attacks them to justify her own wisdom and its superior utility; she argues that wisdom brings about its own limitations by learning to depend on saints and superstitions; she equates pride with felicity. Most of her confirmatio, and so much of her oration, is an anthology of paradoxes, traditional and innovative, realizing the root significance of *para doxa,* running counter to our expectations or to appearances, illogical logic that "teases the intellect as an optical illusion teases the eye," as A. E. Malloch puts it.[63] Pushed hard, Malloch writes, "paradoxes do not really have natures at all; they are nothings. They exist only within the antithetical action of the reader, and if he allows them (i.e., allows them an existence), he is making another paradox, viz., That Nothing Is" (p. 192). John Donne recognizes this form of humanist rhetorical wit in a letter sent to a friend around 1600: "they are rather alarūs to truth to arme her then enemies: & they haue only this advantadg to scape frō being called ill things yt are nothings: therfore take heed of allowing any of them least ye make another,"[64] and Thomas More realizes it best of all, his *Utopia,*

Nowhere, being the ideal response to Erasmus's Nothing—More's apt reply to *Moria*. In a century dominated by a humanist poetics in prose, however, stretching from the *Encomium Moriae* to Thomas Nashe's *Lenten Stuffe*, Erasmus is also at the start of an especially fruitful tradition that will include in Nashe's England, besides Newton's translation of Cicero and A. M.'s (Anthony Munday's) Englishing of Ortensio Landi's *Paradossi* (*The Defence of Contraries* [1593] in which Declamation 5, sigs. G1–H2v, is "For the Foole"), Sir John Harington's *New Discourse of a Stale Subject; Called the Metamorphosis of Ajax* (1596), Richard Barnfield's *Encomium of Lady Pecunia; or, The Praise of Money* (1598)—and D. D.'s (Edward Dyer's) *Prayse of Nothing* (1585) itself, a hotchpotch of the unknown, the inexplicable, and the irrelevant.

Erasmus helps to establish such a humanist poetics by composing a fictive encomium that relies for its meaning and method on works by Plato, Cicero, and Lucian in an attempt to teach social utility and individual piety. But in the spirit of the two-faced Silenus, Erasmus also uses the *Encomium* to parody the misuse of such learning. The obvious irony on man's folly and the open satire on the estates of man, as well as the Diotima-like vision that, merging with a Pentecostal sense of tongues, concludes the work, are all welded together because all mock the misuse of grammar, rhetoric, and logic. The prosopopoeia who would play the sophist with us is, in saying that, wiser than she knows from the outset. By parodying the methods and practices of the humanist grammar schools in her exposure of fallen man, Folly shows us how we too are among the fallen while reserving by implication a *locus* for wisdom to which she may (and in the end does) retreat.

We do not at first think of the teaching of grammar when approaching the *Encomium Moriae*—that laborious, careful, and often sensitive construing of the sense of a passage, what we would now call a close reading—but we must not forget that Erasmus's first work was a translation of Valla, whom Agostino Nifo calls in his *Dialectica ludicra* of 1520 "that most learned and methodical grammarian" and in his *Dialecticae disputationes* (1522) "that book which he wrote on dialectic from the point of view of a grammarian" (f. 23v).[65] Erasmus himself sets out his understanding of the practice of grammar for us in the *Ratione Studii* he wrote for St. Paul's and for its schoolmaster William Lily.

Deinceps quam potest & dilucide, & breviter summam explicet argumenti. Carminis genus diligenter indicet. Post ordinet simplicius, deinde singula fusius explicet. Ad haec, si qua insignis elegantia, si quid prisce dictum, si quid novatum, si quid Graecanicum, si quid obscurius, aut longius redditum, si durior aut perturbatior ordo, si qua etymologia, si qua derivatio aut compositio scitu digna, si qua orthographia, si qua figura, si qui loci Rhetorici, si qua exornatio, si quid depravatum, diligenter admoneat.

[He (The schoolemaster) should explain plot.] Then he should make a simple arrangement of these points and then explain each one in greater detail. In this respect he should carefully draw their attention to any purple passage, archaism, neologism, Graecism, any obscure or verbose expression, any abrupt or confused order, any etymology, derivation, or composition worth knowing, any point of orthography, figure of speech, or rhetorical passages, or embellishment or corruption.[66]

In the *Encomium Moriae,* however, the misuse of this foundation of the New Learning—a foundation Erasmus used through a lifetime of translation—is mocked in several ways. Within the text itself, Folly's continuing practice of twisting her allusions—or misusing those *Adagia* which for many were the chief source of Erasmus's reputation—and so showing her ignorance forces sixteenth-century humanist readers (as well as ourselves) to take her remarks at a critical distance while enjoying the direct challenge of her statements. Thus her initial citation to defend self-praise (that according to the proverb a man who has no one to praise him may praise himself, *laudes celebrarit* [LB 4:407B; sig. A2]) inverts the traditional proverb, which says that a man may praise himself when he has bad neighbors and so no one to do the praising. Within sentences, Folly juxtaposes two antonymous proverbs: that she will say one thing and mean another; that she looks exactly like what she is (*LB* 4:408B; sig. A3). A short time later, she misquotes Homer by alluding to his remark that men spoke with soft voices (*LB* 4:414B; sig. B3v) when actually Homer writes that they speak nonsense (*Iliad* 3.149–52). All three practices run concurrently throughout her speech; and the superb edition of the *Encomium* by Clarence H. Miller (1979) provides a number that are incorporated in Folly's epideictic oration. The last example here, that from Homer, is pointed out by Erasmus's friend Girardus Listrius, whose running commentary was included in a number of early editions, beginning with Frobenius's edition of 1515. Often it is accurate, but Erasmus apparently had a hand in this too (when Listrius fell ill), and the whole act of commentary (as well as certain deliberately obscuring glosses) thus parodies grammar further still. Often, these annotations, rather than illuminating the text, merely confound the problem of reading it. "Aside from identifying key quotations and emblematic references," William J. Kennedy writes concerning this commentary, its imposition only adds to the reader's puzzlement in coming to terms with the text. Nothing is more ironic than Folly's early assurance that the audience will understand every word; for speech, she claims, is "the least deceptive mirror of the mind." What Folly conceals (or perhaps foolishly reveals) is its function as a possible vehicle of deceit, not to mention plain confusion. In his commentary Listrius asserts, "Above all in speech a man's frame of mind is opened up"; and then, apparently unhappy with his own half-truth and its hazardous misapplication, he adds a marginal notation that only confirms the problematic irony: "Folly shines forth in the expression on her face." Together with Listrius' commentary, the corruscating ironies and almost impenetrable paradoxes of Folly's monologue supply the best example of how speech can be a very deceptive mirror of the mind—especially the speech of a fool who, we come to learn, is a very special type of fool.[67]

The joking becomes still more preposterous in the last third of Folly's declamation when she cites accurately the Church Fathers, difficult as they may be, and then misapplies biblical Scripture, especially the plainspoken words of Saint Paul. Her quotation from 2 Corinthians 11:23—"I speak as a fool: I am more"—is a case in point. She claims that the trilinguists led by Erasmus himself might not agree with her because they make Paul claim to be foolish so as not to sound arrogant before the Apostles; but, as Kennedy has it, "Folly prefers her own explanation, and thus provides a splendid example of taking the wrong turn even when she has access to the right one" (p. 88). Beyond Folly's erratic authority, the seriocomic remarks of Listrius (and Erasmus), and Folly's own references to Erasmus and others, there is the work of additional scholiasts as supplied by the series of letters. Beginning with the dedicatory epistle to More and the appended explanation to Dorp, these at once encrust the *Encomium* in layer upon layer of grammatical exegeses and exercises which, though not always intended as parody, nevertheless leave the text as a box within boxes of annotation and interpretation.

We have already seen the rhetorical structure in which Folly attempts to order her remarks; they follow the traditional pattern of major Platonic dialogues and Lucianic satires. They also follow the traditional pattern of encomium that Richard Rainolde illustrates in his *Foundacion of Rhetorike* (1563) with a speech praising Epaminondas (sigs. K4v–L3v) and for which he sets out the traditional rules:

> In praise, we extoll the persone: First by his countree.
> Then by his auncestours and parentes.

In the third place, by his education and institucion.

Then in the fowerth place, of his actes in life.

In the fifte place vse a comparison, comparyng the persone with other, whiche are more inferiour.

Then the conclusion. [Sig. L3v]

This is an order that the foolish Folly can manage only partway. But "everyone knows that those who wish to praise a person must attribute to him a larger number of good qualities than he really possesses," the sophist Isocrates writes in his mock encomium of *Busiris* (4),[68] while Cicero and his student Quintilian declare that the proper function of panegyric is to amplify and embellish (*amplificare et ornare*) its themes (*Institutiones Oratoriae* 3.7.6). For Aphthonius, whose rhetoric Rainolde translates in his popular Tudor English text, such embellishment could come in the variation of stating the theme as well as the enlarging of the argument by a long string of examples, and it is this which is the basis of Erasmus's parody of rhetoric in the *Encomium*; as he mocks his own *Adagia* in his parody of the grammarian, so Erasmus mocks his own *De Copia* in parodying rhetoricians.

The *De Copia* tells the sixteenth-century student at the outset (1.1) how to amplify things: by relating matters at length, by adding details, by showing steps in an argument more fully, by enumerating concomitant or resultant circumstances, by description, by incorporating a digression, by employing epithets, by running circumstances through Aristotelian topics, and by heaping up words and *sententiae*. Such stockpiling of *copia* results in the style of *volubilitas*, the rolling and rushing like a river that characterizes folly, according to John Dickenson in his latter-day humanist fiction *Greene in Conceipt* (1598; sig. B4), and characterizes, too, Erasmus's style in the *Encomium Moriae*. Here "Folly is madness and pleasure and sloth," Sister Geraldine Thompson writes; "it is pedantry, solemnity, greed; it is puritan and libertine; it is hatred and love; it is misfortune, unavoidable and innocent, and sin, humanly willed and active; it is temporal happiness; it is the pearl of great price for which man can foolishly sell all tangible pleasure" (*Under Pretext of Praise*, p. 56). So excited is Folly—and so excitable—in locating fools among lovers, eaters, drinkers, hunters, dice players, and alchemists, among kings, princes, lords, merchants, popes, bishops, and priests as well as among doctors, lawyers, and teachers, that her own rhetoric, both in her choice of words and in her ordering of issues, becomes not only sophistic but solipsistic, often demolishing a logical progression of ideas, threatening to become non-sense. Her disposition and elocution threaten our perception and memory, get at the root skills of oratory. Leonard Coxe knows the significance of this in his Tudorwork on the *Art or craft of Rhetoryke* (1532), especially in application to those in the pulpit where Folly now stands: "the vnapt disposicion of the precher (in orderyng his mater)," Coxe warns, "confoundeth the memory of his herers" (sig. A3). In the art of rhetoric this means it confounds comprehension.

It is also Coxe who states as clearly as anyone among the Tudors the distinction between logic and rhetoric.

> Yf any Theme compounde: be it Logicall or Rhetorycall / it must be referred to the rules of Logike by thē to be proued trew or fals. For this is the dyfference that is betwene these two sciences / that the Logician in dysputynge obserueth certayne rules for the settynge of his wordes being solicitous that there be spokē no more nor no lesse than the thynge requyreth / & that it be euin as plaīly spokē as it is thought. But the Rhetorician seketh about & boroweth where he can asmoche as he may for to make the symple and playne Logicall argumentes gaye & delectable to the eare. So than the sure iugement of argumentes or reasons must be lerned of the logician / but the crafte to set thē out with pleasaunt figures and to delate the mater belongeth to the Rhetorician. [Sigs. A8v–B1]

This distinction is clear in both the Tudor curriculum and the Tudor practice before Ramus and Talon ever seize the distinction to make their reputation on the Continent; and one of the central texts of logic to survive—the Englishman Thomas Wilson's *Rule of reason* (1551) as distinct from his *Arte of Rhetorique* (1553)—shows that for the humanists the study of logic was at root Aristotelian. Thus for Wilson logical arguments are conducted by proceeding through the *topica* of genus, species, differences, property, and accident (sigs. B4v–C2) as well as the predicaments of substance, "quantitie, qualitee, relacion, maner of doing, suffring, when, where, the settelling, and the appareiling" (sig. C5v ff.) while a handy if minute chart on sig. I7 shows the relationships of certain "loci interni" and "Externi." At least as much attention is paid fallacious reasoning, and Wilson is at pains at the first to explain the fallacy of *sorties,* in which a definition of a pile is tested by building it grain by grain or part by part (sigs. H8v), a favorite argument with the sophists of antiquity, and the dilemma,

> when the reason cōsisteth of repugnaūt membres, so that what so euer you graunt, you fall into the snare, and take the foile. As yf I should aske whether it were better to marie a faire woman, or a foul. If you say a faire. Then answer I,

that is not good, for thei comōly say, she wilbe comō. If you say it wer good to mary an hard fauored woman, then I answere, she wilbe lothsome, and so ye fall into an incouenience. Notwithstandyng if either of the partes maie be turned into the aduersaries necke againe, or both of them, it is a faulty Argument, and you maie confute the same by inuersiō, that is to say, turning his taile cleane contrarie, as thus. If I shall marie a faire womā, I shal haue great pleasure, and cōfort in her: yf I marie a browne woman, she shal not be common to other, for few men wil seke after her. Therfore, I shall haue comfort both waies.

[Sigs. I1–I1v]

This logical partitioning is strongly resonant of Folly, just as her ability to take on many prosopopoeias in the course of her address relies on the skill taught at grammar schools to play both parts in a disputation—or many parts in a play. Wilson (following Aristotle) traces many of these fallacies back to the inherent property of words, the basis of Erasmian wordplay: "Deceiptfull argumentes" come in the "doubtfulnesse of a worde," in "the double meanyng of a sentence," in "the ioynyng of wordes that shuld be parted," as well as parting those that should be joined, and in "the maner of speche" or "*Coniunctio distrahendorum*" (sig. Q3v). Folly openly eschews poor logic as she avoids bad rhetoric—at least if we believe her—and she makes a point of her virtue early on:

> Tum autem quae res Deciis persuasit, ut ultro sese Diis Manibus devoverent? Quod Q. Curtium in specum traxit, nisi inanis gloria, dulcissima quaedam Siren, sed mirum quam a Sapientibus istis damnata?

> But I praie you, what prouoked bothe the *Decians* willingly to bequethe thē selfes to the *Infernall Gods?* And likewise egged *Quintus Curtius* to cast hym selfe into the greate caue and swallowe of the grounde, that whilome opened in the marcasteede of Rome, sauyng onely *Vainglorie? Vainglorie* (I saie) that moste faire, and sweete bayted Mermaide, but (lord) how wonderously yet condemned by these sages? [*LB* 4:426B; sigs. E1v–E2]

For Wilson, and for the logic of the New Learning, Folly has already become illogical in confusing verbal fallacies and logical subtleties. Of these latter, which Wilson calls "trappyng Argumentes" (sig. U6v), he lists seven. It is to Folly's discredit that her declamation is a clever Erasmian parody of all of them. Wilson defines them rather briefly.

> *Crocodilites,* is suche a kynde of subtiltie that when we haue graunted a thyng to our aduersarie beyng asked before what we will say: the same turneth to our

harme afterward: and causeth an inconueniēce thervpō to eschew. Authors do feigne that the Crocodile beyng a monster in Egypt did take a womans childe from her, and spake with the mother in this wise: Womā I wil geue the thy child again, if thou wilt saye truth to me, & tel me assuredly, whether I will geue the thy childe againe or no? She aunswered, I knowe assuredly thou wilt not geue me my childe again, and therfore it is reason I haue my child again because I haue said truth, Nay, saied the Crocodile, I wil not geue the thy childe again because thou maist be seen to haue said truth, lesse that yf I geue the thy child again, thou shouldst haue made a lie: neither yet woulde I haue giuen the thy child again, if thou hadst said otherwise, because thē thou hadst not said truth. [Sig. U7]

Antistrephon, is nothing els, then to turne a mans saiyng into his owne necke againe, and to make that whiche he bryngeth for his owne purpose, to serue for our purpose, in Latine it may be called, *Inuersio.* [Sig. U7v] [The example given is the story of Pythagoras who charges a student who in turn sues him to avoid the fee for his sophistical training. Pythagoras wins, for if the student wins at court he was well taught; if the boy loses at court, Pythagoras need not pay.]

Ceratine argumentationes, are called horned argumentes, the which are so daūgerous to aunswere vnto, for both partes propouned, that it wilbe hard to escape a foyle. [Sig. X1v] [His illustration is the Pharisees' attempt to trick Christ related in Matthew 22. The Pharisees ask Christ] Sir may we lawfully pay tribute to Cesar, or no? Or how thynke you, doth it stand with Goddes worde, that we maie paie, or no? Here Christe was beset twoo waies, first it was daungerous for him, to hold his peace: for then he might seme by so doyng, to haue respect to the person of men, and for feare not open the truth, in suche a weightie matter, and so stain the glory of God. Of the other part, if he should answer it ware a daungerous pece of worke, in like maner, for thei thought, he would either speake on Cesars side, & allowe payeng of Tribute, and so incurre the hatred of all the people, whereby thei might more boldly afterward, put him to death: or els thei thought, he would speake against Cesar, and so he should commit treason, and be apprehended therevpon, as a Traitour. [Sigs. X2—X2v]

Cacosistata are suche argumentes that beyng propounded, betwene twoo persones, thei serue aswell for the one parte, as the other, as thus. You muste forgeue hym, because he is but a child, no mary, therfor wil I beate hym, because he is a childe. [Sig. X3]

Asistata are such argumentes, as are impossible to be true, as when a child of two yeres old, should be accused of adulturie, as though it wer like, that he could offende in such filthinesse. [Sig. X3v]

Vtis is nothyng els, but when one goth aboute to proue a thynge, and maketh that which shoulde proue, to bee as vncertain, as that thyng, which is proued, as thus. In Purgatorie synnes are forgeuē, by vertue of the Masse, ergo we must say Masse still. [Sig. X3v]

Pseudomenos. This is called a liynge argument, for what so euer ye shall saye, ye must nedes saie amisse. [Sigs. X3–X4] [The example is that of the Cretan who said, "All Cretans are liars."]

Folly's attempt to make grotesque women lovely by awarding us the power to form illusions turns on us when she suggests that those who may not be grotesque in our eyes will surely be in the eyes of others: She uses the crocodile fallacy she claims to abhor. Asking the man in the theater whether he approves of his make-believe play is to attack by way of *ceratine argumentationes*. The refusal of monks to read in order to maintain piety results also in illiteracy, an example of *cacosistata*. The hairsplitting questions Folly assigns to theologians exemplify *utis*. And to argue that Folly is being praised and therefore is praiseworthy but that what Folly lauds is hardly laudatory is, as Clarence Miller notes, to be guilty of employing *pseudomenos* (Introduction, p. xvii). Doubtless it was piling fallacy upon fallacy, subtlety upon subtlety, as if we today were to rack up a score in Boggle, that helped to make *Encomium Moriae* so delightful and so popular—and so influential—a work among Continental and English humanists.

The audacious feature about the *Encomium Moriae* is that, in openly pursuing humanist thought by alluding to such respected works as Plato's dialogues, Erasmian wit mocks their means; while proceeding to argue with obvious inconsistency and illogicality, it means to uphold the New Learning seriously by showing how dreadfully vulnerable it is to misuse and corruption. For Folly parodies all the learning she touches. She lays claim to respect grammar, but she uses the Greek tags she dismisses (*LB* 4:409B–C; sig. A3v) and satirizes the grammarian Thomas Linacre (*LB* 4:458C; sig. K4v). In her rhetorical ordering, she loses a sense of her own persona (*LB* 4:457B; sigs. K4v ff.), and the cruelty of her later attacks ruins any possibility of her regaining proper decorum (*LB* 4:462C ff.; sigs. L4 ff.). Finally, her admission that she frequently attends disputations (*LB* 4:495A; sig. R3) invites her to corrupt Plato's allegory of the cave by using it for two opposite meanings (*LB* 4:451D,

500D; sigs. I4, S4). Thus her encomium, which begins not as a speech of praise but as a eulogy, ends not with a peroration but with an apparent failure of nerve.

Dramatically, the *Encomium Moriae* continually pays allegiance to the lessons of the grammar school trivium while frustrating the expectations those lessons teach us; philosophically, Folly's respect for classical and biblical learning is constantly undercut by her own misunderstanding and perversion of the ideas she claims to respect. At such times, we must accept her values yet deny her application of them. But there are at least as many instances, especially in the later sections, where her satire is unerring and she upholds just those values we share with her, given the implied set of fundamental humanist values on which the *Encomium Moriae* rests so equivocally. The situation is compounded when Folly makes up her own sources (*LB* 4 : 491C, 495A; sigs. R1, R3) or provides a series of nesting observations within one another, as in the disputation within the disputation on the punishment of heretics (*LB* 4 : 495A–496A; sigs. R3–R4). A last marginal gloss in the Chaloner text also manages this equivocation to which the use of form and parody of form, idea and parody of idea, have led: "Marke how Folie dalieth in hir wordes which: are to be construed to a good sense or els to be but as a talke of Folie" (sig. T2). Such equivocation is a clear signal of Ciceronian paradox; it also reminds us that this first significant work of humanist fiction rests on references common to the humanist community but outside the text itself. It can exist *only* by such references, by such understood acts of imitatio.

As paradox too, the *Encomium Moriae* resists closure in statement and renders a summary impossible. "In any paradoxical argument," Malloch reminds us, "there is a central pivot of equivocation upon which two arguments (logically connected) meet and turn. And a paradoxical argument proceeds, not by deduction, but by a series of such pivots. Hence it is impossible to summarize or condense a paradoxical argument" ("Techniques," p. 194). Yet we are not passive witnesses either; we must refute paradoxes or they are voided of meaning. Malloch continues by pointing out that

> paradoxes have a nature which is revealed in the act of meeting (or, more accurately, resisting) them. And their nature is revealed then because their being remains unfulfilled until they become part of a dialectic action. They do not become themselves until they are overthrown. They are written to be refuted, and unless they are refuted their true nature is hidden. Thus the paradox may

be said to present one part in a verbal drama (truly a word play); the other part is not written out, but is supplied by the reader as he tries "to find better reasons." [P. 195]

What Joel B. Altman calls the "interlaying of arguments" caused by statement, parody, and shifting perspective leads to a work he terms "an instrument of continuous inquiry."[69] Because he would remain the humanist educator, Erasmus takes from us the customary role of audience as privileged receiver of a given text and puts us to work on it as his students.

Such paradox and equivocation, however, do not mean the same thing as permanent incoherence. Folly maintains throughout her rhetorical address that fools believe in their allegiance to the instinctive rather than to the ritualistic, the merely formal, or the repressive; and that fools believe in the invisible rather than the material or corporeal, the illusory rather than the lusory or delusory. In the first, they become men; in the second, they become like Christ. "Nisi mortales stultos esse, etiam pios?"; "*Mortall men beyng fooles, are godly also*" (LB 4:498A; sig. S1). For her as for us the last fool here is the fool of Saint Paul in his letter to the people of Corinth: "If any man among you seemeth to be wise in this world, let him become a fool [*môros genesthô*] that he may be wise" (1 Cor. 3:18 ff., 4:10). The final folly is "Stultitiam crucis," "the *Folie of the crosse*" (LB 4:498B; sig. S1v). At the climax, Folly echoes Thomas à Kempis— "It will then be seen that he who learned to be counted a fool and despised for Christ's sake in this world was indeed wise"[70]—and the original feast of fools is transformed into the heavenly banquet, the Eucharist and the banquet of sapience. The speech is "an optimistic reaffirmation," George Faludy contends, "that the aims of humanism," like its rhetorical means, "will, slowly but surely, prevail" (*Erasmus*, p. 132).

As she descends from her platform, significantly occupied by a pulpit rather than a podium, Folly commands us to applaud her, to live, and to drink. These remarks of farewell also demand our active interpretation to fare well, because the context persuades us to differing significations. If we relate Folly's last words to the opening of her speech, she invites us to celebrate her pride, to laugh at her stupidity, and to join her own father in insobriety, giving birth to further foolishness. "Quare valete, plaudite, vivite, bibite, MORIAE celeberrimi Mystae;" "Fare ye well therfore, clappe your hands in token of gladnesse, liue carelesse, and drinke all out, ye the trustie seruants & solemne ministers of Folie" (LB 4:504C; sig. T3v). But her rhetoric has transformed these into other possibilities—Rebhorn calls this "the perfect ambiguity of her valediction" ("Metamorphoses," p. 473)—and her triadic oration invites us to choose still another set of terms, to catch her impermanent words in the amber of our own understandings. Hence she may also ask for something like thoughtful reflection based on experience and an imaginative vision (a secular dispensary of what Saint John of the Cross calls purgative and illuminative truth); if so, we are invited to drink of humanist truth and of the truth of the Eucharist.

> Nunc alacres, nunc dejecti, nunc lacrymant, nunc rident, nunc suspirant; in summa, vere toti extra se sunt.

> For now shall ye see theim of glad chere, now of as sadde againe, now thei wepe, now thei laugh, now they sighe, for briefe, it is certaine that they are wholy distraught and rapte out of theim selues. [*LB* 4:504B; sig. T3]

Folly seems always to imply (and mean) other (and more) than what she declaims. But by being ironic and not just ingenious, Erasmus uses the imitatio of humanist educators—his art referential in its dynamics—to suit a serious purpose to a delightful fiction. Folly's address is aimed at the sophisticated humanists of her day, the maturest of minds which, presented two sides of an equation or given implied antique texts as alternatives, will develop the fiction's true significance. Thus the ability of reason to question itself consigns its own wisdom. Erasmus's Christian humanism comes with just this superb trust in us as an audience of not only thoughtful but potentially redemptive men and women—and he shares that trust too with Folly.

THREE

Della mortal oblivione questa chiara memoria: Baldassare

Castiglione, *Il Libro del Cortegiano,*

and the Poetics of Eloquence

FIGURING FOLLY AS MAIEU-
TIC NARRATOR IS ERASMUS'S
REMARKABLY SUCCESSFUL WAY OF
UTILIZING (AND EVEN EXPLOITING)
HUMANIST RHETORIC BOTH TO ADMIT THE
HIGHER POSSIBILITIES OF HUMANIST PHILOSO-
phy and to confront the essential cognitive indeterminacy and textual instability that might result from a newly developing culture in which ideas are
as much exploratory as declarative and words are acts of mediation rather than
authoritative counters. Indeed, the very *tentativeness* of the *Encomium Moriae,*
masked more or less by its self-delight in wordplay, suggests that Erasmus
understood that humanist declamation, disputation, and treatise closely approach—may even at their basis be forms of—fiction. Both work as much from
hypothesis as from thesis.

Such an understanding of the propositional quality of speech and debate,
resting as it must on methexis, is shared by Baldassare Castiglione in *Il Libro del
Cortegiano.* This extraordinary Italian humanist fiction of the sixteenth century
vastly extends the voices, attitudes, and allusions of Erasmus's fiction by setting
its rhetorical investigations within a highly cultivated social and political
setting: Here *prosopographia* rather than *prosopopoeia* is elevated to a marmoreal
art. Given the refinements of the civilization he means to portray, Castiglione
fashions a fiction that is deliberately a work of elegance and eloquence. He
eschews the troubled inconsistencies that Erasmus employs to characterize
Folly, and that always threaten to undo the order and sense of Folly's presentation by distributing such conflicting views among the several disputants that

characterize *his* work. For Castiglione's is a studied eloquence. The work is thoroughly grounded in a review of humanist values and concludes with a wonderful example of Christian humanism. *Il Libro del Cortegiano* does not ignore or deny but merely presents more subtly the same concerns—often urgent concerns—that we find in Erasmus regarding man's ability to achieve the stature the humanist taught as possible for all mankind. Nor is it surprising that Castiglione's great work moves openly and consciously toward fictionality; it means to argue (as Folly did of illusion) the preserving and saving powers of the imagination while at the same time it senses the imagination's power to evade by enhancement, distraction, or avoidance. Castiglione's art of eloquence, then, is different only in degree and expression from Erasmus's wit and wordplay.

This is not initially apparent. Wayne A. Rebhorn has recently spoken of the consensual view of *Il Cortegiano* as a work that mediates the issues of humanism through the moderating philosophy of Aristotle. "In the subtly controlled art" of Castiglione's fiction, he notes,

> as in the art of its significantly greater coevals—Raphael's Stanza della Segnatura and Michelangelo's Sistine Chapel ceiling—the humanism of the fifteenth century comes to glorious fruition and strikes a momentary balance with the love of beauty, elegance, and refinement that would soon become the hallmark of later Mannerist courts. For just two short decades at the beginning of the sixteenth century, these masterpieces of High Renaissance culture magically harmonize moral ideals with elegant manners, optimistic ideals of political and social action with aesthetic self-cultivation, and virile, directed energy with grace and refinement.[1]

Seen in retrospect, this reifying consonance of the physical, intellectual, and spiritual attributes of man begun with the revived Greek and Roman texts urged by the humanists is momentous, spectacular, visionary. It far surpasses the more earthbound wit and wordplay of Folly. It soars. No moment in Western cultural history can match it. Humanist models of behavior instruct thought and speech, gesture and act, political purpose and social response in ways that are at once instructive, ethical, elegant, *felicific*. Human possibilities prophesied by the New Learning are epitomized in the contagious conceptualizations provided by Castiglione's *Cortegiano;* it supplies all Europe with an idealistic self-portrait in an apparent pursuit of life in which substance and style are inseparable, coterminous, even synonymous, promising a *speculum principis,* a mirror of princes, as *speculum humanis*, shaping the noble qualities and ennobling reason inherent in all men and women. The style of Castiglione's Urbino is soon the style of Henri's Paris, of Philip's Escorial, and of Elizabeth's Whitehall. It is a style resulting from the highest of principles, as Thomas Hoby makes clear to Lord Henry Hastings in the epistle preceding his 1561 English translation of the 1528 Italian original. "To men growen in yeres," Hoby tells us, *Il Cortegiano* is "a pathway to the behoulding and musing of the minde, and to whatsoeuer elles is meete for that age" (sig. A3v). For Hoby such values are insistent, admonitory, obsessive. "You may see him confirme with reason the Courtly facions, comely exercises, and noble vertues," he explains, "that unawares haue from time to time crept in to you and already with practise and learning taken custome in you" (sig. A3v).

Yet such extravagant encomia, like the euphoric mood that prompts them, seriously mislead. They are, like Pico's rhetorical praise of rhetoric, *self-fulfilling* prophecies. In protesting too much man's potentiality, they chart their own exposed uncertainty. The primary humanist *yearning* for the moral perfectibility of man lurks just beneath the polished surfaces of *Il Cortegiano*. All the postured rhetoric of the debates and dialogues in Castiglione's Urbino about the *uomo universale*, the many-sided man, and all the definitions of courtier and prince rest on an unending pursuit of *proof* that man is educable, moral, and potentially perfect. Such a task is as monumental as it is vital, and Castiglione reveals his own troubling doubts by drawing upon a remarkably diversified arsenal of humanist teachings. Frequent applications of Plato, Aristotle, Ovid, and Livy, Cicero, Plutarch, Quintilian, and Seneca show us that his boyhood lessons while at Milan, in Latin from Giorgio Nerula and in Greek from Demetrios Chalcondylas, were as indelible as they were necessary.[2] Part of Castiglione's early years were also spent at the court of Lodovico Sforza—what Isabella d'Este once called "the Court of the *cognoscenti*"[3]—where he learned to conflate the life of the warrior with that of the scholar, the virtues of a Christian with the aims of a classical hero, and the stoicism of *virtù* with dutiful service to prince and to pope. Such a curriculum was meant to make Castiglione and his followers civilized, to reawaken in them the classical Roman *urbanitas* which "involved such qualities as likeability, good taste, restraint, sobriety, fine language, and charm. It called for the shunning of vices like affectation, weakness, ridicule, avarice, pedantry, and excessive craving for honor, and it was informed by the idea of *mezura* and the golden mean."[4] In designing (or redesigning) life at the ducal palace of Urbino by persistently invoking the moral and rhetorical values of Cicero's villa near Tusculum—a significant Senecan original for the Urbino of *Il Cortegiano*—Castiglione avails himself of the past for his every direction to the present. "Hardly a page of *The Courtier* turns without a bold plagiarism," George Bull notes after translating *Il Cortegiano,*[5] as if Castiglione meant his single literary achievement to be a contemporary encyclopedia of classical learning. And even in his own day his close friend Raphael signaled Castiglione's reliance—or his dependence—by creating a fresco for the Vatican in which Castiglione (as Zoroaster) stands between Aristotle, carrying a copy of the *Ethics* written for his son Nicomachus, and Plato holding a copy of his *Timaeus.*[6] It is as if, by resurrecting the past in the refinements of his own civilization, Castiglione would force time to have a stop. The twin motives that inspire and govern *Il Cortegiano* (and initially govern us) are the inductive establishment of the pure humanist community and the securing of its permanence. The fatal difficulty is that, in so shaping Urbino, Castiglione insists on realizing perfectability in an imperfect society, one whose flaws are caught in a discernible time and place and written—at least in manuscript—as a tribute to those participants who will know from the outset that it is successful only as a deliberately willed act of the imagination, a verbal act of *admiratio.*

Despite Castiglione's quiet act of creative desperation, however, there remain in his open association with other humanists indelible moments of buoyant wit: in the catalogue of jokes that seems, at least at first, misplaced and disproportionate at the end of Book 2; in the descriptions of Gaspare Pallavicino (in his remarks on women) and Ortono da Morella (in his remarks on his own wisdom). The endless *paragore,* the clashes of rhetoric and competitions of accomplishment that humanize the participants and enliven their *conversazioni,* are symbolically positioned in the spacious Sala della Veglie at the ducal palace of Urbino atop the summit of a sharp rock overlooking the functioning city below. There, in the thin, high mountain air of a remote city where the impotent Duke Guidobaldo Montefeltro's thirty or forty copyists are transcribing authentic Greek and Latin manuscripts that constitute the New Learning, a handful of courtiers and court ladies fastidiously debate the superiority of sculpture or painting, ancient or vernacular languages, as well as politeness and rudeness, nature and art, love and hate, passion and spirit, duty and freedom. In these continuing battles of wits that mingle the philosophic, the essential, and the trivial, Castiglione's authorial voice moves deliberately but often imperceptibly from bemused and distanced irony to sharpened satire and even to poignant acceptance of what fools mortals may be. These miniature colloquies, which in sequence form the bulk of *Il Libro del Cortegiano,* owe much in form and even substance to the Erasmian collections that appeared during the composition of *Il Cortegiano:* such works as the *Monita paedogogia* (1522), the *Proci et puellae* (1523), and the *Convivium fabulosum* (1524). *Il Cortegiano* in turn anticipates Erasmus's *Ars notaria* (*The Art of Learning,* 1529), which encapsulates for humanist poetics much of what Castiglione finally accomplishes in an internal debate between two interlocutors named Desiderius and Erasmus.[7] For Erasmus, the true lovers of learning—what the men of *Il Libro del Cortegiano* profess to be despite what they in fact prove to be—are isolated with their books, Folly's notorious satiric Schoolmen anticipating the duke's translators and perhaps the duke himself. Conversely, the courtiers (like Folly) must constantly perform in public. Their pronouncement of their learning prevents further learning, for what they teach each other, in Castiglione's fiction, are not the facts that constitute knowledge but the opinions and gestures that compose *performance.* Their praise is, essentially, a self-praise, their own specialized and refined *encomium moriae.*

Il Libro del Cortegiano, then, like the humanist fiction preceding it, is rooted in paradox. In perpetuating shallow manners before each other and trivializing talk about issues that had been far more serious to their predecessors in the Quattrocento, the guests at Urbino confirm their own mortality in realizing the immortality of the topics they dream.[8] They ignore both the serious theological and political struggles that have swept Rome and the papal states as they turn to the glorious ideals captured in Plato's understanding of forms and Aristotle's disquisition on the cardinal virtues. Yet we cannot forget the fact that Castiglione also chooses to immortalize these very guests at Urbino. A personal remembrance of things past, *Il Libro del Cortegiano* is also his continuing, lifelong commitment to use that past to teach a tarnished present. In his splendid reconstruction of the composition of *Il Cortegiano,* Ghino Ghinassi shows us how the book was begun in 1514 as a relatively traditional commentary on *il valore delle donne,* the merits of women as compared with men (MS. Vat. lat. 8204).[9] Later patchwork additions and embellishments contributed the discussions of arts and letters, the anthology of jokes, and the Neoplatonic revelation of love which, combed and recombed by the young widower Castiglione (although he seems never to have planned publication), led to what is for Jakob Burckhardt "the high school of polished manners" and for W. B. Yeats "the grammar school of courtesies."[10] What rescues *Il Cortegiano* from such superficial concerns, however, is the last major addition, the fourth book in which all the social and rhetorical skills of the members of the court are turned to counseling the prince—are brought to bear, that is, through Ottaviano's understanding of public needs and Bembo's revelation of private visions that energize and shape such counsel, on the most pressing political and social issues confronting the humanists. By undoing one paradox (that of trivial discourse on important matters in the opening books), Castiglione insures another (that of using courtly eloquence for directing extracourtly events). In his sustained humanist paradox of perfecting what may be imperfectible, Castiglione oscillates between the eloquence of Isocrates and that of Cicero, the one based in a sense of literary culture, the other in that of actual civil rule and achievement. By bringing together these disparate sources through the eloquence that unites them, Castiglione realizes the ambiguity in the Greek term *paradoxon* (Latin *para doxa*), which both Cicero and Quintilian translate appropriately with words derived from the Latin verb *admiror,* meaning "to wonder or marvel at"—an ambiguity George Puttenham will comment on in his *Arte of English Poesie* (1589) when he considers paradox as a figure of speech by calling it, instructively, "the wondrer" (sig. Ccl).[11] It is by this richer, deeper, and more profound sense of a poetics of eloquence for humanist fiction that Castiglione earns his title of *arbiter elegantiarum.*

All of this highly significant dynamic for a humanist poetics is explicitly set forth by Castiglione himself in his prefatory letter to Don Michel de Silva, composed after the completion of *Il Cortegiano.* Castiglione begins with a profoundly moving *memento mori,* a moving litany of the dead, in which name after name tolls like a church bell. Revising his work for publication because an inferior copy of his book was about to appear, he tells Don Michel,

> e sùbito nella prima fronte, ammonito dal titulo, presi non mediocre tristezza, la qual ancora nel passar più avanti molto, si accrebbe, ricordandomi la maggior parte di coloro, che sono introdutti nei ragionamenti, esser già morti: ché, oltre a quelli de chi si fa menzione nel proemio dell'ultimo, morto è il medesimo messer Alfonso Ariosto, a cui il libro è indrizzato, giovane affabile, discreto, pieno di suavissimi costumi ed atto ad ogni cosa conveniente ad omo di corte. Medesimamente il duca Iuliano de' Medici, la cui bontà e nobil cortesia meritava più lungamente dal mondo esser goduta. Messer Bernardo, cardinal di Santa Maria in Portico, il quale per una acuta e piacevole prontezza d'ingegno fu gratissimo a qualunque lo conobbe, pur è morto. Morto è il signor Ottavian Fregoso, omo a' nostri tempi rarissimo, magnanimo, religioso, pien di bontà, d'ingegno, prudenzia e cortesia e veramente amico d'onore e di virtù e tanto degno di laude, che li medismi inimici suoi furono sempre constretti a laudarlo; e quelle disgrazie,

che esso constantissimamente supportò, ben furono bastanti a far fede che la fortuna, come sempre fu, così è ancor oggidi contraria alla virtù. Morti sono ancor molti altri dei nominati nel libro, ai quali parea che la natura promettesse lunghissima vita.

sodeinlie at the first blush by reason of the title, I tooke no litle grief, which in proceadinge forward encreased much more, remembringe that the greater part of them that are brought in to reason, are now dead. For beside those that are mentioned in the Proheme of the last booke, M. Alphonsus Ariosto him self is dead, unto whom the booke was dedicated, a noble yonge Gentilman, discreete, full of good condicions, and apt unto every thing meete for one livinge in court. Likewise Duke Julian de Medicis, whose goodnesse and noble Courtesy deserved to have bene a longer time enjoyed of the world. Also M. Bernard, Cardinall of S. Maria in Portico, who for his livelie and pleasant promptness of witt, was most acceptable unto as manie as knew him, and dead he is. The Lord Octavian Fregoso is also dead, a man in oure tymes verie rare, of a most noble courage, of a pure lief, full of goodnesse, witt, wisdome and Courtesie, and a verie frende unto honour and vertue, and so worthy prayse, that his verie ennemies could say none other of hym, then what sounded to his renoume: and the mishappes he hath borne out with great steadinesse, were sufficient inoughe to geve evidence, that fortune, as she hath always bene, so is she in these dayes also an enemie to vertue. There are dead in like maner manie other that are named in this boke, unto whom a man wold have thought that nature had promised a verie longe lief.[12]

A more extended and more moving tribute to the dead duchess follows; *Il Cortegiano* is first meant, then, as a golden monument to combat the swift erasures of fortune and of time; "Per non tardare adunque a pagar quello, che io debbo alla memoria de così eccellente Signora e degli altri che più non vivono, indutto ancora dal periculo del libro, holo fatto imprimere e publicare, tale qual dalla brevità del tempo m'è stato concesso" (p. 25). The sentiment catches up the more drastic images that open Castiglione's final draft of Book 2 with a striking passage that draws upon Vergil's *Aeneid* (6.306 ff.) and closes with a reference to Cicero's *De Oratore* (2.74.299): "Però dei cori nostri in quel tempo, come allo autunno le foglie degli alberi, caggione i suavi fiori di contento a nel loco dei sereni e chiari pensieri entra la nubilosa e turbida tristizia, di mille calamita compagnata". "Therefore the sweete flowers of delyte vade away in that season out of our harts, as the leaves fall from the trees after harvest, and in steade of open and cleare thoughts, there entreth cloudie and troublous heavinesse accompanied with a thousand heart griefes" (pp. 103–4; pp. 86–87). The powerful and irrevocable fact of mortality is inescapable, perhaps irremediable, a stark challenge to a naive humanist view of man's inherent possibilities, to which the vibrant Folly wishes to entitle us. In response to such a different, wrenching, *uncompromising* reality such as that enjoyed by Folly's man in the empty theater—and to avoid further beguiling the mind and misdirecting judgment—Castiglione proposes an uncompromising view of art that will teach men to forget what is painful, admit what elevates, and so preserve further possibilities of human development. *Il Cortegiano*, then, is meant not simply as a memoir, or a tribute to those now dead, or even as a reliable record of a high moment of accomplishment in Castiglione's civilization but as a deliberate opposition to those forces that eradicate human achievement and so threaten the very bases of humanism. Its *roots* are dialectic.

This rather elaborate argument strikes us now as circular and therefore limited in its usefulness. But it does not seem so to Castiglione, coming to his theory after first working out its implications in the long act of composing and revising *Il Cortegiano*. Reconstructing that activity, we can see how at each step his painstaking selection of particular simple truths transforms reality into desirable prototype, making his *acts* of imitatio the *sources* for imitatio. To achieve such ends, Castiglione stresses positive features. Thus the steep mountains, rugged terrain, and harsh climate of Urbino are subordinated to a description of the fertile countryside surrounding the city ("che intorno il paese è fertilissimmo e pien di frutti") which is blessed by Heaven ("il cielo favorevole") (1.2). The very name means "tiny city," from the Latin *urbs,* and according to Castiglione is thought by many if not all ("la opinione di molti") the most beautiful to be found anywhere in Italy. The palace is so well furnished that it seems not to be a palace at all but a city—for the humanists, the height of civilization—in the form of a palace ("che non un palazzo, ma una città in forma de palazzo esser pareva"). This is not seen primarily as the ducal home of Guidobaldo, but as the legacy of the former Duke Federico, who serves as Castiglione's model, for it is an estate Federico has selectively furnished himself with only the richest of silver vases, cloths of gold, statues of marble and bronze, rare paintings and musical instruments, and, climactic and most important, the ancient humanist texts in Greek, Latin, and Hebrew (p. 33). Later, Montaigne will find in his travels to Urbino a large pile of rock, which is too big to have much charm; but for Castiglione, it is a mellowed landscape in which courtly men and women forming a perfect circle sit defining the ideal courtier. Elevating their descriptions and judgments, they renew Duke Federico's legacy while allowing Castiglione to fashion them, in turn, as a further legacy worth preserving.

Nor does he merely select what is best about Urbino; he also omits much that is damaging. What continues to grieve us about *Il Cortegiano* is that in preserving its elegance Castiglione sacrifices so much of the truth. For instance, there is no suggestion, as Rebhorn has noted,

> that just a few months after the discussions of his book supposedly took place, the seventeen-year-old heir-apparent to Urbino's dukedom demonstrated his *virtù* by treacherously stabbing to death his sister's unarmed lover while Duke Guidobaldo was temporarily out of the palace. Nor does Castiglione note that Francesco Maria's *vivacità dello ingegno* would manifest itself throughout his life in a violent brutality that would lead him to murder Cardinal Alidosi in the streets of Ravenna, knock the famous ambassador Guicciardini to the ground, and order his servants to beat to death three Venetian sentries who challenged his right to bear arms on Venetian soil. Likewise, Castiglione says nothing of the murders and bloody deeds performed by Febus da Ceva, his brother Ghirardino, and the Unico Aretino. Nowhere does he provide any hint that the courtiers and ladies of Urbino fell short of their expressed ideal of perfect chastity, even though some evidence points to the philandering ways of Bembo and Bibbiena, and a bastard son born in 1511 offers indisputable proof of the liaison at the court between Giuliano de' Medici and Pacifica Brandono. [*Courtly Performances*, p. 56].

In addition, Castiglione is not above shaping his work by personal tastes and enmities. He features one Medici, the Magnifico Giuliano, but omits his more famous brother Giovanni, later Pope Leo X, thereby avenging himself on Leo for awarding Urbino to his landless nephew Lorenzo and forcing the exile of the duchess and of Castiglione; he remains silent too about the marqués di Pescara, responsible in 1521 for the death of Ottaviano Fregoso.[13] Nor is there any suggestion of his separation from his mother and wife and his exile to Mantua. Instead, Castiglione's intention further dictates that he choose a happier and earlier *time,* that of a papal visit through Urbino that underscores the virtue and importance of the courtiers he portrays (1.6; pp. 54–56). Modesty causes him to fabricate his absence by some months (and create an anonymous but reliable and omniscient narrator) by redating his own mission to England to receive the Order of the Garter for Duke Guidobaldo in the autumn and winter of 1506–7 (1.1; 4.38). By such selection, omission, and modification, real people who doubtless had somewhat similar conversations at Urbino are presented primarily as ideal types ("onorati esempi di virtù"; 4.2).

But Urbino is no Utopia; nor is Castiglione's golden handbook for courtiers void of verisimilitude. Rather, he writes in his letters that he means to present his characters historically, with all their individual *proprietà e condicioni*. Many of the details are incidental, such as Bibbiena's self-confession of his grace and beauty of countenance ("La grazie e 'l volto bellissimo penso per certo che in me sia e perciò interviene che tante donne, quante sapete, ardeno dell'amore mio") in which the self-portrayal capsizes on his further admission that his legs are too small and sharply disproportionate ("ma della forma del corpo sto io alquanto dubbioso, e massimamente per queste mie gambe, che in vero non mi paiono così atte com'io vorrei"; 1.19). More general attitudes help to dramatize the *conversazioni,* such as the continuing misogyny of Gaspare and Niccolò Frisio, which sharply modifies the Magnifico's extravagant praise of women (Book 3), and Signor Morella's remarks, which temper the idea of wisdom as attributable to the elderly (3, 4). The further reality of the courtiers' affectations—their art within a work of art pretending to realism—is clearly and repeatedly called to our attention. Unico Aretino feigns a spontaneous sonnet but is accused of preparing it beforehand ("che da molti fu estimato fatto all'improvviso, ma, per esser ingenioso e culto più che non parve che comportasse la brevità del tempo, si pensò pur che fosse pensato"; 1.9). Jokes are at times excessively belabored (2.55–56), and metaphysical subtleties, according to the Magnifico, often spur courtiers to speak beyond the bounds of their abilities (3.18). Even Ottaviano's crucial discussion of the proper end of the courtier is preceded by numerous remarks about the length of time he took to prepare his remarks, thus suggesting that this highest declamation of wisdom is also (and necessarily) a presentation that is artfully contrived (4.1–3). This presumptive acknowledgment of artifice within artifice—like the boxes within boxes that characterize the argument of Folly—further argues Castiglione's *propositio* that humanist art perfects nature, that the highest form of art not only captures indelibly the emulous dignity of man but, paradoxically, is "an arte to teach us to forget" ("un'arte che è scordar insegnasse"; 2.1). The simulated behavior of the self-designed courtier that Castiglione's characters jointly describe, then, is a deliberate analogy to Castiglione's own simulation of history in his portrayal of the ducal court at Urbino in 1506. Such an artificial but edifying account, filled with elaborate set speeches of instruction, has its classical antecedents as well: Castiglione's poetics is itself an imitatio of the poetics of that selectively detailed and idealized sort of history we see practiced generally by Sallust and

Livy, antique Romans whose art serves Castiglione as distant but useful Senecan originals.

Castiglione's syntagmatic anatomy of *Il Cortegiano* in his letter to Don Michel is a wonderfully accurate accounting of its design and purpose. The outlines of his humanist fiction presumably remained clear from the time he began putting down notes for his treatise around 1508 until he rushed the first manuscript of a completed version to Bembo in 1518 for his response—much as Thomas More had rushed a copy of *Utopia* in manuscript to Erasmus a short time earlier—through the final publication (under duress, according to Castiglione) in 1528. For most of this period, *Il Cortegiano* was in three books, modeled closely on the three books of Cicero's *De Oratore,* his fashioning of an ideal courtier through dialogue and debate similar to Cicero's fashioning of an ideal orator. *Il Cortegiano* was finally published, in more than eighty editions in Italian and various translations between 1528 and 1619; in this ultimate presentation, the theoretical definition of the courtier (Book 1) is joined to the actual performances of courtiers (Book 2) and to those of equally exemplary women (Book 3), precept joined with practice. Then the whole was further elaborated in a later, fourth book, without precedent in Cicero, on the end or purpose of the courtier, whose function is serving and counseling the prince. Thus Ciceronian practice gives way to Aristotelian precept at the end. Thus *Il Cortegiano* fashions a courtier both in the theoretical imagination and in the pragmatic acts of reasonable service: Lodovico Canossa's extended definition in Book 1 is realized in Ottaviano Fregoso's prescriptive program in Book 4, clear coordinates for the particular skills of a courtier listed in Book 2 and the more generalized encomia of admirable women in Book 3. No book of *Il Cortegiano,* that is, works alone; at the least they work in pairs (1 and 4, 2 and 3), and at best they all work together. The entire fiction is finally—like the characters and their discussions in its component books individually—*com-posed.*

This larger dialectic is developed through the more limited dialectics of each book which, implying the art of triangulation once more in its open disputations, suggests humanist moderation through our supplying an Aristotelian mean that responds to competing ideas by reconciling them. Book 1, for example, first examines Castiglione's authorial propositio, to fashion a courtier (*formiamo un cortegian*) by juxtaposing the magnificent ducal palace of Urbino alongside its present impotent and deformed inhabitant. The glories of Urbino bequeathed by Federico, which caused the principality to be renowned for his patronage (1.2), is continued into the time of his son Guidobaldo, the duke at the time of *Il Cortegiano.* Guidobaldo inherits a palace where the Montefeltro autobiography is carved in wooden crests on doorways beside other carvings depicting the glories of arts and letters, the seven liberal arts, and the Petrarchan triumphs. He emulates his father,

> sopra ogni altra cosa procurava che la casa sua fusse di nobilissimi e valorosi gentilomini piena, coi quali molto familiarmente viveva, godendosi della conversazione di quelli: nella qual cosa non era minor il placer che esso ad altrui dava, che quello che d'altrui riceveva, per esser dottissimo nell'una e nell'altra lingua, ed aver insieme con l'affabilità e piacevolezza congiunta ancor la cognizione d'infinite cose; ed oltre a ciò tanto la grandezza dell'animo suo lo stimulava che, ancor che esso non potesse con la persona eserciter l'opere della cavalleria, come avea già fatto, pur si pigliava grandissimo placer di vederle in altrui; e con le parole, or correggendo or laudando ciascuno secondo i meriti chiaramente dimostrava quanto guidicio circa quelle avesse.

> [for he] set his delight above all thinges to have his house furnished with most noble and valiant Gentlemen, with whom hee lived verie familiarly, enjoying their conversation. Wherein the pleasure which hee gave unto other men was no lesse, than that he received of other, because hee was verie well seene in both toongs, and togither with a loving behaviour and pleasantnesse hee had also accompanied the knowledge of infinite things. And beside this, the greatnesse of his courage so quickned him, that where hee was not in case with his person to practise the feates of Chivalrie, as he had done long before, yet did he take verie great delight to beholde them in other men, and with his wordes sometime correcting, and otherwhile praising every man according to his deserts, he declared evidently how great a judgement hee had in those matters.

> [Pp. 34–35; p. 19]

What startles us, then, and begins *Il Cortegiano* with a crucial, ironic, but representative cleavage is that this intellectual paragon is, physically, a failure. Indeed,

> la fortuna in ogni suo disegno tanto gli fu contraria, ch'egli rare volte trasse ad effetto cosa che desiderasse; e benché in esso fosse il consiglio sapientissimo e l'animo invitissimo, parea che ciò che incominciava, e nell'arme e in ogni altra cosa o piccola o grande, sempre male gli succedesse: e di ciò fanno testimonio molte e diverse sue calamità

> fortune was so contrarie to him in al his purposes, that verye seldome he brought to passe any thing to his mind. And for all hee had in him most wise counsaile,

and an invincible courage, yet it seemed that whatsoever he tooke in hand, both in feates of armes, and in everye other thing small or great, it came alwaies to ill successe. And of this make proofe his manye and diverse calamities.

[P. 34; pp. 18–19]

At their best, Guidobaldo's actions mock Federico's. Thus the duke, deformed by gout, is absent from the disputations of the courtiers, for his warped figure would mar their presence and thwart their idealistic explorations. Significantly too, Guidobaldo was impotent; thus his presence would remind Castiglione's courtiers that he was the last of the line that made their gatherings possible.

Guidobaldo's imperfections, like the presence of death hovering over the palace of Urbino, are described by Castiglione at the outset to establish the necessary reservations for the flights of imagination that follow. We are meant to join Lodovico and Ottaviano in their sketches of a more perfect man under the tutelage of the humanist curriculum detailed in Book 2, but we are also meant to realize that Urbino is special because the imaginative ends it proposes are beyond probable realization. This double-edged awareness will be further advanced at every point in *Il Cortegiano* where argument or dialogue comes to momentary rest. Moreover, the carpings of Gaspare and Frisio are meant to function as continual reminders that even healthy courtiers may display weaknesses of character, understanding, or will and may do so even in the midst of higher speculations. Cardinal Pietro Bembo's inspired rhetorical vision at the close of Book 4, then, is only the climactic event in a series of speeches where the highest of hopes is dashed by the realities of existence, as Bembo's Neoplatonic understanding of love is abruptly terminated by the sunrise.

Yet this two-sided awareness, reminiscent of the works of Erasmus, is in its initial instance reconciled within the text. Castiglione claims that Guidobaldo's ability to contain his misfortunes shows his triumph over fate and illustrates a way in which a man sorely tested and found imperfect can nevertheless set an example for others who are unfortunate.

Che mai la virtù dalla fortuna non fu superata; anzi, sprezzando con l'animo valoroso le procelle di quella, e nelle infirmità come sano e nelle avversità come fortunatissimo, vivea con somma dignità ed estimazione appresso ognuno; di modo che, avvenga che cosi fasse del corpo inferno, militò con onorevolissime condicioni a servicio dei serenissimi re di Napoli Alfonso e Ferrando minore; appresso con papa Alessandro VI, coi signori Veneziani e Fiorentini.

Vertue never yeelded to fortune. But with a bold stomacke despising her stormes, lived with great dignitie and estimation among all men: in sicknesse, as

one that was sounde, and in adversitie, as one that was most fortunate. So that for
all hee was thus diseased in his bodie he served in time of warre with most
honourable entertainement under the most famous kings of Naples, Alphonsus
and Ferdinande the yonger. Afterward with Pope Alexander the sixt, with the
Lordes of Venice and Florence. [P. 34; p. 19]

There is no hint here that Guidobaldo will have venereal disease, will frustrate
the duchess, will die young. Partly this too would harm those premises of
humanism Castiglione wishes to explore by seeming to deny them outright.
More importantly, however, these facts are for Castiglione and for *Il Cortegiano*
unimportant, inessential. What alone matters is that Guidobaldo is exemplary
in a negative way; he teaches us how to combat misfortune when we are *unable*
to approximate the ideal. Within *Il Cortegiano,* Guidobaldo's early and sustained absence tells us in advance how we are to accommodate the deaths
announced at the beginning of Books 1, 2, and 4; to those readers of *Il
Cortegiano* who also knew the events surrounding the publication of Castiglione's lifelong testimony to humanism, Guidobaldo's stoic *virtù* is notably
matched by Castiglione's enduring faith in correcting and publishing his portrait of the ideal courtier in the midst of the horror of the sack of Rome.

The exemplary treatment of Guidobaldo limns in miniature the dynamics of
the remainder of Book 1. The games the courtiers entertain as possibilities are
tempered by the presence of the duchess, and the various suggestions are
reconciled in the most comprehensive suggestion, that of the diplomat, soldier, politician, and student of philology Federico Fregoso, who proposes

> di formar con parole un perfetto cortegiano, esplicando tutte le condicioni e
> particulare qualità, che si richieggono a chi merita questo nome; ed in quelle
> cose che non pareranno convenienti sia licito a ciascun contradire, come nelle
> scole de' filosofi a chi tien conclusioni

> to shape in wordes a good Courtier, specifying all such conditions and particular
> qualities, as of necessitie must bee in him that deserveth this name. And in such
> thinges as shall not appeare necessarie, that it may bee lawfull for everie man to
> reply against them, as the maner of Philosophers schooles is against him that
> keepeth disputations. [P. 45; p. 29]

The first disputation is whether or not the courtier needs to be of noble birth.
Lodovico, chosen by Emilia Pia as the first speaker, concedes that study and
diligence may correct many faults of nature. This reconciliation between noble
and plain birth—that those not born to nobility may study to achieve noble

behavior—confirms the Aristotelian mean by which *Il Cortegiano* is structured and at the same time insures the validity of humanist education. The next debate, which advocates arms as the principal and true profession of the courtier (1.17) countered by the utility of wise speech and philosophy (1.18), is meant to be resolved by seeing the courtier as a man equally adept at arms *and* letters. Art or discipline limits and controls nature, so that human perfection is a matter of natural endowments in harness with an artful (and educated) sense of control. We see the disputations here as bifocal, implying their own resolutions. We are also to keep our eye on the end of these debates—to form *in words* a *perfect* courtier—and on the imperfect scraps of information, opinion, and vision by means of which the courtly men and women at Urbino trade ideas and share their understanding to achieve that end.

We might do so, at least at the first, because of the very charm shown by even the least and most petulant of Castiglione's courtiers. "They never lose their social, indeed, playful, tone," Joseph Anthony Mazzeo comments.[14] At the same time, however, Kenneth Burke notes, their endowments are preeminently those of argumentative appeal.[15] Their refined language is a deliberate and deliberating art in which what is most calculated and persuasive is meant to appear casual, and even the heaviest investments of thought and passion are transformed into the incidental comments of polite conversation. What binds these courtiers together and suspends their fundamental divisions of attitude or perspective is what Castiglione terms *sprezzatura:* Elegant style alone resolves fundamental antagonisms and basically irreconcilable beliefs as well as the deep fractures caused by ambiguity and paradox. This eloquence, according to Count Lodovico, who serves here as Castiglione's spokesman, insures an acquired (and vital) grace for social discourse and diplomacy. In the key passage for understanding all of *Il Libro del Cortegiano,* Lodovico calls the art he advocates, and the art Castiglione is himself deliberately practicing, a universal rule,

la qual mi par valer circa questo in tutte le cose umane che si facciano o dicano più che alcuna altra, e ciò è fuggir quanto più si po, e come un asperissimo e pericoloso scoglio, la affettazione; e, per dir forse una nova parola, usur in ogni cosa una certa sprezzatura, che nasconda l'arte e dimostri ciò che si fa e dice venir fatto senza fatica e quasi senza pensarvi. Da questo credo io che derivi assai la grazia; perché delle cose rare e ben fatte ognun sa la difficultà, onde in esse la facilità genera grandissima maraviglia; e per lo contrario il sforzare e, come si dice, tirar per i capegli da somma disgrazia e fa estimar poco ogni cosa, per grande ch'ella si sia. Però si po dir quella esser vera arte che non pare esser arte; né più in altro si ha da poner studio, che nel nasconderla: perché se è scoperta, leva in tutto il credito e far l'omo poco estimato. E ricordomi io già aver letto esser stati alcuni antichi oratori eccellentissimi, i quali tra le altre loro industrie sforzavansi di far credere ad ognuno sé non aver notizia alcuna di lettere; e dissimulando il sapere mostraven le loro orazioni esser fatte simplicissimamente, e più tosto secondo che loro porgea la natura e la verità, che 'l studio e l'arte; la qual se fosse stata conosciuta, arìa dato dubbio negli animi del populo di non dover esser da quella ingannati. Vedete adunque come il mostrar l'arte ed un così intento studio levi la grazia d'ogni cosa.

which in this part (me thinke) taketh place in all things belonging to a man in word or deede, above all other. And that is to eschue as much as a man may, and as a sharpe and daungerous rocke, too much curiousnesse, and (to speake a new word) to use in everye thing a certaine disgracing to cover arte withall, and seeme whatsoever he doth and saith, to doe it without paine, and (as it were) not minding it. And of this doe I believe grace is much derived, for in rare matters and well brought to passe, every man knoweth the hardnesse of them, so that a readinesse therein maketh great wonder. And contrariwise to use force, and (as they say) to hale by the haire, giveth a great disgrace, and maketh everie thing how great so ever it bee, to be litle esteemed. Therefore that may bee saide to be a verie arte, that appeareth not to be arte, neither ought a man to put more diligence in any thing than in covering it: for in case it be open, it looseth credite cleane and maketh a man litle set by. And I remember that I have redde in my dayes, that there were some most excellent Orators, which among other their cares, enforced themselves to make everie man believe, that they had no sight in letters, and dissembling their cunning, made semblant their Orations to be made verie simply, and rather as nature and truth ledde them, than studie and arte, the which if it had beene openly knowne, would have put a doubt in the peoples minde, for feare least hee beguiled them. You may see then, how to shew arte, and such bent studie taketh away the grace of every thing.

[Pp. 61–62; p. 46]

This central doctrine of the *necessity of eloquence,* an art that seems not to be art, and nature that is not nature, goes unquestioned theoretically and practically.

But Lodovico introduces his fundamental principle by two differing con-textual corollaries that warn us not to accept this sort of eloquence without caution, much as the early portrait of Guidobaldo warns us not to be ensnared by the desirability of Lodovico's ideal courtier without reserved judgment. For one thing, we are told that *sprezzatura* disguises the practitioner and may delude him; for another, it is (at least initially) deceptive and false—and so treacherous.

Chi adunque vorrà esser bon discipulo, oltre al far, le cose bene, sempre ha da metter ogni diligenzia per assimiliarsi al maestro e, se possibil fosse, transformarsi in lui. E quando già si sente aver fatto profitto, giova molto veder diversi omini di tal professione e, governandosi con quel bon giudicio che sempre gli ha da esser guida, andar scegliendo or da un or da un altro varie cose. E come la pecchia ne' verdi prati sempre tra l'erbe va carpendo i fiori, cosi il nostro cortegiano averà da rubare questa grazia da que' che a lui paterà che la tenghino e da ciascun quella parte che più sarà laudevole; e non far come un amico nostro, che voi tutti conoscete, che si pensava esser molto simile al re Ferrando minore d'Aragona, né in altro avea posto cura d'imitarlo, che nel spesso alzare il capo, torzendo una parte della bocca, il qual constume il re avea contratto cosi da infirmatà. E di questi molti si ritrovano, che pensan far assai, pur che sian simili ad un grand'omo in qualche cosa; e spesso si appigliano a quella che in colui è sola viciosa

He therefore that will bee a good scholler, beside the practising of good thinges must evermore set all his diligence to be like his maister, and (if it were possible) chaung him selfe into him. And when hee hath had some entrie, it profiteth him much to behold sundrie men of that profession: and governing him selfe with that good judgement that must alwaies be his guide, goe about to picke out, sometimes of one, and sometime of an other, sundrie matters. And even as the Bee in greene medowes fleeth alwaies about the grasse, choosing out flowers: So shall our Courtier steale his grace from them that to his seeming have it, and from eche one, that parcell that shall be most worthie prayse. And not to do as a friend of ours, whom you all know, that thought he resembled much Ferdinande the younger of Aragon, and regarded not to resemble him in any other point, but in the often lifting up of his heade, wrything therewithall a part of his mouth, the which custome the king had gotten by infirmitie. And many such there are that thinke that they doe much, so they resemble a great man in somewhat, and take many times the thing in him that worst becommeth him. [P. 61; p. 45]

The art of nonchalance, then, can deceive *both* the actor *and* his audience, whereas frequent practice can turn, as Erasmus's Folly had noted, all the world into a stage and make the actor, like the lone man in Folly's Horatian theater, foolish or mad. On one hand, then, sprezzatura is a saving flexibility that alone cements courts together by centripetal appeal; on the other, it confounds things by infinite centrifugal disguisings and protean shiftings so that nothing can surely be known. It eliminates the basis for knowing anything or anyone. It allows one man to play many parts, as we all must do in our daily existences. But it also may rob us of any singular identity that is our own.

Looked at one way, sprezzatura shows how we make of ourselves fictional characters and thus find ourselves wedded to the characters of *Il Cortegiano*. Conversely, it suggests in their subtle but obvious maneuvering and their limitations at posturing how *unlike* these characters we are. Sprezzatura is Castiglione's central paradox, and it may remind us, as it should, of Folly's double role. It is not only the means of life at court; it is the stuff of fiction about courts. "The individual's public life," William J. Kennedy writes, "signaled by the roles that he plays in relation to others in accordance with certain social norms, complicates his character." Kennedy goes on to remark that

> No single role ever fully represents or covers his entire fictive nature. He plays instead many roles, some complementary, others contrasting, though even their totality fails to express completely his moral essence. The rhetorical act thus generates a dramatic interest in how the speaker clings to a certain role, shifts to another, moves through a succession of them, or enacts two or more opposing ones simultaneously, and how he squares or fails to square these roles with his moral selfhood.[16]

Sprezzatura, that is, always entails conscious subterfuge. His disposition and conduct always conceal a courtier's intentions to a greater or lesser degree; the elaboration of the self is mirrored in the elaboration of speech, but it is an eloquence that hides rather than reveals purpose. The art of sprezzatura is the art of *dissimulation*—or an art opposed to Castiglione's *simulation* of Urbino— and this further tension adds to the dynamic art of *Il Cortegiano*. At its most extreme, it echoes Pico's remarks in his correspondence with Ermalo Barbaro in their humanist *controversia* in the latter years of the Quattrocento that "the task of the rhetor is nothing else than to lie, to entrap, to circumvent, to practice sleight-of-hand."[17] Little wonder, then, that in its own time *Il Cortegiano* prompted a variety of responses, from Roger Ascham's straightforward recommendation that Castiglione "aduisedlie read, and diligentlie folowed, but one yeare at home in England, would do a yong ientleman more good, I wisse, then three yeares trauell abrode spent in *Italie*" (sig. G4v) and George Whetstone's admiring and derivative *Heptameron of Ciuil Discourses* (1582), which recounts "the ciuill disputations and speaches of sundry well Courted Gentlemen, and Gentlewomen his Guestes during the time of my intertainment, with Segnior Phyloxenus" (sig. A2v), to the more knowing cynicism of Aretino, whose *La Cortigiana,* the story of the grooming of Messer Maco to become a courtier, is a scurrilous satire on Castiglione's putative idealism.[18]

At our distance, it is easy to be suspicious of sprezzatura and, with Aretino, to disparage those foolish enough to follow Ascham's advice to take *Il Cortegiano* with complete seriousness. But we would be at fault if we did so. The eloquence that fosters sprezzatura was worth memorializing for Castiglione because it meant for him, as it did for his master, Cicero, the sort of freedom of speech that comes only at times of political liberty, the sort of liberty that Urbino symbolizes against an aftermath of political and religious constriction and decline. "Nec enim in constituentibus rem publicam nec in bella gerentibus nec in impeditis," Cicero tells us in his rhetorical treatise named after Brutus, "ac regum dominatione devinctis nasci cupiditas dicendi solet. Pacis est comes otique socia et iam bene constitutae civitatis quasi alumna quaedam eloquentia"; "For the ambition to speak well does not arise when men are engaged in establishing government, nor occupied with the conduct of war, nor shackled and chained by the authority of kings. Upon peace and tranquillity eloquence attends as their ally, it is, one may say, the offspring of well-established civic order."[19] Rhetoric and dialectic were admirable disciplines because they served as propaedeutic to philosophy and they embodied, extended, and applied its wisdom;[20] moreover, they extended practical diplomacy by supplying a language that had "the subtlety of chess."[21] In *Il Cortegiano,* however, Castiglione's ardent and audacious honesty shows how the art of exploratory eloquence also becomes the art of attempted *self*-definition; as Lodovico counters Gaspare, Bibbiena, and the Magnifico Giuliano in Book 1, his continuing modifications not only mirror the subsequent waning of the court of Urbino but insistently demand our attentive judgments and reevaluations. Urbino, like More's earlier Utopia and Rabelais's later Thélème, is on trial in *Il Cortegiano,* and the paradoxical employment by the courtiers of sprezzatura demands our active and ongoing interpretation.[22]

Whereas Book 1 provides the theoretical basis of *Il Cortegiano* in its purpose (*di formar con parole un perfetto cortegiano*) and in its paradoxical means (sprezzatura), Books 2 and 3 apply these precepts to the practices of court gentlemen and ladies, respectively. Federico is obliged "a dimostrare in qual modo e maniera e tempo debba il cortegiano usar le sue bone condicioni, ed operar quelle cose che già s'è detto convenirsegli" (2.6), but instead he catalogues their qualities, and the Magnifico goes even further, undermining his analogous responsibility by speaking "di questa donna eccellente come io la vorrei; e formata ch'io o'avero a modo mio, non potendo poi averne altra, terrolla come mia a guisa di Pigmalione" (3.4). He will fashion his own ideal *donna di palazzo* by creating one himself. From the outset, then, both books elude testing the ideas of Book 1 through the clever practice of sprezzatura. The act is indispensable since, without the art of forgetting or feigning, only the stark reality of the fall confronts the disputants at Urbino (p. 105; pp. 88–89). The anonymous authorial voice that sings the dirge for the dead and admits the fall of the present also offers, within this somber context, the grace that comes with prudence, here proposed by Federico (p. 100; p. 93). Such active prudence implies the moderating force of reconciling later oppositions such as age and youth (3.15), success and failure (3.24), dress (3.27), walk (3.28), and even friendship (3.30); in each instance, we are invited to steer a middle course between excess and deficiency. Book 3 thus confirms and extends Book 2. It is in this way that we too practice art like the courtiers who,

> come i boni pittori, i quali con l'ombra fanno apparere e mostrano i lumi de' rilevi, e così col lume profundano o'ombre dei piani e compagnano i colori diversi insieme di modo, che per quella diversità l'uno e l'altro meglio si dimostra, e 'l posar delle figure contrario l'une all'altre le aiuta a far quell'officio che è intenzion del pittore.
>
> as the good painters with a shadow make the lights of high places to appeare, and so with light make low the shadowes of plaines, and meddle divers colours together, so that through that diversitie both the one and the other are more sightly to beholde, and the placing of the figures contrarie the one to the other is a helpe to them to doe the feate that the painters mind is to bring to passe.
>
> [P. 111; pp. 94–95]

Such diligence and the care for excellence are the principal aim, although the means remains an affected nonchalance (2.11).

The continuing need for sprezzatura is further confirmed when Castiglione turns, with a certain degree of ruthlessness, from the lesser urgencies of the courtier's excessive or deficient behavior and deceit to the evil of which men are capable. As he unrolls an anthology of wit in Book 2, the grimmer tones of the opening passages in Book 3 are anticipated. For what begins, once more, as humanist in its outlook of promise—a formal oration and encomium on entertainment beginning with its history (2.45)—grows constantly cruder, "radically dark" as Robert Grudin puts it. "Under cover of laughter," he sums, "we are ushered away from the smiling courtliness of the Urbino palace into a gross 'real' world where the traditional courtly standards are hollow, inoperative, or totally reversed. In this new world villainy not virtue is the norm, and success lies not in moral rectitude but in superior cunning." [23] As it proceeds, Book 2 is progressively more somber, questioning (as it unfolds) the very efficacy of the notions of beauty and art with which it begins and testing the longevity and utility of the sprezzatura by which it is conveyed; like the *Encomium Moriae*, *Il Cortegiano* becomes self-reflexive. So the gentlemen of Urbino who first talk about fooling and deceiving soon share stories in which "cardinals are characterized as heretical, dishonest, shameful and quintessentially wicked," "priests are unabashedly maligned," and "Florentines are derided as money-mad, Brescians as hopelessly silly, Siennese as thievish and Romans as sexually perverted," as Grudin has it (p. 201). Just as Federico would transform the courtier even into the prince his master (1.26), Castiglione has transformed the discussions at Urbino into a general metaphor to characterize the potentialities of man's baser nature. Thus the question of whether art can train and refine nature becomes immeasurably more serious even as the intuitive need to further discussion moves the courtiers themselves beyond entertainment. They enter into a protracted disputation in which more and more of them feel the urge to participate, a debate in which formal presentations, such as Lodovico's and Federico's, are splintered by Gaspare's persistent probings and Bembo's disruptive claims for various forms of love. These two outsiders become, by the close of Book 2, Castiglione's carefully delineated representations of man's dual possibilities. When Emilia tries, at evening's end, to continue the investigation on the related topic of courtly women to provide some relief during their common pursuit, she turns to the greatest of them, Lord Giuliano de' Medici, Giuliano the Magnifico, only to be frustrated by his own gnawing doubt. Madam, he replies,

> io non so come bon consiglio sia il vostro impormi impresa di tanta importanzia, ch'io in vero non mi vi sento sufficiente; né sono io come il Conte a messer Federico, i quali con la eloquenzia sua hanno formato un cortegiano che mai non fu né forse po essere.

> I wot not whether your devise be good or no, to commit into my handes an enterprise of so great waight, for (to tell you the truth) I thinke not my selfe able inough. Neither am I like the Count and Sir Fredericke, which with their

eloquence have shaped such a Courtier as never was; nor I believe ever shall be.

[P. 205; p. 184]

Nor . . . ever shall be: At midpoint Castiglione's melancholy is justified since in this last confrontation of idealized courtier and fallen man, the whole scheme of forming a hypothetic synthesis seems to fall apart, like a house of cards.

The chief point of contention in *Il Cortegiano,* then, is not whether a courtier must be born or can be made—a common humanist debate—but whether, given man's propensities, a courtier can be reliably fashioned *in any way at all* and whether sprezzatura can be authenticated as a sufficient means. In raising the underlying doubt about the perfectibility of man, Castiglione raises the central dilemma of humanism and couples it with his own frank examination of humanist rhetoric and humanist fiction as accommodating methods—or as methods potentially redolent with failure. Book 3, with its album of good women to emulate, counters the hollow jest prefacing the book, which wittily argues that, as Pythagoras deduced the size of Hercules by mathematical formula, so we can deduce the true state of Urbino by examining the portraits of heroic women of a past never associated with that ducal palace. The Magnifico's catalogue of exemplary characteristics—gentle birth, good manners, cleverness, prudence, and grace; affability, modesty, quick vivacity of spirit, chastity, wit, and discretion (3.4–5), as well as speech that is fluent, prudent, virtuous, and pleasant (3.6)—is undercut, however, when his only applications are from the remote classical past, in which commendable women illustrate only single virtues. Thus Alessandra, wife of Alessandro, king of the Jews, is a model for political prudence alone (3.22), Epicare and Leona figure forth only constancy (3.23), Aspasi and Diotima demonstrate wisdom (3.28), and Anne of France and Margherita embody justice (3.34). Such morals as we are able to draw often conflict with each other, as justice and prudence, constancy and chastity, often do; more importantly, what a single episode seems to say and what it is intended to signify are often at odds. Thus the lesson of Alessandra, which appears to honor courage and fortitude, actually emphasizes impiety and ruthlessness; the Trojan women ostensibly honored for their part in founding Rome are characterized by their trickery and deceit (3.29); and the Sabine women learn that it is wiser and more expedient to accept the fact of their rape than to seek justifiable revenge (3.30).[24] Imitatio is surely implied yet just as surely denied by the careful reader, who will *not* follow the Trojan women into crucial acts of betrayal or Sabine women into acquiescence to rape. In displaying such vulnerability, these women become ironic counterparts to those men whose crude jokes revealed an even cruder nature. In the anecdotes in both Book 2 and Book 3, men and women alike betray their darker purposes, despite the encomia of Petrarch and Solomon (3.52). Challenges and objections even to such praise as this are voiced by Gaspare and Bernardo Accolti, the Unico Aretino, and in the dialectic of Book 3 they are answered by the presence of the duchess and by the spirited replies of the younger Emilia. Emilia's position—that true love pleases the beloved and awakens love in him (3.63)—answers the charge of evil not by ignoring it but by subsuming it, making love the greater force. This reply, like Aretino's proposed marriage of true souls (3.63), so simply put and in so seemingly tangential a cause, would disappear from our perception of the grosser issues we are meant to contest and resolve were it not for the emphasis Castiglione gives to his own nostalgia, to his own confidence that despite such issues the loss of the Urbino he knew is grievously significant. Although Emilia's answer to Aretino may be of insufficient weight to answer the larger problems introduced in Books 2 and 3, it nevertheless, within the narrower confines of the discussion of women, *is* adequate to handle the barbs of the misogynist attitudes she is forced to encounter. Thus she too manages an understanding of the Aristotelian mean; and her moderating stance is echoed in Ottaviano Fregoso's remarks concluding Book 3.

These three books—for many years constituting all of *Il Cortegiano*—attempt to portray both the realities and the dreams of Urbino figuring forth a larger Italy. "He makes his little court into an image of an entire civilization," Rebhorn reminds us (*Courtly Performances,* p. 87), drawing his characters together from the various regions and cultures of Renaissance Italy. His characters are also types. Gaspare and Frisio are incurable misogynists; Unico Aretino is hyperbolic and petulant; Emilia witty and mischievous; Morella irritable and forgetful; Bembo impractical and visionary; the Duchess Elisabetta remote. Such broad representatives of Italy and of human character are both individualized and brought together as a composite of mankind generally. This oscillation, this art of synergism, which ends in a gathering up of parts to make a greater whole, follows the poetics of Castiglione's friend Raphael (and is derived in turn from the Ciceronian definition of imitatio): "per dipingere una bella, mi bisogneria veder più belle"; "to paint a beauty, I would have to see many beautiful women."[25] Such a movement is not unrelated to sprezzatura, which moves from natural fact to artistic casualness and disguise, gathering up the bits and pieces of reality and transforming them into an artifice with the designed purpose of heightening, pleasing, and persuading. The same sort of development—anticipating the transformation in Book 4 from the pragmatic

Ottaviano to the visionary Bembo—can be seen in the accretive prologues to the four books of *Il Cortegiano*. The prologue to the first book describes the beauty of Urbino and the nobility of its former ruler; the prologue to Book 2 goes further by arguing the superiority of Urbino to all courts past and present. The opening to Book 3 goes further yet, analogizing the superior stature of Urbino with the superior size of Hercules to suggest that the court has about it a heroic quality; and Book 4 opens with a reference to the Trojan horse, continuing the heroic quality of Urbino but now transforming it into the realm of epic. This latter comparison is more than a general one, for Castiglione continues his final prologue by giving epic stature to those courtiers dramatized at Urbino, now dead, in a moving set of particularized eulogies.[26] Urbino generally is transfigured in the course of *Il Cortegiano,* from its straightforward geographical placement on the slopes of the Apennines (1.2) to its elevated positioning in history, which transcends particular place and time ("ché veramente del caval troiano non uscirono tanti signori e capitani, quanti di questa casa usciti sono omini per virtù singulari e da ognuno sommamente pregiati," (4.2). This ennobling act of sprezzatura by Castiglione, leaving behind the Roman authorities of Cicero and Quintilian to allude to the more ancient Greek texts, reactivates as well the Greek concept of *kalokagathia,* the understanding of man as both ethical agent and artistically constructed self.[27]

Although Book 4 of *Il Cortegiano* is more somber and more serious, its statements are richer, more purposeful. A jarring abruptness shakes us from the setting of 1507 to the time of publication (1528) with a long list of the actual deaths that have intervened, robbing the present of the possibility of continuing forever the *conversazioni* that constitute *Il Cortegiano.* They belong now to the historic past. When we return to Urbino for the last time, then, it is with the understanding that we are being given one final privileged view of that happier and more perfect time; our concluding visit is weighted by its proximity to oblivion and therefore charged with extra power and significance. All this prefaces the remarks of Ottaviano (which took longer than usual to prepare), his declamation displacing a dance as soon as he is announced,[28] his speech carrying into the long, dark night. As we are led by such indicators to expect, Ottaviano Fregoso's purpose is the most important of all, for it is concerned with the final Aristotelian cause, the end or purpose of the courtier rather than the passing traits of his daily behavior. It is, moreover, an end that passes through and beyond sprezzatura.

> Il fin adunque del perfetto cortegiano, del quale insino a qui non s'è parlato, estimo io che sia il guadagnarsi per mezzo delle condicioni attributtegli da questi

signori talmente la benevolenzia e l'animo di qual principe a cui serve, che possa dirgli e sempre gli dica la verità d'ogni cossa che ad esso convenga sapere, senza timor o periculo di despiacergli; e conoscendo la mente di quello inclinata a far cosa non conveniente, ardisca di contradirgli, e con gentil modo valersi della grazia acquistata con le sue bone qualità per rimoverlo da ogni intenzion viciosa ed indurlo al camin della virtù; . . . certo è che l'animo di colui, che pensa di far che 'l suo principe non sia d'alcuno ingannato, né ascolti gli adulatori, ne i malèdici e bugiardi, e conosca il bene e 'l male ed all'uno porti amore, all'altro odio, tende ad un ottimo fine.

The ende therefore of a perfect Courtier (whereof hetherto nothing hath beene spoken) I believe is to purchase him, by the meane of the qualities which these Lordes have given him, in such wise the good will and favour of the Prince he is in service withall, that he may breake his minde to him, and alwaies enforme him franckly of the truth of every matter meete for him to understand, without fear or perill to displease him. And when hee knoweth his minde is bent to commit any thing unseemely for him, to be bold to stand with him in it, and to take courage after an honest sorte at the favor which he hath gotten him through his good qualities, to disswade him from every ill purpose, and to set him in the way of vertue. . . . sure it is that the minde of him which thinketh to worke so, that his Prince shall not bee deceived, nor lead with flatterers, railers, and lyers, but shall know both the good and the bad, and beare love to the one, and hatred to the other, is directed to a verie good end. [Pp. 287–88; pp. 261–62]

Ottaviano argues for services to the prince, not transformation into the prince. His position is precisely that of Thomas More-persona standing before Hythlodaye outside the unfinished Church of Notre Dame in Antwerp. But whereas *Utopia* breaks openly into halves, two sides of an unreconciled choice, Castiglione always pursues a more complex combination of forces and issues while leaving the reconciliation to us. Ottaviano, therefore, addresses a wide spectrum, from the position that witnesses to man as essentially good (4.27) to a bitter attack on princes as not merely corruptible but historically evil (4.8); his praise catches the tone of hope in Book 1, his denunciation that of villainy in Book 2 and brutalities endured in Book 3. The prince, moreover, may threaten the courtier; and both may fall prey to sycophancy (4.6) and luxuriousness (4.7). The awareness that these possibilities may occur at any time and at any station in life gives to Book 4 a certain wariness we have not seen in Castiglione before and brings to his closing section an unmistakable urgency.

But it is not only the grave pressures of time and perspective that change

Book 4 so decisively; it is also the *direction* in which it takes the formation of the ideal courtier. In stressing the courtier's purpose rather than his skills or behavior, Ottaviano merges the salon with the schoolroom and transforms the ideal gentleman into a humanist *maestro di scuola*. His function now is redirected into teaching—that is, cultivating—the prince.

> Però, come nell'altre arti, così ancora nelle virtù è necessario aver maestro, il qual con dottrina e boni ricordi susciti e risvegli in noi quelle virtù morali, delle quai avemo il seme incluso e sepulto nell'anima, e come bono agricultore le cultivi e loro apra la viâ, levandoci d'inortno le spine e 'l loglio degli appetiti, i quali spesso tanto adombrano e suffocan gli animi nostri, che fiorir non gli lassano, né produr quei felici frutti, che soli si dovriano desiderar che nascessero nei cori umani. . . . ché se il bene e 'l male fossero ben conosciuti ed intesi, ognuno sempre eleggeria il bene e fuggiria il male. Però la virtù si po quasi dir una prudenzia ed un sapere eleggere il bene, e 'l vicio una imprudenzia ed ignoranzia che induce a giudicar falsamente; perche non eleggono mai gli omini il male con opinion che sia male, ma s'ingannano per una certa similitudine di bene

> Therefore even as in the other artes, so also in the vertues it is beholefull to have a teacher, that with lessons and good exhortations may stirre up and quicken in us those moral vertues, whereof wee have the seede inclosed and buried in the soule, and like the good husbandman till them and open the way for them, weeding from about them the briers and darnell of appetites, which many times so shadow and choke our mindes, that they suffer them not to budde nor to bring forth the happie fruites, which alone ought to be wished to growe in the harts of men. . . . For in case good and ill were well knowne and perceived, every man woulde alwaies choose the good, and shunne the ill. Therefore may vertue be saide to be (as it were) a wisedom and an understanding to choose the good: and vice, a lacke of foresight and an ignorance that leadeth to judge falsely. Because men never choose the ill with opinion that it is ill, but they are deceived through a certaine likenesse of good. [Pp. 294–95; pp. 268–69]

Ottaviano's doctrine is not that of courtesy books but that of humanist writings; and his advice is markedly similar to that of Erasmus, More, and Ascham. Moreover, the proposed curriculum, which leans heavily on Aristotle, is similar; the courtier as instructor would teach the prince justice above all (4.32) but also prudence, piety, and love (4.32–35). Cesare Gonzaga catches the point: Ottaviano's ideal would rather deserve the name of schoolmaster than of good courtier, and the best prince would be the ideal governor ("più presto meritareste nome di bon maestro di scola che di bon cortegiano ed esso più presto di bon governatore che di gran principe," (4.36).

Il Cortegiano, then, undeniably culminates in humanist doctrine as developed by Ottaviano at the beginning of Book 4. His sense of human nature is taken, as it is with all the humanists, from the humor psychology of Aristotle (4.16): Reason controls passion and promotes knowledge. But the waste of time and expense of shame in learning by experience are short-circuited by Ottaviano, by the precepts of the humanist teacher. In the battle-ravaged states of Cinquecento Italy, what is desirable for Roger Ascham in *The Scholemaster* is vital for Castiglione, and for his prince; and Ottaviano advises the instruction of such lessons alongside concrete examples:

> a poco a poco infundergli nell'animo la bontà ed insegnarli la continenzia, la fortezza, la giustizia, la temperanzia, facendogli gustar quanta dolcezza sia coperta da quella poca amaritudine, che al primo aspetto s'offerisce a chi contrasta ai vicii; li quali sempre sono dannosi, dispiacevoli ed accompagnati dalla infamia e biasimo, così come le virtù sono utili, giocunde e piene di laude; ed a queste eccitarlo con l'esempio dei celebrati capitani e d'altri omini eccellenti, ai quali gli antichi usavano di far statue di bronzo e di marmo e talor d'oro; e collocarle ne' lochi publici, cosi per onor di quegli, come per lo stimulo degli altri, che per usa onesta invidia avessero da sforzarsi di giungere essi ancor a quella gloria

> by litle and litle distil into his mind goodnesse, and teach him continencie, stoutnesse of courage, justice, temperance, making him to tast what sweetnesse is hid under that litle bitternesse, which at the first sight appeareth unto him that withstandeth vices, which are alwaies hurtfull, displeasant and accompanied with ill report and shame, even as vertues are profitable, pleasant and prayseable, and enflame him to them with examples of manye famous captaines, and of other notable personages, unto whome they of olde time used to make images of mettal and marble, and sometime of golde, and to set them up in common haunted places, as well for the honour of them, as for an encouraging of others, that with an honest envie, they might also endevor themselves to reach unto that glorie. [P. 291; pp. 264–65]

Such an explicit summary confirms the dynamics of precept in Book 1 of *Il Cortegiano* joined to the examples of Books 2 and 3, translating the preceding three books, as Cicero does in *De Oratore,* into a fundamentally *humanist* fiction.

To supply us with further direction, Castiglione has Ottaviano develop the active behavior of the prince turned governor into the exercise of moderation, the continuing reconciliation of excess and deficiency that mirrors our own need to moderate the extremes argued in Books 1, 2, and 3 and to unwind such paradoxical behavior as that caused by sprezzatura. In the tradition of humanist fiction, moreover, such counsel comes in the form of a *responsio:*

> Si che non chiamate, messer Cesare, per minuzia cosa alcuna che possa migliorare un principe in qualsivoglia parte, per minima che ella sia; ne pensate già ch'io estimi che voi biasmiate i [mici] documenti, dicendo che con quelli più tosto si formaria un bon governatore che un bon principe; che non si po forse dare maggior laude né più conveniente ad un principe, che chiamarlo bon governatore. . . . di levare ed abbreviar le liti tra i sudditi; di far fare pace tra essi, e legargli insieme di parentati; di far che la città fosse tutta unita e concorde in amicizia, come una casa privata; populosa, non povera, quieta, piena di boni artifici; di favorir i mercatanti ed aiutarli ancora con denari; d'esser liberale ed onorevole nelle ospitalità verso i forestieri e verso i religiosi; di temperar tutte le superfluità; perché spesso per gli errori che si fanno in queste cose, benché paisano piccoli, le città vanno in ruina.

> Therefore my (Lord Cesar) doe you not call a small matter any thing that may better a Prince, how small so ever it be. Nor thinke that I judge it to bee in the reproofe of my lessons, where you say, that a good governour might better thus bee formed, than a good Prince. For perhaps there can not be a greater praise nor more comely for a Prince, than to call him a good governour. . . . [Such precepts, moreover, are experentially realized.] To breake and to ende controversies among his subjects. To take up matters betweene them, and to knitte them together in allyance by marriage. To provide so, that the citie may be all joyned together and agreeing in amitie, like a privat house, well peopled, not poore, quiet, and full of good artificers. To shew favour to marchant men, and to helpe them also with stockes. To be liberall and honourable in house keeping toward straungers and relegious persons. To temper all superfluous matters, because through the offences committed in these thinges, albeit they appeare but small, Cities many times fall in decay. [Pp. 319–20; pp. 293–94]

Such lessons, found in Aristotle's *Nicomachean Ethics 2,* are coordinated with his *Politics 2–4* (4.21) and taught by imitatio at various levels: The courtier's examples will teach the prince, whose life will act as an example for his people while he in turn emulates God (4.22, 23). By understanding the force of both precept and example (4.29), the prince will correctly administer rewards and punishments (4.27), thus cultivating proper behavior in his subjects as the courtier has, in less forceful ways, fostered it in him. The secret to success in such instruction is the inculcation of self-discipline; the end is a harmonious state; in addition, laws and regulations help insure the peace and tranquillity that for Castiglione function as the basis of an ideal government. "Però è ancor officio del bon principe instituire talmente i populi suoi, e con tali leggi ed ordini, che posano vivere nell'ocio e nella pace senza periculo e con dignità e godere laudevolmente questo fine delle sue azioni che deve esser la quiete" (4.27). Such a prince and such a government resemble the ideals of Plato's Republic—and may be just as unrealizable, as Frisio is quick to point out. Ottaviano's inspired portrait of the prince teaches and persuades all the men and women in the ducal palace at Urbino, so much so that his subtle change of subject usurps all concern with the ideal courtier, which had been the single subject in the preceding books until Frisio's abrupt reminder. You (and we) can go no further than this, Frisio sums, but his interjection is more wistful than satiric: "che sia come la republica di Platone e che non siamo per vederne mai un tale, se non forse in cielo"; "he is like the common weale of Plato, and wee shall never see such a one, unlesse it bee perhaps in heaven." (p. 321; p. 294). At the highest pitch of his argument, Ottaviano confronts the fundamental humanist dilemma that seems to have motivated Castiglione's own late additions to his manuscript and the slow reformation of *Il Cortegiano* into the fiction described to Don Michel in the book's preface.

For an understanding of Castiglione's deep desire to confirm the possibility of humanist thought and practice, despite the savage attacks on Rome and the cleavage between Church and state, it is crucial to see what he does here: He introduces Bembo, whose private raptures on the possibilities and power of love confirm that human nature needed by Ottaviano to realize his perfect prince and perfect state. All of the effect of *Il Cortegiano* and much of its meaning rest on our ability to reconcile this apparent fracture between the public declamation on state and leadership and the private revelation of man's impulsion toward beauty and goodness—and to do so we agree to Ottaviano's vision (as well as to Bembo's) and answer Frisio's fundamental challenge. Much talk of love has been scattered throughout the books composing *Il Cortegiano,* from the opening suggestions for evening games preceding the decision to fashion an ideal courtier through the behavior of courtiers and court ladies to Ottaviano's own insistence on love as the efficient cause of peace. For Ottaviano the success of any government rests finally on love, on the prince's love for his people (4.33) and on the people's love for their ruler (4.34). It is the last lesson of the curriculum that he assigns to the courtier as humanist schoolmaster (4.32—35). The introduction of Bembo and his affective revelation of the Neoplatonic *scala amoris,* combining precept and example in a single presentation (for the first and only time in *Il Cortegiano*), is the culmination of a major theme and the definitive response to the last unanswered need. In addition to these functions, explored by Lawrence V. Ryan,[29] Bembo's vision renews hope for Ottaviano's ideal counselor *and* his ideal prince, and awards new possibility for the sort of ideal government that Frisio despairs of finding.

Bembo's mystical declamation, moreover, is the culmination—by demonstration and analysis—of Castiglione's poetics of eloquence. Ottaviano has already allied the enticements and beauties of art with the salutary medicine of doctors (4.10); Bembo extends the argument by making love the motivating force for understanding beauty, a force governed by knowledge (4.51), seeing beauty as the outer circumference of that which is goodness and God (4.57) and therefore seeing beauty now indistinguishable from love as the gateway to both goodness and holiness (4.68—69). The intensity of feeling that causes such a vision—clearly evident in Bembo's impassioned speech, the mystical counterpart in rhetoric to Ottaviano's committed blueprint for governance—is the last awareness to be shed before absorption by God.

Quando adunque il nostro cortegiano sara giunto a questo termine, benchè assai felice amante dit si possa a rispetto di quelli che son summersi nella miseria dell'amor sensuale, non però voglio che se contenti, ma arditamente passi più avanti, seguendo per la sublime strada diretto alla guida che lo conduce al termine della vera felicità; e così in loco d'uscir di se stesso col pensiero, come bisogna che faccia chi vol considerar la bellezza corporale, si rivolga in se stesso per contemplar quella che si vede con gli occhi della mente, li quali allor cominciano ad esser acuti e perspicaci, quando quelli del corpo perdono il fior della loro vaghezza; pero l'anima, aliena dai vicii, purgata dai studi della vera filosofia, versata nella vita spirituale ed esercitata nelle cose dell'intelletto, rivolgendosi alla contemplazion della sua propria sustanzia, quasi da profundissimo sonno risvegliata, apre quegli occhi che tutti hanno e pochi adoprano, e vede in se stessa un raggio di quel lume che è la vera imagine della bellezza angelica a lei communicata, della quale essa poi communica al corpo una debil umbra; però, divenuta cieca alle cose terrene, si fa oculatissima alle celesti; e talor, quando le virtù motive del corpo si trovano dalla assidua contemplazione astratte, o vero dal sonno legate, non essendo da quelle impedita, sente un certo odor nascoso della vera bellezza angelica, e rapita dal splendor di quella luce comincia ad infiammarsi e tanto avidamente la segue, che quasi diviene ebria e fuor di se stessa, per desiderio d'unirsi con quella, parendole aver trovato l'orma di Dio, nella contemplazion del quale, come nel suo beato fine, cerca di riposarsi: e però, ardendo in questa felicissima fiamma, si leva alla sua più nobil parte, che è l'intelletto; e quivi, non più adombrata dalla oscura notte delle cose terrene, vede la bellezza divina; ma non però ancor in tutto la gode perfettamente, perché la contempla solo nel suo particular intelletto, il qual non po esser capace della immensa bellezza universale. Onde, non ben contento di questo beneficio, amore dona all'anima maggior felicità; che, secondo che dalla bellezza particular d'un corpo la guida alla bellezza universal di tutti i corpi, così in ultimo grado di perfezione dalla intelletto particular la guida allo intelletto universale. Quindi l'anima, accesa nel santissimo foco del vero amor divino, vola ad unirsi con la natura angelica e non solamente in tutto abbandona il senso, ma più non ha bisogno del discorso della ragione; ché, transformata in angelo, intende tutte le cose intelligibili, e senza velo o nube alcuna vede l'amplo mare della pura bellezza divina ed in sé lo riceve, e gode, quella suprema felicità che dai sensi è incomprehensibile.

When our Courtier therfore shall bee come to this point, although hee may bee called a good and happie lover, in respect of them that be drowned in the miserie of sensuall love, yet will I not have him to set his hart at rest, but boldly proceede farther, following the high way after his guide, that leadeth him to the point of true happinesse. And this in steade of going out of his wit with thought, as he must doe that will consider the bodily beautie, hee may come into his wit, to beholde the beautie that is seene with the eyes of the minde, which then begin to be sharpe and throughly seeing, when the eyes of the bodie lose the floure of their sightlinesse. Therefore the soule ridde of vices, purged with the studies of true Philosophie, occupied in spiritual, and exercised in matters of understanding, turning her to the beholding of her owne substance, as it were raised out of a most deepe sleepe, openeth the eyes that all men have, and few occupie, and seeth in her selfe a shining beame of that light, which is the true image of the Angelike beautie partened with her, whereof she also partneth with the bodie a feeble shadow. Therefore waxed blinde about earthly matters, is made most quicke of sight about heavenly. And otherwhile when the sturring vertues of the bodie are withdrawne alone through earnest beholding, either fast bound through sleepe, when she is not hindred by them, she feeleth a certaine privie smell of the right Angelike beautie, and ravished with the shining of that light, beginneth to be inflamed, and so greedely followeth after, that (in a menner) she waxeth dronken and beside her selfe, for coveting to couple her selfe with it, having found (to her weening) the footesteps of God, in the beholding of whom (as in her happie ende) she seeketh to settle her selfe. And therefore burning in this most happie flame, she ariseth to the noblest part of her which is the understanding, and there no more shadowed with the darke night of earthly matters, seeth the heavenly beautie: but yet doth she not for all that enjoy it altogether perfectly, because she beholdeth it onely in her particular understanding, which can not conceave the passing great universall beautie. Whereupon not throughly satisfied with this benefit, love giveth unto the soule a greater happinesse. For like as through the particular beautie of one bodie hee guideth her to the universall beautie of all bodies: Even so in the least degree of perfection through particular understanding hee guideth her to the universall understanding. Thus the soule kindled in the most holy fire of true heavenly love, fleeth to couple her selfe with the nature of Angels, and not onely cleane forsaketh sense, but hath no more neede of the discourse of reason, for being chaunged into an Angell, she understandeth all thinges that may be understood: and without any veil or cloud, she seeth the maine sea of the pure heavenly beautie and receiveth it into her, and enjoyeth the soveraigne happinesse, that can not be comprehended of the senses. [Pp. 345–46; pp. 318–19]

It is difficult to interrupt the sweep and power of Bembo's eloquent rhetoric, for its artistry, having nothing to do with the feigned casualness of sprezzatura, is all of a piece. It is an artistry so intertwined with the nature of the thought and the nature of the speaker that, like the courtiers at Urbino, we can only observe in awe. Bembo's ecstatic vision is more than an adequate response to the problem posed at the beginning of *Il Cortegiano—di formar con parole un perfetto cortegiano*—for in the enactment of his intellectual and verbal passion Bembo *incarnates* words—*parole*—and so makes word and act as inseparable as life itself. He too recognizes this, and Castiglione's constant references to Bembo's eloquence (as in 4.65, 69) and the unprecedented silence of his audience show us that he is meant to be the embodiment of the poetics outlined in the letter to Don Michel. At the singular moment of his extraordinary vision—for which he barely finds an accommodating rhetoric—*nothing* else occurs, nothing else *matters*.[30]

So magnificent is Bembo's set oration that it little concerns us that the ideas are drawn from Plato's *Symposium*—by which Castiglione joins other humanist writers of fiction in acknowledging the original master of Continental humanist fiction—or that some passages are taken almost verbatim from Marsilio Ficino's commentary on that Greek dialogue. *Il Cortegiano* 4.57, for instance, about the relationship of beauty, goodness, and God, relies for its fullest force on Castiglione's courtiers drawing on their knowledge of Ficino, as he might expect his original readers to do.

Materia vero et corporis moles, orbis est ab alio et in alio mobilis. Ab alio quidem, quoniam ab anima necessario agitatur. In alio autem, quia in loci spatio motus corporis agitatur. Iam quam ob causam bonitatem in centro, in circulo pulchritudinem, theologi collocent, aperti intelligere possumus. Bonitas si quidem rerum omnium unus ipse est Deus, per quem cuncta sunt bona. Pulchritudo autem Dei radius quattuor illis insitus circulis, circa Deum quodammodo revolutis. Huiusmodi radius omnes rerum omnium species in quattuor illis effingit: species illas in mente, ideas; in anima, rationes; in natura, semina; in materia, formas appellare solemus. Idcirco quattuor in circulis quattuor splendores esse videntur. Idearum splendor in primo, rationum in secundo; in tertio seminum, formarum in ultimo.

But Corporal Matter is a circle movable both *by* another and *in* another: "by another" because it is necessarily moved only by soul; and "in another," because the motion of a body is brought about in the space of place. We can now clearly understand why the ancient theologians agree in placing Goodness in the center, and Beauty on the circumference. The goodness of all things is the one God himself, through whom everything partakes of good. Beauty, then, is the light of God infused in these four circles revolving, so to speak, around God. This light forms in those four circles all the images of every thing. Those images we call, in the Mind, Ideas; in the Soul, Concepts; in Nature, Seeds; and in Matter, Shapes. Thus in the four circles we see four splendors: in the first, the splendor of Ideas; in the second, those of Concepts; in the third, that of Seeds; and in the last, that of Shapes.[31]

Ficino's Latin commentary carries the same assurance as Bembo's declamation, but it lacks the visionary fire and eloquence. Next to Castiglione's dramatization, Ficino's labored explication falls flat; and his cautious and repetitive parsing of issues has more in common with scholastic disputations than with the impassioned humanist art of *Il Cortegiano*. Yet elsewhere in Ficino's commentary there is a gloss on Alcibiades that employs Augustine's sense of the image and that may well be an indication of how Castiglione also saw his courtiers serving as poetic images.

Si in turba hominum quaerat Socrates Alcibiadem, sitque illum aliquando reperturus, necesse est Socratis menti aliquam Alcibiadis figuram, ut sciat quem hominem quaerat prae caeteris, ac repertum in coetu multorum Alcibiadem ab alio discernere valeat. Ita necque indagaret ea quattuor animus, neque aliquando inveniret, nisi haberet illorum, id est veritatis, bonitatis, honestatis, utilitatis, aliquam notionem, per quam illa quaereret inventurus, ut quotiens reperit quae investigaverat, recognoscat, atque ab eorum discernat contrariis.

If sometime Socrates had to find Alcibiades, and looked for him in a crowd of men, there would have to be in the mind of Socrates some picture of Alcibiades, in order for him to know which man he was seeking, instead of the others; and, if he found Alcibiades in a group of several men, to be able to distinguish him from the others. So the soul would neither seek these four concepts nor find them anywhere unless it had some notion of them, that is, of Truth, Goodness, Nobility, and Utility, through which it would seek them in its search, so that when it found what it had been seeking it might recognize them and distinguish them from their opposites. [P. 95; p. 205]

Ficino's analogy between the image of a person and the imaging of Truth tells us (as it doubtless told Castiglione) how Bembo's declamation complements Ottaviano's speech and answers Frisio's objection.

Ficino is only one of many sources on which Castiglione drew during the long gestation of *Il Cortegiano*. Aside from Rabelais's fiction with its remarkable compendium of classical and contemporary references and allusions, Castiglione's work of Continental humanist poetics is surely the most syncretic. There is some truth in George Bull's observation that Castiglione attempts to "synthesize the idea of the warrior and the scholar, the Christian believer and the classical hero, the self-contained man of *virtù* and the dutiful servant of the prince," in his composite courtier (Introduction, p. 14). But beyond frequent specific allusions, there are a number of antique texts, such as the histories of Livy and Sallust, which seem to have served Castiglione as models in elevating men and events to exemplary emblems. Yet the best known of his Senecan originals is Cicero's *De Oratore*, a dialogue between Cicero's two teachers, the theorist Crassus and the practitioner Antonius; like Castiglione's humanist fiction it is an attempt to preserve the memory of the dead (2.2.8). Testimony that this source was widely recognized in the sixteenth century can be found in Hoby's letter to Hastings (p. 3). Nor need we seek far to locate the similarities. The premise of *De Oratore* is clearly Castiglione's starting point in *Il Cortegiano* 1.12:

Quare ego tibi oratorem sic iam instituam, si potuero, ut, quid efficere possit, ante perspiciam. Sit enim mihi tinctus litteris; audierit aliquid, legerit, ista ipsa praecepta acceperit: tentabo quid deceat, quid voce, quid viribus, quid spiritu, quid lingua efficere possit. Si intellegam posse ad summos pervenire, non solum hortabor, ut elaboret, sed etiam, si vir quoque bonus mihi videbitur esse, obsecrabo: tantum ego in excellenti oratore, et eodem viro bono, pono esse ornamenti universae civitati.

"And so I shall now begin making an orator for you, if I can, by first discovering the extent of his capacity. I would have him be a man of some learning, who has done some listening and some reading, and received those very teachings we have mentioned; I will make trial of what suits him, and of his powers of intonation, physique, energy and fluency. If I find him capable of reaching the highest class, I will not merely encourage him to work out his purpose but will positively implore him so to do, provided that I also think his character sound— so much glory to the whole community do I see in an outstanding orator who is also a man of worth." [32]

Antonius's ideal orator, like Castiglione's ideal courtier, is a man of natural gifts (1.28.128) and a liberal education (1.34.158–59), "a man of finish, accomplishment, and taste" ("hominem significat, quod eruditum, quod urbanum," 2.58.236), who is taught by cultivation (2.21.88–89) and imitatio:

Ergo hoc sit primum in praeceptis meis, ut demonstremus, quem imitetur atque ita ut, quae maxime excellant in eo, quem imitabitur, ea diligentissime persequatur. Tum accedat exercitatio, qua illum, quem delegerit, imitando effingat, atque ita exprimat.

"Let this then be my first counsel, that we show the student whom to copy, and to copy in such a way as to strive with all possible care to attain the most excellent qualities of his model. Next let practice be added, whereby in copying he may reproduce the pattern of his choice." [2.22.90]

By precept and practice, this ideal orator as an ideal student will be a master of language; he will be liberally educated in physical and intellectual skills, and he will use his talents and training to serve the political and social life of the state. Other debts are more specific, such as Castiglione's discussion of wit and several of his jokes are taken directly from the long digression in *De Oratore* 2.219–90. But the most attractive feature to Castiglione was doubtless his view of *De Oratore* as a superb defense of eloquence, "the soulbending sovereign of all things"; "flexanima atque omnium regina rerum" (2.44.187), which serves as "the orator's godlike power and excellence . . . a style elegant, copious and diversified"; "oratoris vis illa divina virtusque cernitur . . . ornate, copiose varieque dicere" (2.27.120). The heightened fluency of language in *De Oratore*, especially in the declamation by Crassus in *De Oratore 3*, is perhaps the work's greatest legacy to Castiglione in his own shaping of a poetics of eloquence; it permeates every sentence of *Il Cortegiano*, as Rebhorn has noted (*Courtly Performances*, p. 92). But nowhere in Castiglione do we find the misuse of rhetoric, the ticks of verbal manipulation that the *De Oratore* outlines (2.24.101–42.178); in *Il Cortegiano*, oratory remains a high and serious art. Castiglione's view of Cicero's work, by selective imitation, is that promoted by Strebaeus Remensis in his commentary on *De Oratore* (Basel, 1541): "Nusquam tam magnifice honore vestitur orator, nunquem ita graviter & ornate demonstratur oratoria facultas"; "Nowhere is the orator clad in such splendid dignity, nowhere is oratory described so gravely and ornately."[33] In *De Oratore* this polished style is openly assigned to Crassus (1, 2) and illustrated in his long speech, which climaxes the work (3). Here the startling poignancy that characterizes the entire *De Oratore* stems from the opening passage about the death of Crassus (and hence of true eloquence, 3.1.1), followed by mourning for the fates of others (3.3) and a *cri de coeur* for mortality:

> O fallacem hominum spem fragilemque fortunam, et inanes nostras contentiones, quae medio in spatio saepe franguntur et corruunt et ante in ipso cursu obruuntur quam portum conspicere potuerunt!

> How hollow are our endeavours, which often break down and come to grief in the middle of the race, or are shipwrecked in full sail before they have been able to sight the harbour! [3.2.7]

The deaths of the great Roman poets and orators who teach eloquence in *De Oratore* stand just behind Castiglione's moving memorial to Urbino.

Still an even closer model for *Il Cortegiano* was a second Ciceronian treatise on rhetoric written a decade later, the *Orator*. Addressed to Cicero's friend Brutus, this Senecan original also begins with an attempt to fashion the ideal orator, but now Cicero is filled with misgiving in doing so because the perfect orator, like the perfect courtier, has never existed (1.3–4). Like Castiglione's courtier, it is a verbal construct, a figure of the mind.

> Ego in summo oratore fingendo talem informabo qualis fortasse nemo fuit. Non enim quaero quis fuerit, sed quid sit illud quo nihil esse possit praestantius, quod in perpetuitate dicendi non saepe atque haud scio an nunquam in aliqua autem parte eluceat aliquando, idem apud alios densius, apud alios fortasse rarius. Sed ego sic statuo, nihil esse in ullo genere tam pulchrum, quo non

pulchrius id sit unde illud ut ex ore aliquo quasi imago exprimatur. Quod neque oculis neque auribus neque ullo sensu percipi potest, cogitatione tamen et mente complectimur.

In delineating the perfect orator I shall be portraying such a one as perhaps has never existed. Indeed I am not inquiring who was the perfect orator, but what is that unsurpassable ideal which seldom if ever appears throughout a whole speech but does shine forth at some times and in some places, more frequently in some speakers, more rarely perhaps in others. But I am firmly of the opinion that nothing of any kind is so beautiful as not to be excelled in beauty by that of which it is a copy, as a mask is a copy of a face. This ideal cannot be perceived by the eye or ear, nor by any of the senses, but we can nevertheless grasp it by the mind and the imagination.[34]

The analogy for Cicero, as for the courtiers at Urbino, is with art; and the definition anticipates the poetics of a Raphael.

Itaque et Phidiae simulacris, quibus nihil in illo genere perfectius videmus, et eis picturis quas nominavi cogitare tamen possumus pulchriora. Nec vero ille artifex cum faceret Iovis formam aut Minervae, contemplabatur aliquem e quo similitudinem duceret, sed ipsius in mente insidebat species pulchritudinis eximia quaedam, quam intuens in eaque defixus ad illius similitudinem artem et manum dirgebat.

For example, in the case of the statues of Phidias, the most perfect of their kind that we have ever seen, and in the case of the paintings I have mentioned, we can, in spite of their beauty, imagine something more beautiful. Surely that great sculptor, while making the image of Jupiter or Minerva, did not look at any person whom he was using as a model, but in his own mind there dwelt a surpassing vision of beauty; at this he gazed and all intent on this he guided his artist's hand to produce the likeness of the god. [2.8–9]

The perfect sculpture for Cicero is not an accurate imitation of reality but the extension of the idea of perfect beauty by the sculptor—who is alone responsible for its conception as much as for its execution—and its perfection is confirmed by the way in which it stimulates further acts of imagination in those who behold it.

The artist, then, is indivisible from his art, just as an ideal orator is indivisible from perfect eloquence (*perfectae eloquentiae*); and the *Orator* is given over to "our task of delineating that ideal orator and moulding him in that eloquence which Antonius had discovered in no one" ("Referamus igitur nos ad eum quem volumus incohandum et ea quidem eloquentia informandum quam in nullo cognovit Antonius," (9.33), just as the courtiers at Urbino, following Lodovico, fashion the courtier through a sprezzatura that embodies, guarantees, and furthers his qualifications to be an ideal courtier (*un perfetto cortegiano*). For Cicero too the key is *performance* (19.61). Yet the style Cicero proposes in this dedicated declamation to Brutus is decidedly not the grandiloquent style, which proclaimed splendid power of thought and majesty of diction, or the plain style, refined, concise, stripped of ornament, but something between them.

> Est autem quidam interiectus inter hos medius et quasi temperatus nec acumine posteriorum nec fulmine utens superiorum, vicinus amborum, in neutro excellens, utriusque particeps vel utriusque, si verum quaerimus, potius expers, isque uno tenore, ut aiunt, in dicendo fluit nihil afferens praeter facultatem et aequalitatem aut addit aliquos ut in corona toros omnemque orationem ornamentis modicis verborum sententiarumque distinguit.

> Between these two there is a mean and I may say tempered style, which uses neither the intellectual appeal of the latter class nor the fiery force of the former; akin to both, excelling in neither, sharing in both, or, to tell the truth, sharing in neither, this style keeps the proverbial "even tenor of its way," bringing nothing except ease and uniformity, or at most adding a few posies as in a garland, and diversifying the whole speech with simple ornaments of thought and diction. [6.21]

The well-knit rhythm of prose realizes the Aristotelian mean: "Meae quidem et perfecto completoque verborum ambitu gaudent et curta sentiunt nec amant redundantia," Cicero insists; "My ear, at any rate, rejoices in a full and rounded period; it feels a deficiency, and does not like an excess" (50.168). Such a moderate style is verbally analogous to the courtier who must constantly juggle disguise and reality in performing a verisimilitudinous sprezzatura; and it is just such a balancing act that is for Cicero the function of a successful orator. Indeed, the orator fashions his speech to the occasion, just as Castiglione's courtier must.

> Semper oratorum eloquentiae moderatrix fuit auditorum prudentia. Omnes enim qui probari volunt voluntatem eorum qui audiunt intuentur ad eamque et ad eorum arbitrium et nutum totos se fingunt et accommodant.

> The eloquence of orators has always been controlled by the good sense of the audience, since all who desire to win approval have regard to the goodwill of

their auditors, and shape and adapt themselves completely according to this and to their opinion and approval. [8.24]

This is not only the cardinal rule; it is also universal (21.71). Cicero describes in more detail than Castiglione's courtiers how one performs appropriately for particular audiences (36.124–25). To this end, and for this end only, Cicero catalogues figures of rhetoric for Brutus, both the figures of style (39.135) and the figures of thought (39.136–40.139), as well as various strategies of disposition (44.149–67.226)—the basis for a subsequent poetics of eloquence. If Castiglione has *De Oratore* in mind during such particular passages as those on mortality and wit, it is likelier that he took his understanding of fashioning an idea, of a poetics of eloquence and sprezzatura, from this later work of Cicero's most mature period. He may also have found a ready resource in Quintilian's derivative portrait of the ideal orator in *Institutio Oratoria 12*, as one who is brilliant, sublime and opulent of speech, the lord and master of all the resources of eloquence whose affluence surrounds him ("Nitidus ille et sublimis et locuples circumfluentibus undique eloquentiae copiis imperat").[35]

Yet, if Castiglione's humanist fiction originates in Cicero—as so much work by Continental humanists does—its expansion and refinements come in holograph additions taken from Aristotle; Castiglione's poetics is equally rooted in the *Politics* and *Nicomachean Ethics*.[36] Books 1 and 2 of *Il Libro del Cortegiano* expand on Aristotle's theory of education as summed in *Politics 8*.

> It is clear . . . that there is a form of education in which boys should be trained not because it is useful or necessary but as being liberal and noble. . . . And it is also clear that some of the useful subjects as well ought to be studied by the young not only because of their utility, like the study of reading and writing, but also because they may lead on to many other branches of knowledge. [8.3.1][37]

The *Politics* is a handbook for forming useful (and free) citizens in a functioning government, as Ottaviano suggests in *Cortegiano 4;* but its program is reinforced by remarks in the *Ethics,* a book of the governor for teaching men how to be good, as Bembo urges in *Cortegiano 4*. Here Aristotle discusses the need for practice. "We learn an art or craft by doing the things that we shall have to do when we have learnt it: for instance, men become builders by building houses, harpers by playing on the harp. Similarly we become just by doing just acts, temperate by doing temperate acts, brave by doing brave acts" (2.1.4). Aristotle means to drill his students into habitual behavior, and the habits are to be formed according to his understanding of the mean, Castiglione's *mezzo*, a basic premise of his *Ethics*.

First of all then we have to observe, that moral qualities are so constituted as to be destroyed by excess and by deficiency—as we see is the case with bodily strength and health (for one is forced to explain what is invisible by means of visible illustrations). Strength is destroyed both by excessive and by deficient exercises, and similarly health is destroyed both by too much and by too little food and drink; while they are produced, increased and preserved by suitable quantities. The same therefore is true of Temperance, Courage, and the other virtues. The man who runs away from everything in fear and never endures anything becomes a coward; the man who fears nothing whatsoever but encounters everything becomes rash. Similarly he that indulges in every pleasure and restrains from none turns out a profligate, and he that shuns all pleasure, as boorish persons do, becomes what may be called insensible. Thus Temperance and Courage are destroyed by excess and deficiency, and preserved by the observance of the mean. [2.2.6–7; cf. 2.7.2–6][38]

To appreciate Castiglione's further refinement of the mean as that act of protean moderation that characterizes a successful courtier's flexibility (*mediocrità*)[39] as well as the latitude given the reader in his responses to the extremes of argument and posturing in *Il Cortegiano,* we must keep in mind, as Castiglione's first readers did, Aristotle's understanding of the mean as relative and not fixed.

By the mean of the thing I denote a point equally distant from either extreme, which is one and the same for everybody, by the mean relative to us, that amount which is neither too much nor too little, and this is not one and the same for everybody. For example, let 10 be many and 2 few; then one takes the mean with respect to the thing if one takes 6; since $6 - 2 = 10 - 6$, and this is the mean according to arithmetical proportion. But we cannot arrive by this method at the mean relative to us. Suppose that 10 lb. of food is a large ration for anybody and 2 lb. a small one: it does not follow that a trainer will prescribe 6 lb., for perhaps even this will be a large ration, or a small one, for the particular athlete who is to receive it; it is a small ration for a Milo, but a large one for a man just beginning to go in for athletics. And similarly with the amount of running and wrestling exercise to be taken. In the same way then an expert in any art avoids excess and deficiency, and seeks and adopts the mean—the mean, that is, not of the thing but relative to us. If therefore the way in which every art or science performs its work well is by looking to the mean and applying that as a standard to its productions (hence the common remark about a perfect work of art, that you could not take from it nor add to it—meaning that excess and deficiency destroy perfection, while adherence to the mean preserves it)—if then, as we say, good craftsmen look to the mean as they work, and if virtue, like nature, is more accurate and better than any form of art, it will follow that virtue has the quality of hitting the mean. I refer to moral virtue, for this is concerned with emotions and actions, in which one can have excess or deficiency or a due mean. For example, one can be frightened or bold, feel desire or anger or pity, and experience pleasure and pain in general, either too much or too little, and in both cases wrongly; whereas to feel these feelings at the right time, on the right occasion, towards the right people, for the right purpose and in the right manner, is to feel the best amount of them, which is the mean amount—and the best amount is of course the mark of virtue. And similarly there can be excess, deficiency, and the due mean in actions. Now feelings and actions are the objects with which virtue is concerned; and in feelings and actions excess and deficiency are errors, while the mean amount is praised, and constitutes success; and to be praised and to be successful are both marks of virtue. Virtue, therefore, is a mean state in the sense that it is able to hit the mean. [2.6.4–14]

Education is therefore an ongoing process for Aristotle, as it is for Castiglione, a matter of *praktikè,* or human endeavor—less stable than the natural phenomena of *theoretikè,* or scientific observation, and thus more needful of constant study, practice, and discipline. For Aristotle, the student is, in short, *fashioned;* and it is in this sense of fashioning that Castiglione proposes *di formar un perfetto cortegiano.* Although Ottaviano takes his psychology (4.16) from the *Ethics* and his discussion of governments (4.21) from the *Politics,* while Castiglione takes his examples of joking from *De Oratore,* it is the sense of *Aristotelian epistemology* that forms the Senecan pattern operating behind *Il Cortegiano.* In forming his perfect courtier of the mind, Castiglione shapes *all four books,* in their final revision, by the progressive sense of learning—of education—in the *Ethics,* by building the courtier through lessons in *technē,* or skills (*Ethics* 6.4); *phronēsis* or prudence, practical wisdom (6.5); *nous,* intelligence or rational wisdom (6.6); and *sophia,* wisdom (6.7). As Erasmus relied on an organizing pattern for the *Encomium Moriae,* so too Castiglione shapes Book 1 by describing the skills of the ideal courtier, Book 2 by showing how these skills are put to practical use, Book 3 by illustrating the wisdom of women through their intuitive responses when their courage or intelligence is tested, and Book 4 through both the rational wisdom of Ottaviano and the mystical and enraptured wisdom of Bembo. This ladder of learning, although less explicit, is as important to the conception of *Il Cortegiano* as Cicero's *De Oratore* or *Orator,* or as the more particularized ladder of love derived from Plato's *Symposium* is to Bembo's particular speech (making him the work's Diotima): As with all significant works of humanist fiction, there are multiple Senecan originals from classical texts.

Plato is of course Castiglione's other chief Greek source among humanist texts recovered from the past. The *Republic* lies distantly behind the idea of Urbino as a palace that imitates the ideal state because of its functioning governance combining both utility and pleasure while maintaining, beyond its walls, an exclusive class structure; and Plato's remark that the best education is a necessary precondition of a functioning state (416B–C) is a premise shared by Castiglione. But the *Symposium* is the primary Platonic influence; and its organizing principle of the *scala amoris* shapes not merely Bembo's remarks on love but the overall disposition of *Il Cortegiano,* from the bantering of physical attraction in Books 1 and 2 to the discussion of the virtue prompted by love in Book 3 and the final transportation of the mystic in Book 4. As with Cicero and Aristotle, there are specific borrowings—the atmosphere and discussion at the beginning of the *Symposium* setting the scene; the employment of Bibbiena, Francesco Maria della Rovere, and Bembo as counterparts to Plato's Aristophanes, Alcibiades, and Socrates [40]—but the primary way in which the *Symposium* functions in *Il Cortegiano* is the form or container it gives to the more specific Ciceronian and Aristotelian ideas. Through cross-cuttings of dialogue and debate, various types of individuals jointly pursue a common goal, the definition of love, first as a game and then as a more serious philosophic exploration. This is the primary indebtedness; and when we recall that *symposium* translates as *drinking party* we see how the levity of *Il Cortegiano*—both its banter and its development of sprezzatura—grows directly out of Plato's paradoxical use of a drinking party that feeds both the body and the mind and a drunkenness that allows pratfalls and visions. Castiglione may have known the other humanist texts of his classical past that also use this pattern; three of them have some connection with *Il Cortegiano.* Xenophon's *Banquet* has the same jovial atmosphere, and the chief discussion, on what men take most delight in, leads to definitions of beauty (4.56–5.7) and the ideal man (8.40–42). Plutarch's *Septem Sapientium Convivium (Dinner of the Seven Wise Men)* opens with a sense of impermanence (*Moralia* 146B) and with a sense of mortality captured dramatically in the *memento mori* of a skeleton (148B). The *Saturnalia* of Macrobius, likewise modeled after Plato's *Symposium* (2.1.2; 7.1.13), is concerned with honoring the past (3.14) and takes up in some detail the importance of rhetoric (4) as preparatory to philosophy (7). But it is to Plato that Castiglione and his contemporaries paid greatest respect; when Tasso divides the various forms of dialogue into nine categories in his treatise on the form, he makes the Socratic model superior to the rest. Leonardo Bruni, in his *Dialogus* of 1401 addressed to the humanist educator Petrus Vergerius, describes how Coluccio Salutati, the renowned humanist of the Quattrocento, reprimanded a group of men who, while visiting him, made no attempt to carry on a discussion, and he has Salutati deliver an eloquent declamation on the art of dialogue. His work follows the Platonic model of the symposium and resembles *Il Cortegiano* by closing at the point of further discussion; other contemporary examples of the symposium known to Castiglione are the *Banquets* of the Greek scholar Filelfo and the *De Amore* of Ficino.[41] It is to this most revered of forms, then, that Castiglione subjects the most precious ideas of his fellow humanists in the orations of Lodovico (1), Federico (2), the Magnifico Giuliano (3), and Ottaviano (4), drawing, at times heavily, on the teaching of Vittorino da Feltre as he learned of it at Urbino and on such works as *De Ingenius Moribus* by Vergerius, *De Studiis et Literis* by Lionardo Bruni d'Arezzo, and *De Liberorum Educatione* by Aeneas Sylvius Piccolomini.[42]

And it is among these humanist symposia that we find, in a masterpiece of the Quattrocento, the last important Senecan model for *Il Libro del Cortegiano*. It is Leon Battista Alberti's *I Libri della Famiglia,* published in 1434 (Books 1–3) and 1437 (Book 4). Alberti's principal theme is the one Castiglione chooses to emphasize in his obsession with mortality—that of *virtù* opposed by *fortuna*—and the prologue to Book 1 of Alberti finds an extraordinary number of echoes in the prologues to Castiglione's four books. It is concerned, once more, with the impermanence of humanist actions.

I lodati studi, la sollecitudine, l'industria, e la diligenzia, il buon governo, le buone assuetudini, e osservanzie, gli onesti costumi, l'umanità, la facilitia, e civiltà rendono le famiglie degne. Debbono adunque studiare i padri, come multiplichi la famiglia, con che mestieri, e uso s'aumenti, e divenga fortunata, e come s'acquisti grazia, benivolenzia, e amista, e con quali discipline s'accresca in onore, fama, e gloria. Sono i vecchi come mente, e animal di tutto il corpo della famiglia; e niuna letizia puo essere a'vecchi maggiore, che vedere la loro gioventù costumata, riverente, e virtuosa. Pertanto, figliuoli miei, io voglio con voi conferire, e communicare quello ho letto, e compresso da altri, e provato in questa mia lunga vita, perche voi con questi documenti, e per vostro studio possiate essere migliori. Non pure debbono i buoni padri essere utili a'figliuoli in ricchezze, quanto in fama, in grazia, ed in consiglio.

Fortune's fickleness and imprudence actually seemed able to seize families rich in heroes, abounding in all that is precious, dear, and most desired by mortal men, endowed with honor, fame, high praise, authority, and public favor, and to cast them down into poverty, desolation, and misery. They were reduced from a great number of ancestors to a very few descendants, from unmeasured riches to strait necessity, and hurled from the brightest splendor of glory. They were drowned in calamity, plunged into obscure, oblivious, tempestuous adversity. How many families do we see today in decadence and ruin! It would not be possible to enumerate and describe all the most noble families among the ancients, like the Fabii, Decii, Drusii, Gracchi, and Marcelli and others. They stood in our land for the public good, for the maintenance of liberty, and for the conservation of authority and dignity in peace and in war. They were modest, wise, and fortunate families, feared by their enemies, but loved and revered by their friends. Of all these families not only the magnificence and greatness but the very men, not only the men but the very names are shrunk away, and gone. Their memory, almost every trace of them, is wiped out and obliterated.[43]

How close to Castiglione's bone this must have cut, enjoying as he did the hospitality of the Montefeltros threatened by the unfortunate impotence of Duke Guidobaldo and the uncertain patronage of the pope. Against such forces, Alberti writes, it was to little avail that the humanists fortified themselves with "just laws, virtuous princes, wise counsels, strong and constant actions," and, more privately, "love of country, fidelity, diligence, highly disciplined and honorable behavior" (p. 26). How, then, he asks with Castiglione's anonymous narrator, "shall we view fortune . . . as the teacher of morals, the moderator of conduct, and the guardian of our most sacred traditions" (p. 27)? "It seems to me," he adds poignantly in the prologue to Book 3, "that our imperial splendor was not wholly extinguished until the light and the far-reaching influence of Latin and of Latin letters faded away" (p. 151); and it is to the resurrection of this ancient culture that the four *Libri della Famiglia,* purporting to record a *conversazione* held during the afternoon and evening in May 1421, is written. To reexamine a whole culture, Alberti chooses the analogous metaphor of the family, as Castiglione will choose the metaphor of the court of Urbino; by approaching this more manageable problem, he too will test the bases and efficacy of humanist thought and practice. In the debate that constitutes Book 1, Alberti discusses the duties of the father and the stimulation of a child's natural aptitudes; the need for physical, intellectual, and moral education; the need to avoid a wholly ascetic or contemplative life;

and, more particularly, the need for literary, physical, and military training. He registers, in short, the humanist program that he means to put on trial, in the coordinate speeches of the philosophic Lionardo and the practical Avardo. The occasion for this gathering is the approaching death of their host, Lorenzo Alberti, the author's father, whose notable absence from the dialogue itself functions as that of Guidobaldo does in *Il Cortegiano*. Alberti's own son Battista enters into debate with Lionardo in Book 2: In a witty and sophistic speech of misogyny that anticipates that of Gaspare, he defines nature as lust; Lionardo responds with a more moderate definition of nature as the source of fecundity, economy, and beauty. For Lionardo, the humanist is characterized by a tempering self-discipline arising from the mean between the fear of shame and the hope of honor. This definition of the humanist is furthered in Book 3 by the elderly Giannozzo's declamation on the value of economy, thrift, and good management of a man's household as of his life—*messerizia*—and his consequent denunciation of waste whether from prodigality or irrational stinginess. The aging diplomat of Book 4, Piero, argues for the calculated friendship of the politician—for the life of sprezzatura—to which Avardo, as Alberti's ideal, juxtaposes the lessons of the humanists' moral philosophy, reminiscent for us of Ottaviano's speech near the conclusion of Castiglione's fiction. As in *Il Cortegiano*, the theme of love unites all the various speeches and books of the *Famiglia*. Lionardo introduces the topic of love in Book 1, Battista corrupts it in Book 2, and Giannozzo goes off to practice it in a charitable errand at the close of Book 3; in Book 4, as a precedent to Bembo, Avardo finds it the most elevating emotion of all. He answers Lionardo's definition of love as the basis for friendship, *amicizia*, by introducing the idea of love as the affection of the soul, *amore* (p. 283). Together, these declamations and disputations that constitute the four books of Alberti's *Famiglia* are orchestrated in such a way as to provide the ideal moderation of thought and an aesthetic balancing and harmony of judgments; and as in *Il Cortegiano*, the problem of mortality is overlooked at the end for the promise of a continuing discussion in the days to come.

It is this very humanist tradition of the symposium as an open, unending form for instructive fiction—as open to our final interpretation as Folly's invitation to us to drink—that has seemed so problematic to critics of *Il Cortegiano*. When the rising dawn puts an end to Bembo's raptures and the shared ecstasy of his auditors, how are we to see this—as nature's light confirming the art of the cardinal's uninterrupted declamation or as the sun which puts an end to the visions and dreams of night that delude more than inform us? Does the appearance of the star of Venus on the horizon—the fixed point of vision for all the courtiers as they turn their attention away from Bembo toward a dazzling light that embraces them all—symbolize nature at one at last with fortune, or does the image of Venus undermine the cardinal's more transcendent ideas about love? It is Castiglione's final, remarkable gesture of eloquence, the courtiers' *maraviglia* precisely caught in the art of *admiratio* with its elevated figures and cadences of Ciceronian style. It is a limited historic moment in a confined historical space, both startling and memorable. It is also a moment profoundly Neoplatonic, as Ficino explains in his commentary on Plato's *Philebus:*

> Attende vim rei naturalis per sensus ad imaginationem per hanc ad mentem pervenire, qua concipitur nominique includitur quasi vita et intelligentia corpori. Vim vero divinam per mentes superiores ad nostram, qua concipitur similiterque nominatur nomine vivo; et tanto magis vivo quam nomina corporum quanto potentior a superioribus in nos provenit motus. In nos inquam cum Deo similiores evadimus, id est, quando mentem ab inferioribus sevocamus.

> Notice that the power of a natural object reaches through the senses to the imagination, through the imagination to the intelligence by which it is apprehended and enclosed in a name, just as life and understanding are enclosed in the body. But notice that the divine power reaches through the heavenly intelligences to our intelligence by which it is apprehended and similarly named with a living name. And this name is more alive than the names of bodily objects to the extent that the movement coming down to us from those above is more powerful—coming down to us, I say, when we become more like God, that is, when we recall our intelligence from lower things.[44]

But in the same commentary, Ficino warns that "ut qui eam [dialectic] tractant sensus et phantasiae illusiones caveant et divino mentis lumine ad hanc incedant"; "those who attempt it [dialectic] must guard against the illusions of the senses and the phantasy and proceed towards it by the divine light of the intelligence" (p. 219; p. 218).

There are also pertinent echoes in a far more distant source of humanist poetics, Cicero's *Tusculan Disputations,* which in its portrait of Tusculum provides a Senecan original for Urbino.

> Est enim gloria solida quaedam res et expressa, non adumbrata: ea est consentiens laus bonorum, incorrupta vox bene indicantium de excellenti virtute, ea virtuti resonat tamquam imago: quae quia recte factorum plerumque comes est, non est bonis viris repudianda; illa autem, quae se eius imitatricem esse vult,

temeraria atque inconsiderata et plerumque peccatorum vitiorumque lauda-
trix, fama popularis, simulatione honestatis formam eius pulcritudinemque
corrumpit.

For true glory is a thing of real substance and clearly wrought, no shadowy
phantom: it is the agreed approval of good men, the unbiassed verdict of judges
deciding honestly the question of pre-eminent merit; it gives back to virtue the
echo of her voice; and as it generally attends upon duties rightly performed it is
not to be disdained by good men. The other kind of glory, however, which
claims to be a copy of the true, is headstrong and thoughtless, and generally
lends its support to faults and errors; it is public reputation, and by a counterfeit
mars the fair beauty of true honour. [3.2.3–4][45]

Bembo's passionate vision—the passage of greatest intensity in *Il Cortegiano*—
unites all the courtiers, but only temporarily; it isolates him in the end when he
seems to be the only one unusually and *permanently* affected by it. Indeed, the
immediate force of Bembo's speech is undermined by Gaspare, whose misogyny
has remained unaffected by the cardinal's various definitions of love, and by
Emilia Pia who, teasing Bembo by pulling at his robe, refuses to see his
declamation as climactic. All the others at Urbino, like the sun and the star of
Venus and the seasons of life and death, propose to continue their round of
discussions the next day, to begin again, belying Castiglione's own placement
of this vision as the concluding speech in his tribute to Urbino. Even this last
light seems, on reflection, to darken.

We are right to see this passage as especially vexing (despite the tradition of
humanist poetics) because, though it balances Ottaviano's speech, it is at odds
with *all the rest* of *Il Cortegiano*—it is the only central moment at which a
reconciling mean is *not* suggested by Castiglione. Thus it disrupts the fabric of
the narrative and the rhythm of its presentation. Moreover, it puts manifestly
on trial the capacity of a poetics of eloquence to manage any reconciliation, to
accommodate the virtues, challenges, doubts and paradoxes fostered by humanism. By refusing, at the end, to pull together sufficiently the act of
eloquence and the effect of eloquence, Castiglione suspends the dynamics of
sprezzatura. Such suspension allows the various dimensions of *Il Cortegiano* to
fall into place—the need for sprezzatura as a manner by which courtiers can
operate with minimum fuss and maximum joy is a need shared by the artist,
who must employ rhetorical ends while *seeming* to pass beyond rhetoric to truth.
It means to be at once artifact and fact. The poet is like the courtier who would
wear his costume partly opened so that others will know it is only a costume;

otherwise, eloquence will lose part of its designed appeal and power. The gestures of a poetics of eloquence, like the gestures of artless art that distinguish the true courtier, both conceal and reveal. The highly patterned yet highly graceful disposition and style of language that Castiglione uses thus reinforce behavior and gesture in *Il Cortegiano* and become in this fictional Urbino the *only* behavior, the *only* gesture. Sprezzatura, the equivocal reconciliation of art and nature, is both *subject* and *style*. *Il Cortegiano* passes before us refined, refining us in turn; it *is* what it is about. Castiglione's book civilizes us by its eloquent occasion for reconciliation, the elegant employment of the Aristotelian mean, and the *in*conclusiveness that results. We can see why at his own passing Castiglione awakened encomia from men as diverse as Tasso and Charles V.[46] Lawrence V. Ryan writes that *Il Libro del Cortegiano* is designed, "obviously, for denizens of salons and council chambers rather than for the schools" ("Book Four," p. 158), but it means, instead, to be for them all, to balance salon *and* school in its use and test of sprezzatura, and then leave them, finally, fused but unreconciled. Urbino is a site where the lessons and practices of humanism reify and renew the humanist poetic vision; as a counselor, Castiglione images the ideal courtier as Phoenix (4.47), continually renewing himself through his persuasive eloquence. Castiglione's accomplishment was to marry the court and the academy as ideal vision and as vital activity—and to give to the one an added significance, to the other a workable style. In this, Castiglione's fiction embraces that of Erasmus and extends it into the courtly life at once remote from and reacting to political and social necessities that humanism could not blinker even if it would. Such a complicated yet straightforward monument to art—a *realistic* triumph of the *imagination*—*Il Libro del Cortegiano* broadens, enriches, darkens, and transfigures the humanist poetics of the sixteenth century. In adding to the growing tradition a special interest in balance and in the grace of thought and style as he denies them any true permanence, Castiglione paves the way for a dialectical use of fiction as both an exploration and a response to the humanist view of life. Such a view will reach its Continental apex in the subsequent works of Marguerite de Navarre, Rabelais, and Cervantes, to which we now turn.

FOUR

Marguerite de Navarre's *Heptaméron des Nouvelles:*

The Poetics of Metaphysics and the

Fiction of *L'inquiétisme*

THE PRISMATIC *CONTES* THAT
CONSTITUTE *L'HEPTAMÉRON* OF
MARGUERITE, THE QUEEN OF NA-
VARRE—"THE PATRON OF THE RE-
NAISSANCE, AND THE CHAMPION OF THE
LEARNED" [1]—ARE COMPOSED, FROM THE
start, to emphasize the caducity of the world we know. Essentially, they share
with Castiglione a universe noted for its frailty, its perishability, its very
impermanence. Together, these *contes* mark a decisive turning point in the development of Continental humanist poetics. Drawing simultaneously and consen-
taneously on the wit and paradox by which Erasmus exposed man's folly and
rescued his wisdom and on the urgent need for cultivation and the strategic use
of manners advanced by Castiglione, Marguerite transforms her predecessors'
inherent disputation and open dialectic wholly into the service of fiction. The
various embedded tales of *L'Heptaméron* function both philosophically and
rhetorically to create a singular—and a memorable—*nouvelle. L'Heptaméron*
(written from 1541; published posthumously in 1558) is a masterpiece of
humanist fiction, a splendid and dazzling accomplishment, propaedeutic in
turn to the great novels of Rabelais and Cervantes that will follow.

Marguerite de Navarre "was the greatest lady of her time," L. Cazamian
writes. He echoes the praise given her at her death in 1544 that she was "certes
tout l'honneur Des Princesses de nostre age"; "She was also the most cultivated
and gifted woman of the French Renaissance," an "epitome" of humanist
culture.[2] But she is no feminist epigone of Boccaccio, just as *L'Heptaméron* is no
mere imitation of the *Decameron.* Whereas the Italian collection of tales remains

a series of escapades with a vitality alternately salacious and satiric, a way to fend off thoughts of the plague, Marguerite's peculiar blending of the sensual, the moral, the sardonic, and the mystical—what Hugh M. Richmond has called "so thoroughly Shakespearean" and "hypnotic"[3]—is far more intricate and considerably more resonant than what we find in her predecessor. Moreover, her deliberate placement of tales, arranged dialectically by speaker, by subsequent commentary, and with each other, orchestrates a far more rhetorical effect than the random presentation of Boccaccio's stories does. *Il Libro del Cortegiano* is consequently a far more accurate measure of Marguerite's intention. Its peculiar combination of salon and schoolroom as instrumental for humanist symposia is compounded in Marguerite by the deliberately chosen setting of a monastery; hers is a profoundly *Christian* humanism, preserved in its consistent ethical, scriptural, and mystical echoes. This tough woman—learned, proud, passionate, grief-stricken, lonely, *regal*—pursues in humanist fiction a factious, schismatic Europe of political contest and religious strife. Thus the form of the symposium introduced to humanist fiction by Castiglione was extraordinarily apt; and Marguerite manages her own fiction, as he did his, with a sprezzatura that supplies a flexible means of communication to maintain, without denying the complexities of competing heterodoxies, a kind of tentative rhetorical harmony, a kind of tentative rhetorical grace.

But as Marcel Tetel has noted: "Marguerite de Navarre remains elusive."[4] It is easy enough to see why. Her multidimensional life—from her birth in 1492 to the house of Angoulême, related both to the house of Orléans and to the ruling house of Valois—made on her unprecedented and often conflicting demands. When in 1515 Louis XII died without issue, Marguerite's brother succeeded him as François I, and he immediately summoned her from her provincial exile in Alençon to share with him the honors and the duties at court. In time she became one of the ruling triumvirate along with him and their mother, Louise de Savoie, administering affairs of state, managing the kingdom when François was away at war, and at least once, when he was imprisoned in Madrid, making a treacherous journey alone to negotiate his release from their Spanish enemy. Despite such public duties—often, for her, social as well as political—Marguerite remained an exemplary humanist, interested in the life of the mind and in the welfare of her people. "In spite of her political and administrative duties," Jules Gelernt writes, "she found time for the reformation of convents and monasteries, the founding of hospitals, the encouragement of artists, writers, and scholars. She sponsored translations, fostered the dissemination of new ideas, and whenever possible intervened when the safety of her protégés [the Reformists] were threatened by the [Catholic] Sorbonne."[5]

During Marguerite's childhood at the dowerhouse of Romarantin, Louise de Savoie surrounded her with books—among them works of Plato and Aristotle, Dante and Petrarch. The vitality of the humanist movement, with its ardent recovery of antique texts, was fortified and furthered in France by Guillaume Budé's *Commentaires sur la Langue Grecque* and Robert Estienne's *Thesaurus Linguae Latinae*. It was advanced even more by those humanist salons, seemingly modeled on Urbino, that Marguerite later sponsored. And François I himself imported both artists and architects from Italy to build, expand, and decorate the magnificent châteaux still to be seen up and down the Loire valley. Until the time of Charles VIII, France had looked backward, to an earlier Renaissance of the twelfth and thirteenth centuries inspired by the Church; now, with fresh editions of Greek and Latin authors and new philological works published almost daily, the Erasmian spirit took hold and the Angoulême rulers were quick to respond. Cultivated themselves since childhood, they sought to cultivate others. It is this desire to preserve the best of humanist values in the midst of a verisimilar world that characterizes the frequent strife and circumstantial realities of life in her own palaces at Alençon and at Navarre and that motivates Marguerite's *Heptaméron*.

Despite the elegance of her courtly life, her interest in humanist texts, and the power she wielded once her brother became king, Marguerite's life always had a pronounced dark side as well. The woman whom Michelet came to call "le pur elixir des Valois"[6] was at birth too distant from the ruling Valois; and the heir presumptive, her father, saw his chances dim when a son born to Charles VIII ended the expectations of all collateral claimants to the throne. It was an omen, had she but recognized it. Her first marriage, to Charles, duke of Alençon, was a political match arranged without her consent when she was seventeen. That was in 1509. It was a drab marriage that gave her no children. In 1523 she lost her beloved aunt, Philiberte de Savoie, her sister-in-law Claude, and, most wrenching for her, her eight-year-old niece Charlotte, whom she nursed to the end. Two years later the disaster of Pavia stunned her as it stunned her country. Her husband just managed to escape the invaders; her brother was taken prisoner and incarcerated in Madrid, seriously ill and perhaps dying. Although she was allowed to nurse him back to health and to negotiate his release on behalf of France, she did so only by agreeing to place in hostage

François's two sons. Following the death of Alençon in 1525 there was a brief respite in her far happier marriage—at least at first—to the handsome, dashing Henri d'Albret, king of Navarre, eleven years her junior; in November 1528 she gave birth to a daughter Jeanne and in 1530 to a son. But the boy lived only a few months, and no later child of hers lived past infancy. The boy's death was followed shortly by the death of Marguerite's mother in 1531 and by an increase in her husband's philandering. Removing herself to Henri's lands in the southwest, Marguerite sought refuge at the capitals of Pau and Nérac, where she held court with Reformers and Evangelicals who came to form the nucleus of her highly literate, highly cultured society.

In light of so mercurial an existence, it is little wonder that Marguerite de Navarre sought the peace and repose first provided by her friendship with the idiosyncratic, mystical Guillaume Briçonnet, bishop of Meaux. Our best evidence suggests that it was Briçonnet who introduced her to an affective faith. His "influence was profound," Gelernt writes. "He encouraged her predilection for a religion of feeling rather than of intellect, and it is he who put her in the habit of bringing everything back to God, leading her to a mystique which, stripped of its symbolic terminology, comes down to an appreciation of love and an indulgence in dreamy speculation" (*World of Many Loves*, p. 16). Briçonnet was also quite probably her first connection with the Evangelicals, who already had the warm support of such humanists as Erasmus and Jacques Lefèvre d'Etaples. He was the author of commentaries on the *Ethics* and *Politics* of Aristotle, the editor of a new psalter and of Saint Paul's Epistles—unlike Erasmus, however, he was also attracted to the Neoplatonism of Pico and Ficino and to the more esoteric writings of Dionysius the Areopagite and Nicholas of Cusa. Briçonnet sympathized with many of Luther's doctrines, especially the belief in salvation through faith rather than works. Though he and other Reformers, including Marguerite, attempted to cleanse the Catholic church from within, they too criticized certain institutions of the Church, demanding the Communion in both kinds and refusing to admit to the strict doctrine of the Real Presence in the Eucharist. Rather than recognize a special sanctity for the Church, they emphasized instead the innate goodness and holiness inherent in each man and woman. Though they acknowledged such Catholic doctrines as the Incarnation, Nativity, Passion, and Resurrection of Christ, they also understood the conception, birth, and spiritual resurrection of every person made perfect through individual meditation, prayer, and penitence. For them the Passion was a symbol of the martyrdom of any true believer, the Sacrament the emblem of any believer's conversion. They preached—and Marguerite came to practice—a religion of intense personalism.

To further the Evangelicals' communal life of prayer and study, Marguerite invited them to join her in the castle at Pau, a fortresslike building in a high-lying, steep little town at the edge of the white peaks of the Pyrenees, Navarre's clear equivalent of Castiglione's Urbino. But outside their insulated salon—as isolated from the world as the monastery setting of *L'Heptaméron*, cut off by flood and mountain range—opposition continued to mount. In 1521 the Faculty of Theology at the Sorbonne formally censured Luther. Before the Church of Notre Dame in Paris, Luther's writings were burned to rubble. Lefèvre d'Etaples was threatened with the stake. Farel, Mazurier, and others were forced to flee. In the face of torture, captivity, and exile, Briçonnet temporized; in October 1523 he issued a decree against those who abused the Gospels by denying Purgatory and the saints: He recanted. It is doubtless this capitulation that caused Marguerite to have a change of heart toward the Franciscan order of which he was a member; it may also have confirmed her plan to establish a sanctuary for Reformist exiles at Nérac. There she gave asylum to Michel d'Arande, Antoine Heroët, and, briefly, to Jean Calvin himself; there she made the exiled Gérard Roussel bishop of Oloron; there she paid for the schooling of Baduel and other young priests; there she harbored Clément Marot, the poet and Lutheran suspect who had once been her secretary at Alençon and was now her gentleman of the chamber along with Bonaventure Desperriers. There she sheltered Lefèvre d'Etaples, too, who, at the age of 101, perished in her presence proclaiming his chastity.

This closely knit community of Reformers thus displaced the earlier courts of Marguerite—the humanist society she knew as a child at Romarantin with her mother, Louise de Savoie, and the political community she knew later at the court of her brother François. This last society, very much hers alone, seems also to have satisfied her most. It may also have blinded her as the others had never done: No one at Nérac was prepared for the morning of Whitmonday 1528 when the statuette of the Virgin and Child that decorated the angle of Monsieur Harlai's house in front of the parish church of Pétit Saint-Antoine in Paris was found mutilated, Mother and Babe decapitated and the heads smashed in the gutter below. Nor were they prepared for the outburst of the Reformers who during the night of 18 October 1534 plastered the cathedrals and town halls of Paris, Rouen, Meaux, and other cities, and even the castle of Amboise where François I was in residence, with posters attacking in gross terms the mysteries of the Catholic faith, the Mass, the Host, and the prayers for the dead—the notorious *affaire des placards,* in which nothing sacred was left untouched or untarnished. Both François and Marguerite reacted with courage and with tolerance for the Evangelicals, but both also felt called upon to renew their deep-seated allegiance to a traditional Catholicism. Through all this she must have learned yet again the high cost of any persistent belief, of any consistent set of values, in a restless and unsettled world, a world of revolution and dissent that was always uncertain and even treacherous. For it is precisely this fundamental dialectic between the fears, anxieties, and genuine pain of the real world of contrary political, religious, and social aims and the Christian humanist's intense personal and interior longing for peace of mind and soul that lies at the very heart of *L'Heptaméron* and that awaits our resolution.

Like all works of Continental humanist poetics, *L'Heptaméron* attempts to civilize its readers by instructing them in the art (and need) of self-discipline. Moderation in behavior, growing out of a sense of self-esteem and self-control and fostering relationships grounded in mutual trust, is unexceptionally rewarded in Marguerite's novel, as in the cases of the wife in story 27 who reports to her husband the illicit favors sought by his friend, the lady in story 13 who receives a diamond from a galley captain and who instead of accepting it returns it to the captain's wife bringing about marital reconciliation, and the young woman of story 26 who remains virtuous despite her attraction to a young man who seeks her love knowing that she is married to a much older man and childless. Such actions as these are sanctioned not only by morality but also by society. The reverse is true of Rolandine who, in story 21, despite her nobility, marries secretly a bastard of noble birth and, despite her father's harsh treatment of her, remains constant to her husband until his death, following which she marries a gentleman who bears the arms of her own family. Clearly, for Marguerite as for the humanists generally, when conscience is in conflict with class or convention, it is virtue that wins out. Story 42 mirrors 21; here the commoner Françoise is the object of the prince's affection, but his overtures—his pleas, his promises, his cajoleries, his threats—all fail to persuade her to make love or marry above her station. The prince, rewarding her virtue, holds her in esteem and eventually marries her to a gentleman in his service for whom marriage to her would be appropriate. In all these instances what Marguerite cultivates through the text of *L'Heptaméron* is the sort of self-regulated moderation we have already seen urged by Castiglione and implied by Erasmus, if not by Folly herself. Natural passion is grounds for rational self-discipline. With Marguerite, moreover, drawing on her Reformist studies, passion must be reconciled with Christian doctrine in which virtue is the controlling factor. In *L'Heptaméron* this is persistently the position Parlamente takes, the position that gives her the leadership among the storytellers—and the position which, each morning, Oisille confirms with the support of Scripture.

In advancing such central ideas of humanist ethics, Marguerite also employs the humanist means of imitatio. But, like Erasmus and Castiglione when they draw on Lucian and Cicero, her use of models as resources by which convergence and divergence will convey meaning to her learned audience—instructed because participant—causes her art of imitatio never to be precise or exacting. Therein, Joachim du Bellay would write in his *Défense et illustration de la langue française* of 1549, lay enslavement or treason. In fact, not unlike *Il Libro del Cortegiano,* Marguerite's chief antique model, Plato's *Symposium,* is a choice largely of *form*—her own latter-day symposium on the varieties of love and the meanings of love, like Plato's original, moves dialectically to suggest a range of meanings which, presented inconclusively, leave open questions of emphasis, preference, and final meaning. Whereas Castiglione sees manners as the means for definition and discriminating judgment, however, Marguerite sees the various forms of love—of which the highest is Saint Paul's sense of *caritas,* invoked repeatedly by Parlamente and Oisille and underscored with references to Paul—as a reliable means for estimating the worth of human behavior and for understanding the inherent possibilities of the human condition.

By focusing on love as she does, Marguerite is thus able to incorporate into *L'Heptaméron,* in a range of emulation and criticism, much of the love poetry that had interceded between the age of classical thought and form and her own comprehensive act of fiction making. Thus *L'Heptaméron* shares with troubadour poetry its concern with romance as it reflects current social behavior and denies social norms through fantasy and idealization, fantasy and idealization that Maurice Valency has traced as psychological necessities in a regulated society.[7] Other poets than Provençal poets, those of the *dolce stil,* idealized love until it was no longer corporeal, until it sublimated the physical into the spiritual, providing a kind of mystical yearning for an absolute, all-embracing love such as Diotima conveys to Socrates in his visionary dream of her in the original *Symposium,* or such as Bembo describes in *Il Cortegiano 4.* Indeed, the choices that lovers are repeatedly, if implicitly, asked to make in *L'Heptaméron* are those Marguerite's beloved Petrarch examines in his *Secretum.* In his three imaginary dialogues with Saint Augustine, he defends his love for Laura by arguing that it has led him to a life characterized by honor and virtue only to hear Augustine reply that neither is so significant as the salvation of the soul, which is a still higher form of love. Gelernt sees Marsilio Ficino's commentary on Plato's *Symposium* as another mediate source of ideas (if not actual situations) that is exemplary for Marguerite.

> Reinterpreting Christian myth in philosophic terms, [Ficino] established a metaphysics which unfolded the dynamic structure of Being through the primacy of the creative principle of love. He found the source of love in God and saw it as the force which cements the created universe and draws all creation back to Him. Love is a desire for Beauty, and Beauty, according to Ficino, is nothing other than the resplendence of Divine Goodness throughout the hierarchy of creation. This desire expresses itself through both the intelligence of the Angelic Mind (Venus Urania) and the generative power of the World Soul (Venus Dione), the one leading to the contemplation of the Supreme Beauty, the other to the creation of this beauty in material form; these, in turn, act in the human soul as the powers of contemplation and generation, enabling the mind to recognize the divine element in beauty and ensuring the propagation of the race. Ultimately Ficino came to define love as a sort of delirious seizure of the soul—"furor" is his term—of which there are two kinds: one, physical in origin, reduces man to the level of an animal, and the other, divine in nature, intoxicates the soul of the lover and binds him most closely to God. [*World of Many Loves*, pp. 43–44]

It is the Platonic dichotomy between Diotima and Alcibiades in their love for Socrates—that of the mystic and visionary and that of the sensualist—which, we are told, makes of Socrates a Silenus, one whose double nature supplies him with a capacity for a range of appearances and responses, that same capacity that Erasmus found conducive either to wisdom or to folly. It is this ongoing dialectic of spirit and body, which reaches back through Ficino's Christian humanist commentary through the poetry of the troubadours to its initial source in the antique Plato, that causes Marguerite to emphasize both the elevated and the vulgar in *L'Heptaméron*. One is robbed of its significance without the other. It is as if the court at Nérac would have no meaning if it did not exist in a world of doctrinaire Catholicism, or as if the library at Romarantin would be useless without the court of François I in which to put into practice its beliefs and its values. As in Castiglione, so here, the worlds of Amboise and Paris are coexistent and interdependent with the worlds of Pau and Nérac, and both are collapsed into the singular abbey of Nostre-Dame de Serrance (p. 5; p. 65),[8] where ten representatives of mankind arrive exhausted and covered with perspiration as if dying and about to be reborn. They will be reborn constantly, in *L'Heptaméron* as in *Il Cortegiano,* through their renewing self-projections in the stories they tell but, unlike *Il Cortegiano,* also in their shifting relationships with each other, their evolving maturity, and the growing awareness that the ritual of Scripture and prayer suggested by Oisille encloses even their most audacious immorality within a routine that forever offers redemption. Even the most ribald tale, the most obscene story, is thus given space only in an environment that seems simultaneously regulated by God's grace.

What is clear at once from such an initial appraisal of *L'Heptaméron* is that Marguerite's *nouvelle* far surpasses any of its predecessors in fiction. The long tradition that incorporates the *Thousand and One Nights,* the *Canterbury Tales,* and even the *Decameron* has no intricate dialectic such as the one that grew out of Marguerite's study and worldly activity. The tales of Bandello, for instance, with their continual mingling of the authentic and the imaginative and with their choric pronouncements preferring truth to fiction such as we find also in Marguerite, are too slim and too incidental to have served her as a model, just as Boccaccio's *Decameron*—for which Marguerite herself commissioned a translation by one of François I's royal councillors, Antoine le Macon, completed in 1545—has, once we scrutinize it, only superficial resemblances. Parlamente suggests in the prologue to *L'Heptaméron* that the guests at Nostre-Dame de Serrance spend their enforced delay telling one another entertaining stories such as she has read in Boccaccio, but whereas those tales are random exposures of passion, concupiscence, and adultery, both the range of Marguerite's tales and their clearly instructive humanist purpose immediately set them apart. Even the occasion for storytelling—plague in one instance, a flood in the other—is distinguished, Boccaccio stressing the frailty of life and Marguerite emphasizing the miraculous deliverance of her narrators. Boccaccio's fiction is enjoyable and escapist; Marguerite's tales—every one of them—are departure points for discussion, debate, and enlightenment. They are, all of them, exemplary narratives that are transformed into premises for rhetorical argumentation, indirect (because dramatized) orations that become, very much like the speech of Folly, inherent disputations. Narrations are the stuff of conversations, of *controversiae.* Gelernt has sensed this distinction, too: "She will keep faith with human experience no matter how confusing or contradictory it may appear," he tells us. "Furthermore, she will stop short of final conclusions. She will put the various theories of love to the test of action," just as Castiglione before her has put the beliefs and principles of his various interlocutors to the test of behavior, "and, having taken note of the consequences in the stories, she will allow her [speakers] to battle it out, . . . with the weapons which are their natural endowment—their sensibility and their measure of reason. Her hope was, I think, that out of this clash truth might emerge" (*World of Many Loves,* p. 56)—the end, always, of a work of humanist poetics.

L'*Heptaméron,* like all great works of humanist fiction, is superbly, and profoundly, informed by classical thought as well as by classical form. The *form* of Marguerite's nouvelle, like the form of *Il Cortegiano,* is that of the Platonic symposium, in which clearly distinguishable voices argue from predisposition and conviction certain attitudes toward the common subject of love as a means, finally, to define and refine human nature—to instruct, to discipline, to cultivate, and to enhance. There is, in the very form of the symposium, a multiplicity of perspectives that is by its nature inclusive and by that same nature inconclusive. But more than the mere form of *L'Heptaméron* is Platonic. The fundamental understanding of good and evil that Marguerite examines in her nouvelle follows Socrates' discussion of epistemology in the *Theaetetus.*

> It is impossible that evils should be done away with, Theodorus, for there must always be something opposed to the good; and they cannot have their place among the gods, but must inevitably hover about mortal nature and this earth. Therefore we ought to try to escape from earth to the dwelling of the gods as quickly as we can; and to escape is to become like God, so far as this is possible; and to become like God is to become righteous and holy and wise.
>
> [176A–B][9]

Man's yearning is directly connected by Socrates to God's nature, as it is in *L'Heptaméron.*

> God is in no wise and in no manner unrighteous, but utterly and perfectly righteous, and there is nothing so like him as that one of us who in turn becomes most nearly perfect in righteousness. It is herein that the true cleverness of a man is found and also his worthlessness and cowardice; for the knowledge of this is wisdom or true virtue, and ignorance of it is folly or manifest wickedness; and all the other kinds of seeming cleverness and wisdom are paltry when they appear in public affairs and vulgar in the arts. Therefore by far the best thing for the unrighteous man and the man whose words or deeds are impious is not to grant that he is clever through knavery; for such men glory in that reproach, and think it means that they are not triflers, "useless burdens upon the earth" [Homer, *Iliad* 18.104; *Odyssey* 20.379] but such as men should be who are to live safely in

a state. So we must tell them the truth—that just because they do not think they are such as they are, they are so all the more truly; for they do not know the penalty of unrighteousness, which is the thing they most ought to know. For it is not what they think it is—scourgings and death, which they sometimes escape entirely when they have done wrong—but a penalty which it is impossible to escape. [176C–E]

In answer to Theodorus's question about the meaning of such penalties, Socrates proceeds to limn the very basis of Marguerite's nouvelle.

Two patterns, my friend, are set up in the world, the divine, which is most blessed, and the godless, which is most wretched. But these men do not see that this is the case, and their silliness and extreme foolishness blind them to the fact that through their unrighteous acts they are made like the one and unlike the other. They therefore pay the penalty for this by living a life that conforms to the pattern they resemble; and if we tell them that, unless they depart from their "cleverness," the blessed place that is pure of all things evil will not receive them after death, and here on earth they will always live the life like themselves—evil men, associating with evil—when they hear this, they will be so confident in their unscrupulous cleverness that they will think our words the talk of fools.

[176E–177A]

Plato's direct sequel to the *Theaetetus* is his *Sophist,* in which Theaetetus is shown in some detail by an Elean Stranger, rather than by Socrates, how men attempt to instruct in the good through an art that imitates ideal concepts rather than the evil of mundane reality: The former, he says, are seers; the latter are sophists who misrepresent, mislead, and misinform because they lack a sense of the good that is to be found in the unity and harmony of things, not in the fragmentation of experience. The Stranger begins his sense of poetics by arguing (as the humanists do) that art is a matter of imitation. "I see," he tells Theaetetus, "two classes of imitation."

I see the likeness-making art as one part of imitation. This is met with, as a rule, whenever anyone produces the imitation by following the proportions of the original in length, breadth, and depth, and giving, besides, the appropriate colours to each part.

THEAETETUS. Yes, but do not all imitators try to do this?

STRANGER. Not those who produce some large work of sculpture or painting. For if they reproduced the true proportions of beautiful forms, the upper parts, you know, would seem smaller and the lower parts larger than they ought, because we see the former from a distance, the latter from near at hand.

THEAETETUS. Certainly.

STRANGER. So the artists abandon the truth and give their figures not the actual proportions but those which seem to be beautiful, do they not?

THEAETETUS. Certainly.

STRANGER. That, then, which is other, but like, we may fairly call a likeness, may we not?

THEAETETUS. Yes.

STRANGER. And the part of imitation which is concerned with such things, is to be called, as we called it before, likeness-making?

THEAETETUS. It is to be so called.

STRANGER. Now then, what shall we call that which appears, because it is seen from an unfavourable position, to be like the beautiful, but which would not even be likely to resemble that which it claims to be like, if a person were able to see such large works adequately? Shall we not call it, since it appears, but is not like, an appearance?

THEAETETUS. Certainly.

STRANGER. And this is very common in painting and in all imitation?

THEAETETUS. Of course.

STRANGER. And to the art which produces appearance, but not likeness, the most correct name we could give would be "fantastic art," would it not?

THEAETETUS. By all means.

STRANGER. These, then, are the two forms of the image-making art that I meant, the likeness-making and the fantastic. [235D–236C] [10]

This precise choplogic is unusual even for Plato—it may be one reason he assigns this particular examination to an Elean Stranger rather than to Socrates, who is nevertheless present—but the point he wishes to make is critical. In the real world, he asks, where does the visionary fit in? And where does reality—such as the world of Nostre-Dame de Serrance—cease to be real, cease to be at all? The answer lies somewhere between the fact that it can never cease to be and that in concentrating on its multiplicity through which man understands the nature(s) of being we are always endangered by our own inventiveness, our own rhetorical sophistry, which is the corruption of wisdom: "We are really, my dear friend," the Stranger points out more succinctly, "engaged in a very difficult investigation; for the matter of appearing and seeming, but not being, and of saying things, but not true ones—all this is now and always has been very perplexing" (236E).

In *L'Heptaméron* Oisille is assigned the task of voicing what is true being, both through her tales and commentary and through her devout practices. Her stout, recalcitrant appeal to piety and to faith becomes the backbone of Marguerite's main humanist fiction. Against Oisille's position are deployed all the other speakers save the ethical Parlamente and the mystical Dagoucin (whose name means "of saintly tastes"). They are caught up in the appearances of details and so, in their imitation of their subject in their narrations, dwell on nonbeing. Philosophically, and rhetorically, they *deceive*—and Marguerite underscores this by causing each of them, again and again, to tell stories of deception, of disguise, of dissimulation, of *un*truth. That is, according to the Elean Stranger, what we should suspect (240D–241A).

Thus, the difficulty and the danger for Marguerite, as well as for the Reformers she housed at Pau and at Nérac, are that such distracting realities, which turn our attention more and more toward nonbeing, or finite and therefore corrupted being, are nevertheless just those tools by which we must begin our ascent toward our understanding of true being which transcends them. With the Elean Stranger of the *Sophist,* too, this is precisely a question of good and bad *art*. The good poet is a seer, a person of faith, belief, and vision, like the devout characters of *L'Heptaméron;* the bad poet resembles the scientist, the ultrarealist, for the Stranger the atomist (246A–C), for Marguerite the sensualist. Ultimately for the Stranger, the good poet is a philosopher, one who "has a clear perception of one form or idea extending entirely through many individuals each of which lies apart, and of many forms differing from one another but included in one greater form, and again of one form evolved by the union of many wholes, and of many forms entirely apart and separate" (253 D–E)—justifying Marguerite's use of the symposium as a structuring device— whereas the bad poet, for the Stranger, is the sophist who "runs away into the darkness of not-being, feeling his way in it by practice, and is hard to discern on account of the darkness of the place" (254A). Again, Marguerite underscores her understanding by her continuing use of light and darkness both within the tales and in the commentary and frames provided for the tales.

What is strikingly absent from the Elean Stranger's complicated and rather long-winded poetic is the matter of *technē:* How is the seer, the philosopher, or the poet to comprehend, translate, and make appealing his inspired sense of being to a world everywhere conditioned and accustomed to nonbeing? Both the answer and the means become Socrates' chief contribution, through the imitation or imaging of the fantastic Diotima, in another Platonic dialogue, the *Symposium*. The answer, Diotima tells Socrates in a vision, is love, the same answer Marguerite borrows for *L'Heptaméron*. For love, Diotima remarks, is

> "A great spirit, Socrates: for the whole of the spiritual is between divine and mortal."
>
> "Possessing what power?" I asked.
>
> "Interpreting and transporting human things to the gods and divine things to men; entreaties and sacrifices from below, and ordinances and requitals from above: being midway between, it makes each to supplement the other, so that the whole is combined in one. Through it are conveyed all divination and priestcraft concerning sacrifice and ritual and incantations, and all soothsaying and sorcery. God with man does not mingle: but the spiritual is the means of all society and converse of men with gods and of gods with men, whether waking or asleep. Whosoever has skill in these affairs is a spiritual man" [202E–203A][11]

—just as Marguerite means for the mundane conversations at Nostre-Dame de Serrance to lead, from morning Mass to evening prayer, to conversation with God and of Him. That love is a natural force as well as a divine one—indeed, the chief force of God and man—is substantiated further by Diotima when she tells Socrates that it is the one means of reaching immortality and that yearning for immortality is the final end of all men; "the mortal nature ever seeks, as best it can, to be immortal. In one way only can it succeed, and that is by generation; since so it can always leave behind it a new creature in place of the old" (207C–D), *generation* for her meaning love and *pro*creation, *generation* for Marguerite, in her later days, being the creation of *L'Heptaméron* itself. In light of this fundamental analogy of procreation and creation, Diotima too supplies a poetics, and one especially useful to Marguerite:

> "When a man has been thus far tutored in the lore of love, passing from view to view of beautiful things, in the right and regular ascent, suddenly he will have revealed to him, as he draws to the close of his dealings in love, a wondrous vision, beautiful in its nature; and this, Socrates, is the final object of all those previous toils." [210E]

This vision alone is what is true (and for the Elean Stranger, what is being), and Diotima's decisive definition here is what informs Marguerite's use of truth and the appeal to truth by her characters in ways far more resonant than the use of "truth" either by Bandello or by Boccaccio.

"Do but consider," she said, "that there only will it befall him, as he sees the beautiful through that which makes it visible, to breed not illusions but true examples of virtue, since his contact is not with illusion but with truth. So when he has begotten a true virtue and has reared it up he is destined to win the friendship of Heaven; he, above all men, is immortal." [212A]

In showing frequent exempla of virtue, Marguerite's *L'Heptaméron* helps illumine truth and lead us to it; by being an immortal work of art it can also function indefinitely to make its readers moral and immortal too if they so choose: *L'Heptaméron* is, profoundly, the work of a *Christian* humanist, in the questions it asks, the models it provides, and the trust it places in its readers to respond to it properly.

Whether Marguerite de Navarre came to the *Theaetetus* and *Symposium* directly or indirectly through the mediation of the *Enneads* of Plotinus we have no real way of knowing. For Plotinus alludes frequently to Plato's comment in the *Theaetetus* that the good for man is to attain likeness to God insofar as he is able, and to Diotima's understanding, in the *Symposium,* that the philosopher's practice of morality is best served by true lovers of beauty who contemplate eternal values and from there await the vision of the one source of Being and Truth. Plotinus sets out to justify this possibility by developing a metaphysic that guarantees the ascent Diotima proposes. He argues that part of man's soul forever remains in contemplation of divine Forms and is never immersed in the daily moral flux of the visible and quotidian world. The other part of the soul is concerned precisely with coping with the everyday details of life. It is man's chief concern, he argues further, to subject the "outer man" operating in the world to the "inner man" who is concerned with contemplation so that eventually he will discard his bodily existence altogether and become pure contemplation; through purification, asceticism, and—notably—love, he will be transported to the world of Soul and beyond the world of Soul to the world of pure Form or intellect, the world of *Nous.* Such an ascent is one toward unity and simplicity, the very demeanor that Marguerite assigns to Oisille as she arranges her characters, from Nircan and Nomerfide through Parlamente to Dagoucin, in their awareness and love of God and of contemplation.

This ascent of the "inner man" is a chief theme of the *Enneads;* at its most succinct, in the fifth tractate of Book 3, its debt to Plato is most apparent.

> Those that desire earthly procreation are satisfied with the beauty found on earth, the beauty of image and of body; it is because they are strangers to the Archetype, the source of even the attraction they feel towards what is lovely here.

There are souls to whom earthly beauty is a leading to the memory of that in the higher realm and these love the earthly as an image; those that have not attained to this memory do not understand what is happening within them, and take the image for the reality. Once there is perfect self-control, it is no fault to enjoy the beauty of earth; where appreciation degenerates into carnality, there is sin.

Pure Love seeks the beauty alone, whether there is Reminiscence or not; but there are those that feel, also, a desire of such immortality as lies within mortal reach; and these are seeking Beauty in their demand for perpetuity, the desire of the eternal; Nature teaches them to sow the seed and to beget in beauty, to sow towards eternity, but in beauty through their own kinship with the beautiful. And indeed the eternal is of the one stock with the beautiful, the Eternal-Nature is the first shaping of beauty and makes beautiful all that rises from it.[12]

This potentiality, he tells us, is universal.

Since not only the pure All-Soul but also that of the Universe contains such a Love, it would be difficult to explain why our personal Soul should not. It must be so, even, with all that has life.

This indwelling love is no other than the Spirit which, as we are told, walks with every being, the affection dominant in each several nature. It implants the characteristic desire; the particular Soul, strained towards its own natural objects, brings forth its own Eros, the guiding spirit realizing its worth and the quality of its Being.

As the All-Soul contains the Universal Love, so must the single Soul be allowed its own single Love: and as closely as the single Soul holds to the All-Soul, never cut off but embraced within it, the two together constituting one principle of life, so the single separate Love holds to the All-Love. Similarly, the individual Love keeps with the individual Soul as that other, the great Love, goes with the All-Soul; and the Love within the All permeates it throughout so that the one Love becomes many, showing itself where it chooses at any moment of the Universe, taking definite shape in these its partial phases and revealing itself at its will. [Pp. 194–95]

Plotinus urges therefore that we understand all events, all data of our earthly existence, as so many signifiers; each is capable alone or with others of leading us to the All-Soul, where we will arrive enraptured and possessed (ὥσπερ αρπαοθείς η ευθυσωδας), in a state of eternal ecstasy. Thus for Plotinus our liberty to act, our self-disposal, must be related not to activity in the outer world, not to doing something or getting something done, but to intellection in the inner world of mediation, to advancing virtue's capacity for vision and enlightenment. Plotinus therefore argues for an authentic self-sufficiency— again, the sort that characterizes Oisille—which precludes us from any communal interests except those of teaching and service, the ends to which Marguerite de Navarre devoted the last years of her life and, quite clearly, the writing of *L'Heptaméron*.

Such a Plotinian poetics as this lies directly behind the conception and writing of Marguerite's nouvelle, but the influence of the Reformers with whom she held court is equally strong, and she is explicit from the outset that the scriptural readings by Oisille each morning are the precise equivalents, as well as the directives, of each afternoon's tales and commentaries. She is also explicit about what those readings are: first, Paul's Epistle to the Romans, a favorite text with the Reformers and Evangelicals because it dictated Christ's teachings of faith and works and laid down an implicit program for the religious life; next, the five chapters of 1 John, which is, as Marguerite herself says, the key text on Christian love; finally, on the seventh day of *L'Heptaméron*, the opening chapters (presumably chapters 1–3) of the Acts of the Apostles, which translates both Romans and 1 John, through its narrative of Pentecost, into the beginning life of the Church. Thus the weekdays are governed within the dialectic structure of *L'Heptaméron* by an increasingly mystical sense of love and faith; on the seventh day, presumably the Sabbath, this is channeled into the Church so that, presumably, the Church will realize the significance of the inner life rather than try to regulate it through doctrine—precisely the position the Reformers took even during the disgraceful *affaire des placards*.

We will thus understand the dynamics behind *L'Heptaméron* if we place the philosophy and poetics of Plato and Plotinus alongside Christian Scripture, Holy Writ. Paul begins Romans by justifying a life of faith rather than works (1 : 16–17).

> For the wrath of God is reueiled from heauen against all vngodlines, and unrighteousnes of men, which withholde the trueth in vnrighteousnes,
>
> For asmuche as y‛, which may be knowen of God, is manifest in them: for God hathe shewed it vnto them.
>
> For the inuisible things of him, that is, his eternal power and Godhead, are sene by the creation of the worlde, being cōsidered in *his* workes, to the intēt that they shulde be without excuse:

Because that when they knewe God, they glorified him not as God, nether
were thankeful, but became vaine in their imaginations, and their foolish heart
was ful of darkenes.

When they professed them selues to be wise, they became fooles. [Geneva
version (1560) 1 : 18–22]

Consequently, "God gaue them vp to their heartes lustes, vnto unclēnes, to
defile their owne bodies betwene thēselues: Which turned the trueth of God
vnto a lie, and worshipped and serued the creature, forsaking the Creator,
which is blessed for euer, Amen" (1 : 24–25). Such an action, however, is the
province of God; though we are to judge good and evil, Paul writes, we are not
to judge each other—"for in that thou iudgest another, thou cōdemnest thy
self: for thou that iudgest, doest the same things" (2 : 1). The disputations of
L'Heptaméron, the *controversiae* that follow each oration or tale, should limit
themselves to questions of good and evil; to be distracted by persons or behavior, by the details of the narration rather than its underlying significance, is to
be guilty of trivialization and to betoken fallen (that is, evil) man.

Proper understanding of each of Marguerite's tales, then—proper belief for
the humanists as much as for the Reformers—lies in the interpretations,
judgments, and applications—precepts turned into experience—that such
tales require. This lesson is provided in *L'Heptaméron* by Oisille as she reads
further from Paul's letter:

For the promes that he shulde be the heire of the worlde, was not *giuen* to
Abraham, or to his seed, through the Law, but through the rightouesnes of
faith. . . .

Then being iustified by faith, we haue peace towarde God through our Lord
Iesus Christ.

By whome also we haue accesse through faith vnto this grace, wherein we
stand, & reioice vnder the hope of the glorie of God. [4 : 13; 5 : 1–2]

Both the philosophy and poetic that Plato and Plotinus advance along with
Paul is reinforced in the first letter of John, which Oisille (and Marguerite) also
introduces into *L'Heptaméron*. John too speaks of the quotidian world as the
manifestation of God—and only when rightly perceived: "if we walke in the
light as he is in the light, we haue felowship one with another, and the blood of
Iesus Christ his Sonne clenseth vs from all sinne" (1 John 1 : 7). For John as for
his predecessors, the rightful means to such an understanding, such a divinely
inspired fellowship, is love, but love of a kind that transcends the physical.

Loue not the worlde, nether the things that are in the worlde, If any mã loue the worlde, ye loue of the Father is not in him.

For all that is in the worlde (*as* the luste of the flesh, the luste of the eyes, & the pride of life) is not of ye Father, but is of the worlde.

And the worlde passeth awaye, and the luste thereof: but he that fulfilleth the wil of God, abideth euer. [2 : 15 – 17]

This then is the true nature of love, and the sort of love advocated in *L'Heptaméron*. Human love is redolent of divine love, and the process for John as for Plato is reversible.

And we haue knowen, and beleued the loue that God hathe in vs, God is loue, & he that dwelleth in loue, dwelleth in God, and God in him. . . .

If anie man say, I loue God, and hate his brother, he is a lyer: for how can he that loueth not his brother whome he hathe sene, loue God whome he hathe not sene?

And this commandement haue we of him, that he who loueth God, shulde loue his brother also. [4 : 16, 20 – 21]

Such a conception as this goes far to show why for Marguerite stories of love must *necessarily* show their phenomenal existence in this world: This world points us toward divine love as divine love is meant to inform and reshape the love of this world. Given her sense of humanist thought and fiction as a means of mediating God's Word—of supplying yet another instance of moral instruction—we can also see why *L'Heptaméron* is *necessarily* dialectical in form.

The contest between reason and the senses for the control of the will and the exercise of love that directs so much of our attention in *L'Heptaméron* finds further support in the Christian poetics of another of the chief influences on Marguerite de Navarre: the work of Saint Augustine. For him, too, love as *caritas* is the primary subject we must learn, the supreme Christian virtue. We are told this first in his *Confessions*, where he sees the proper understanding of divine love precisely as Plato's Elean Stranger sees it—as the forsaking of rhetoric as mere sophistry for something more divinely inspired. Augustine first characterizes rhetoric in the *Confessions* as pagan, materialistic, and deceptive.

Docebam in illis annis artem rhetoricam, et victoriosam loquacitatem victus cupiditate vendebam, malebam tamen, domine, tu scis, bonos habere discipulos, sicut appellantur boni, et eos sine dolo docebam dolos, non quibus contra caput innocentis agerent, sed aliquando pro capite nocentis. et, deus, vidisti de longinquo lapsantem in lubrico, et in multo fumo scintillantem fidem meam, quam exhibebam in illo magisterio diligentibus vanitatem et quaerentibus mendacium, socius eorum.

I taught in those years the art of rhetoric, and myself being overcome with a desire of gain, made sale of a loquacity, to overcome others by. Yet I desired rather (Lord, thou knowest) to have honest scholars, as they are now-a-days accounted; and those, without all deceit, I taught how to deceive; not that they might plead against the life of any innocent person, though sometimes to save the life of the guilty. And thou O God, from afar perceivedst me falling in that slippery course, and in much smoke sparkling out some little faith, which I then made show of in that schoolmastership of mine to those that loved vanity and sought a lie, becoming their companion. [4.2].[13]

"For Augustine," Thomas O. Sloane writes in connection with this passage, "rhetoric is on the one hand a commodity, something to be bought and sold. On the other it is evil itself, parodying the actions of God, and substituting lies and insane battles for the truth and peace God alone can give."[14] According to Sloane, Augustine attacks pagan rhetoric in several ways. First, he distinguishes between the attraction of words—charming eloquence, *suaviloquentia*—and its antithesis, truth. This was shown him, Augustine tells us, in the person of Faustus, whom he met at the age of twenty-nine.

iam venerat Carthaginem quidam Manichaeorum episcopus, Faustus nomine, magnus laqueus diaboli, et multi inplicabantur in eo per inlecebram suaviloquentiae. quam ego iam tametsi laudabam, discernebam tamen a veritate rerum, quarum discendarum avidus eram, nec quali vasculo sermonis, sed quid mihi scientiae comedendum adponeret nominatus apud eos ille Faustus intuebar.

There came in those days unto Carthage a certain Bishop of the Manichees, Faustus by name: a great snare of the Devil he was, and many were entangled by him in that gin of his smooth language: which though myself did much commend in him, yet I was able to discern betwixt it, and the truth of those things which I then was earnest to learn: nor had I an eye so much to the curious dish of oratory, as what substance of science their so famous Faustus set before me to feed upon. [5.3]

Truth is not something constructed but something that proceeds from the source of all truth, which is God "Deus ipsa Veritas" (12.25). Eloquence may reinforce truth, as it does in the words of Saint Ambrose (5.13–14), but that is because truth, not eloquence, is at the root of what is being thought and said. The characters in Marguerite's nouvelle thus protest too much their telling of truth, their knowing at first hand, their reliance on unimpeachable witnesses for their tales. The tales themselves will make the truth known, if there is indeed truth in them: It is Marguerite's knowing joke with us, and just possibly her stern attempt to divorce herself from the likes of Bandello and Boccaccio.

Augustine also reinforces Marguerite's sense of time as she has it from Plato, from Plotinus, and from Scripture. It is a second way Sloane claims that Augustine finds cause to challenge pagan rhetoric.

> Dicturus sum canticum, quod novi: antequam incipiam, in totum expectatio mea tenditur, cum autem coepero, quantum ex illa in praeteritum decerpsero, tenditur et memoria mea, atque distenditur vita huius actionis meae, in memoriam propter quod dixi, et in expectationem propter quod dicturus sum: praesens tamen adest attentio mea, per quam traicitur quod erat futurum, ut fiat praeteritum. quod quanto magis agitur et agitur, tanto breviata expectatione prolongatur memoria, donec tota expectatio consumatur, quum tota illa actio finita transierit in memoriam.

> I am about to repeat a psalm that I know. Before I begin, my expectation alone reaches itself over the whole: but so soon as I shall have once begun, how much so ever of it I shall take off into the past, over so much my memory also reaches: thus the life of this action of mine is extended both ways: into my memory, so far as concerns that part which I have repeated already, and into my expectation too, in respect of what I am about to repeat now; but all this while is my marking faculty present at hand, through which, that which was future, is conveyed over, that it may become past: which how much the more diligently it is done over and over again, so much more the expectation being shortened, is the memory enlarged; till the whole expectation at length vanished quite away, when namely, that whole action being ended, shall be absolutely passed into the memory. [11.28]

This exercise in hermeneutics is made possible by divine wisdom, which is always complete and always present; it resembles the divine will, which Marguerite, through Oisille and Parlamente, will tell us already inhabits each act of love and which is known by believers before, during, and after its momentary, phenomenological existence. Truth is a priori to events that realize it, just as God is present before, during, and after human perception and judgment; yet if truth always *is*—if essence precedes and succeeds existence—then there is no grounds for rhetoric to claim the powers of creation but only to claim the powers of realization or expression. Augustine thus provides Marguerite, and *L'Heptaméron,* as Plato and Plotinus and even Paul and John have, with a *metaphysics* for poetics.

This sense of the eternal is vital if we are, finally, to judge Marguerite's use of controversiae. What has frustrated many readers of *L'Heptaméron* is either their inconclusiveness or their apparent digressiveness. Both are Marguerite's points, of course, just as they are precisely *not* her point: As the resources of her poetics should now make sufficiently plain, the fragmentary opinions voiced in the controversiae, the petty questions and petty debates, are finite and partial perceptions of a divine truth from men and women who have not yet learned the true significance of love as Oisille means to teach it, as Parlamente means to persuade them, or as Augustine defines it in his sense of *caritas.* For those who understood the tales of *L'Heptaméron* at the outset, no discussion would be necessary. The stories surpass human understanding unaided by divine love as God's love itself can surpass understanding. The tales of folly and wisdom simply are, as God's love simply is. To splinter it, to redefine it, to debate it is (as both the Elean Stranger and Augustine note) a matter of sophistic rhetoric. Yet the other side of *L'Heptaméron* is to show that we as earthbound creatures often have precious little *but* rhetoric—even sophistic rhetoric—by which to determine our own judgments and proceed to share them with others. If God needs only signs, if Diotima has visions, men often have only *words.* This dilemma too is at the root of *L'Heptaméron,* giving to the controversiae there a haunting and plangent quality that can stick in the mind long after the tale that evoked it has passed from easy recall. Augustine goes on to say in *De doctrina christiana* that specific words at some point no longer matter because they are merely shadows of God's eternal truth (1.13.12). His final counsel, therefore, is that man surpass rhetoric by surpassing words, through prayer (4.15–16). If Marguerite means for us to see Augustine's sense of *caritas,* and his sense of rhetoric, behind her stories of the varieties of love and the controversiae that attempt to confront them—and it seems clear that she does—then (as du Bellay advises us), the *absence* of prayer within the action detailed in *L'Heptaméron* shows us how far the souls stranded at Nostre-Dame de Serrance have yet to go.

Nearly all the implications of her Platonic, Plotinian, scriptural, and Augustinian poetics are set out plainly by Marguerite in the prologue that opens her nouvelle. What seems the most accurate and journalistic of beginnings, we learn soon enough, is a passage of signs for the initiated.

Le premier jou de septembre, que les baings des montz Pirenées commencent entrer en leur vertu, se trouverent à ceulx de Cauderès plusieurs personnes tant de France que d'Espaigne; les ungs pour y boire de l'eaue, les autres pour se y baigner et les autres pour prendre de la fange; qui sont choses si merveilleuses que les malades habandonnez des medecins, s'en retournent tout guariz.

On the first day of September, when the springs of the Pyrenees are just beginning to be at their most potent, there were a number of people staying at the spa town of Cauterets. They had come from Spain [and other countries] as well as from France, some to drink the waters, some to bathe in them, and some to be treated with the mud. These are all very remarkable cures, so remarkable that patients long given up by their physicians go home completely restored to health.[15]

We shall soon learn that such earthbound remedies, substitutes for true faith, are not at all restorative and that those who believe in such "remarkable cures" are God's fools. Divine beneficence instructs them (and us) by creating a flood so extraordinary that it is compared to Noah's own, a raging torrent that prevents many from leaving the mountains and reaching home. Some who are foolhardy enough to wade into the swollen stream or who think they can manufacture their own escape routes are killed in their attempts to depart, but others, like the aged Oisille, who knows the meaning (and limitations) of human struggle; Hircan, who risks his life for his wife Parlamente; and Dagoucin and Saffredent, who follow two women out of selfless concern for their welfare, are all saved because, we are told, they trust to God's guidance (p. 3; p. 62). Two others, Nomerfide and Ennasuite, who are chased by a bear, are also spared: "Et le matin ouyrent la messe bien devotement, louans Dieu des perilz qu'ilz avoient eschappez"; "The next morning they heard mass with great devotion, praising God for delivering them from the perils of the mountains" (p. 4; p. 63). Even Simontaut, whose encircling body of servants drown when he attempts to cross the swollen river on horseback, provides a "very moving spectacle" ("il avoit veu une bien grande pitié," p. 5; p. 64), and the older Geburon, who is saved from bandits because he is lightly dressed, knows enough instinctively to thank God (p. 4; p. 63). The intention of the prologue as parable is quite clear: Those whose trust goes beyond natural cures to divine faith are miraculously saved; theirs is not only a tale of curing but a tale of *deliverance*. Moreover, naturally or through the instruction of others, making their several ways to a nearby monastery, they give the abbot and monks there an occasion for charity ("où elle fut charitablement receue des religieux," p. 2; p. 61).

All the characters who assemble at Nostre-Dame de Serrance, then, are men and women who see in God's salvation of their lives a cure far greater than that proclaimed by the healthiest of natural spas. Yet even here, in the holiest of earthly settings, the monastery, they have much to learn. Uprooted, they are soon bored and appeal to the older, wiser Oisille for a suggestion of how best to spend their time. Her reply, to lead a life of devotion, becomes Marguerite's *propositio*—it is what the entire *L'Heptaméron* throughout its long rounds of tales and discussions, orations and disputations, will veer toward and diverge from. Some, most notably Parlamente and Dagoucin, will tell stories that confirm the wisdom of Oisille; others, such as Hircan and Longarine, will rebel against it. Thus Oisille's initial speech is one side of the disputation, against which the remainder of *L'Heptaméron* will, in its multivocality, take issue.

"Mes enfants, . . . si vous me demandez quelle recepte me tient si joyeuse et si saine sur ma viellesse, c'est que, incontinant que je suys levée, je prends la Saincte Escripture et la lys, et, en voiant et contemplant la bonté de Dieu, qui pour nous a envoié son filz en terre anoncer ceste saincte parolle et bonne nouvelle, par laquelle il permect remission de tous pechez, satisfaction de toutes debtes par le don qu'il nous faict de son amour, passion et merites, ceste consideration me donne tant de joye que je prends mon psaultier et, le plus humblement qu'il m'est possible, chante de cueur et prononce de bouche les beaulx psealmes et canticques que le sainct Esperit a composé au cueur de David et des autres aucteurs. Et ce contentement là que je en ay me faict tant de bien que tous les maulx qui le jour me peuvent advenir me semblent estre benedictions, veu que j'ay en mon cueur par foy Celluy qui les a portez pour moy. Pareillement, avant soupper, je me retire pour donner pasture à mon ame de qualque leçon; et puis au soir faictz une recollection de tout ce que j'ay faict la journée passée pour demander pardon de mes faultes, le remercier de ses graces; et en son amour, craincte et paix, prends mon repos asseuré de tous maulx."

"My children, . . . if you ask what the prescription is that keeps me happy and healthy in my old age, I will tell you. As soon as I rise in the morning I take the Scriptures and read them. I see and contemplate the goodness of God, who for our sakes has sent His son to earth to declare the holy word and the good news by which He grants remission of all our sins, and payment of all our debts, through His gift to us of His love, His passion and His merits. And my contemplations give me such joy, that I take my psalter, and with the utmost humility, sing the beautiful psalms and hymns that the Holy Spirit has composed in the heart of David and the other authors. The contentment this affords me fills me with such well-being that whatever the evils of the day, they are to me so many blessings, for in my heart I have by faith Him who has borne these evils for me. Likewise, before supper, I withdraw to nourish my soul with readings and meditations. In the evening I ponder in my mind everything I have done during the day, so that I may ask God forgiveness of my sins, and give thanks to Him for his mercies. And so I lay myself to rest in His love, fear and peace, assured against all evils."

[Pp. 7–8; pp. 66–67]

Hircan's reply—to combine such a spiritual exercise and regimen with a more worldly one—establishes the basic dialectic.

Hircan print la parolle et dist: "Ma dame, ceulx qui ont leu la saincte Escripture, comme je croy que nous tous avons faict, confesseront que vostre dict est tout veritable; mais si fault il que vous regardez que nous sommes encore si mortiffiez qu'il nous fault quelque passetemps et exercice corporel; car si nous sommes en noz maisons, il nous fault la chasse et la vollerye, qui nous faict oblier mil folles pensées; et les dames ont leur mesnaige, leur ouvraige et quelquesfois les dances où elles prennent honneste exercice; qui me faict dire (parlant pour la part des hommes) que vous, qui estes la plus antienne, nous lirez au matin de la vie que tenoit nostre Seigneur Jesus-Christ, et les grandes et admirables euvres qu'il a faictes pour nous; pour après disner jusques à vespres, fault choisir quelque passetemps qui ne soit dommageable à l'ame, soit plaisant au corps; et ainsy passerons la journée joieusement."

Then Hircan spoke: "Madame, anyone who has read the holy Scriptures—as indeed I think we all have here—will readily agree that what you have said is true. However, you must bear in mind that we have not yet become so mortified in the flesh that we are not in need of some sort of amusement and physical exercise in order to pass the time. After all, when we're at home, we've got our hunting and hawking to distract us from the thousand and one foolish thoughts that pass through one's mind. The ladies have their housework and their needle-work. They have dances, too, which provide a respectable way for them to get some exercise. All this leads me to suggest, on behalf of the men here, that you, Madame, since you are the oldest among us, should read to us every morning about the life of our Lord Jesus Christ, and the great and wonderful things He has done for us. Between dinner and vespers I think we should choose some pastime, which, while not being prejudicial to the soul, will be agreeable to the body. In that way we shall spend a very pleasant day. [P. 8; p. 67]

Other minor disputes follow at once: whether the pastime should be for two participants or for all of them; whether there should be a single leader or all should have equal rights; whether the discussions they decide to hold about tales they decide to tell should be public or private; and whether the tales themselves should be stories, events witnessed by the narrator, or, regardless of either, tales simply "worthy of belief" ("et assuy de paour que la beaulté de la rethoricque feit tort en quelque partye à la verité de l'historie"; "dira chascun quelque histoire qu'il aura venue ou bie oy dire à quelque homme digne de foy"; pp. 9–10; pp. 68–69). Ironically—but deliberately—Marguerite so ends the prologue that *both* sides *lose:* The day of meditation Oisille suggests breaks into open and unresolved debate, and the physical exercise that Hircan proposes ends in a rhetorical free-for-all. It is a clear sign that we are in the fallen world despite the recent deliverance and that all the characters—save perhaps Oisille—have much to learn before their deliverance becomes possible, or actual. Before such dissension the putative narrator backs off, riddling: "Et ne faillirent pas à midy de s'en retourner au pré, selon leur delibération, qui estoit si beau et plaisant qu'il avoit besoin d'un Bocace pour le depaindre à la verité"; "At midday they all went back as arranged to the meadow, which was looking so beautiful and fair that it would take a Boccaccio to describe it as it really was" (p. 10; p. 69). But Boccaccio is dead.

The dialectic established with such artistry and wit in the prologue is continued by the very structure of *L'Heptaméron:* Tales are deliberately placed alongside antithetical stories; they are countered by the commentaries made on them; they are often at odds with the narrators who supply them; and they are sometimes internally inconsistent in plot and characterization. Some, moreover, argue carnal love whereas others support spiritual love; some propose the wisdom of dissimulation whereas others condemn it as hypocrisy or worse. Even as we wrestle with such local and relatively confined problems of interpretation and judgment as these—for how are we, as those to be instructed, meant to respond?—the stories also release our imaginations into the widest of arenas: Geographically, they move beyond Europe to Canada and the New World; historically, they move from the timeless past through the reign of Charles VIII and into the present; in attitude they move from the crudest and coarsest of tales—such as the fabliau of the frozen feces (story 52)—to the most idealistic of romances—such as the story of the prince who falls in love with a commoner (story 42). Such stories are as old as the world and as fresh, and, as Geburon tells us (and them), such stories are endless (pp. 326–27; p. 427). In such a world of erring fools, the precise relationships of the characters to each other—Hircan seems to represent Henri II as Parlamente seems to represent Marguerite herself—and to the actual world outside the frame of the novel are deliberately blurred. The final dialectic is therefore a dilemma: This fiction may have little actual fiction.

In a work whose boundaries are so indistinct, we may expect to be robbed of any clarity of meaning provided by an authority other than ourselves, and in this we shall not be disappointed. The morality of the very first tale, for instance, of a procurator's wife who indiscriminately accepts the advances of the ordained bishop of Sées and the secular son of the lieutenant-general of Alençon, would seem clear and pronounced enough; if there were the slightest doubt, the teller of the tale, Simontaut, seems to dispel it at the end. He says of the procurator who butchers one of his wife's lovers and of the sorcerer in whom he has placed his faith,

> ce que luy fut octroyé, et furent envoiez luy et Gallery à Marseilles, aux galleres de Sainct Blanchart, ou ilz finerent leurs jours en grande capitivité et eurent loisir de recongnoistre la gravité de leurs pechez. Et la mauvaise femme, en l'absence de son mary, continua son peché plus que jamais et mourut miserablement.

> Saint-Aignan and Gallery were sent to Baron de Saint-Blancard's galleys at Marseilles. In the galleys they ended their days, and with plenty of time to reflect on the seriousness of their crimes. As for the depraved wife, she led a more immoral life than ever, once her husband was out of the way, and died a most miserable death. [P. 17; p. 77]

Yet Simontaut both limits and apparently misunderstands his own tale in the erupting conversation that follows: He sees it as exemplary only of women as the cause of evil. Thus the procurator and sorcerer are excused from murder and sin because the procurator's wife was the first to stoop to folly. Nor, before Oisille, does Simontaut see any depravity in turning for aid to a sorcerer rather than to the Lord. Even the authorities in *L'Heptaméron,* then, can be ignorant of the meaning of their *own* tales from the outset.

As the tales continue, "the language," Marcel Tetel notes, "hovers at a theoretical and argumentative level and because of the contrasting points of view never quite settles on any one opinion" (*Marguerite's "Heptameron,"* p. 15). Although the tangled state in which manuscripts and editions of *L'Heptaméron* have come down to us prevents our finally knowing the authoritative version or even in what order the stories are to be printed or even, for that matter, what stories Marguerite meant to include [16]—Donald Stone, Jr., demonstrates clearly that even the traditionally corrupt first edition of 1558 printed in Paris by Pierre Boaistuau has some irrevocable claim on our attention [17]—the order now generally assumed follows this initial tale of a woman who prostitutes herself with that of a woman who is exemplary: Oisille's abbreviated story of a muledriver's wife from Amboise who refuses to surrender to her husband's servant when he attempts to rape her and dies rather than submit. Oisille notes how the women of the village held the muledriver's wife in great respect for her virtue, as she herself does, and for once there is no opposition from her audience. But there seems to be no secure lesson, either, for in telling the next tale Saffredent reveals how the queen of Naples, to take revenge on her unfaithful husband, takes in adultery the husband of the king's mistress. Nor is there any moral justice, such as that supplied by Oisille. In Saffredent's story, the king never suspects his wife's infidelity, and both remain unfaithful until their deaths. The fourth story, once again by contrast, tells of a virtuous woman who defends her honor and teaches a presumptuous young man the value of modesty and respect. Later stories continue to function dialectically during the Première Journée, including that of two evil Franciscans who are outwitted by a chaste boatwoman (story 5) and that of a trickster who is himself tricked (story 6). Such varying stances are—ironically—exposed by Saffredent himself: "Pource que l'homme croit voluntiers ce qu'il veoit," he tells us; "men see and believe just what they want to" (P. 23; p. 83).

So many men, so many minds: Marguerite's sense of earthbound epistemology, as opposed to that of antique and Christian teaching, realizes one of Erasmus's best-known adages. Splintering the possibilities of the epistemology of fallen man—of those who have not yet learned from Plato, Plotinus, or Paul that love can transport men to divinity or, from Augustine, the essential need for *caritas*—among the various *devisants* of *L'Heptaméron* may find its Senecan original in Plato's *Symposium,* as it surely finds its model in the symposium as a formal method of instruction, but it is nevertheless a method Marguerite uses elsewhere, most notably and most successfully in her drama. [18] In her early play *Le Mallade* (1535?) she juxtaposes worldliness (a Sick Man), superstition (a Wife), wisdom (a Doctor), and ecstasy or faith (a Chambermaid). As Tetel sums it, "No attempt will be made to cure the wife, a hopeless case. But the chambermaid, counseled by the physician who is just as rapacious as he is sagacious, will heal the husband, without even any bloodletting" (*Marguerite's "Heptaméron,"* p. 141). In the *Comédie du parfait amant* (1549), written the year of Marguerite's death, an old woman tries fruitlessly to discover a faithful love to crown. Her first choice is a wife who is faithful until her husband is forced to leave her for three months; a second wife has remained faithful, it is true, but only because her husband has never left home and so, dialectically to the first, she has had no opportunity for infidelity; a third wife remains faithful while her husband is absent for six months, but she says that if she learns that he has been unfaithful to her she will respond in kind. At last the old woman is successful, but when she offers the crown to a perfect married couple, neither will accept it, since each is certain the other deserves it more. But the richest of Marguerite's plays is the *Comédie de Mont-de Marsan* (1548), which examines dramatically and dialectically four women: La Mondaine, who represents the materialism of an amoral society; La Superstitieuse, or religious bigotry and hypocrisy; La Sage, enlightened faith; and La Ravie de l'Amour de Dieu, or mysticism resulting from a direct union with God. What is most striking about this work is the complicated way in which such relatively allegorical persons interact. La Mondaine lives for self-pleasure, *philautia,* reserving all her attention for the welfare and joy of her body; she therefore has no use for the self-punishment of La Superstitieuse, whose chief interest seems to be in castigating and reforming others. (La Superstitieuse probably is meant to represent the smug orthodoxy of the Sorbonne rather than the inward-looking theology of the Evangelicals.) La Sage's doctrine, by contrast, is a workable harmony between the physical and spiritual sides of man; reason will lead man to virtue and thus to God: "L'homme raisonnable / Est faict agréable / A Dieu et au monde" (lines 171– 73). She finds her instruction, she says, in reading the Bible, and she distributes copies of the Old and New Testament to La Mondaine and La Superstitieuse. But she is interrupted when La Ravie, as a shepherdess, suddenly walks before them singing of her passion for an unnamed lover (God). She is ecstatic; she neither names her lover nor comprehends the state she is in. Thus the play's two debates work in opposite directions: La Sage is able to persuade La Mondaine and La Superstitieuse to redeploy their gifts to the service of God; but no one is able to communicate with La Ravie, and she is unable to communicate with them.[19] All three plays reinforce the sense of multiple perspective and of irresolution, then, that characterizes the first day's tales in *L'Heptaméron.*

Despite the shared characteristics of the *devisants* of Marguerite's nouvelle— their aristocratic background, their Reformist attitudes, their exercises of Catholic ritual and doctrine—they differ considerably in age, station, and outlook. Oisille is the oldest and most authoritative, but her authority comes more from Scripture than from theology; she is alive with the spirit of evangelical reform. Parlamente, who may be Marguerite's self-fictionalization, is morally upright; associated with purity and perfection, she defends the honor of women and will not allow generalizations to be made about them despite what stories are told. Her husband Hircan—who may be the handsome, dashing, and unfaithful Henri II—is especially masculine; he is a warrior, a hunter, and a lover who supports a double standard for men and women and, though liberal in his love matches, he is rigid about the class system in connection with marriage. Longarine is given to laughter and good times; she is so concerned with matters of this world, in fact, that she is especially interested in reputations, including her own. Dagoucin is the Neoplatonist of the group, given to silence generally—he does not speak at all until story 8—and the gentlest of the company. Saffredent, on the other hand, is fun-loving and consequently casual in his attitudes, activities, and moral standards. Ennasuite is the most quick-tempered, sensitive to criticism, and given to a sharp tongue; she is also strongly anticlerical and antimonastic. The youngest of the group is Nomerfide; she too is enthusiastically worldly, finding clerics generally distasteful. Geburon is the oldest of the men and presently or formerly of the military. He is also, with Oisille, one of the most sensible, frequently quoting the Bible or citing proverbs to defend his position in debate; his view of love, however, is pessimistic. Simontaut is the other military man and a misanthrope; like Ennasuite he is touchy and easily angered. He has little interest in religion, thinking it appeals largely to dreamers. Such clear demarcations change little in the course of *L'Heptaméron;* the complexity comes in various interplays among such clearly defined and often antagonistic storytellers.[20] Yet all of them share an underlying concern with the sharp disjunction between the life of virtue and faith and the life of sin and infidelity—and all of them remain more or less conscious of their good fortune in being delivered to the monastery in the midst of the great flood.

It is precisely to this disjunction that Parlamente responds at the close of the first day with the longest story of all, a story that pulls together all the salient themes of her predecessors and reshapes them. Her story is about a virtuous woman, the Lady Floride, who successfully resists the advances of young Amadour and withdraws to the religious life; he in turn learns courage and devotion from her example. Notably, this tale opens with Parlamente's description of Amadour as the ideal humanist.

> Et, entre les autres, y en avoit ung nommé Amadour, lequel, combien qu'il n'eust que dix huict ou dix neuf ans, si avoit-il grace tant asseurée et le sens si bon, que on l'eust jugé entre mil digne de gouverner une chose publicque. Il est vray wue ce bon sens là estoit accompaigné d'une si grande et native beaulté,

qu'il n'y avoit oeil qui ne se tint contant de le regarder; et si la beaulté estoit tant exquise, la parolle la suyvoit de si près que l'on ne sçavoit à qui donner l'honneur, ou à la grace, ou à la beaulté, ou au bien parler. Mais ce qui le faisoit encores plus estimer, c'estoit sa grande hardiesse, dont le bruict n'estoit empesché pour sa jeunesse; car en tant de lieux avoit deja monstré ce qu'il sçavoit faire, que non seullement les Espaignes, mais la France et l'Ytallie estimerent grandement ses vertuz, pource que, à toutes les guerres qui avoient esté, il ne se estoit poinct espargné; et, quand son pais estoit en repos, il alloit chercher la guerre aux lieux estranges, où il estoit aymé et estimé d'amys et d'ennemys.

Amongst these men there was one by the name of Amador. Although he was only eighteen or nineteen years of age, he had such confidence, and such sound judgement, that you could not have failed to regard him as one of those rare men fit to govern any state. Not only was he a man of sound judgement, he was also endowed with an appearance so handsome, so open and natural, that he was a delight for all to behold. This was not all, for his handsome looks were equally matched by the fairness of his speech. Poise, good looks, eloquence—it was impossible to say with which gift he was more richly blessed. But what gained him even higher esteem was his fearlessness, which, despite his youth, was famed throughout all lands. For he had already in many different places given evidence of his great abilities. Not only throughout the kingdom of Spain, but also in France and Italy people looked upon him with admiration. Not once during the recent wars had he shrunk from battle, and when his country had been at peace, he had gone to seek action in foreign parts, and there too had been loved and admired by friend and foe alike. [Pp. 55–56; pp. 122–23]

Despite these attributes, he is also subject to human passion, and he falls in love with Floride, the twelve-year-old daughter of the countess of Armade. He has sufficient self-discipline to bide his time and to approach her through her servant, but he is called to war and imprisoned, and upon his return, he finds her married. Although his initial advances before his departure were eloquent, as were her denials at the time (p. 62; p. 130), his approach now—that they may have an affair since she is married and it will not stain her honor—is repulsive to Floride. She admonishes him in Reformist terms, the shift from humanist dialogue to spiritual counsel marked if subtle. The truth, in fact, by which Parlamente has guaranteed her tale has now become the Truth of God.

"Helas! Amadour, sont-ce icy les vertueux propos que durant ma jeunesse m'avez tenuz? Est-ce cy l'honneur et la conscience que vous m'avez maintesfoys conseillé plustost mourir que de perdre mon ame? Avez-vous oblyé les bons exemples que vous m'avez donnez des vertueuses dames qui ont resisté à la folle amour, et le despris que vous avez tousjours faict des folles? Je ne puis croire, Amadour, que vous soyez si loing de vous-mesmes, que Dieu, vostre conscience et mon bonneur soient du tout mortz en vous. Mais, si ainsy est que vous le dictes, je loue la Bonté divine, qui a prevenu le malheur où maintenant je m'alloys precipiter, en me monstrant per vostre parolle le cueur que j'ay tant ignore."

"Alas! Amador," she began, "what has happened to all the virtuous things you used to say to me when I was young? Is this the honour, is this the conscience, for which you so often told me to die, rather than lose my soul? Have you forgotten all the lessons you taught me from examples of virtuous ladies who resisted senseless and wicked passion? Have you forgotten how you have always spoken with scorn of women who succumb to it? It is hard, Amador, to believe that you have left your former self so far behind that all regard for God, for your conscience, and for my honour is completely dead. But if it really is as you seem to say, then I thank God that in His goodness He has forewarned me of the disaster that was about to befall me. By the words you have uttered God has revealed to me what your heart is really like." [P. 74; p. 142]

This is a crucial turning point, not only in the tale but in Parlamente's telling of the tale. For she has been alert all day long both to the ways in which the stories have revealed the character and outlook of their narrators and to the way in which her husband Hircan has approved of just such a plan as Amadour proposes to Floride: She has purposely chosen a story by means of which she can expose Hircan's own disgraceful behavior and her own virtuous suffering. Continually frustrated over the years in his attempt to win Floride, even with the aid of her mother and with knowledge of her loveless marriage, Amadour at last gives his life to God on the battlefield ("en baisant la croix de son espée, rendant corps et ame à Dieu, s'en donna ung tel coup, qu'il ne luy en fallut poinct de secours," p. 82; p. 152). His battlefield conversion leads to Floride's own.

Les nouvelles en coururent par toute l'Espaigne, tant que Floride, laquelle estoit à Barselonne, où son mary autresfois avoit ordonné estre enterré, en oyt le bruict. Et, après qu'elle eut faict ses obseques honorablement, sans en parler à mere ne à belle-mere, s'en alla randre religieuse au monastere de Jesus, prenant pour mary et amy Celuy qui l'avoit delivrée d'une amour si vehemente que celle d'Amadour, et d'un ennuy si grand que de la compagnye d'un tel mary. Ainsi tourna toutes ses affections à aymer Dieu si parfaictement, que après avoir vescu longuement religieuse, luy rendit son ame en telle joye, que l'espouse a d'aller veoir son espoux.

The news of his death spread throughout Spain, and eventually reached Florida, who was at Barcelona, where her husband had expressed his wish to be buried. She conducted the obsequies with due honour. Then, saying not a word either to her own mother or to the mother of her dead husband, she entered the Convent of Jesus. Thus she took Him as lover and as spouse who had delivered her from the violent love of Amador and from the misery of her life with her earthly husband. All her affections henceforth were bent on the perfect love of God. As a nun she lived for many long years, until at last she commended her soul to God with the joy of the bride who goes to meet her bridegroom. [Pp. 82–83; p. 152]

Floride's final act of marriage neatly resolves her honor, devotion, and passion—in all ways, an exemplary act. But whereas the tale reaches resolution, what follows does not: In the succeeding controversia, Parlamente, after apologizing for the length of her story—it is one of the longest—asks Hircan for approval of Floride's actions, but he refuses and, what is more, he gains support from Saffredent! Thus the *day's* resolution—in which Oisille leads them all to vespers—only thinly covers the irresolution of the narrators and the divisiveness of their values and attitudes. The instruction of Parlamente's tale—so clearly argued, so eloquently presented, and received by so attentive an audience—has no lasting effect, and the final indication of the Première Journée is that no "story"—whether true or not—has the capacity to convert those in need of moral (and religious) instruction. The Première Journée ends, that is, by questioning the very value of *L'Heptaméron* itself.

Marguerite thus openly tests—as all writers of Continental humanist poetics do—the efficacy of literature. The Première Journée constantly examines, and in the end confirms, Simontaut's reaction to Dagoucin's hopes for instructing men in the ways of virtue, which he suggests during the controversia for tale 8: Things may sound very fine in writing, as they do, say, in Plato's *Republic,* but they are hardly true to experience and therefore hardly functional ("qui s'escript et ne s'experimente poinct," p. 48; p. 113). The Deuxiesme Journée repeats the pattern. It begins with holy lessons, which will be put to the test.

Le lendemain, se leverent en grand desir de retourner au lieu où le jour precedent avoyent eu tant de plaisir; car chascun avoit son compte si prest, qu'il leur tardoit qu'il ne fust mis en lumiere. Après qu'ilz eurent ouy la leçon de madame

Oisille, et la messe, où chascun recommanda à Dieu son esperit, afin qu'il leur donnast parolle et grace de continuer l'assemblée.

The next day they got up, eager to return to the spot where they had had so much pleasure the day before, for they had all prepared their stories, and could hardly wait to tell them. They listened to Madame Oisille's lesson and to mass, each of them offering their hearts and minds to God that He might inspire their words and grant His grace to continue their gathering. [P. 87; p. 155]

Some of the stories are exemplary—even tale 11 in which beshitting is conveyed as the stain of original sin. But these stories also run into difficulty. Tale 12, for instance, in which the duke of Florence asks the brother of the woman he loves to seduce her only to cause him to murder the duke in his bed, thus ridding the woman, and the land, of a tyrant, is now cause for dissension, despite the fact that it is told by the mild-mannered Dagoucin.

> Ceste histoire fut bien ecoutée de toute la compaignye, mais elle luy engendra diverses oppinions; car les ungs soustenoient que le gentil homme avoit faict son debvoir de saulver sa vie et l'honneur de sa seur, ensemble d'avoir delivré sa patrie d'un tel tirant; les autres disoient que non, mais que c'estoit trop grande ingratitude de mectre à mort celluy qui luy avoit faict tant de bien et d'honneur. Les dames disoient qu'il estoit bon frere et vertueux citoyen; les hommes, au contraire, qu'il estoit traistre et meschant serviteur.

> Everyone had listened attentively to Dagoucin's story. But it was a story that engendered diverse opinions. For some, the gentleman had clearly done his duty in saving his sister's life and honour, and in ridding his homeland of a tyrant by the same stroke. Others, however, did not agree. They said that it was the height of ingratitude for the gentleman to murder the very man from whom he had received such honour and advancement. The ladies said that he was a good brother and virtuous citizen. The men, taking the contrary view, insisted that he was a traitor and a bad servant. [P. 95; p. 163]

This opposition is reinforced in tales 18 and 19, when Hircan tells a story of perfect love with obvious cynicism and Parlamente replies with a story of *Amour* in its most elevated sense, the man becoming an Observant Franciscan, the woman a nun of Saint Clare. Again Parlamente's tale does not have the desired effect: Saffredent next tells of a patient and devoted lover who, when he finally finds the courage to make an advance, finds his beloved in the arms of a stableboy—a fabliau that returns us, at day's sacred end, to Hircan's story instead. And the monks, entranced by such stories, are found eavesdropping intently—so intently they nearly miss vespers.

En disant ces parolles, Parlamente meit son touret de nez, et, avecq les autres, entra dedans l'eglise, où ils trouverent vespres très bien sonnées, mais ilz n'y trouverent pas ung religieux pour les dire, pource qu'ilz avoient entendu que dedans le pré s'assembloit ceste compaignye pour y dire les plus plaisantes choses qu'il estoit possible; et, comme ceulx qui aymoient mieulx leurs plaisirs que les oraisons, s'estoient allez chacher dedans une fosse, le ventre contre terre, derrière une haye fort espesse. Et là avoient si bien escoucté les beaulx comptes, qu'ilz n'avaient poinct oy sonner la cloche de leur monastere. Ce qui parut bien, quant ilz arriverent en telle haste, que quasi l'alaine leur failloit à commencer vespres.

On saying these words Parlamente raised her mask to her face, and went into the church. They found that although the bell had been ringing heartily for vespers, not a single monk had yet appeared. The fact was that they had heard that the ladies and gentlemen were meeting together in the meadow to recount all manner of amusing tales and, preferring their pleasures to their prayers, they had been hiding in a ditch behind a thick hedge, flat on their bellies, so that they could overhear. So attentively had they been listening, they had not even heard their own monastery bell ringing. The consequence was that they came scurrying to their places in such a hurry that they hardly had enough breath left to start singing the service! [P. 156; p. 234]

This appears at first a delicate balance between the appeal of stories of passion and final reconciliation with worship at evensong. But it is not really so equivocal as all that. The tale of the monks provided by the narrator—that is by Marguerite—is itself a fabliau in line with the tales of Hircan and Saffredent. Moreover, corruption has now not only invaded the church but left the inset stories (confirming Parlamente's accusations of Hircan embedded in tale 10) and entered the very grounds of Nostre-Dame de Serrance itself.

The accumulating gravity of *L'Heptaméron* is compounded in the course of the Troisiesme Journée, when the world of most of the tales becomes one of dissimulation and disguise, the last, tale 30, resulting in tragic incest. Rolandine and her lover, a bastard, meet in church disguised in monastic habits (tale 21). A Franciscan plots with a devoted follower to sleep with his wife and jumps into bed with her when she thinks it is her husband (tale 23). "The protagonists in the novellas move about in a world of screens that shield their true thoughts and intentions from others," Marcel Tetel writes (*Marguerite's "Heptameron,"*

p. 74). "The naked face would become a metaphor of honesty" (p. 90). They read books, feign sickness, pretend to be at prayer; they spy through holes, stand in closets, wait secretly in neighboring rooms; they feign journeys and absences; they put on costumes and masks. Nor can speech redeem such appetites and such practices. Rolandine's extraordinary Ciceronian eloquence in her classical oration to her mother the queen on behalf of her bastard lover fails to convince (21), as the gentle, honest, unworldly Dagoucin has already discovered and warned us:

> Las! mon Parler foible et plein de langueur,
> Tu n'as povoir de bien au vray luy paindre
> Comment son oeil peult un bon cueur contraindre?
> Encores moins à louer sa parolle
> Ta puissance est pauvre, debille et molle.

> Alas, poor Speech, your weary strength is slight,
> You cannot paint for her, with all your art,
> How her pure eye can take a steadfast heart,
> Nor can you praise the words that she can speak,
> Your power is only faltering and weak.
>
> [P. 102; pp. 171–72]

For in a fallen world language too has been so frequently corrupted that there seems no way now to restore it when truth and proper intentions call it into service.

Yet Marguerite opposes such mounting abuses during the Troisiesme Journée with a growing emphasis on true religion. Story 26 is a retelling of the parable of the wise and foolish virgin; stories 27 and 28 are clearly meant to be parables, too. Paul's letter to the Corinthians is invoked in the controversia following story 22; the Gospel of Saint Matthew is quoted following story 23. Small passages of overt theology intrude at the start of 23 and in the course of 26. The day itself ends, in fact, with Saffredent calling upon the example of Saint Jerome!

> —Vrayement, dist Geburon, c'est bien l'extremité de la folye de se voulloir randre de soy-mesmes, impecable et cercher si fort les occasions de pecher!" Ce dist Saffredent: "Il y en a qui font au contraire, car ilz fuyent tant qu'ilz peuvent les occasions: encores la concupiscence les suict. Et le bon sainct Jherosme, après s'estre bien foueté et s'estre caché dedans les desers, confessa ne povoir eviter le feu qui brusloit dedans ses moelles. Parquoy se fault recommander à Dieu, car, s'il ne nous tient à force, nous prenons grand plaisir à tresbucher."

"Really," said Geburon, "it's the extreme of folly to want to put oneself through one's own efforts above sin, and then actually to go looking for situations where a sin may be committed!"

"Some people do the opposite, however," said Saffredent, "and avoid such situations as much as they can—but even then their concupiscence goes with them. The good Saint Jerome, even after he had flagellated himself and hidden himself away in the wilderness, confessed that he could not get rid of the fire that burned in the marrow of his bones. So we should commend ourselves to God, for if He does not hold us in His grip, we stumble and take great pleasure in so doing." [P. 234; pp. 322–23]

Hircan has just told a prolonged and ugly story of incest, in which a man fathers a daughter with his mother, and we should expect Saffredent, at least, to find joy in such an outrageous "entertainment." But he counters even Geburon by responding to Hircan's *story* and Geburon's *hypothesis* with the recorded *history* of Saint Jerome as a model of *truth* for all of them to emulate in the *actuality* of the abbey at Serrance. The increased dissimulation that is recounted—that is appealed to—on the Troisiesme Journée, then, is also reversible, applying to both fiction and fact, the tales of the narrators but also their own lives, so that the reversibility between story and frame, which was broken on the Deuxiesme Journée by Hircan and Parlamente, is extinguished. From now on, *L'Hep-taméron* means to tell tales that are no longer simply tales. The analogy is clear: *L'Heptaméron* has as its real audience not the ten persons stranded at Serrance but ourselves.

Marguerite's account of the Quatriesme Journée is now distinguished by the increasing interest in Serrance. As the stories quicken and shorten, the symposia that succeed each of them grow considerably longer and more complex. The tales are merely texts for interpretation and analysis—secular Scriptures for the day's many lessons on love and on faith, those on infidelity (following tale 32), on sin and vengeance (following tale 36), and on love, finally submitting to the will of God (following tale 40), only the most noticeable and the most important. The passions that men and women fail to control and the Word of God, which is meant to hold them in check, are further exacerbated on the Cinquiesme Journée, when a husband and his friends take vengeance on some lustful Franciscans who have dishonored the man's wife: "car, après les avoir bien battuz, leur couperent les bras et les jambes, et les laisserent dedans les vignes à la garde du dieu Baccus et Venus, dont ilz estoient meilleurs disciples que de sainct François," "They beat them, cut off their arms and legs, and left them in the vines in the care of Bacchus and Venus, for they were better disciples of the god of wine and goddess of love than of Saint Francis" (pp. 316–17; p. 415)—and when Parlamente makes her most decisive claim: "ne vouluz croire en parolle de prescheur, si je ne la trouve conforme à celle de Dieu, qui est la vraye touche pour sçavoir les parolles vraie ou mensongeres"; "I have refused to believe [even] these preachers, unless what they say seems to me to conform to the word of God, which is the only true touchstone by which one can know whether one is hearing truth or falsehood" (p. 304; p. 400). The words of Scripture that Oisille reads to all of them at the start of each day—those words we have already examined—thus become the only index by which Parlamente, and by association Oisille and Marguerite, can now find security when dealing with stories that become increasingly dreadful.

Perhaps it is for this reason that Oisille changes her reading on the Sixiesme Journée from Paul's prescriptions for the Christian life in his letter to Rome to John's more philosophical (and warmer) letter on love. But, sadly, it seems misplaced. The first tale—which takes place in Urbino, corrupting the refined manners and mores of *Il Cortegiano*—is a tale of confinement and restriction; instead of edification and joy, it calls up during the subsequent controversia another account of mutilation supplied by Geburon.

> —Vrayement, dist Geburon, quant Rivolte fut prins des François, il y avoit ung cappitaine Italien, que l'on estimoit gentil compaignon, lequel, voiant mort ung qui ne luy estoit ennemy que de tenir sa part contraire de Guelfe à Gibelin, luy arracha le cueur du ventre, et, le rotissant sur les charbons à grand haste, le manges, et, respondant à quelques ungs qui luy demandoient quel goust il y trouvoit, dist que jamais n'avoit mengé si savoureux ne si plaisant morceau que de cestuy-là.

> "Yes, indeed," said Geburon. "When Rivolta was taken by the French there was an Italian captain whom everybody regarded as a valiant comrade-at-arms and who came across a man lying dead, a man who was only an enemy in the sense that he had been a Guelph, while the captain was a Ghibelline. He tore the dead man's heart out of his chest, roasted it over a charcoal fire, and ate it. When some people asked what it tasted like, he replied that he had never tasted a more delicious or enjoyable morsel." [Pp. 331–32; pp. 431–32]

Against such a horrible account, Geburon's proverbial sense of justice only a few moments later—"Je n'ai jamais veu, dist Geburon, mocqueur qui ne fut mocqué, trompeur qui ne fut trompé, et glorieulx qui ne fut humillyé"; "I have never seen," said Geburon, "a mocker who was never mocked, nor a deceiver who was never himself deceived, nor arrogance that was never in the end humiliated" (p. 332; p. 433)—seems to us all but inconsequential, and it is further undermined by the later abuse of Saint Raphael (tale 56) and the parody of the Resurrection in which a curate digs up the body of the mistress he would make love to (tale 60). The gentle and optimistic Dagoucin seems nearer the mark, in fact, when he is forced to say—surprisingly, tellingly—that "la felicité de ce monde, qui avecq soy porte une mutabilité"; "in this world happiness never lasts for long" (p. 312; p. 410).

And yet—and yet—as Simontaut says with excitement and joyful conviction following tale 34—all ten *devisants* have started out with tales of folly and wound up with philosophy and theology (p. 254; pp. 344–45). He may be remembering Parlamente's long and warm support of Platonic and Plotinian thought following tale 19.

—J'appelle parfaictz amans, luy respondit Parlamente, ceulx qui cerchent, en ce qu'ilz aiment, quelque parfection, soit beaulté, bonté ou bonne grace; tousjours tendans à la vertu, et qui ont le cueur si hault et si honneste, qu'ilz ne veullent, pour mourir, mectre leur fin aux choses basses que l'honneur et la conscience repreuvent; car l'ame, qui n'est creée que pour retourner à son souverain bien, ne faict, tant qu'elle est dedans ce corps, que desirer d'y parvenir. Mais, à cause que les sens, par lesquelz elle en peut avoir nouvelles, sont obscurs et charnelz par le peché du premier pere, ne luy peuvent monstrer que les choses visibles plus approchantes de la parfection, après quoy l'ame court, cuydans trouver, en une beaulté exterieure, en une grace visible et aux vertuz moralles, la souveraine beaulté, grace et vertu. Mais, quant elle les a cherchez et experimentez, et elle n'y treuve poinct Celluy qu'elle ayme, elle passe oultre, ainsy que l'enfant, selon sa petitesse, ayme les poupines et autres petites choses, les plus belles que son oeil peult veoir, et estime richesses d'assembler des petites pierres; mais, en croissant, ayme les popines vives et amasse les biens necessaires pour la vie humaine. Mais, quant il congnoist, par plus grande experience, que es choses territoires n'y a perfection ne felicité, desire chercher le facteur et la source d'icelles. Toutesfois, si Dieu ne luy ouvre l'oeil de foy, seroit en danger de devenir, d'un ignorant, ung infidele philosophe; car foy seullement peult monstrer et faire recevoir le bien que l'homme charnel et animal ne peult entendre.—

"Those whom I call perfect lovers," replied Parlamente, "are those who seek in what they love some perfection, whether it be beauty, goodness or grace, those whose constant goal is virtue and whose hearts are so lofty and so pure that they would die rather than make their goal that which is low and condemned by honour and conscience. For the soul, which was created solely that it might return to its Sovereign Good, ceaselessly desires to achieve this end while it is still within the body. But the senses, by means of which the soul is able to have intelligence of its Sovereign Good, are dim and carnal because of the sins of our forefather Adam and consequently can reveal to the soul only those things which are visible and have some nearer approximation to perfection. The soul runs after these things, vainly thinking that in some external beauty, in some visible grace and in the moral virtues it will find the sovereign beauty, the sovereign grace and the sovereign virtue. But once the soul has searched out these things and tried and tested them, once it has failed to find in them Him whom it loves, it passes beyond. In the same way children, when they are small, like dolls and all manner of little things that are attractive to the eye and think that the pebbles they collect will make them rich; but then, as they grow up, the dolls they love are living people and the things they collect are the necessities of human life. [Then,] when they learn through experience that in earthly and [transitory] things there is neither perfection nor felicity, they desire to seek the source and maker of these things. Yet, if God does not open the eyes of faith, they will be in danger of leaving ignorance behind only to become infidel philosophers. For only faith can reveal and make the soul receive that Good which carnal and animal man cannot understand." [Pp. 151–52; p. 229]

Surely the slippage here from Sovereign Good to our forefather Adam is no accident. Through Parlamente, Marguerite means to show how antique philosophy from the humanists—how the whole culture of the Renaissance—is imbued with Christianity, and incomplete without it. And in a sense, despite the tales of lust and vice that follow, *L'Heptaméron* also keeps constantly before us—and not just before the *devisants* with their morning Scripture and Mass and their evening prayers—the meaning of what is sacred: in tales 27 and 28, 38 and 40, 49, 57, 63, 64, 67, and 70, the last tale (told, fittingly, by Oisille herself) ending with the aggrieved duke of Burgundy withdrawing into the religious life at the very abbey where his wife and her two lovers lie buried. Scripture too becomes irrevocable and irreversible authority: in references to John (tale 19), to the Purification of the Virgin (tale 23), to the Psalmist (following tale 30), to John (following tale 36), to James (following tale 48), to Paul (following tales 55, 57, and 67), to name only a few. It is such passages as these that Parlamente draws together when she comments elsewhere that she believes those words that conform to the Word of God ("conforme à celle de Dieu," p. 304; p. 400).

On the Septiesme Journée Oisille senses, too, that the company is reaching a forceful conclusion to its debates and changes texts once more, this time to another confined group of persons, Christ's disciples awaiting him in the Upper Room: the glorious story of Pentecost that opens the Acts of the Apostles. And, following the tale of a man and woman of exemplary virtue (63), she speaks in an oration that is the companion piece to the one just cited from Parlamente:

"Ce n'est poinct de miracle, dist Oisille, car où le cueur s'adonne, il n'est rien impossible au corps.—Non aux corps, dist Hircan, qui sont desjà angelisez." Oisille luy respondit: "Je n'entens poinct seullement parler des ceulx qui sont par la grace de Dieu tout transmuez en luy, mais des plus grossiers esperitz que l'on voye ça-bas entre les hommes. Et, si vous y prenez garde, vous trouverez ceulx qui ont mys leur cueur et affection à chercher la perfection des sciences, non seulement avoir oblyé la volupté de la chair, mais les choses les plus necessaires, comme la boire et le manger; car, tant que l'ame est par affection dedans son corps, la chair demeure comme insensible; et de là vient que ceulx qui ayment femmes belles, honnestes et vertueuses, ont tel contentement à les veoir et à les oyr parler; et ont l'esperit si contant, que la chair est appaisée de tous ses desirs. Et ceulx qui ne peuvent experimenter ce contentement sont les charnelz, qui, trop enveloppez de leur graisse, ne congnoissent s'ilz ont ame ou non. Mais, quant le corps est subgect à l'esperit, il est quasi insensible aux imperfections de la chair, tellement que leur forte opinion les peult randre insensibles.

"It is no miracle," said Oisille, "for when the heart is true, nothing is impossible to the body."

"For bodies already transformed into angels, maybe!" Hircan replied.

"I do not only mean the bodies of those who through God's grace have been transmuted into Him," she went on, "but also those bodies that belong even to the basest spirits we see here on earth among men. If you look closely at the matter, you will find that those who have given their heart and affections to the pursuit of the perfection of knowledge, have not only forgotten the pleasures of the flesh, but even the most basic needs, such as eating and drinking. For, as long as the soul is by affection within its body, the flesh remains as if it were insensible. Thus it is that those men who love beautiful, honorable and virtuous women find such contentment in seeing them and hearing them speak. Thus it is that their minds are so contented that the flesh finds peace and is rid of all desires. Those who cannot experience such contentment are men of carnal natures, who, being too much enveloped in their flesh, do not even know whether they have a soul or not. But when the body is subject to the spirit it is almost insensible to the imperfections of the flesh, so much so that the strong conviction of such people may render them insensible." [P. 382; p. 490]

Parlamente is prompted to respond in kind to this extraordinary synthesis of Platonic, Plotinian, Augustinian, and scriptural thought by both comment and story (63):

> —Par ce compte, dist Parlamente, mes dames, vous regarderez deux fois ce que vous vouldrez refuser, et ne vous fier au temps present, qu'il soit tousjours ung; parquoy, congnoissans sa mutation, donnerez ordre à l'advenir.

> "This, Ladies," began Parlamente, "is a tale that will teach you to think twice before you refuse something. It will teach you not to place trust in the present, hoping that things will remain the same for ever, [but] to recognize that the present is in constant change and to have thought for the future."

> [P. 383; p. 491]

Such summary statements sweep now into insignificance Nomerfide's stumbling attempt at a pallid Aristotelianism such as humanists might have first entertained—"trop d'amour trompe et luy et vous, car partout il y a le moien"; "Too much love could lead you both astray. There's a happy medium for everything" (p. 395; pp. 505–6)—and Oisille guarantees the greater weight of her opinion by following Parlamente's lead: She too tells a story that realizes her statements and her beliefs, turning precept into experience, truth into the world's business. She closes *L'Heptaméron* with the exemplary study of the duke of Burgundy at which we have already glanced, a long story full of compassion, love, sacrifice, and faith. And she follows the story with her own commentary, transporting her earlier compound of antique and Christian thought into the most moving—as it is the most Christian humanist, the most *Augustinian*— passage in all of Marguerite's fiction.

> "Voilà, mes dames, l'histoire que vous m'avez priée de vous recompter; que je congnois bien à voz oeilz n'avoir esté entendue sans compassion. Il me semble que vous debvez tirer exemple de cecy, pour vous garder de mectre vostre affection aux hommes, car, quelque honneste ou vertueuse qu'elle soyt, elle a tousjours à la fin quelque mauvays desboire. Et vous voiez que sainct Pol, encores aux gens mariez ne veult qu'ilz aient ceste grande amour ensemble. Car, d'autant que nostre cueur est affectionné à quelque chose terrienne, d'autant s'esloigne— il de l'affection celeste; et plus l'amour est honneste et vertueuse et plus difficille en est à rompre le lien, qui me faict vous prier, mes dames, de demander à Dieu son Sainct Esperit, par lequel vostre amour soyt tant enflambée en l'amour de Dieu, que vous n'aiez poinct de peyne, à la mort, de laisser ce que vous aymez trop en ce monde."

"That, Ladies, is the story you asked me to tell you. I can tell from the looks in your eyes that it hasn't left you unmoved. I think you should let it stand as an example to you not to fix your affection on men, for, however pure and virtuous your affection may be, it will always lead to some disastrous conclusion. You will remember that Saint Paul preferred love such as this not to exist even between husband and wife. For, the more one fixes one's affection on earthly things, the further one is from heavenly affection. And the more one's love is virtuous and noble, the more difficult it is to break the bond. And so, Ladies, I beg you to pray to God [at all times] to grant you His Holy Spirit, that your hearts may be so inflamed with love of Him that at the hour of your death you will be spared the suffering that comes from loving too dearly things that must be left behind on earth." [P. 418; p. 532]

Even Hircan protests only slightly, thus incorporating men into Oisille's grand statement. At the end, "la compaignie se leva, et allerent oyr vespres, n'oublians en leurs bonnes prieres les ames des vraiz amans, pour lesquelz les religieux, de leur bonne volunté, dirent un *de Profundis*"; "the whole company rose, and went to hear vespers. In their prayers they did not forget to pray for the souls of the true lovers, and the monks agreed of their own free will to say a *De profundis* for them" (p. 420; p. 534).

But the repose, the *settledness,* of this conclusion comes at an undisclosed price. Shortly after the controversia that follows tale 69—the one preceding Oisille's final story—Nomerfide reveals at last what Parlamente and others seem to have suspected, that she is Hircan's mistress. In fact, it is a verbal debate between Parlamente and Hircan that forces this confession. What Oisille does in the final story, then, is to suggest by means of the duke of Burgundy a way for Hircan to transform himself and, in her final speech, a way for Parlamente to resign herself to the situation. This becomes significantly more important (and poignant) if we note with most who have studied *L'Heptaméron* that the names are thinly disguised anagrams of authentic persons of Marguerite's acquaintance and that Parlamente and Hircan are her own fictional explorations of herself and her relationship with Henri de Navarre. Yet, to hint at their actuality while refusing to guarantee historicity leaves us suspended between fact and fiction, just as the characters at the close of *L'Heptaméron* are suspended between their own earthly follies and confessions and the Reformist and even Catholic rituals they have come to practice and even advocate. No matter how hard we search *L'Heptaméron* for resolutions to these problems, it will not yield them. In fact, it only confirms such equivocation, much like the humanist fictions of Erasmus and Castiglione. Some tales are set with geographical detail and accuracy and with historical time, yet M. Ritte, according to A. J. Krailsheimer,

> living in the shadow of the Pyrenees, has exposed in detail the errors of his predecessors for whom topography apparently means toponymy, with no regard for the lie of the land. He proves quite conclusively that neither Marguerite nor anyone else could have made the journeys described, and M. Febvre's perfect illusion does not survive a course in basic map-making. As for the encounters with brigands, bears and things that go bump in the night, everyone has recognized this to be the purest fantasy. The adventure (but not necessarily the discussion) in the Prologue is thus an additional story, with no claim to veracity.[21]

So it is with nearly everything in *L'Heptaméron:* What seems true is often just a matter of appearance; yet what merely appears true to the characters—both those in the tales and those telling them—has the ring of fact. The same equivocation is true of the presentation of people and places central or incidental to the embedded narratives. P. A. Chilton has commented that

> Just as in the Prologue the storytellers visit a "good" and a "bad" monastery, so the monastic institutions portrayed in the stories are double-edged. On the one hand there is sexual aggression and abasement; friars attack women, intrude into the family, disrupt the social order. On the other hand, there is sexual suppression and sublimation; frustrated lovers leave society in order not to transgress its rules, entering the inner mystical world in order to resolve their conflicts with such rules. Thus the obverse of the image of the monk as rapist is the image of the secular person ravished by divine love.[22]

Just as the boundary between the tales told and the tale of the tellers is continually blurred, so is the boundary between the lives in *L'Heptaméron* and our own. In a humanist fiction of boxes within boxes that Erasmus could not help but admire, historic (authentic) persons are turned into fictional characters (by disguised names, by superlative descriptions, by exemplary plots and attitudes) and, as fictional characters, teach real people (the "people" listening in the meadow; the actual, living readers then and now) about moments and actions in "history." The distinctions are impossibly, and so forever, confounded. But that of course is the point. As Tetel notes, for Marguerite de Navarre (and so she would mean it too for us), "this world" in which she lived and we live is forever "in flux between seeming and being" (*Marguerite's "Heptameron,"* p. 64).

We can perhaps understand Marguerite's accomplishment more precisely if we glance at two similar works that appeared just before and just after hers. *Ragionamento de la Nanna et de la Antonia fatto a Rome sette una ficia: composto dal divino Aretino per suo capricio a corretio de i tre stati delle donne (Conversation of Nanna and Antonia carried on at Rome under a fig-tree; composed by the divine Aretino as a whim, for the improvement of the three states of women)* describes a world that, in the words of Antonia, demonstrates that everything is tinged with deceit. The *Ragionamento* is a series of three *converzatione* in reply to Nanna asking Antonia where she should send her sixteen-year-old daughter Pippa. With a cynicism matching that of Hircan and Saffredent, Antonia urges the life of a courtesan. Part 1 tells the story of Nanna, who as young girl joined a convent where from the first moment she saw sin (gluttony) and from the first night was herself violated; part 2 is a series of fabliaux on married women who are unhappy or dissatisfied with their husbands and the affairs they engage in. Part 3 is a cony-catching book of scams by courtesans used to cheat customers (or to attract them). Aretino's work is therefore another set of tales told by characters in an authentic setting as exemplary and directive. But, if it is humanist in form and ostensible purpose, it is surely antihumanist in content, emphasis, and values.

Vies des dames galantes by l'abbé de Brantôme is a direct imitation of *L'Hep-taméron*. It too is divided into seven parts, each with a series of stories loosely linked, dialectical with one another at times, and each claiming veracity. Brantôme, like Marguerite, mixes past and present, dissolving time as a force; he uses authentic settings; and he even borrows some plots from *L'Heptaméron* (stories 3, 16, 26, 32, 49). But the titles given to the seven sections by a recent translator reveal how Brantôme debases his original:

First Essay. On ladies who make love and their cuckold husbands.

Second Essay. Essay on the question as to what gives most satisfaction in love-making, the sense of touch, the sense of sight, or speech.

Third Essay. Another essay, on the beauty of a lovely leg and the virtue there is in it.

Fourth Essay. An essay on Married Women, Widows and Girls to ascertain which class of them is hotter in love than the others.

Fifth Essay. An essay on the love-making of some elderly women and on how some of them are more given to love-making than others, and how this can be seen from several examples, without naming or disgracing anybody.

Sixth Essay. Essay on its not being seemly to speak badly of estimable ladies although they do have love affairs and on the great trouble that slandering them about their conduct has caused.

Seventh Essay. An essay on lovely estimable ladies liking brave men and brave men liking courageous ladies.[23]

Just as the view here is crude and one-dimensional, corrupting the eloquence Brantôme pretends to imitate, so he finds it only natural, in the course of the First Essay, even to debase Saint Augustine.

Beside such works as these, but even beside the *Encomium Moriae* and *Il Libro del Cortegiano*, *L'Heptaméron* of Marguerite de Navarre shimmers with its manifold tales, its multivalent perspectives, and its equivocations and ambiguities as it places before us the transient nature of our own lives. If *L'Heptaméron* finally defies classification, it is because Marguerite is certain that the clearest vantage point from which to see life's mundane realities as well as its deeper mysteries is beyond what Sir Philip Sidney calls, in his *Defence,* our clayey beings. *L'Heptaméron* must have circulated in manuscript through much of Marguerite's later years, at least in parts, but it was not published until after her death. Subsequent to that, fragments of an eighth book have been discovered in which Oisille returns to John for her morning Scriptures, Parlamente chooses to tell a story of a foolish saddler, and—less representative yet—Dagoucin relates a scurrilous tale in which, during the course of Extreme Unction and while laying out a corpse, a monk gets a nun with child. Although both tales seem unlikely and in any case are unmoored, they reinforce the overarching metaphor for *L'Heptaméron,* the bridge which, when repaired, will lead all the *devisants* from their temporary isolation back into the real world. When *L'Heptaméron* ends, the bridge is still unfinished. All ten storytellers thus remain in suspension, telling the same stories over and over, engaging in the same debates about them. Even the fragment ends in midthought, about to begin another tale. Nomerfide takes over from Dagoucin and says, "Aussy ay-je ung compte tout prest, . . . digne de suyvre le vostre, car je parle de religieux et de mort. Or, escoutez le bien, s'il vous plaist"; "Well, I have a story ready to tell you, and it's a very appropriate one after the one you've told. It's about death, and it's about a monk. So please all listen carefully" (p. 428; p. 543)—and then stops. We are left, breathless, waiting, expecting. But that is as it should be: With Marguerite de Navarre, no final closure is possible in this world, and although our own meaning, our own sense of what she has been telling us, will forever rest separately with each of us, what she has been telling us all along in this superbly crafted humanist fiction is that we too are at best in midprocess. From God's eyes, and Augustine's, and Plato's and Plotinus's, we are only in the act of becoming. "Sa religion, le quiétisme?" her distinguished editor Saulnier once wrote; "Tout le contraire. L'inquiétisme, si l'on veut."[24]

FIVE

Abstracteur de Quinte Essence and *Docteur en Médecine:*

Rabelais's Fiction of *Summa Humanistica*

and the Poetics of Copia

FOLLY AND WISDOM, STYLE
AND SUBSTANCE, DESPAIR
AND HOPE ALTERNATE IN THE HU-
MANIST WORKS OF ERASMUS, CAS-
TIGLIONE, AND MARGUERITE DE NAVARRE;
WITH FRANÇOIS RABELAIS THE SAME POWER-
ful humanist concerns are buried in a copious language generated by an un-
quenchable love of learning. "Rabelais plays with words as children do with
pebbles," Anatole France writes of his Renaissance predecessor; "He piles them
up into heaps."[1] Rabelais's irresistible taste for humanist copia is a direct
consequence of enormous energies, of fiercely unlimited thought, and of un-
bounded vitality that move him and his gigantic singular novel far beyond the
deliberately more concentrated and focused Lucian poetics of Erasmus, or the
Ciceronian poetics of Castiglione, to something akin to Marguerite's Plotinian
interests in being and becoming. Unlike Marguerite, however, Rabelais is a
man of many diverse parts and of a complicating rather than a unifying vision.
He is a textual scholar (like Erasmus) who translated Book 2 of Herodotus's
fabulous *Historia,* prepared an edition of Giovanni Manardi's detailed Latin
letters on medicine (for which he composed a Latin preface), and edited his own
volume of Hippocrates' scientific *Aphorisms,* based on his medical lectures at
Montpellier; yet he also stoutly remains a novelist who, like his three Continental predecessors, keeps confronting what Mary E. Raglund calls "an uncertain and cryptic universe."[2] The bibliographer's precision and the mystic's
propensity for the ineffable are both encompassed in the sweep of his prose
fiction. Both are exposed and central to his characteristically ebullient passages,
with their stacks of words and accretive phrases that always hover near repeti-

tion but continue to drive us forward while apparently going nowhere. Thus, throughout the many volumes of the untitled work we call *Gargantua and Pantagruel*, it is not only the humanists' love of antique thought but (primarily) the humanists' love of language that remains the center of its gravity—center of both its weight and its seriousness. In Rabelais, language becomes, in the powerful smithy of this *maître ès langues*, the match for his urgent need to create, explore, and test. His language, writes Alice Fiola Berry, is

> a matter much like clay to be pulled and stretched and twisted at will into new and unknown forms. . . . Their sounds are savored, their senses are scrambled, and when the available stock of words runs out, Rabelais, like Panurge, unhesitatingly creates new ones—even whole new languages if it suits him. Why did Panurge use thirteen languages instead of answering directly and straightaway in French? Because it is the principle of his creativity that thirteen is better than one; that the multiple is preferable to the simple; that verbal *gaspillage* is infinitely more fun than verbal *économie*.[3]

Like Erasmus's Folly and Castiglione's Gaspare, nearly all of Rabelais's characters are inveterate talkers and, more open than the characters of *L'Heptaméron*, incurably loquacious about *themselves*. Together they compose the whole, apparently formless sprawl of *Gargantua and Pantagruel* with their various speeches and grammatical gambols, reveal Rabelais's deep-seated *ivresse lexicographique*, his lexicographical intoxication, and make his fiction of copia a polyglot thesaurus of a unique—and miraculous—kind. Yet, with Rabelais as with those before him, the humanist compulsion to exploit language coupled with the humanist's need to prove its viability amid gnawing doubts about its vulnerability makes the exuberant wordplay in Rabelais a matter of *critical gravity*, too.

There are other ways, of course, in which Rabelais demonstrates his fundamental allegiance to humanism. For him as for Erasmus and Castiglione, life is a matter of ever-receding horizons.[4] *Gargantua* (our present Book 1) conspicuously digs into the past in order to comprehend the present. It opens with the discovery of a bronze tomb containing a little, moldy book, which contains the genealogy of Gargantua—Rabelais's fiction is a book that begins with a book and so becomes the continuation of that antique relic—and closes with a bronze plate unearthed at the digging of the foundations for the Abbey of Thélème. In both instances, these ancient texts—the first secular, the last sacred—are awarded doctrinal significance. Yet the first is a list of *fanfreluches antidotées*, corrective conundrums that are initially chewed away by vermin, the other an enigmatic riddle. Such bewildering signals of the past force speculation, yet their meanings must establish interpretations that will pass into an indefinite future. The same is true of the tales, parables, and orations in the later books of *Gargantua and Pantagruel*. The last of these, *Le Cinquième Livre*, closes with a similarly oracular but explained prophecy from the Dive Bouteille, the Divine Bottle of Bacbuc, insuring the triangulation we have seen to be characteristic of humanist poetics in which two or more meanings of crucial texts must be resolved by the reader. It is this humanist intermingling of past and present that allows Rabelais to locate his contemporary "histoire . . . veridicque" (2.28) in assorted quotations, imitations, and parodies of humanist commonplace books and rhetorical formularies and that causes him to document and gloss contemporary biographies by employing a vast assemblage of humanist authorities including Plato, Aristotle, Lucian, Plutarch, Pliny, Aulus Gellius, and Cicero. Rabelais's own style, in fact, in such patently serious passages as the prologue to *Gargantua*, Gargantua's letter to his son in *Pantagruel*, and Gargantua's speech on marriage in *Le Tiers Livre*, are carefully crafted in an elevated Ciceronian style at times resembling speeches in Castiglione.

This humanist learning, which shapes so much of Rabelais's fiction, is the mature fruit of a lifetime devoted to works of classical Greece and Rome. As a young student at the Franciscan monastery of Fontenay-le-Comte, he applied to learn Greek with his friend Pierre Lamy until, sometime around 1524, the Church confiscated his books, causing him to leave the order and to join the Benedictines to pursue his own studies. Later he joined the circle of scholars that included Tiraqueau and Bouchard, carried on a correspondence with Budé, and purchased his own copies of Ficino's Plato and the *Opuscula* of Dionysius the Areopagite. His favorite author of all was Erasmus. "Patrem te dixi," he writes this ideal mentor from Rotterdam in November 1532,

matrem etiam dicerem, si per indulgentiam mihi id tuam liceret. . . . quidquid sum et valeo, tibi id uni acceptum. . . . Salve itaque etiam arque, Pater amantissime, pater decusque patriae, litterarum adsertor αχεξσαχις veritatis propugnator invictissime.

I have called you father, I would even call you mother if I were allowed to by your indulgence. . . . Whatever I am and am worth, I have received from you alone. . . . Therefore I hail you again and again, most loving father, father and ornament of the fatherland, savior of letters who protects them from evil, invincible champion of the truth.[5]

The sentiment echoes a surviving letter of 1521 to Budé in which he comments on the singular mastery of Greek and Latin that Budé's correspondence displays; "Epistula tua . . . utriusque linguae peritiam singularem redolens."⁶ To his own work in Greek, Latin, and even a smattering of Hebrew, Rabelais added extensive knowledge in Roman law unhampered by medieval commentary, the classical medicine of Hippocrates and Galen coupled with practical lessons in medicine and surgery, military art and the art of navigation, education, architecture, sports, dress, and mores.⁷ His ranging humanism resulted, says Balzac, in "The greatest mind in modern humanity, the man who sums up Pythagoras, Hippocrates, Aristotle, and Dante."⁸ In this last, he also embraces many interests of Marguerite's more insistently Christian humanism.

And it is in just this context of such broad and deep humanist learning that we can now best gauge the impulses that propel the five books of Rabelais into a rainbow of rhetorical effects. Like the preceding works of humanist fiction, "The whole of Rabelais's book is concerned with education," A. J. Krailsheimer writes. "The first two books deal with the initial studies of their heroes, and the latter two with what one might call the post-graduate application of these studies."⁹ The last of the five, only partially by Rabelais as near as we can now tell, furthers this application. Thus *Pantagruel*, our Book 2 but the first volume Rabelais wrote, deals largely with Erasmian copia, the grammatical practice that served as a foundation of humanist culture. Book 1, *Gargantua*, the second book to be written, attempts to control the verbal inebriety of Gargantua by realizing the forms and limitations of rhetoric and logic, completing the review of the trivium; *Le Tiers Livre*—pointedly dedicated to Marguerite de Navarre—anatomizes this curriculum in a symposium on marriage and cuckoldry that employs the lessons of grammar to examine the uses and shortcomings of rhetoric and logic; and the adventures of *Le Quart Livre* further subject all these lessons to the Grand Tour, which completes the education of Pantagruel (but, noticeably, not of Panurge). *Le Cinquième Livre*, for which Rabelais may have written the opening and closing chapters, carries forward the humanists' concern with the texts and meanings of Holy Scripture as the final end of a Christian humanist education. In sum, Rabelais's great fictive act of *bouffonnerie* is extravagant wordplay along the lines of study laid down by Erasmus; but it is also, at the same time, as deeply serious as Castiglione's *Il Cortegiano* and as religious and mystical in its final import as Marguerite's *Heptaméron*. In addition, Rabelais supplies humanist fiction with the exactitude of the doctor of medicine (with which he signed, in his own name, Books 3 and 4) and with the mysterious and ineffable truths that lie just beyond that discipline as his anagrammatic pseudonym, Alcofribas Nasier, indicates in Books 1 and 2 when he also identifies himself as "abstractor of the quintessence." As a single work, these ranging, comprehensive adventures of Gargantua and Pantagruel stand, then, as Rabelais's consciously designed *summa humanistica*.

When it first appeared on the Lyons bookstalls in 1532, Rabelais's initial work of humanist fiction, *Pantagruel*, subtitled *Les horribles et espouenta bles faictz et prouesses du tresrenomme Pantagruel, Roy des Dipsode filz du grand geant Gargantua* (*The Horrible and Frightful Acts and Prowesses of the Very Renowned Pantagruel, King of the Dipsodes, Son of the Giant Gargantua*), must have looked considerably different, must have seemed little more than a parodic continuation of an anonymous chapbook called *Les grandes et inestimables Chronicques: du grant et enorme geant Gargantua* (also 1532?) about two giants, Gargantua and Grand-gosier, created by Merlin to defend King Arthur. Some episodes, such as the theft of the bells from Notre Dame in Paris, are even taken directly from that book. But from the outset, *Pantagruel* is more complicated because, like *Encomium Moriae*, *Il Libro del Cortegiano*, and *L'Heptaméron*, it is grounded in equivocation.

Pantagruel opens with his birth. It causes his mother's death, yet it is richly comic, tellingly symbolic, and—ultimately—sophistic.

> Quand Pantagruel fut né, qui fut bien esbahy et perplex? Ce fut Gargantua son pere. Car, voyant d'un cousté sa femme Badebec morte, et de l'aultre son fils Pantagruel né tant beau et grand, ne sçavoit que dire ny que faire, et le doubte que troubloit son entendement estoit assavoir s'il devoit plorer pour le dueil de sa femme, ou rire pour la joye de son fils. D'un costé et d'autre il avoit argumens sophisticques qui le suffocquoyent, car il les faisoit très bien *in modo et figura*, mais il ne les povoit souldre, et par ce moyen, demouroit empestre comme la souriz empeigée ou un milan prins au lasset.

> When Pantagruel was born no one could have been more astonished and per-plexed than his father Gargantua. For, seeing on the one side his wife Badebec newly dead, and on the other his son Pantagruel newly born, and so big and handsome, he did not know what to say or do. His mind was troubled with the doubt whether he ought to weep in mourning for his wife, or laugh out of delight at his son. On either side he found sophistical arguments which took his breath away. For he framed them very well *in modo et figura*, but he could not resolve them. And consequently he remained trapped, like a mouse caught in pitch, or a kite taken in a noose.[10]

The irresolution of Gargantua's dilemma, exacerbated by numerous *argumens sophisticques* (2.3), adumbrates the incoherent disputation between the two lords Baisecul and Humevesne (2.10–13), the oration of a learned Limosin student whose multivalent language combines macaronic Latin and bastardized French (2.6), and the library of Sainct Victor where a huge collection of learned treatises seem to be all jokes and nonsense (2.7). This sequence reaches its climax in Pantagruel's meeting with Panurge whose thirteen languages—some real, some apparently made up on the spot—show us how copia says many things on a single theme while declaring a single idea in various ways (2.9). Rabelais's first book is further complicated and compromised by placing between the library of Sainct Victor and the multiple replies of Panurge the single-minded and highly serious letter of Gargantua to his son. This humanist epistle, at first a respectable testimonial to the values of a humanist education (2.8), then an apparent critique of it, sums the entire book. "Voluntiers me delecte à lire les *Moraulx* de Plutarche, les beaulx *Dialogues* de Platon, les *Monumens* de Pausanias, et *Antiquitez* de Atheneus"; *"I find great delight in reading the* Morals *of* Plutarch, *Plato's magnificent* Dialogues, *the* Monuments *of* Pausanius, *and the* Antiquities *of Athenaeus,"* Gargantua writes, but he adds that these, along with the Talmudists and Cabalists and the Old and New Testaments of the Holy Scriptures in the original Hebrew and Greek, lead to "un abysme de science"; *"a veritable abyss of knowledge."* His pregnant but puzzling conclusion looks forward to the learned Epistemon (Knowledge) whose journey to the underworld teaches Pantagruel lessons that undercut both the heroism of his own classical texts and the Christian epistemology of Hell (2.30). All of these divisions of belief and revelation stem from the divided thesis of the book itself: It is the story of a devil in the form of a saint's life. The giant Pantagruel is named for the legendary (but tiny) sea-devil who personifies Thirst and whose sole function is to throw salt into the mouths of drunkards, despite the factitious etymology Alcofribas gives us (2.2); but the life of this lazy and conniving thief whose natural ally is the inventive prankster Panurge—he of the coat of many pockets—is told with spiritual overtones, beginning with a miraculous birth (2.2) and ending with both the resurrection of Epistemon through the healing powers of Panurge (2.30) and the visions of other worlds supplied by the revelations of Epistemon after his visit to Limbo (2.30) and by Alcofribas in Pantagruel's mouth (2.32).

We should not know what to make of such a cacophonous and splintered series of events were Rabelais's focus not steadily on Pantagruel's education: his childhood games and lessons, his Grand Tour through the universities of France and the great city of Paris, his companionship with Panurge, and the final tests of his knowledge, skills, and mercy in the war between the Dipsodes and the Amaurots, the battles with the giants and their captain Loup Garcia (2.28–29). The author makes clear in his prologue, moreover, that Pantagruel's learning is to be matched by our own.

> Et a la mienne volunté que chascun laissast sa propre besoigne, ne se souciast do son mestier et mist ses affaires propres en oubly, pour y vacquer entierement sans que son esperit feust de ailleurs distraict n'y empesché; jusques à ce que l'on les tint par cueur, affin que, si d'adventure l'art de l'imprimerie cessoit, ou en cas que tous livres perissent, on temps advenir un chascun les peust bien au net enseigner à ses enfans, et à ses successeurs et survivens bailler comme de main en main, ainsy que une religieuse Caballe; car il y a plus de fruict que par adventure ne pensent un tas de gros tolvassiers tou croustelevez, qui entendent beaucoup moins en ces petites joyeusetes que ne faict Raclet en l'*Institute*.

> *So far as I am concerned, I would have every man put aside his proper business, take no care for his trade, and forget his own affairs, in order to devote himself entirely to this book. I would have him allow no distraction or hindrance from elsewhere to trouble his mind, until he knows it by heart; so that if the art of printing happened to die out, or all books should come to perish, everyone should be able, in time to come, to teach it thoroughly to his children, and to transmit it to his successors and survivors, as if from hand to hand, like some religious Cabala. For there is more profit in it than may be imagined by a rabble of scabby swaggerers, who understand far less of these jolly little productions than Raclet does of the* Institutes. [1.215–16; p. 167]

The litany of chapter titles—"Comme. . . ," "Comme. . . ," "Comme. . . ."—further demonstrates this interest in teaching.

Even so, the lessons are negative ones; the humanist world turned upside down provides us with models *not* to imitate. That is the singularly grand joke behind Rabelais's first book. The hero's first lesson as a baby results in his attempt to eat the whole cow whose teats alone were to provide his sustenance (2.4), and Panurge's first instructions for him detail the building of walls around the city of Paris by using the private parts of women (2.15)! As he grows older, Pantagruel's youthful deeds either interrupt his studies—as when he provides the Upright Stone to his teachers at Poitiers so as to give them means of recreation from their studies (2.5)—or parody the places and possibilities of higher education, as in the initial portion of his Grand Tour to Bordeaux, Toulouse, and Montpellier, where he learns to play games, draw swords, and drink wines. Because the passions of the men Pantagruel meets in the course of his education have misconstrued and corrupted the sources of humanism, the lessons and forms they teach him run riot; and we see this, reflected wherever we turn, in Rabelais's rampant copia of etymologies, analogies, references, catalogues, non sequiturs, letters, declamations, disputations, and reportage that together constitute the bulk of *Pantagruel*.

These rapid word formations lead to a deliberately jumbled copia of ideas, as in the treatment of Pantagruel's birth: He is born, we are told, at a time of cosmological and astrological confusion, nature and science at one in their massive disorientation. This intoxication of the heavens effects a drunken state in men.

En icelle les Kalendes feurent trouvées par les breviaires des Grecz. Le moys de mars faillit en Karesme, et fut la my oust en may. On moys de octobre, ce me semble, ou bien de septembre (affin que je ne erre, car de cela me veulx je curieusement guarder) fut la sepmaine tant renommée par les annales, qu'on nomme la sepmaine des troys jeudis: car il y en eut troys, à cause des irreguliers bissextes, que le soleil bruncha quelque peu, comme *debitoribus,* à gauche, et la lune varia de son cours plus de cinq toyzes, et feut manifestement veu le movement de trepidation on firmament dict *aplane,* tellement que la Pleiade moyene laissant ses compaignons, declina vers l'Equinoctial, et l'estoille nomme l'Espy laissa la Vierge, se retirant vers la Balance, qui sont cas bien espoventables et matieres tant dures et difficiles que les Astrologues ne y peuvent mordre; aussy auroient ils les dens bien longues s'ilz povoient toucher jusques la!

Faictes vostre compte que le monde voluntiers mangeoit desdictes mesles, car elles estoient belles à l'oeil et delicieuses au goust; mais tout ainsi comme Noe, le sainct homme (auquel tant sommes obligez et tenuz de ce qu'il nous planta la vine, dont nous vient celle nectaricque, delicieuse, precieuse, celeste, joyeuse et deificque liqueur qu'on nomme le piot) fut trompé en le beuvant, car il ignoroit la grande vertu et puissance d'icelluy, semblablement les hommes et femmes de celluy temps mangeoyent en grand plaisir de ce beau et gors fruict.

In that year the Kalends were fixed by the Greek date-books, the month of March was outside Lent, and mid-August fell in May. In the month of October, I believe, or perhaps in September—if I am not mistaken, and I want to take particular care not to be—came the week so famous in our annals, that is called the Week of Three Thursdays. For it had three of them on account of the irregular bissextiles, since the sun strayed a little to the left *as we forgive our debtors,* and the moon veered more than ten feet from her course, and the movement of trepidation in the firmament, which is called Aplanes, was clearly observed. For the middle Pleiad left her companions and declined towards the Equinoctial, and the star called Spica left the constellation of the Virgin and moved away towards the Scales; which are very alarming happenings, and so hard and difficult that the astrologers cannot get their teeth into them. Their teeth would have been pretty long, indeed, if they could have reached as far as that! Account it a fact that everybody gladly ate those medlars, for they were pleasant to the eyes and a delight to the taste. But just as Noah, the holy man to whom we are so much obliged and indebted for his having planted us the vine, from which comes that ambrosial, delicious, precious, celestial, joyous, and deific liquor which is called *drink,* made a mistake in drinking it, since he did not know its great virtue and power, so the men and women of that time ate this fine, big fruit with great delight. [1.221−22; pp. 171−72]

Noah's agricultural gift eventually signifies a world of inebriation. Such world-wide chaos, however, is set beside the orderly generation of *begats* which, drawn from its Senecan original in Holy Scripture rather than from astrological treatises and secular prognostications, joins Noah with Nimrod, Atlas, Goliath, Polyphemus, Alexander the Great, Sisyphus, Hercules, Grandgousier, Gargantua, and Pantagruel (2.1): Rabelais's first outrageous catalogue is an initial attempt to find a pattern in events. But the equivocating set of perspectives he applies—in embryonic form the fluid authorial viewpoint he will develop in later books—causes not a season of order but a season of disputations, thirst acknowledged in a dry year. Pantagruel's formal lessons, then, have no effect except in the need for words and for the knowledge they ought to advance. Nor is a solution to be found in the vast catalogue of books in the Abbey of Sainct Victor near Paris, for the titles of these books are mostly make-believe, parodying the classical and sacred by placing them alongside the nonsensical.

Behind this wordplay regarding humanist education are various *loci classici* on the proper and improper use of language. There is, for example, a central passage from Quintilian's *Institutio 2.*

Sequitur quaestio, an utilis rhetorice. Nam quidam vehementer in eam invehi solent, et, quod sit indignissimum, in accusationem orationis utuntur orandi viribus: eloquentiam esse, quae poenis eripiat scelestos, cuius fraude damnentur interim boni, consilia ducantur in peius, nec seditiones modo turbaeque populares sed bella etiam inexpiabilia excitentur; cuius denique tum maximus sit usus, cum pro falsis contra veritatem valet. . . . Equidem nec urbium conditores reor aliter effecturos fuisse ut vaga illa multitudo coiret in populos, nisi docta voce commota; nec legum repertores sine summa vi orandi consecutos, ut se ipsi homines ad servitutem iuris astringerent. Quin ipsa vitae praecepta, etiamsi natura sunt honesta, plus tamen ad formandas mentes valent, quotiens pulchritudinem rerum claritas orationis illuminat. Quare, etiamsi in utramque partem valent arma facundiae, non est tamen aequum id haberi malum, quo bene uti licet.

There follows the question as to whether rhetoric is useful. Some are in the habit of denouncing it most violently and of shamelessly employing the powers of oratory to accuse oratory itself. "It is eloquence," they say "that snatches criminals from the penalties of the law, eloquence that from time to time secures the condemnation of the innocent and leads deliberation astray, eloquence that stirs up not merely sedition and popular tumult, but wars beyond all expiation, and that is most effective when it makes falsehood prevail over the truth." . . . Never in my opinion would the founders of cities have induced their unsettled multitudes to form communities had they not moved them by the magic of their eloquence: never without the highest gifts of oratory would the great legislators have constrained mankind to submit themselves to the yoke of law. Nay, even the principles which should guide our life, however fair they may be by nature, yet have greater power to mould the mind to virtue, when the beauty of things is illumined by the splendour of eloquence. Wherefore, although the weapons of oratory may be used either for good or ill, it is unfair to regard that as an evil which can be employed for good. [16.1–10][11]

This passage, a crucial text behind Book 1, is the sort that teaches Pantagruel the deceptiveness of words as well as their value and causes him, at important times, to pass beyond language altogether. Thus it is that Pantagruel learns to love Panurge instinctively, *before* that prankster dishes up a banquet of real and fictitious languages (2.9); indeed, his *condition*—

un homme beau de stature et elegant en tous lineamens du corps, mais pitoyablement navré en divers lieux, et tant mal en ordre qu'il sembloit estre eschappé es chiens, ou mieulx resembloit un cueilleur de pommes du pais du Perche

a man of handsome build, elegant in all his features, but pitifully wounded in various places, and in so sorry a state that he looked as if he had escaped from the dogs, or to be more accurate, like some apple-picker from the Perche country [1.263; p. 196]

—communicates an essential meaning that the *words* only *obscure*. What Pantagruel learns from this encounter, Panurge uses in debate with Thaumaste—conceivably a joking reference to Thomas More [12]—when he substitutes gestures for words (2.18). But this analysis of the use and misuse of language, as well as the use of the metalanguage of gesture and act, does not escape Rabelais's searching parody either. The grammatical practices that the exempla of copia nearly exhaust find their countermovement in parodic acts of creativity where Panurge's necromantic drug used to attract dogs only converts the Parisian lady to an object for urine and beshitting (2.22), and Pantagruel's victory over the giants and Dipsodes is accomplished only by drowning them in his urine (2.28). One alternative is no better, but perhaps no worse, than the other.

The clue to a workable grammar in so duplicitous and nefarious a world comes at last for Rabelais in Quintilian's understanding of the *good* orator. Reliable grammar appears in *Pantagruel* to depend on the speaker's intention. Gargantua's very human letter advocating a humanist curriculum that sharply contradicts the pranks and judgments of the wayward Pantagruel remains a set of principles that stoutly resists denial by the adventures surrounding them (2.8). "Often called a humanist manifesto," Krailsheimer sums,

> this letter is a stirring hymn to the New Learning based on the recently restored Classical tongues, and championed by Rabelais's heroes Erasmus and Budé. This embraced not only the whole of the antique wisdom enshrined in Greek and Latin authors, but led directly to study of the Bible in the original, for which Hebrew and Syriac are also to be mastered. The style and content of this letter (some half dozen pages long) are of such sustained solemnity that they create the most striking impression. . . . While all the other chapters show Pantagruel as a giant, albeit uttering sentiments of notable sagacity from time to time, this one alone is on a purely human scale, and it is serious. [13]

Gargantua's desires for his son are put into action, moreover, in 2.14 when Panurge tells of his miraculous escape from the Turks, in which reason and ingenuity play as great a part as cunning and instinct in bringing about a kind of rough justice; by the end of *Pantagruel* and its lessons of the Grand Tour, Panurge will even pass beyond justice to mercy in his salvation of Pantagruel's tutor Epistemon (2.30). This final, unexpected union of word and act, learning (of medicine) and life (of battle), is not much enlightenment in the dark world of Pantagruel where the sun flies off course and a week can have three Thursdays. Through such Gothic darkness as that represented by the shelves of useless learning at the Abbey of Sainct Victor, it is the merest glimmer of a humanist dawn. But digging beneath the parodies and the jokes, the exuberant nonsense that dances across the exhilarating surfaces of Rabelais's inventive (and sometimes intractable) style, we find the serious human needs that give rise to humanist education. *Pantagruel,* for all its incoherence and irresistible clowning, always stands ready as a potentially serious prolegomenon, seriously setting the stage for the *Gargantua* that follows two years later (1534).

At first glance, this second book to be written and published (but the first narrative chronologically) is twin to *Pantagruel.* It too recounts the life and education of its titular protagonist through random and outrageous incidents—Gargantua's birth through the ear of his mother Gargamelle after she has consumed too much tripe (1.4, 6); Gargantua's boyish prank of stealing the bells of Notre Dame for cowbells (1.17); and the incredible but sobering conflict between the bakers of Lerne and the shepherds of Grandgousier's provinces that threatens to set all Western civilization at war (1.24–48)— combined with the customary parodying of the technē of humanist grammar and rhetoric. There is the catalogue of Gargantua's wardrobe (1.8) and the seemingly endless listing of his childhood games (1.22); the treatises on livery and on the significance of colors (1.9, 10); the disquisition on the perfect arse-wipe that first awakens Grandgousier to the intelligence of his son (1.13); and the judicial oration by Master Janotus de Bragmardo in which honest and responsible feelings are lost in the thickets of bastardized Latin (1.19). All of these seem to function, moreover, with a kind of aimless sophistry that is anticipated in the tumultous drinking party—Socrates' symposium turned upside down—that celebrates Gargantua's birth with a jangling revelry (1.5). Thus the baby Gargantua's initial contribution, a cry for some drink himself (1.6), makes him at once a disciple of Socrates and of Noah (2.1) and another prime candidate for the bottle of the priestess Bacbuc (5.45). Furthermore, when we learn that the mishaps of the pilgrims who are first swallowed by Gargantua and then pissed on by him have scriptural authority in Psalms (1:145–46, 122) or when Frère Jean, asked why he swears, replies, "Ce n'est . . . que pour orner mon langaige. Ce sont couleurs de rethorique Cicero-niane"; "It's only to embellish my language. . . . It's rhetorical colouring, Ciceronian" (1.150; p. 125), we seem once more to have lost our traditional humanist bearings.

Yet, though the fluid authorial viewpoint in *Gargantua* may be as problem-atic as it is in *Pantagruel,* the tone is grimmer, the reasoning more compacted and resonant, the perspective actually more consistent. *Gargantua* is no longer mere grammatical wordplay but a more straitened examination of humanist rhetoric and logic; the writing here has advanced considerably. We see this, for instance, in Alcofribas's digression on the meaning of the colors white and blue (1.10).

> Aristoteles dict que, supposent deux choses contraires en leur espece, comme bien et mal, vertu et vice, froid et chauld, blanc et noir, volupté et doleur, joye et dueil, et ainsi de aultres, si vous les coublez en telle facon q'un contraire d'une espece convienne raisonnablement à l'un contraire d'une aultre, il est consequent que l'autre contraire compete avecques l'autre residu. Exemple: *vertus* et *vice* sont contraires en une espece; aussy sont *bien* et *mal;* si l'un des contraires de la premiere espece convient à l'un de la seconde, comme *vertus* et *bien,* car il est sceut que *vertus* est bonne, ainsi feront les deux residuz qui sont *mal* et *vice,* car *vice* est maulvais.
>
> Ceste reigle logicale entendue, prenez ces deux contraires: *joye* et *tristesse,* puis ces deux: *blanc* et *noir,* car ilz sont contraires physicalement; si ainsi doncques est que *noir* signifie *dueil,* à bon droict *blanc* signifiera *joye.*
>
> Et n'est cette signifiance par imposition humaine institué, mais receue par consentement de tout le monde, que les philosophes nomment *jus gentium,* droict universel, valable par toutes contrées.

> Aristotle says that if you take two things opposite in kind, such as good and evil, virtue and vice, cold and hot, white and black, pleasure and pain, joy and grief, and so on, and if you couple them in such a way that one of one kind logically agrees with one of the other, it follows that the second of the first pair agrees with the second of the second. For example: *virtue* and *vice* are opposites in one kind, and so are *good* and *evil.* If one of the first pair of opposites agrees with one of the second, as do *virtue* and *good,*—for it is well known that *virtue* is *good*—the remaining two—*evil* and *vice*—will do the same, for *vice* is *evil.*
>
> Once this logical rule is understood, take the two opposites, *joy* and *sadness;* then the two, *white* and *black,* for these are physical opposites; so, therefore, if *black* stands for *grief, white* will rightfully stand for *joy.*
>
> Nor is this significance based on a mere human interpretation. It is accepted by that common consent which philosophers call *jus gentium,* universal law, valid in all countries. [1.43–44; p. 59]

The pseudologic is Aristotelian, the fallacy one of false analogy. We are playing here not merely with syntactic arrangements but with syllogistic means of conceptualizing data and idea: What is under analysis is nothing less than the *Prior Analytics*. As a slightly different instance, we may take the lively and apparently foolish defense of the bells of Notre Dame by the well-intentioned Janotus de Bragmardo (1.19). Because he is the most authoritative member of the university faculty, he is chosen to defend the people of Paris "après avoir bien ergoté *pro et contra;* "After a thorough argument *pro et contra*" (1.70; p. 75). His harangue combines straightforward argument and simple Attic style— "Ce ne seroyt que bon que nous rendissiez nos cloches, car elles nous font bien besoing"; "It would only be right if you were to give us back our bells, for we are greatly in need of them" (1.72; p. 77)—with an inept floridity even Cicero would condemn as too Asiatic:

> "Nous en avoions bien aultresfoys refusé de bon argent de ceulx de Londres en Cahors, sy avions nous de ceulx de Bourdeaulx en Brye, qui les vouloient achapter pour la substantificque qualité de la complexion elementaire que est intronificquée en la terresterité de leur nature quidditative pour extraneizer les halotz et les turbines suz noz vignes, vrayement non pas nostres, mais d'icy aupres."

> "Often in the past we have refused good money for them from the people of London in Cahors, and also from the people of Bordeaux in Brie, who wanted to buy them for the substantific quality of the elementary complexion which is inherent in the terrestriality of their quidditive nature, in order to extraneize the hailstorms and whirlwinds from our vines—not really from ours, though, but from some close by." [1.72–73; p. 77]

This is not simply the speech of a foolish man but that of an authority who begins with wise issues wisely put being transformed into a fool as if the *logic of his argument* or the *rhetorical form of his defense* leads him astray. It is a very different case from that of Panurge in *Pantagruel,* whose sophistry was a crafty smoke screen for base motives, and clearly more sophisticated. Janotus has the right motives and ideas. Yet words, or the occasion, or both, pull him off track. Rabelais makes his case best, perhaps, with the analogous Ulrich Gallet, Grandgousier's Master of Requests, who is ordered to seek peace from the raging Picrochole (1.31). Again he relies on the best humanist form of the deliberative oration; he marshals logical and emotional issues with sureness and force (1.31). *And he fails.* "Où est foy? Où est loy? Où est raison? Où est humanité? Où este craincte de Dieu?"; "Where is faith? Where is law? Where is reason? Where is humanity? Where is the fear of God?" (1.119; p. 105). In his anxiety and passion, Ulrich Gallet's rhetorical reasoning threatens to become irrational, and Picrochole virtually ignores him (1.32); it takes the active intervention of Gargantua and the butchery of Frère Jean to defeat the armies raised against the irenic, passive Grandgousier. Such stern trials of the word are considerably distant from the lessons of the sophist Thubal Holoferne (1.14) or Gargantua's random exercises (1.11) and his meandering search for soft toilet paper (1.13), it is true, but they are of a piece with the more enlightened humanist curriculum of Panocrates (1.21, 23, 24), which has already produced Eudemon, subject of an impressive *chreia* (1.15) and Gargantua's fellow student and friend. Still, all of the designs and hopes of Grandgousier for his son as suggested in his moving letter (1.29) and all of Panocrates' instructions are called into question when the unlessoned Frère Jean, using only his right instincts and his force of will, is able to hold the abbey close of Seuillé as no one else can (1.27). Frère Jean turns astonishingly savage, parting company with any common concept of the Christian humanist.

> Es uns escarbouilloyt la cervelle, es aultres rompoyt bras et jambes, es aultres deslochoyt les spondyles du coul, es aultres demoulloyt les reins, avalloyt le nez, poschoyt les yeulx, fendoyt les mandibules, enfonçoyt les dens en la geule, de seraulloyt les omoplates, spaceloyt les greves, desgondoit les ischies, debezilloit les fauciles.
>
> Si quelq'un se vouloyt cascher entre les sepes plus espès, à icelluy freussoit toute l'arest du douz et l'esrenoit comme un chien.
>
> Si aulcun saulver se vouloyt en fuyant, à icelluy faisoyt voler la teste en pieces par la commissure lambdoide.
>
> Si quelq'un gravoyt en une arbre, pensant y estre en seureté, icelluy de son baston empaloyt par le fondement.
>
> Si quelqu'un de sa vielle congnoissance luy crioyt: Ha, Frere Jean, mon amy, Frere Jean, je me rend!
>
> "Il t'est (disoit il) bien force: mais ensemble tu rendras l'ame a tous les diables."
>
> Et soubdain luy donnoit dronos.

> He beat out the brains of some, broke the arms and legs of others, disjointed the neck-bones, demolished the kidneys, slit the noses, blackened the eyes, smashed the jaws, knocked the teeth down the throats, shattered the shoulder-blades, crushed the shins, dislocated the thigh-bones, and cracked the fore-arms of yet others. If one of them tried to hide among the thickest vines, he bruised the whole ridge of his back and broke the base of his spine like a dog's. If one of

them tried to save himself by flight, he knocked his head into pieces along the lambdoidal suture. If one of them climbed into a tree, thinking he would be safe there, Friar John impaled him up the arse with his staff. If any one of his old acquaintance cried out: "Ha, Friar John, my friend, Friar John, I surrender!" he replied: "You can't help it. But you'll surrender your soul to all the devils as well." And he gave the fellow a sudden thumping. [1.109–10; p. 99]

However vicious, however desirous to damn the enemy, Frère Jean is portrayed as more effectual—and indeed more necessary—than Plato's philosopher king Grandgousier (1.45). Or so it seems.

Such strange turns as these, which we find repeatedly in *Gargantua* despite its apparent grounding in the thorough course of New Learning set out at the center of the book (1.21–24), lead to—in Floyd Gray's terms—"a disequilibriated perspective." [14] A more complicated and substantial book than *Pantagruel*, *Gargantua* is heralded by a more complicated and substantial prologue by the putative Alcofribas Nasier. It begins with an image familiar to humanist poetics, that of the Silenus, in open homage to Socrates and Erasmus: *Gargantua* begins also with an echo of the *Encomium Moriae*.

Beuveurs tres illustres, et vous, Verolez tres precieux,—car à vous, non à aultres, sont dediez mes escriptz,—Alcibiades, ou dialogue de Platon intitulé *Le Bancquet*, louant son precepteur Socrates, sans controverse prince des philosophes, entre aultres parolles le dict estre semblable es Silenes. Silenes estoient jadis petites boites, telles que voyons de present es bouticques des apothecaires, pinctes au dessus de figures joyeuses et frivoles, comme de harpies, satyres, oysons bridez, lievres cornuz, canes bastées, boucqs volans, certz limonniers et aultres telles pinctures contrefaictes à plaisir pour exciter le monde à rire (quel fut Silene, maistre du bon Bacchus); mais au dedans l'on reservoit les fines drogues comme baulme, ambre gris, amonon, musc, zivette, pierreries et aultres choses precieuses.

Most noble boozers, and you are my very esteemed and poxy friends—for to you and you alone are my writings dedicated—when Alcibiades, in that dialogue of Plato's entitled The Symposium, *praises his master Socrates, beyond all doubt the prince of philosophers, he compares him, amongst other things, to a Silenus. Now a Silenus, in ancient days, was a little box, of the kind we see to-day in apothecaries' shops, painted on the outside with such gay, comical figures as harpies, and other devices of that sort, lightheartedly invented for the purpose of mirth, as was Silenus himself, the master of good old Bacchus. But inside these boxes were kept rare drugs, such as balm, ambergris, cardamum, musk, civet, mineral essences, and other precious things.* [1.5; p. 37]

Once again we seem to be back in Folly's world of doubleness, of inside-outside. Even the drunken atmosphere reminds us of Erasmus's mock encomium. It is as if, by authenticating Silenus boxes at the local druggists in the Lyons of 1534, Rabelais wishes, first and foremost, to ally himself with the broader world of Renaissance humanism. But whereas Folly addresses us as a sober audience when she invokes the Silenus, Alcofribas talks to us like those poxy boozers at the original symposium who were so drunk on the wisdom of Socrates that when he came to define comedy they were asleep and his wisdom passed them unheard. Triangulation of a textual dialectic and the reader could not be announced more strongly, and yet the persistent references to drinking and drunkenness also suggest that the text to follow may prove incomprehensible or irrelevant.

Alcofribas continues by pursuing with apparent seriousness the Socrates/Silenus analogy. Viewing Socrates from the outside, he remarks, we remain ignorant; looking more deeply we become in-formed with "entendement plus que humain" and

> vertus merveilleuse, couraige invincible, sobresse non pareille, contentement certain, asseurance parfaicte, deprisement incroyable de tout ce pourquoy les humains tant veiglent, courent, travaillent, navigent et bataillent.
>
> *superhuman understanding, miraculous virtue, invincible courage, unrivalled sobriety, unfailing contentment, perfect confidence, and an incredible contempt for all those things men so watch for, pursue, work for, sail after, and struggle for.* [1.5–6; p. 37]

The searching man is transported. This promise—from Erasmus and also from what must have been a common source, the *Dionysius,* then assigned to Lucian, which adds the element of drinking—suggests that Alcofribas's book hides the same sort of treasurehouse of wisdom (and not folly). He seems to confirm this by turning to medieval *allegoresis* and scriptural *exegesis,* which Rabelais had learned from the Franciscans and Benedictines, in calling on the image of the dog that has Senecan models in both Aristotle and Jerome.

> Mais veistes vous oncques chien recontrant quelque os medulare? C'est, comme dict Platon, *lib. ij de Rep.,* la beste du monde plus philosophe. Si veu l'avez, vous avez peu noter de quelle devotion il le guette, de quel soing il le guarde, de quel ferveur il le tient, de quelle prudence il l'entomme, de quelle affection il le brise, et de quelle diligence il le sugce. Qui le induict à ce faire? Quel est l'espoir de son estude? Quel bien pretend il? Rien plus qu'un peu de mouelle. . . .
>
> A l'example d'icelluy vous convient estre saiges, nour fleurer, sentir et estimer ces beaulx livres de haulte gresse, legiers au prochaz et hardiz à la rencontre; puis, par curieuse leçon et meditation frequente, rompre l'os et sugcer la substanti-

ficque mouelle—c'est à dire ce que j'entends par ces symboles Pythagoricques—
avecques espoir certain d'etre faictz escors et preux à ladicte lecture; car en icelle
bien aultre goust trouverez et doctrine plus absconce, laquelle vous revelera de
très haultz sacremens et mysteres horrificques, tant en ce que concerne nostre
religion que aussi l'estat politicq et vie oeconomicque.

Or did you ever see a dog—which is, as Plato says, in the second book of his Republic, *the
most philosophical creature in the world—discover a marrow-bone? If ever you did, you
will have noticed how devotedly he eyes it, how carefully he guards it, how fervently he
holds it, how circumspectly he begins to gnaw it, how lovingly he breaks it, and how
diligently he licks it. What induces him to do all this? What hope is there in his labour?
What benefit does he expect? Nothing more than a little marrow. . . . Now you must
follow this dog's example, and be wise in smelling out, sampling, and relishing these fine
and most juicy books, which are easy to run down but hard to bring to bay. Then, by
diligent reading and frequent meditation, you must break the bone and lick out the
substantial marrow—that is to say the meaning which I intend to convey by these
Pythagorean symbols—in the hope and assurance of becoming both wiser and more
courageous by such reading. For here you will find an individual savour and abstruse
teaching which will initiate you into certain very high sacraments and dread mysteries,
concerning not only our religion, but also our public and private life.* [1.7–8; p. 38]

It is a subtle but treacherous turn in reasoning: The wisdom we seek may be so
mysteriously encoded that it is beyond our intellectual grasp. The text of
Gargantua may reveal, but it may also conceal. The delicately juggled equiva-
lency then falls just as suddenly at the close of the prologue.

Si ni le croiez, quelle cause est pourquoy autant n'en ferez de ces joyeuses et
nouvelles chronicques, combien que, les dictans, n'y pensasse en plus que vous,
qui par adventure beniez comme moy? Car, à la composition de ce livre seigneu-
rial, je ne perdiz ne emploiay oncques plus, ny aultre temps que culluy qui estoit
estably à prendre ma refection corporelle, sçavoir est beuvant et mangeant.

*If you do not believe those arguments, what reason is there that you should not treat these
new and jolly chronicles of mine with the same reserve, seeing that as I dictated them I gave
no more thought to the matter than you, who were probably drinking at the time, as I was?
For I never spent—or wasted—any more—or other—time in the composing of this lordly
book, than that fixed for the taking of my bodily refreshment, that is to say for eating and
drinking.* [1.8–9; p. 39]

But we all give considerable time to eating and drinking, for these are matters
not only of refreshment but of life itself. Perhaps we are to give these chronicles

little conscious thought because their lessons, like our daily activities of bodily sustenance, are now instinctive and habitual. Or perhaps in seeking Pythagorean truths we stumble and fall from high aspirations; perhaps such heady truths will make us drunk on wisdom so that we emulate Socrates and become perfect drinkers ("In a sense," notes Thomas M. Greene, the "whole work composes a lesson in how and how not to drink").[15] Or it may be that, sufficiently warned, we do not settle for the *poton* or *sympotos,* the drink and the fine dinner we await, but insist instead on *deipnon* or *syndeipnon,* the main banquet of sapience. If this range of pointers is initially confusing or discouraging, it also signals us to look for other matter in *Gargantua* than simply the given skepticism toward humanist learning we have initially discovered there.

For one thing, the composed picture of Grandgousier at home roasting chestnuts, writing, and reciting history (1.28) is an ideal portrait of an aging humanist that stands out in sharp contrast to the restless greed, rapacity, and ambition that consistently characterize the easily duped Picrochole. That Grandgousier is meant to be ideal is reinforced by his choice of the tutor Panocrates for his son (1.15) and, subsequently, in his letter to his son rousing him to decisive action (1.29): "ainsi comme debiles sont les armes au dehors si le conseil n'est en la maison," he says; "arms are powerless abroad unless there is good counsel at home" (1.115; p. 103). Rabelais has no more compacted definition of humanist thought than this. And Grandgousier's wisdom is measured too by the growth of Gargantua. Although he is clever in military strategy and the development of forces when it is necessary (1.49), his stirring address to the vanquished (1.50) demonstrates how much he has learned. It is the first oration in *Gargantua* in which humanist thought and humanist rhetoric are perfectly married.

"Nos peres, ayeulx et ancestres de toute memoyre ont esté de ce sens et ceste nature que des batailles par eulx consommées ont, pour signe memorial des triumphes et victoires, plus voluntiers erigé trophees et monumens es cueurs des vaincuz par grace que, es terres par eulx conquestées, par architecture: car plus estimoient la vive souvenance des humains acquise par libertalité que la mute inscription des arcs, colomnes et pyramides, subjecte es calamitez de l'air et envie d'un chascun."

"Our fathers, grandfathers, and ancestors from time immemorial have been of such nature and disposition that as a memorial to the victories and triumphs they have won in the battles they have fought, they have preferred to erect monuments in the hearts of the vanquished by a display of clemency, than to raise trophies in the form of architecture in the lands they have conquered. For they have valued the lively gratitude of men, won by their liberality, more highly than mute inscriptions on arches, columns, and pyramids, which are subject to the injuries of climate and all men's spite." [1.182; p. 145]

Moreover, Gargantua matches his deeds to his words (1.51).

> Puis ceulx qui la estoient mors il feist honorablement inhumer en la vallée des Noirettes et au camp de Bruslevielle. Les navrés il feist panser et traicter en son grand nosocome. Après advisa es dommaiges faictz en la ville et habitans, et les feist rembourcer de tous leurs interestz à leur confession et serment, et y feist bastir un fort chasteau, y commettant gens et guet pour à l'advenir mieulx soy defendre contre les soubdaines esmeutes.

> Then he had those who had died there honourably buried in the Walnut-tree valley and in Burn-hag field, and he had the wounded dressed and treated in his great *Nosocomion,* or hospital. Afterwards he ascertained what damage had been done to the town and its inhabitants, and had them reimbursed for all their losses, on their sworn declaration. He had a strong fort built there also, which he garrisoned with a guard of his people, so that he could be defended better in the future against sudden uprisings. [1.187; pp. 148–49]

The grotesque baby giant has grown like Socrates into a man of wisdom. As the symposium of the prologue to *Gargantua* is succeeded by the precious drugs inside the Silenus box, so the drunken revelry at Gargantua's birth is succeeded by the growth of a humanist.

But the precious contents of the Silenus do not conclude the prologue, which ends instead with the ambiguity about the wisdom or folly of us poxy boozers; and *Gargantua* concludes not with the rewards of justice, clemency, and preparedness that Gargantua assigns but with the reward of Thélème to Frère Jean for his courage and his singular defense against the rebels. The praise awarded Thélème (1.52–58) is unique in *Gargantua,* the tone describing it more earnest and more subdued; it has often been excerpted as the work's most enduring achievement. Yet the facts that surround this description are unsettling, much as our introduction to the world of Urbino in Castiglione or of the Abbey of Nostre-Dame de Serrance in Marguerite warned us not to accept any place without first scrutinizing it. Thélème is a suitable reward for the changeable Frère Jean, who is not only a brave soldier but also a bold swaggerer and robust drinker, a monk whose breviary is both book and bottle. The unforeseen—but willful—war that brought Thélème into being is surely a comment on the abbey named by the Greek word *thelēma,* meaning *will* or *desire,* found chiefly in the New Testament and in ecclesiastical writers. The abbey's motto, moreover, "Fay ce que vouldras" ("Do what you want"; "Do what you will"), is curiously unsuited to a place where a restricted elite, obeying their instincts and compulsions, seem nonetheless because of their refined and identical training to be will-less. It may be noteworthy that Rabelais's composition of this episode swiftly follows the debate over free will between Erasmus and Luther.[16] In any event, Thélème is by design antimonastic: The abbey has no walls, admits women as well as men, permits marriage but requires no vows of chastity, obedience, or poverty. And it differs not only spiritually but materially from a holy community. Further characteristics—the hunting and hawking, archery and riding for men, and the lovely chambers with embroidered beds and tapestries and plentiful barbers and perfumers for women—seem to point not to an abbey at all but to the imaginary Urbino of *Il Cortegiano,* the life of the monastery linked with that of the Renaissance French château so as to provide a life of "culture, civilization, courtesy, urbanity," as Greene puts it, "manners, with the graceful carriage of the body and the alert suppleness of the mind" (*Rabelais,* p. 51). There is yet a third shadowy model in Thomas More's *Utopia.* Both Thélème and Utopia keep out strangers; both are rigidly hierarchical; both insure peace by identical education and training of the citizenry daily reinforced by communal dinner and activity (in Thélème in a common hall on which everyone's stairway converges). If Thélème measures life by delight, if all seems providentially given and self-sustaining because Gargantua, as a kind of god at the close of his story, supplies sufficient money and luxurious if similar clothing (1.56), the awkward references to a Senecan model in More disconcert us. Moreover, at Thélème as in Utopia, books are made available for leisure time, days are regulated by bells (here the absence of locks is only nominal), and there is a pointed absence of lawyers. And as if to recall the impossible mathematical geography of Utopia, Alcofribas provides Thélème with mathematically improbable architecture: 9,332 identical apartments (in this "unregulated" society!) are cramped into a space that allows no more room for each of them than the width of a single meter.[17] Thus *Gargantua,* ironically published the year of More's execution, also concludes the tribute to Thélème and the work itself with a statement—whether due to the outrageous *affaire des placards* of 17 October 1534 or not—in which Frère Jean has serious reservations about the significance of the inscription, the "substantificque mouelle," on the bronze plate found during excavation for the abbey and, by extension, pointing to the very foundation of the community of Thélème itself. Gargantua thinks the riddle is indicative of Holy Writ (1.58), but the monk believes it is only a description of tennis wrapped up in strange language, like the harangue of Janotus de Bragmardo, and Frère Jean has no hesitation in leaving this gift to follow Pantagruel and Panurge. Even here, at the close of *Gargantua,* Frère Jean dismisses contemplating the meaning of Thélème, the antiabbey of willful will-lessness, with a quick drink (1.58). On reflection, the most damaging thing about Thélème is that its static presence admits no education, no practice of humanist thought and no occasion for humanist rhetoric. Although *Gargantua,* in its many jostling perspectives, promotes the cause of humanism, the conclusive movement with its focus on the abbey still leaves open basic questions concerning the nature, if not the potential dignity, of man. The embryonic, episodic narrative of *Pantagruel* around linked humanist concerns thus coalesces by the close of the more advanced *Gargantua.* The growth of narrative control here, along with the deepening concerns of humanism—the identity and educability of man—seems to measure the growth of Rabelais's mind itself.

The search to determine humanist identity, in France and abroad, is likewise a concern common to many of the episodes in the remainder of Rabelais's humanist fiction—and the portion to which he openly subscribed his name. The organizational principle of *Le Tiers Livre* (1546) is the good-natured agreement to disagree, between the stoically tolerant Pantagruel and the urgently inquiring Panurge, concerning the nature of man (his fear of self-deception and his vulnerability) and the responsibility of the humanist (whether to marry and propagate) in which both men are at times wisely foolish (in being content not to know, in asking impossible riddles) and foolishly wise (in stoutly refusing to settle for easy answers, in claiming any single solution as universal and eternal). *Le Tiers Livre,* then, is a generally long, imaginative, and convoluted gloss on the *Encomium Moriae* seen most quickly in Panurge's Folly-like *declamatio* in 3.46.

—"Au rebours (respondit Panurge). Non que je me vueille impudentement exempter du territoire de follie, j'en tiens et en suys, je le confesse. Tout le monde est fol. En Lorraine Fou est près Tou, par bonne discretion. Tout est fol. Solomon dict que infiny est des folz le nombre. A infinité rien ne peut decheoir, rien ne peut estre adjoinct, comme prouve Aristotles, et fol enragé seroit si, fol estant, fol ne me reputois. C'est ce que pareillement faict le nombre des maniacques et enraigez infiny. Avicenne dict que de manie infinies sont les especes."

"Quite the contrary," said Panurge. "Not that I wish shamelessly to exempt myself from allegiance to the realm of folly. I am its vassal, and I belong to it; that I confess. Everyone is foolish, and it is quite right that the village of Foul in Lorraine is close to Toul, or, as you might say that *fool* and *all* almost rhyme. All are fools. Solomon says that the number of fools is infinite; nothing can be added to infinity, and nothing can be subtracted from it, as Aristotle proves. And I should be a raging fool if, being a fool, I did not consider myself one. That is exactly what makes the number of maniacs and madmen infinite. Avicenna says that there are infinite varieties of madness." [1.592–94; pp. 14–15]

This speech resembles the university sophister defending a proposition in the most flamboyantly rhetorical way, but when we try to untangle the threads of Panurge's rhetoric to find what is true and what fantastic, what logical and what illogical, we shall find that sorting things out is not so simple as separating a worthwhile end from debatable or misapplied means. The etymology of towns in Lorraine may be sheer exuberant foolishness, but Solomon and Aristotle are correctly cited although the context distorts them both. The reference to Avicenna, however, is not a matter of distortion alone; context here makes the use of him, quite simply, wrong. Yet, such use of rhetoric insists, how negatively are we to judge the clever use of such a various bundling of evidence when the cause being advanced—that all men are sometimes fools—ought to be defended as cleverly and convincingly as possible? The false use of Avicenna argues something beyond the boundaries of paradoxy, takes the problem into the area of the conundrum (where 1.2 has from the start placed us). And this step is perilously close to the possible infinitude of foolishness that Panurge is advocating—that he himself embodies. Even as the range (and size) of Rabelais's achievement is grander than that of his predecessors, so the intricacies of wit embedded in a fundamentally humanist poetics here become enormously more complex. At some points, such as the one just cited, it becomes so confusing that we are tempted to sort it out by instinct alone—or to pass it by with an equally equivocal smile or laugh. "Such language," Richard A. Lanham notes, "can only remind us that what it points to, by the nature of language, it cannot describe." [18]

But in *Le Tiers Livre* as in *Gargantua* a reference point is provided by Rabelais's prologue. The former prologue concludes with a passage taken verbatim from the *Dionysius;* this prologue recalls Lucian's satiric *How to Write History,* although subjected to Rabelais's delightfully Erasmian *copia.* The core incident, as Lucian records it, is relatively simple. He is recounting the Parthian War to Philo.

As I saw and heard all this [the war against the barbarians, the disaster in Armenia, and the run of victories], friend, I was reminded of the story of the man of Sinope. When Philip was said to be already on the march, all the Corinthians were astir and busy, preparing weapons, bringing up stones, underpinning the wall, shoring up a battlement and doing various other useful jobs. Diogenes saw this, and as he had nothing to do—nobody made any use of him—he belted up his philosopher's cloak and very busily by himself rolled the crock in which, as it happens, he was living up and down Cornel Hill. When one of his friends asked: "Why are you doing that, Diogenes?" he replied: "I'm rolling the crock so as not to be thought the one idle man in the midst of all these workers."

From this incident, Lucian draws his own poetic.

So in my own case, Philo, to avoid being the only mute in such a polyphonic time, pushed about open-mouthed without a word like an extra in a comedy, I thought it a good idea to roll my barrel as best I could; not to produce a history or even merely chronicle the events—I'm not so bold as that: don't be afraid that I should go that far. I know the danger of rolling it over rocks, particularly a poorly baked little barrel like mine. Just as soon as it hits against a tiny piece of stone we shall have to pick up the pieces. . . .

[Anyone feels he can write history, but] history is not one of those things that can be put in hand without effort, and can be put together lazily, but something which needs, if anything does in literature, a great deal of thought if it is to be what Thucydides calls "a possession for evermore." [19]

History, he continues, cannot admit fiction (11), pomposity (27), dialectic (27), or eloquence (29), the dramatic or the marvelous (33). But Lucian's own practice denies his theory (it is in part another Lucianic joke): After insisting on fearlessness, incorruptibility, and impartiality (57), he goes on to argue that the historian's mind should "have a touch and share of poetry, since that too is lofty and sublime. . . . The task of the historian is . . . to give a fine arrangement to events and illuminate them as vividly as possible" (59, 65). The historian, that is, should be a writer of truthful and instructive fiction.

Rabelais also likens himself to the Cynic of antiquity in various and discontinuous ways.

Prins ce choys et election, ay pensé ne faire exercice inutile et importun, si je remuois mon tonneau Diogenic qui seul m'est reste du naufrage faict par le passé on far de Mal'encontre. A ce triballement de tonneau, que feray-je en vostre advis? Par le vierge qui se rebrasse, je ne sçay encores. Attendez un peu que je hume quelque traict de ceste bouteille: c'est mon vray et seul Helicon, c'est ma fontaine caballine, c'est mon unicque enthusiasme. Icy beuvant je delibere, je discours, je resoulz et concluds. Après l'epilogue je riz, j'escripz, je compose, je boy. Ennius beuvant escrivoit, escrivant beuvoit. Aeschylus (si a Plutarche foy avez *in Symposiacis*) beuvoit composant, beuvant composoit. Homere jamais n'escrivit à jeun. Caton jamais n'escrivit que après boyre. Affin que ne me dictez ainsi vivre sans exemple des biens louez et mieulz prisez. Il est bon et frays assez, comme vous diriez sus le commencement du second degré: Dieu, le bon Dieu Sabaoth (c'est à dire des armées) en soit eternellement loue. Si de mesmes vous autres beuvez un grand ou deux petitz coups en robbe, je n'y trouve inconvenient aulcun, pourveu que du tout louez Dieu un tantinet.

Puys doncques que telle est ou ma sort ou ma destinée (car à chascun n'est oultroyé entrer et habiter Corinthe) ma deliberation est servir et es uns et es autres: tant s'en fault que je reste cessateur et inutile. Envers les vastadours, pionniers et rempareurs, je feray ce que feirent Neptune et Appolo en Troie soubs Laomedon, ce que feit Renaud de Montauban sus ses derniers jours: je serviray les massons, je mettray bouillir pour les massons, et, le past terminé, au son de ma musette mesureray la musarderie des musars. Ainsi fonda, bastit et edifá Amphion, sonnant de sa lyre, la grande et celebre cité de Thebes. . . . De ce poinct expedié, à mon tonneau je retourne. Sus à ce vin, compaigns! Enfans, beuvez à pleins goudetz. Si bon ne vous semble, laissez-le.

Having made my choice, having made up my mind, I decided that I should perform no useless or tiresome role if I were to tumble my Diogenic tub, which is all that is left to me from the shipwreck of my past in the Straits of Misfortune. Now, how do you advise me to set about my tub-rumbling? By the Virgin who ups her skirts, I do not yet know. Wait a little, till I've swallowed a draught from this bottle. It is my true and only Helicon, my one Pegasus spring, my sole enthusiasm. As I drink here deliberate, discourse, resolve, and conclude. After the epilogue I laugh, write, compose, and drink again. Ennius wrote as he drank, drank as he wrote. Aeschylus, if you put any trust in Plutarch's Symposiacs, used to drink as he composed, to compose as he drank. Homer never wrote on an empty stomach, Cato never wrote except after drinking. So do not say that I am not following the example of good and praiseworthy men. It is fine fresh stuff, as you might say, entering into its second, or rarified state. God, the good lord Saboath—that is to say, the Lord of Hosts—be eternally praised for it! So if at the same time the rest of you will take one large or two little gulps under your hoods, I can see no objection, providing that you give God a pinch of thanks for it.

So since this is my lot or my destiny—for it is not granted to everyone to go and live in Corinth—I am resolved to serve both attackers and defenders. For I will not stand by as a useless idler. Amongst the diggers, pioneers, and engineers, I will do what Neptune and Apollo did under Laomedon in Troy, what Renaud of Montauban did in his latter days. I will help the masons, I will set the pot boiling for them, and when the meal is finished I will measure the musings of the bemused with the music of my little pipe. Even so did Amphion found, build, and complete the great and celebrated city of Thebes, to the sound of his lyre. . . . With this point settled, I return to my cask. "Up, lads, and to the wine! Gulp it down, my boys, in brimming cups. Or, if you do not like it, leave it alone."

[1.398–401; pp. 284–86]

What holds the passage together is the elaborate interweaving of certainty and uncertainty in which drink is both inebriation and inspiration, escape from responsibility and the grace given by God. The stances at each end of the shifting perspective here—the fluid authorial viewpoint that is Rabelais's fundamental contribution to a humanist poetics of fiction—are the self-indulgent foolishness that will characterize the Panurge of *Le Tiers Livre* and the accepting aloofness of one's lot or destiny that will delineate Pantagruel's abiding response. There is a vast difference between this range of lessons derived from the exemplum of Diogenes before the siege of Corinth and Ralph Robynson's citation of Diogenes in his preface to More's *Utopia* some five years earlier—not all of it due to Rabelais's love of copia—in which Robynson sees in the Cynic philosopher a learned man who daily puts forth new inventions for his poor talent to emulate. By contrast, Rabelais's Diogenes as *substantificque mouelle* is Protean: a cynic, a Stoic, and a philosopher king who succeeds the Socrates of *Gargantua*.

True to such hints, *Le Tiers Livre* has as its Senecan model the Platonic *Symposium*, in which a wide array of intellectual positions are advanced but final judgment of them is often suspended, positions that sometimes grasp and sometimes fail to grasp the key philosophic issues of humanism just beneath Panurge's apparently frivolous questions about human nature and human destiny. "The *Tiers Livre*," M. A. Screech writes, "is a book about decision and indecision; it centres round the problem of how men can, or cannot, reach right decisions in a divinely ordained universe in which God reigns supreme but the Devil remains prince of this world." [20] Screech helps us recall that Pantagruel is named for a devil and Panurge (from Greek *panourgos*) means *jack-of-all-trades* or *rascal;* and that the two first meet near the Abbey of Sainct-Antoine (2.9), a saint best known for *his* various encounters with the devil. It is in just this light—with Panurge as a kind of Everyman torn between angelic aspirations and devilish inclinations—that we are to read the *locus classicus* of 3.3–4,

Panurge's famous *encomium moriae* in praise of debts. For Rabelais's learned audience, this formal speech is at once rational, irrational, and blasphemous; it catches up, uses, and misapplies a storehouse of classical antecedents such as Plutarch's *De Vitando Aere Alieno* (*Moralia* 827D–832A)—"I am pointing out to those who are too ready to become borrowers how much disgrace and servility there is in the practice and that borrowing is an act of extreme folly and weakness" (*Moralia,* 829F)[21]—and Cicero's *De Officiis:* "nec enim ulla res vehementius rem publicam continet quam fides, quae esse nulla potest, nisi erit necessaria solutio rerum creditarum"; "For there is nothing that upholds a government more powerfully than its credit; and it can have no credit, unless the payment of debts is enforced by law."[22] There is no more certain clue that Panurge lacks full humanist training at the hands of a Panocrates than in this oration where he concentrates on form at the expense of substance. For him the borrowing and lending of money bind men into a community, whereas the opposite state of being is a bestial one in which dog eats dog (3.3). But then the powers of logic slip from his grasp. Whether through sly cleverness or accidental ignorance, Panurge likens borrowing to an exercise in the four cardinal virtues of prudence, justice, fortitude, and temperance as well as the Christian virtues of faith, hope, and (especially) charity—but he seems not to see how delusions of rhetorical grandeur cause him to set himself up as God.

"que sus l'opinion de tous philosophes (qui disent rien de rien n'estre faict) rien ne tenent, ne matiere premiere, estoys facteur et createur."

"For—notwithstanding the universal opinion of philosophers, who say that out of nothing nothing is made—although I possessed nothing and had no prime substance, in this I was a maker and creator." [1.416; p. 296]

Panurge means to defend both borrowing and the intention to borrow without meaning to make good the debt; his community is a parody of the humanist commonwealth. Pantagruel's *responsio* (3.5) is brief and pointed: He underscores Panurge's blasphemy by citing Scripture, but rather than using the antique texts of the New Learning he adds evidence from experience.

"J'entends (respondit Pantagruel) et me semblez bon topicqueur et affecté à vostre cause. Mais preschez et patrocinez d'icy à la Pentecoste, en fin vous serez esbahy comment rien ne me aurez persuadé, et par vostre beau parler, ja ne me ferez entrer en debtes. Rien (dict le sainct Envoyé) à personne ne doibvez fors armours et dilection mutuelle.

"Vous me usez icy de belles graphides et diatyposes, et me plaisent très bien;

mais je vous diz que, si figurez un affronteur efronté et importun emprunteur entrant de nouveau en une ville ja advertie de ses meurs, vous trouverez que à son entrée plus sermont les citoyens en effroy et trepidation, que si la Peste y etroit en habillement tel que la trouva le philosophe Tyanien dedans Ephese.*"*

"I understand," answered Pantagruel. "You seem to me good at argument and an enthusiast for your cause. But if you preach and sermonize from now till Whitsun, you'll be astonished to find me finally unconvinced. With all your fine talk you will never make me a debtor. Owe no man anything, says the holy Apostle, save love and mutual delight. You provide me with fine illustrations and figures, which please me greatly. But let me tell you that if one of your shameless swaggerers and tiresome borrowers were to make a second visit to a city that knew his habits, you would find the citizens more worried and alarmed by his entrance than if the plague had come in person, dressed up as the Tyanian philosopher saw it at Ephesus." [1.424−25; p. 302]

Still, Panurge remains a singularly poor student to Pantagruel. He does not learn from others' precepts. Instead, he must learn by direct experience—and that is what frightens him. Having failed to convince Pantagruel with one foolish encomium, he delivers another, this time in defense of codpieces (3.8). Now, Panurge finds, Pantagruel refuses to debate or counsel him at all. He must teach himself.

This trilogy of speeches—two on debts and one on codpieces—introduces a full-scale symposium with a series of diviners and scholars of the New Learning who give advice freely, without establishing any indebtedness. Whether such a community is characterized by aggressive behavior (as in borrowing), withheld action (as in using codpieces), or mutual commitment (as in marriage), it is the larger context of humanist thought that Rabelais is exploring. Panurge's simplistic problems—and there are two, not one: shall I marry? and, will I be cuckolded if I do?—are actually ways of getting to a definition of the *humanist* community, its basis, interaction, and stability. The remainder of *Le Tiers Livre* is, then, a sequence of implicit disputations between Panurge and a host of authorities and quasiauthorities. This book is the story of Panurge's education, as the first and second books chart the education of Gargantua and Pantagruel.

Panurge first experiments with divination (3.12−20) before making formal inquiries of an artist (the poet Raminagrobis, who supplies a paradoxical Petrarchan sonnet by way of reply) and a scientist (the astrologer Her Trippa, who predicts certain cuckoldry, allowing Rabelais to satirize horoscopes and Frère Jean to praise male testicles). Angered, frustrated, dispirited, Panurge approaches those authorities representing the advanced faculties of the New Learning. On the surface, they seem to perform no greater service. The theologian Hippothadée (3.30) can only reply, when Panurge asks if he will be cuckolded, "si Dieu plainst" (1.530); "if it please God" (p. 371). The doctor Rondibilis (3.31–33) cites the opposing schools of Hippocratic and Galenic medicine, and the philosopher Trouillogan (3.33–36) follows the scholastic *pro et contra*. His answer is *tous les deux, ne l'un ne l'autre,* both and neither, neither one nor the other; *scelon la recontre,* according to circumstances. We are in for a pleasant surprise, however, when Panurge turns to the last, the lawyer Bridoye, separated from the other three by an actual fool, for he is, among them all, the wisest. It is true that he treats all cases identically, as *causae perplexae,* which, according to Roman law, may be decided by the casting of dice.[23] But it is for just this practice that Pantagruel, not Panurge, defends him (3.43)—a certain clue—since in letting justice rest on the fall of dice, which he does not even pretend to understand, Bridoye shows his faith in things unknown, whether fate, God, or both. He is a learned man doubtless—the extraordinary appeals he makes correctly to humanist florilegia and Roman law are meant to show us that—and yet, what he finally *knows* is that he knows nothing. Bridoye is a key Silenus because he is, in his knowledgeable ignorance, the whole fiction's Socrates. He is the focal point of *Le Tiers Livre* that looks back to the Silenus in the prologue to *Gargantua* and forward to the image of the Silenus in *Le Cinquième Livre* (5.35). No other authority of the New Learning in *Le Tiers Livre* is as paradoxical and as simply profound; his singular humility is *both fou* and *tou.* M. A. Screech agrees: Bridoye is a holy fool, like the Christ of Folly.

> Such a man rejects the standards of this world and refuses to accept the self-centred, self-advancing suppositions of the worldly-wise. The wisdom of this world is recognised by the heavenly intelligences for what it really is: sheer stupidity in the sight of God. A man who wishes to appear wise in the estimation of the angels must be selfless and foolish after the manner of Christians. To vulgar men he will appear a fool in the usual pejorative sense. But a man, in Pantagruel's belief, lives his life in the sight of these *Intelligences coelestes.* Rabelais makes his point with the help of serious wordplay, linking together *sage* (wise) and *praesage* (endowed with prophetic wisdom through foreknowledge).[24]

Bridoye is, finally, the fiction's Diogenes. He rolls his dice as Diogenes rolls his tub, participating in life but allowing a greater will than his to dispose of events and judgments. To do any more is to *over*allegorize. Yet in other ways Bridoye is like Hippothadée, Rondibilis, and Trouillogan: In refusing to supply Panurge or Pantagruel with any ready solution, he implies, as all humanists would imply, that the answer is in one's self. All the scholars in *Le Tiers Livre* promote the humanist belief in self-choice and self-determination, and they all agree that once man has made these choices, by whatever means is best for him, he must learn to live with them. And that too was Pantagruel's initial response in 3.9. To teach yourself is to know yourself. And "knowing thyself" is the humanist lesson that joins the words of Socrates with the words of Christ.

Against so prolonged and so highly pitched a moment, the closing dissertation in *Le Tiers Livre* on the herb pantagruelion, tracing its etymology, its properties, its applications and uses, and its indestructibility (3.49–52), may seem an afterthought. But in a book so carefully developed as *Le Tiers Livre,* this too has point. It sums the book's lessons for both Panurge and us and reviews the most important issues. The pantagruelion, like the humble Bridoye, has small roots, but it has large branches and many leaves. It is a miraculous growth, both *divins et mystérieux* (3.49). It may be used as a salve for a scald or burn, a remedy for colic in horses, or a poison for vermin (3.51). Pantagruel uses it to build Thélème (3.52). The idea is not that this wonderful herb can do anything or everything but that it is so wonderful that it awakens faith, like Bridoye's dice. It asks us to *trust* in what is *marvelous.* A truly splendid example of the Rabelaisian copia of words now inseparable from a copia of thought and belief, this special herb, closing *Tiers Livre* as the enigmatic riddle concluded *Gargantua,* invites us to speculate on the things in this world beyond the boundaries of reason.

Panurge attracts us immediately in *Le Tiers Livre* because his rascality has softened into an endearing concern for humanity; his love for Pantagruel has transformed him. "Vous vivent joyeulx, guaillard, dehayt," Panurge tells his companion as the newly installed warden of Salmiguondin, "je ne seray riche que trop"; "So long as you're alive, and jolly, sprightly and merry, I shall be more than rich" (3.2). But he has not lost his sparkle; a moment later he is defending the most improbable propositions by misquoting Hippocrates and tossing in vague references to Plato and Cicero for good measure. His good measure is also Rabelais's. Although Rabelais's greatest debts are to the *Encomium Moriae, Adagia,* and *De Copia* of Erasmus[25] and to the *Symposium* of Plato, he likewise makes considerable use of Hippocrates and Cicero as well as Herodotus, Plutarch, and Galen. These important shaping influences for Rabelais's humanist fiction are not as specific citations or identifiable allusions in the work—what A. J. Krailsheimer suggestively calls *actes de présence;*[26] rather, they are the broader Senecan models from whom he chiefly learned and so those on which his ranging fiction, and his fluid viewpoint, come to rely.

Rabelais's understanding of the humanist belief in the dignity of man, for example, owes much to the *De Officiis* of Cicero (to which he also turns, more specifically, for Panurge's praise of debtors). It is a perspective that has great appeal for Rabelais: a capsule view of rational man as a natural creature whose instincts for self-preservation and reproduction are disciplined by speech and act.

Principio generi animantium omni est a natura tributum, ut se, vitam corpusque tueatur. . . . homo autem, quod rationis est particeps, per quam consequentia cernit, causas rerum videt earumque praegressus et quasi antecessiones non ignorat, similitudines comparat rebusque praesentibus adiungit atque annectit futuras, facile totius vitae cursum videt ad eamque degendam praeparat res necessarias. . . .

In primisque hominis est propria veri inquisitio atque investigatio. Itaque cum sumus necessariis negotiis curisque vacui, tum avemus, aliquid videre, audire, addiscere cognitionemque rerum aut occultarum aut admirabilium ad beate vivendum necessariam ducimus. Ex quo intellegatur, quod verum, simplex sincerumque sit, id esse naturae hominis aptissimum. Huic veri videndi cupiditate adiuncta est appetitio quaedam principatus, ut nemini parere animus bene informatur a natura velit nisi praecipienti aut docenti aut utilitatis causa iuste et legitime imperanti; ex quo magnitudine animi existit humanarumque rerum contemptio.

Nec vero illa parva vis naturae est rationisque, quod unum hoc animal sentit, quid sit ordo.

First of all, Nature has endowed every species of living creature with the instinct of self-preservation . . . while man—because he is endowed with reason, by which he comprehends the chain of consequences, perceives the causes of things, understands the relation of cause to effect and of effect to cause, draws analogies, and connects and associates the present and the future,—easily surveys the course of his whole life and makes the necessary preparations for its conduct. . . .

Nature likewise by the power of reason associates man with man in the common bonds of speech and life. . . .

Above all, the search after truth and its eager pursuit are peculiar to man. And so, when we have leisure from the demands of business cares, we are eager to see, to hear, to learn something new, and we esteem a desire to know the secrets or wonders of creation as indispensable to a happy life. Thus we come to understand that what is true, simple, and genuine appeals most strongly to a man's nature. To this passion for discovering truth there is added a hungering, as it were, for independence, so that a mind well-moulded by Nature is unwilling to be subject to anybody save one who gives rules of conduct or is a teacher of truth or who, for the general good, rules according to justice and law. From this attitude come greatness of soul and a sense of superiority to worldly conditions.

And it is no mean manifestation of Nature and Reason that man is the only animal that has a feeling for order, for propriety, for moderation in word and deed. [1.4.11−14]

Here too is a passage analogous to the plot of *Gargantua* and *Pantagruel* and to the characterizations of Pantagruel and Panurge.

Omnes enim trahimur et ducimur ad cognitionis et scientiae cupiditatem, in qua excellere pulchrum putamus, labi autem, errare, nescire, decipi et malum et turpe ducimus. In hoc genere et naturali et honesto duo vitia vitanda sunt, unum, ne incognita pro cognitis habeamus iisque temere assentiamur; quod vitium effugere qui volet (omnes autem velle debent), adhibebit ad considerandas res et tempus et diligentiam. Alterum est vitium, quod quidam nimis magnum studium multamque operam in res obscuras atque difficiles conferunt easdemque non necessarias.

For we are all attracted and drawn to a zeal for learning and knowing; and we think it glorious to excel therein, while we count it base and immoral to fall into error, to wander from the truth, to be ignorant, to be led astray. In this pursuit, which is both natural and morally right, two errors are to be avoided: first, we must not treat the unknown as known and too readily accept it; and he who wishes to avoid this error (as all should do) will devote both time and attention to the weighing of evidence. The other error is that some people devote too much industry and too deep study to matters that are obscure and difficult and useless as well. [1.6−18−19]

This warning, which sounds very much like the implicit counsel of Pantagruel to Panurge in *Le Tiers Livre* and *Le Quart Livre,* is repeated by Cicero in *De Officiis* 1.30.106.

It is this comprehensive anthology of ideas we find in Cicero that Rabelais weds to the fabulous storytelling technique of Herodotus, which he learned when translating Book 2 of the *Historia,* the long independent digression on the marvelous history and customs of Egypt; here too he may have taken the idea of seeing his fiction as a *chronicle*[27] from one of the authors respected by the New Learning. For Cicero, Herodotus was known as the Father of History, but for Plutarch the Father of Lies: Herodotus of Halicarnassus is a writer, like Rabelais, of great personal charm and of enormous learning and scope but one whose observations always test our credulity. His work, episodic and sprawling like Rabelais's, is also meant to record the great deeds of heroic man; *Herodotus of Halicarnassus: Researches*, the *Historia* begins, as Rabelais begins his first two books researching genealogies. In the *Historia* 2 of Herodotus, moreover, we find the same delight in discovering and portraying a world upside down that characterizes Rabelais's humanist fiction—

> As the Egyptians have a climate peculiar to themselves, and their river is different in its nature from all other rivers, so have they made all their customs and laws of a kind contrary for the most part to those of all other men. Among them, the women buy and sell, the men abide at home and weave; and whereas in weaving all others push the woof upwards, the Egyptians push it downwards. Men carry burdens on their heads, women on their shoulders. Women make water standing, men sitting. They relieve nature indoors, and eat out of doors in the streets, giving the reason, that things unseemly but necessary should be done in secret, things not unseemly should be done openly. No woman is dedicated to the service of any god or goddess; men are dedicated to all deities male or female. Sons are not compelled against their will to support their parents, but daughters must do so though they be unwilling[28]

—and the same joy in storytelling:

> Now, indeed, there are no men, neither in the rest of Egypt, nor in the whole world, who gain from the soil with so little labour; they have not the toil of breaking up the land with the plough, nor of hoeing, nor of any other work which men do to get them a crop; the river rises of itself, waters the field, and then sinks back again; thereupon each man sows his field and sends swine into it to tread down the seed, and waits for the harvest; then he makes the swine to thresh his grain, and so garners it. [Chap. 14]

Again and again Herodotus's narrative works by surprise (46, 66) or deflation (47); it is heavily rhetorical, often hugely reliant on copia; it tells the most fabulous events while maintaining a shameless, straightforward pretense of authenticity. As with Rabelais, Herodotus displays a delight in numbers (such as the length of the Egyptian coastline (chap. 7), etymology (as in determining that the *Asmach* are those who stand on the left hand of the king (chap. 29), and obscenity when describing the festival of Dionysus, celebrated with puppets whose genitals are as big as their bodies (chap. 48). There is also the sense of gallimaufry: here a recipe for embalming (86), there a dissertation on sacred animals (69–73), at the end a detailed description of the labyrinth of the twelve kings (148) that anticipates the complex description of the Temple of the Dive Bouteille in Rabelais (5.37–42). To the work of this historian of the wholly fabulous—or so Rabelais and his contemporaries believed, although we have since learned differently—Rabelais added the customs and sense of storytelling in Plutarch's shared interest in Egyptology in the *Moralia* (351C–438E). Rabelais also imitates the use of multiple significations for explaining the ineffable, which Plutarch attempts in an ingenious catalogue in *De E Apud Delphos* and the passage on other worlds in *De Defectu Oraculorum*, 22, and the sense of play and satire in Lucian with its notable mixing of fantasy and reality, distance and engagement, the marvelous and the commonplace, that we have already seen in Rabelais's borrowings from *How to Write History*.[29]

Besides being Herodotean, Rabelais's poetics for fiction are also Hippocratic and Galenic, as his abiding preoccupation with medicine testifies. Rabelais lectured on the Greek text of Hippocrates as part of his qualifying examination for the bachelor of medicine at Montpellier in 1530; later, he lectured further on Hippocrates and wrote a commentary for his *Aphorisms* in Greek and Latin (1532). It may be, however, that it is the Hippocratic pledge—"I will use treatment to help the sick according to my ability and judgment, but never with a view to injury and wrong-doing"[30]—he has in mind when he presents his own theory of the therapeutic value of fiction in the prologue to *Pantagruel* (also 1532).

> J'en ay congneu de haultz et puissans seigneurs en bon nombre, qui, allant à chasse de grosses bestes ou voller pour canes, s'il advenoit que la beste ne feust rencontrée par les brisées ou que le faulcon se mist à planer, voyant la proye gaigner à tire d'esle, ilz estoient bien marrys, comme entendez assez; mais leur refuge de reconfort, et affin de ne soy morfondre, estoit à recoler les inestimables faictz dudict Gargantua.
>
> Aultres sont par le Monde (ce ne sont fariboles) qui, estans grandement affligez du mal des dentz, après avoir tous leurs biens despenduz en medicins sans en rien profiter, ne ont trouvé remede plus expedient que de mettre lesdictes *Chroniques* entre deux beaulx linges bien chaulx et les appliquer au lieu de la douleur, les sinaprizand avecques un peu de pouldre d'oribus.
>
> *I have known high and mighty noblemen in great numbers, hunters of great game or hawkers after ducks, who if the game happened not to be caught where it was expected, or the hawk saw her prey gaining on her by power of wing and began to hover, grew most annoyed, as you know well enough. But their refuge and comfort, and their method of avoiding a chill was to re-read the inestimable deeds of the said Gargantua. There are*

others in the world—these are no fairy-tales—who, when greatly afflicted with tooth-ache, after expending all their substance on doctors without any result, have found no readier remedy than to put the said Chronicles *between two fine linen sheets, well warmed, and apply them to the seat of the pain, dusting them first with a little dry-dung powder.* [1.216; p. 167]

Ever since the humanists had rediscovered the idea of poetry and philosophy as medicine in Plato's *Gorgias,* mental health and physical health were for them closely allied, as they are even in this Rabelaisian parody. Another Senecan original shaping Rabelaisian poetics is Hippocrates' *Laws,* where the natural analogy for medicine is the same as that used in humanist grammar books.

The learning of medicine may be likened to the growth of plants. Our natural ability is the soil. The views of our teachers are as it were the seeds. Learning from childhood is analogous to the seeds' falling betimes upon the prepared ground. The place of instruction is as it were the nutriment that comes from the surrounding air to the things sown. Diligence is the working of the soil. Time strengthens all these things, so that their nurture is protected. [3]

Things however that are holy are revealed only to men who are holy. The profane may not learn them until they have been initiated into the mysteries of science. [5]

The care (and pride) with which Rabelais describes Panurge's surgery on Epistemon (2.30) or Frère Jean's anatomical butchery (1.27) shows how man was for him a physical phenomenon capable of scientific dissection. Conversely, Rabelais believes with humanists generally that the educated man is the healthy man, that the good teacher is the good "docteur en médecine." There is a certain way in which the questions Panurge poses in *Le Tiers Livre* are prognoses, the answers he receives diagnoses, each resembling the aphorisms of Hippocrates. Hippocrates' sense of disease in the *Laws,* moreover, unites microcosmic man with the larger universe.

He who would make accurate forecasts as to those who will recover, and those who will die, and whether the disease will last a greater or less number of days, must understand all the symptoms thoroughly and be able to appreciate them, estimating their powers when they are compared with one another. . . . However, one must clearly realize about sure signs and about symptoms generally, that in every year and in every land bad signs indicate something bad, and good signs something favourable, since the symptoms described above prove to have the same significance in Libya, in Delos, and in Scythia. [25]

This is the same conceptualization of the human body writ large as the human commonwealth that Panurge uses in his *encomium moriae* on debts:

"Adoncques chascun membre se praepare et s'esvertue de nouveau à purifier et affiner cestuy thesaur. Les roignons par les venes emulgentes en tirent l'aiguosité, que vous nommez urine, et par les ureteres la découllent en bas. Au bas trouve receptacle propre, c'est la vessie, laquelle en temps oportun la vuide hors. La ratelle en tire le terrestre et la lie, que vous nommez melancholie. La bouteille du fiel en soubstraict la cholere superflue. Puys est transporté en une autre officine pour mieulx estre affiné, c'est le coeur. Lequel par ses mouvemens diastolicques et systolicques le subtilie et enflambe, tellement que par le ventricule dextre le mect à perfection, et par les venes l'envoye à tous les membres. Chascun membre l'attire à soy et s'en alimente à sa guise: pieds, mains, orelz, tous: et lors sont faictz debteurs, qui paravant estoient presteurs. Par le ventricule gausche il le faict tant subtil, qu'on le dict spirituel, et l'envoye à tous les membres par ses arteres, pour l'autre sang des venes eschauffer et esventer. Le poulmon ne cesse avecques ses lobes et souffletz le refraischir. En recongoissance de ce bien le coeur luy en depart le meilleur par la vene arteriale. En fin tant est affiné dedans le retz marveilleux, que par parès en sont faictz les espritz animaulx, moyennans les quelz elle imagine, discourt, juge, resoust, delibere, ratiocine et rememore."

"Then each member prepares itself and strives anew to purify and refine this treasure. The kidneys, by the renal conduits, draw off that liquid which you call urine, and pass it down through the ureters. Below is its proper receptacle, the bladder, which in the course empties it out. The spleen draws off the earthy part and the lees, which you call melancholy. The bile duct extracts the superfluous choler. Then the blood is transported for further refinement to another workshop, that is the heart, which by its diastolic and systolic movements so subtilizes and fires it that it is perfected in the right ventricle, and sent through the veins to all the members. All the members—the feet, the hands, the eyes, and all the rest—absorb it, and take nourishment from it, each in its own way. Thus they become debtors who previously were lenders. In the left ventricle the heart so subtilizes it that it is called spiritual, and then sends it to all the members through its arteries to heat and ventilate the rest of the blood in the veins. The lungs never cease to refresh it with their lappets and bellows and in return for this service the heart gives them of its best blood through the pulmonary artery. In the end it is so refined in the *miraculous network,* that it later becomes the material of the animal spirits, which endow us with imagination, reason, judgement, resolution, deliberation, ratiocination, and memory." [1.423; pp. 300–1]

This devilish connection between the interaction of bodily functions and the need for creditors and debtors is an especially comic development of Hippocratic anatomy, but the sense of humors is Galenic. Galen begins his study of medicine, as Rabelais begins his fiction, by citing books of the past. He is essentially inductive; unlike Hippocrates, Galen is an empiricist. The need for investigation on which Galen insists is the same need Pantagruel sees for Panurge in *Le Tiers Livre*—that Panurge must seek his own answers to the issues of marriage and cuckoldry, of human nature and human society. Indeed, Galen's description of his method in *The Diagnosis and Cure of the Soul's Errors* sounds like a rough definition of the humanism behind Panurge's Grand Tour:

> The man who wishes to be free from error must consider whether demonstration of an obscure matter is possible; then, when he shall find this out, he must seek, not alone and cursorily, but for a long time and with the help of men who are most truthful, prudent by nature, and well practiced in intellectual speculation to discover what the method of demonstration is; then, he must thereafter exercise himself anew in it for a long time before he goes in search of the most important things.[31]

Galen goes on to discuss the passions as irrational impulses, errors, and false opinions (3), which through lifelong discipline may be effectively trained (4, 5). "The education of children," he remarks, "in some way closely resembles horticulture" (7). In *De Captationibus* he attacks ambiguity in language; the characteristics he lists (4) have a particular relevance to Panurge's linguistic tricks in *Le Tiers Livre* when he attempts to console himself before adversary opinion.[32] Throughout Rabelais's fiction, then, Panurge is essentially Hippocratic in his outlook, whereas Pantagruel remains Galenic.

Medicine in particular (but also science generally) is given its greatest emphasis in *Le Quart Livre*. It is as if Rabelais, having determined the search for self-knowledge is ultimately an embracing of divine mystery—what Greene acutely calls "the predicament of the conditional, the contingent, the unforeseen, the enigmatic ground of our condition" (*Rabelais,* pp. 70–71)—is a sufficient definition of the nature of truth and the nature of man, has now turned his attention and his capacious energies to the nature of nature—cosmology, botany, zoology, anatomy, and pharmacology—and to the nature of the human imagination—fiction, myth, and fantasy. The prologue to *Le Quart Livre,* therefore, although the longest and in many ways the most abstruse, is unified by the theme of curing misfortune as we cure poor health: We must serve as our own physicians as the humble Couillatris does in choosing the return of his hatchet. We must choose our cures, heal ourselves by becoming lowly wise. This new poetics, of a kind of religion of medicine, prefaces the voyage of Pantagruel, Panurge, and Frère Jean into the world of reality and fiction beyond the lands of Europe, a world imaged largely by hunger, greed, and rapacity. The allusions to drink that have often thickened the pages of preceding books are now crowded out by images of eating, as in the case of Bringuenarilles, who eats windmills but is killed by a lump of butter in his throat (4.17). Other strange creatures, such as the Andouilles or sausages (whose natural enemy is Lent), are shaped like common foods (4.35–42). Science and eating are further joined in Rabelais's longest exercise in copia, Xenomanes' anatomy of Quaresmeprenant (or Lent), which stretches through three chapters (4.30–32), preceding the portrait of an inverse cosmography (4.32) and the myth that, standing as the book's central panel, unites science with fantasy and legend. It is the parable of Physis and Antiphysis—a story within a story—recited by the wise Pantagruel (4.32).

—"Physis (c'est Nature) en sa première portée enfanta Beaulté et Harmonie sans copulation charnelle, comme de soy mesmes est grandement feconde et fertile. Antiphysie, laquelle de tout temps est partie adverse de Nature, incontinent eut envie sus cestuy tant beau et honorable enfantement: et au rebours enfanta Amodunt et Discordance par copulation de Tellumon. Ilz avoient la teste sphaerique et ronde entierement, comme un ballon; non doulcement comprimée des deux coustez, comme est la forme humaine. Les aureilles avoient hault enlevées, graundes comme aureilles d'asne; les oeilz hors la feste, fichez sur des os semblables aux talons, sans soucilles, durs comme sont ceulx des cancres; les pieds ronds comme pelottes, les braz et mains tournez en arriere vers les espaules. Et cheminoient sus leurs testes, continuellement faisant la roue, cul sus teste, les pieds contremont. Et (comme vous scavez que es cingesses semblent leurs petits cinges plus beaulx que chose du monde) Antiphysie louoit et s'efforcoit prouver que la forme de ses enfans plus belle estoit et advenete que des enfans de Physis: disant que ainsi avoir les pieds et teste sphaeriques, et ainsi cheminer circulaire-ment en rouant, estoit la forme competente et perfaicte alleure retirante à quelque portion de divinité: par laquelle les cieulx et toutes choses eternelles sont ainsi contournées. Avoir les pieds en l'air, la teste en bas, estoit imitation du createur de l'univers: ven que les cheveulx sont en l'home comme racines, les jambes comme rameaux. Car les arbres plus commodement sont en terre fichees sus leurs racines que na seroient sus leurs rameaux. Par ceste demonstration alleguant que trop mieulx, plus aptement estoient ses enfans comme une arbre droicte, que ceulx de Physis, les quelz estoient comme une arbre renversée. . . . Ainsi, par le tesmoignage et astipulation des bestes brutes, tiroit tous les folz et insensez en sa sentence, et estoit en admiration à toutes gens ecervelez et desguarniz de bon jugement et sens commun. Depuys elle engendra les Matagotz, Cagotz et Papelars; les Maniacles Pistoletz, les Demoniacles Calvins, imposteurs de Geneve; les enraigez Putherbes, Briffaulx, Caphars, Chattemittes, Canibales, et aultres monstres difformes et contrefaicts en despit de Nature."

"Physis—Nature, that is—in her first delivery brought forth Beauty and Harmony, without physical copulation. For she is most fertile and prolific in herself. Antiphysis, who has always been Nature's enemy, was immediately jealous of these beautiful and noble offspring and, to be even with her, gave birth to Misharmony and Discord, by copulation with Tellumon. They had spherical heads, as round as footballs, and not delicately flattened on either side as human beings have theirs. Their ears were high on their heads, and stuck up like asses' ears. Their eyes stood out of their heads on the ends of bones like heel-bones, without eyebrows, and were as hard as crabs' eyes. Their feet were round, like tennis balls, and their hands and arms faced backwards, in reverse. They walked on their heads, continually turning cartwheels, arse over tip, with their legs in the air.

"Now, just as mother-apes—as you know—think their offspring the prettiest things in the world, so Antiphysis was loud in her children's praise, and took great pains to prove that they were prettier and more attractive than Physis's. A spherical head and spherical feet, she said, were the nicest possible shape; and a circular motion, like that of a cartwheel, was not only the most proper and perfect means of travelling, but smacked somewhat of the divine. For the heavens and all things eternal were made to revolve in just that way. To have one's feet in the air and one's head down, therefore, was to imitate the creator of the Universe, seeing that hair in men was like their roots, and their legs were like branches. Furthermore, trees are far more securely attached to the earth by their roots than they would be by their branches. By this argument she claimed that her children were far better off and far better shaped than Physis's, being formed like standing trees, while her rival's offspring resembled trees upside down. . . . So, basing her argument on evidence drawn from the brute creation, she attracted every fool and madman to her side, and won the admiration of every brainless idiot, of everyone, indeed, who lacked sound judgement and common sense.

"Since that time, she has brought forth the pious apes, holy hypocrites, and

pope-mongers; the maniacal nobodies, demoniacal Calvins, and imposters of
Geneva; the furious Puy-Herbaults—Pfui, how they stink!—the belly-stuffers,
church-lice, holy-holy men, cannibals, and other deformed monsters, misshapen in Nature's despite." [2.135–37; pp. 519–20]

This uncharacteristically bitter passage was written at a time when Rabelais
mistakenly thought his beloved France, under Henri II, was free of the Catholic
church at last. It gathers up the central idea in *Le Quart Livre*, that pride (Papi-
manes), hunger (Bringuenarilles), fear (Quaresmeprenant), self-indulgence
(Andouilles), avarice (the Chicquanous), and even foolishness (Dindenault) are
all monstrosities of human nature, diseases of the mind that result in grotesque
bodies and behavior. By contrast, Physis, or humanist nature, which breeds
beauty and harmony, or the orderly natural world fused with the world of
Christianity and Neoplatonism, is fertile, self-sustaining—and *content*. The
absence of pride in Physis suggests a trust in the natural order of things that
parallels Rabelais's humanism, his sense of medicine at one with his notion of
the quintessence. Yet this heavily scientific book—written as if the thought of
voyaging by star and compass set his mind to thinking of the laws of nature and
the corrupting inventions of man—culminates in the allegory of Gaster, the
belly, as the chief pagan god who, for such misguided people as the Gas-
trolatres, is the father of creation, of science and of art, and of the history of the
world (4.61).

> Dès le commencement, il inventa l'art fabrile et agriculture pour cultiver la
> terre, tendant à fin qu'elle luy produisist grain. Il inventa l'art militaire et armes
> pour grain defendre; medicine et Astrologie, avecques les mathematicques ne-
> cessaires, pour grain en saulveté par plusieurs siècles guarder et mestre hors les
> calamités de l'air, deguast des bestes brutes, larrecin des hriguans.
>
> So, in the beginning, he invented the blacksmith's art and the cultivation of
> the earth by agriculture, so that he might produce himself grain. He invented
> the art of war and arms in order to defend his corn; and medicine and astrology
> together, with the necessary mathematics, to keep corn in safety for many
> centuries, and to safeguard it from climatic disasters, the depredations of brute
> beasts, and the thieving of brigands. [2.224; p. 580]

Plutarch's discussion of oracles (*Moralia*, 435B) and Holy Scripture (Phil.
3:18) are both degraded in this inwardly turning self-indulgence, which is the
antithesis of the lessons of searching, self-knowledge, and trust in the greater

community of men and of God that Panurge learned in *Le Tiers Livre*. Here in *Le Quart Livre,* the comic but aging Everyman (who had every right, with his white hair, to fear cuckoldry) is reduced to a childlike coward; it is up to Pantagruel, not Panurge, to furnish a communal banquet of sapience at the book's close (4.64–65), to amend and correct the misuse of hunger that has been the main distraction of their voyage abroad. Only in this way can we see what Screech means when he remarks that the 1552 *Quart Livre,* written near the end of Rabelais's life, "shows a sustained concern with humanist learning and Christian humanist values." [33]

Le Quart Livre opens with homage once more to Erasmus, in a storm scene based on the Erasmian colloquy *Naufragium* (1523), and is frequently indebted to Herodotus, Plutarch, and Pliny as well as the scientific treatises of Aristotle and Galen (*Historia Animalium; On the Natural Faculties*), but the Senecan original (comparable to the shaping influence of Plato's *Symposium* for *Le Tiers Livre*) is Lucian's *True History*. Here Lucian's pretended voyage through the Pillars of Hercules to the moon and lands beyond combines authentic geography with incredible fantasy. "I observed some strange and wonderful things" about creatures on the moon, Lucian writes,

> that I wish to speak of. In the first place there is the fact that they are not born of women but of men; they marry men and do not even know the word woman at all! Up to the age of twenty-five each is a wife, and thereafter a husband. They carry their children in the calf of the leg instead of the belly. When conception takes place the calf begins to swell. In course of time they cut it open and deliver the child dead, and then they bring it to life by putting it in the wind with its mouth open. It seems to me that the term "belly of the leg" came to us Greeks from there, since the leg performs the function of the belly with them. But I will tell you something else, still more wonderful. They have a kind of men whom they call the Arboreals, who are brought into the world as follows: Exsecting a man's right genital gland, they plant it in the ground. From it grows a very large tree of flesh, resembling the emblem of Priapus: it has branches and leaves, and its fruit is acorns a cubit thick. When these ripen, they harvest them and shell out the men. Another thing, they have artificial parts that are sometimes of ivory and sometimes, with the poor, of wood, and make use of them in their intercourse. [34]

Such a passage as this—with its wide arc of exaggeration coming to an abrupt halt on the lucid image of dildos—stands behind the myth of Physis and

Antiphysis, whereas Lucian's subsequent *Odyssey*-like travels to the Isle of the Blest, the Isles of the Wretched, and the Isle of Dreams incorporate such realistic descriptions as that of the old man irrigating his garden for cabbages (p. 289). In the same way, reality interpenetrates the fiction of *Le Quart Livre*, as in the fictional Epistemon's presence at the actual funeral of Guillaume du Bellay (4.26–27), a funeral Rabelais himself attended.[35]

With Rabelais, however, such a loosened form as the imaginary voyage is still largely governed by humanist thought and rhetoric. The humanist's self-knowledge and tolerance, embodied in the ship under Pantagruel's command, must avoid or contain the disputatious worlds they persistently encounter, must form *within* the novel now the same triangular reaction that characterizes the humanist poetics of the earlier books. Pantagruel's overtly normative role throughout *Le Quart Livre*, as our representative, is a decided advance, but it is necessary in a fiction in which, from the early Council of Chesil (as the Council of Trent), we are subjected to entire worlds populated by fools in a long catalogue of islands (4.9–66). Beginning with Medamothi, Nowhere (4.2), Rabelais's most splendid tribute to Thomas More, these Lucianic worlds, drawn from their joint original, all harbor a delightful collection of tales, such as that of the junior devil and his losing bargains with a farmer (4.46) and the invention of boomeranging ammunition (4.62). Unlike Lucian, however, but closer to More, all such fanciful accounts are subjected to and metamorphosed by an enlightened Christian humanism. Events in *Le Quart Livre* are distinguished by transcendent and holy truths: The poetics here is a poetics of the *religion* of medicine.

Through Claudius, we are told in the prologue, the pagan Galen had some feelings for the Christian Bible. Drinking from Diogenes' tub has become a drink of the Eucharist. The herb pantagruelion reemerges as the philosophy Pantagruelism: "c'est certaine gayeté d'esprit conficte en mespris des choses fortuites"; *"a certain lightness of spirit compounded of contempt for the chances of fate,"* which finds its source in the admonition for the physician to heal himself recounted in Luke 4 (2.11–12; p. 439). Indeed, *Le Quart Livre* proper and the voyage for the Dive Bouteille at the hands of *la dive Bacbuc* (4.1 title) *set off* in religious ceremony.

En la Thalamege doncques feut l'assemblée de tous. La Pantagruel leur feist une briefe et saincte exhortation, toute auctorisée de propous extraictz de la Saincte Escripture, sus l'argument de naviguation. Laquelle finie, feut hault et clair faicte priere a Dieu, oyans et entendes tous les bourgeoys et citandins de Thalasse, qui estoient sus le mole accourruz pour veoir l'embarquement.

Après l'oraison feut melodieusement chanté le psaulme du sainct Roy David, lequel commence: *Quand Israel hors d'Aegypte sortit.* Le pseaulme parachevé, feurent sus le tillac les tables dressées et viandes promptement apportées. Les Thalassiens, qui pareillement avoient le pseaulme susdict chanté, feirent de leurs maisons force vivres et vinage apporter. Tous beurent a eulx. Ilz beurent a tous.

So the general assembly was on the *Thalamège,* and there Pantagruel gave them a short and pious exhortation on the subject of navigation, wholly based on arguments drawn from Holy Writ. When this was over, prayers were raised to God in high clear tones, distinct enough to be heard and understood by all the burgesses and citizens of Thalassa, who had rushed out on to the mole to witness their departure. After the prayer, there was a melodious singing of that psalm of the blessed King David which begins, *When Israel went out of Egypt.* Then, after the psalm was finished, tables were set up on deck and the meats promptly served. The Thalassians, who had sung this psalm with them, sent to fetch a quantity of food and wine from their houses. All drank to them; they drank to all. [2.33–34; p. 452]

This strikingly new tone in Rabelais's fiction has its pronounced effect for the entire *Quart Livre,* as when, for example, Panurge says farewell to the tricked Dindenault (2.51; p. 467).

If, then, *Le Quart Livre* seems at the first disappointing—slacker in tone, more loosely organized, more coarsely drawn—that is because its energies are now more intellectual than dramatic. From this point on (4.8), Panurge functions as the wayfaring but wayward *pilgrim,* Pantagruel as the enlightened, tolerant *believer;* and their running dispute (dramatized as cowardice versus courage) supplies both a firm framework and sufficient mortar to bind the otherwise discrete episodes. This basic dialectic, in which skepticism and faith are set against each other as running exempla of bad and good health, is reconciled at the most exceptional moment in all of Rabelais when we actually hear a god speak directly to men. It is a stunning and poetic passage, if somewhat long.

"Estant là abourdée, aulcuns des voyagiers dormans, aultres veiglans, aultres beuvans et souppans, feut de l'isle de Paxes ouie une voix de quelqu'un qui haultement appeloit *Thamoun.* Auquel cry tou feurent espovantez. Cestuy Thamous estoit leur pilot, natif de Aegypte, mais non congneu de nom, fors à quelques uns des voyagiers. Feut secondement ouie ceste voix: laquelle appelloit *Thamoun* en cris horrificque. Persone ne respondent, mais tou restans en silence et trepidation, en tierce foys ceste voix fut ouie plus terrible que davant. Dont advint que Thamous respondit: 'Je suis icy, que me demande tu? que veulx tu que je face?' Lors feut icelle voix plus haultement ouie, luy disant et commandant, quand il seroit en Palodes, publier et dire que Pan le grand Dieu estoit mort.

"Ceste parolle entendue, disoyt Epitherses tou les nauchiers et voyaigiers s'estre esbahiz et grandement effrayez; et entre eulx deliberans quel seroit meilleur ou taire ou publier ce que avoit esté commandé, dist Thamous son advis estre, advenent que lors ilz eussent vent en pouppe, passer oultre sans mot dire; advenent qu'il feust calme en mer, signifier ce qu'il avoit ouy. Quand doncques furent près Palodes advint qu'ilz n'eurent ne vent ne courant. Adoncques Thamous montant en prore, et en terre projectant sa veue, dist ainsi que luy estoit commandé: que Pan le grand estoit mort. Il n'avoir encores achevé le dernier mot quand feurent entendez grands souspirs, grandes lamentations et effroiz en terre, non d'une persone seule, mais de plusieurs ensemble.

"Ceste nouvelle (parce que plusieurs avoient esté praesens) feut bien toust divulguée en Rome.

"Et envoya Tibere Caesar, lors empereur en Rome, querir cestuy Thamous. Et, l'avoir entendu parler, adjousta foy a ses parolles. Et se guementant es gens doctes qui pour lors estoient en sa court et en Rome en bon nombre, qui estoit cestuy Pan, trouva par leur raport qu'il avoit esté filz de Mercure et de Penelope. Ainsi au paravant l'avoient escript Herodote, et Ciceron on tiers livre *De la Nature des dieux*. Toutes foys je le interpreteroys de celluy grand Servateur des fideles, qui feut en Judée ignominieusement occis par l'envie et inquité des Pontifes, docteurs, prebstres et moines de la loy Mosaicque. Et ne me semble l'interpretation abhorrente: car à bon droict peut il estre en languaige Gregoys dict Pan, veu que il est le nostre Tout, tout ce que sommes, tout ce que vivons, tout ce que avons, tout ce que esperons est luy, en luy, de luy, par luy. C'est le bon Pan, le grand pasteur, qui, comme atteste le bergier passionné Corydon, non seulment a en amour et affection ses brebis, mais aussi ses bergiers. A la mort duquel feurent plaincts, souspirs, effroys et lamentations en toute la machine de l'Univers, cieulx, terre, mer, enfers. A ceste miene interpretation compete le temps, car cestuy tresbon, tresgrand Pan, nostre unique Servateur, mourut lez Hierusalem, regnant en Rome Tibere Caesar."

Pantagruel, ce propous finy, resta en silence et profonde contemplation. Peu de temps après, nous veismes les larmes decouller de ses oeilz grosses comme oeufz de austruche. Ja me donne à Dieu, si j'en mens d'un seul mot.

"Now, as some of the passengers were sleeping and some awake, as some were eating and some drinking, a voice was heard from the island of Paxon of someone loudly crying, *Thamous!* This cry terrified them all. This Thamous was their captain, an Egyptian. But he was only known by name to one or two of the passengers. The voice was heard a second time, loudly and terrifyingly calling, *Thamous!* No one replied, but all stood silent and trembling. Then the voice was heard a third time, more terrible than before. Upon which Thamous answered: 'I am here. Who is calling me? What do you want me to do?' Then the voice was heard again, even louder, commanding him, when he reached the port of Paloda, to announce the news that the great god Pan was dead.

"Epitherses related that when they heard this speech all the sailors and passengers were amazed and greatly frightened. They debated amongst themselves whether it would be better to say nothing or to proclaim the news they had been given. Thamous gave his decision that if they had a favourable wind behind them they ought to pass by and say nothing, but if they were becalmed he would declare what he had heard. When they came close to Paloda, it happened that both wind and tide failed them. So Thamous climbed on the prow and, facing towards the land, declared, as he had been told to, that the great Pan was dead. No sooner had he spoken the last word than loud sighs, lamentations, and shrieks were heard from the shore, coming not from one person alone, but from many together.

"Since there had been several witnesses, this news soon spread to Rome; and Tiberius Caesar, who was then Emperor, sent for this Thamous. When he had listened to him, he believed his story and, on inquiring from men of learning, who were plentiful at that time at his court and in Rome, who this Pan was, he gathered from their answers that he was the son of Mercury and Penelope, as he had been recorded at an earlier day by Herodotus and by Cicero, in his third book *On the Nature of the Gods*.

"I should interpret this anecdote, nevertheless, to refer to that great Saviour of the Faithful, who was shamefully put to death in Judea through the envy and wickedness of the pontiffs, doctors, priests, and monks of the Mosaic Law, and I do not consider my reading of the story far-fetched. For he can rightfully be called, in the Greek tongue, Pan; seeing that he is our All. All that we are, all that we live by, all that we have, all that we hope for is from him, in him, of him, and by him. He is the good Pan, the great shepherd who, as the lovesick swain

Coridon affirms, loves not only his sheep with a great love, but his shepherds also. At his death there were wailings, sighs, fears, and lamentations throughout the whole mechanical universe, throughout the heavens, the earth, the sea, and hell beneath. The date agrees with this interpretation of mine. For that most good and mighty Pan, our Saviour, died outside Jerusalem in the reign of Tiberius Caesar."

When Pantagruel had finished his story he remained silent, in a profound meditation. A little while afterwards we saw the tears rolling down from his eyes, as big as ostrich eggs. God take my soul, if every word I say isn't the truth."

[2.123–25; pp. 510–12]

The story—clearly superior to the myth of Physis and Antiphysis—is from Plutarch's *De Defectu Oraculorum* 17 (*Moralia,* 419B–E), where it is treated seriously, as a historic event. Humanists of Rabelais's time considered the story serious and historical, too, because they were convinced it was an allegory of the Resurrection. Thus Pantagruel's story within our story is astonishingly plain-spoken, void of Erasmian and Rabelaisian copia, nearly evangelical in its tenor. The exegesis is scriptural. Pantagruel weeps because *Pan* is part of *Pan*urge and himself, *Pan*tagruel: The story is of *their* mortality and its connection to the salvation promised by the divine exemplum of Christ. This extraordinary tale, which takes us to an entirely new plane of experience in Rabelais's humanist fiction (and one from which we shall never quite return), gathers up the miraculous resurrection of Epistemon in Book 2, the miraculous birth of Gargantua in Book 1, and the miraculous herb pantagruelion in Book 3 to imply that the whole world of the book—including these journeys to its outermost limits—is overseen by a deity more powerful than man. Little wonder, then, that when at the close of *Le Quart Livre* Pantagruel offers a grand banquet, an occasion for communion (4.65–66), he can find no language to respond to religious doubt (4.64); little wonder that he engineers a final salvo against the false Muses (4.66) who had not inspired him (and Plutarch before him) with the story of Pan. *Scientia sine conscientia ruina animae,* he tells us; science without conscience is the ruin of the soul.

Le Quart Livre differs from its predecessors by Rabelais because it is a narrative of ideas written in the author's last years. Its center is a subject new for Rabelais, Stoic *ataraxia,* which Thomas M. Greene defines as "a lofty indifference to the contingencies of Fortune, an inner fortitude which renders the individual impervious to prosperity or adversity, even to joy or sorrow" (*Rabelais,* p. 71). That is not always the case with Pantagruel, as we have just seen. But it is clear that Rabelais has replaced his copy of Cicero's *De Officiis* with a copy of the Ciceronian *De Finibus,* where Tully honors the Stoic Posidonius, his renowned teacher of rhetoric in Rhodes, with an analysis of Stoicism in Book 3. Here the empirical outlook (which Pantagruel enacts by voyaging) leads to an understanding of the world as guided by the mind of God, man's function as the lofty submission of his will to nature.

Prima est enim conciliatio hominis ad ea quae sunt secundum naturam; simul autem cepit intellegentiam vel notionem potius, quam appellant ἐωθυαν illi, viditque rerum agendarum ordinem et ut ita dicam concordiam, multo eam pluris aestimavit quam omnia illa quae prima dilexerat, atque ita cognitione et ratione collegit ut statueret in eo collocatum summum illud hominis per se laudandum et expetendum bonum; quod cum positum sit in eo quod ϑηολο Stoici, nos appellemus convenientiam, si placet,—cum igitur in eo sit id bonum quo omnia referenda sunt, honeste facta ipsumque honestum, quod solum in bonis ducitur, quamquam post oritur, tamen id solum vi sua et dignitate expetendum est, eorum autem quae sunt prima naturae propter se nihil est expetendum. . . . Est tamen ea secundum naturam multoque nos ad se expeten-dam magis hortatur quam superiora omnia. . . . Cum autem omnia officia a principiis naturae proficiscantur, ab iisdem necesse est proficisci ipsam sapien-tiam. Sed quemadmodum saepe fit ut is qui commendatus sit alicui pluris sum faciat cui commendatus quam illum a quo sit, sic minime mirum est primo nos sapientiae commendari ab initiis naturae, post autem ipsam sapientiam nobis cariorem fieri quam illa sint a quibus ad hanc venerimus. . . . Sapientia enim et animi magnitudinem complectitur et iustitiam et ut omnia quae homini acci-dant infra se esse indicet. . . . Cum igitur hoc sit extremum, congruenter naturae convenienterque vivere, necessario sequitur omnes sapientes sem-per feliciter, absolute, fortunate vivere, nulla re impediri, nulla prohiberi, nulla egere.

Man's first attraction is towards the things in accordance with nature: but as soon as he has understanding, or rather becomes capable of "conception"—in Stoic phraseology *ennoia*—and has discerned the order and so to speak harmony that governs conduct, he thereupon esteems this harmony far more highly than all the things for which he originally felt an affection, and by exercise of intelligence and reason infers the conclusion that herein resides the Chief Good of man, the thing that is praiseworthy and desirable for its own sake; and that inasmuch as this consists in what the Stoics term *homologia* and we with your approval may call "conformity"—inasmuch I say as in this resides that Good which is the End to which all else is a means, moral conduct and Moral Worth itself, which alone is counted as a good, although of subsequent development, is nevertheless the sole thing that is for its own efficacy and value desirable, whereas none of the primary objects of nature is desirable for its own sake. . . . Again, as all "appropriate acts" are based on the primary impulses of nature, it follows that Wisdom itself is based on them also. But as it often happens that a man who is introduced to another values this new friend more highly than he does the person who gave him the introduction, so in like manner it is by no means surprising that though we are first commended to Wisdom by the primary natural instincts, afterwards Wisdom itself becomes dearer to us than are the instincts from which we came to her. . . . For Wisdom includes also magnanimity and justice and a sense of superiority to all the accidents of man's estate. . . . Inasmuch then as the final aim is to live in agreement and harmony with nature, it necessarily follows that all wise men at all times enjoy a happy, perfect and fortunate life, free from all hindrance, interference or want.[36]

Physis, as Harmony, needs no lengthy discussion by Pantagruel because, in discussing Pan, the All, he has already defined her; moreover, his every action in *Le Quart Livre* has realized her teachings. She would Christianize Cicero too. Instead, Pantagruel condemns Antiphysis, to make certain that this rejection of the sick, the deformed, and the immoral will instruct his passengers, regardless of what form such forces may take on whatever islands they must visit. All are simply so many temptations set by nature and by the gods between them and the Dive Bouteille. That the voyage is long between the two points—between the streets of Paris and the land of Bacbuc—does not bother him, however, because as a Stoic he sees all life as a learning experience. Nature is a lesson book for him every bit as much as it is for Hippocrates or Galen or Cicero (*De Finibus* 3.4.17–18). Thus Pantagruel nourishes an inner equilibrium at odds with the strict hierarchy of passengers and crew aboard the ship named for the egalitarian Thélème; he teaches instead an egalitarianism of mind and attitude. We may find him remote, chilly, less interesting as a character; but in terms of the meaning of Rabelais's humanist fiction he emerges clearly in *Le Quart Livre,* as he has not before, as the fiction's superior hero. Next to him, the recalcitrant Panurge seems too self-centered. In the context of *Le Quart Livre,* Panurge still has far to go and much to learn. He is still the fallen, unclean man (who even beshits himself on one occasion) who must go the distance to the oracle of Bacbuc to cleanse himself, and to be reborn.

There is one final startling passage in *Le Quart Livre,* one of the most crucial in all of Rabelais's fiction: the strange interlude of the frozen words (4.55–56). In a fiction writer so heavily reliant on words as Rabelais, this is an extraordinary examination of humanist grammar, and at its deepest brilliance and its widest fantasy.[37] If Rabelais's chief premise and theme are identical to the opening of Aristotle's *Metaphysics,* "πάτες ανθρωποη ποδ ειδθναι δρέγουπαι φθοει (980a21) (all men naturally desire knowledge), then the tales, myths, monologues, dialogues, declamations, and disputations all work to that end. Yet such language conspires against experience since in stopping time and event it distorts actions and accomplishments. The singular means at the humanist teacher's disposal betray his purposes, as antique texts, too narrowly codified, are likely to mislead or to become dead issues. This is one reason for Rabelais's dependence on Erasmian copia, as if his restless mind would escape reducing or killing concepts by multiplying his expressions of them. The wise Pantagruel seems to want the same thing when he notes in 3.19 that

"C'est abus, dire que ayons languaige naturel. Les languaiges sont part institutions arbitraires et convenences des peuples; les voix (comme disent les dialecticiens), ne signifient naturellement, mais a plaisir."

"It's nonsense to say that we have a natural language; languages arise from arbitrary conventions and the needs of peoples. Words, as the dialecticians say, have meanings not by nature, but at choice." [1.480; p. 339]

He has good authority in Aristotle (*On Interpretation* 26a28–30); he himself cites others. But behind his observation—and indeed behind Rabelais's humanist poetics, as made clear finally in the episode of the frozen words—lies his last major Senecan original, the *Cratylus* of Plato. This dialogue, to which Rabelais pays open homage in 4.37, is the earliest extant attempt to discuss the origin and functioning of language; it is occasioned when Hermogenes realizes that the literal etymology of his own name is not true, and is treated more extensively and seriously by Socrates, who sees in the flux of Heraclitus the possible denial of any eternal truths or forms. The dialogue begins rapidly with Hermogenes' complaint before Cratylus and Socrates.

Cratylus, whom you see here, Socrates, says that everything has a right name of its own, which comes by nature, and that a name is not whatever people call a thing by agreement, just a piece of their own voice applied to the thing, but that there is a kind of inherent correctness in names, which is the same for all men, both Greeks and barbarians. . . . For my part, Socrates, I have often talked with

Cratylus and many others, and cannot come to the conclusion that there is any correctness of names other than convention and agreement. For it seems to me that whatever name you give to a thing is its right name; and if you give up that name and change it for another, the later name is no less correct than the earlier, just as we change the names of our servants; for I think no name belongs to any particular thing by nature, but only by the habit and custom of those who employ it and who established the usage.[38]

Socrates argues for words as natural, not conventional, citing the need for a natural language in the law courts (389D). How else, he asks later, could man question, discover, or learn (493B)? In *Le Quart Livre,* it is the wise Pantagruel who first hears the frozen words and senses their profound significance (4.55).

En pleine mer nous banquetans, gringotans, divisans et faisans beaulx et cours discours, Pantagruel se leva et tint en pieds pour discouvrir à l'environ. Puys nous dist: "Compaignons, oyez vous rien? Me semble que je oy quelques gens parlans en l'air, je n'y voy toutesfoys personne. Escoutez." A son commandement nous feusmes attentifz, et à pleines aureilles humions l'air, comme belles huytres en escalle, pour entendre si voix ou son aulcun y seroit espart: et pour rien n'en perdre, a l'example de Antonin l'Empereur, aulcuns oppousions nos mains en paulme darriere les aureilles. Ce neantmoins protestions voix quelconques n'entendre.

Pantagruel continuoit affermant ouyr voix diverses en l'air, tant de homes comme de femmes, quand nous feut advis, ou que rous les oyons parseillement, ou que les aureillies nous cornoient. Plus perseverions escoutans, plus discernions les voix, jusques à entendre motz entiers. Ce que nous effraya grandement, et non sans cause, personne ne voyans et entendens voix et sons tant divers, d'homes, de femmes, d'enfans, de chevaulx.

As we were banqueting, far out at sea, feasting and speechifying and telling nice little stories, Pantagruel suddenly jumped to his feet, and took a look all round him. "Can you hear something, comrades?" he asked. "I seem to hear people talking in the air. But I can't see anything. Listen."

We all obeyed his command, and listened attentively, sucking in the air in great earfuls, like good oysters in the shell, to hear if any voice or other snatches of sound could be picked up; and so as to miss nothing, some of us cupped the palms of our hands to the backs of our ears, after the manner of the Emperor Antoninus. But, notwithstanding, we protested that we could hear no voice whatever. Pantagruel, however, continued to affirm that he could hear several voices on the air, both male and female; and then we decided that either we could hear them too, or else there was a ringing in our ears. Indeed, the more keenly we listened, the more clearly we made out voices, till in the end we could hear whole words. This greatly frightened us, and not unnaturally, since we could see no one, yet could hear voices and different sorts of sounds of men, women, children, and horses. [2.203; pp. 566–67]

Panurge immediately cries out in alarm and asks Frère Jean to draw his cutlass to protect him—a natural reaction, we are told. But *Le Quart Livre* is a book about the *un*natural: the imaginary and the fantastic and the religious. Like the herb pantagruelion, like the holy fool of Folly, the vision of Bembo, and the directives of Oisille, Book 4 is meant to awaken our *faith*. The spiritually advanced Pantagruel advocates this position by finding in the voices cause for mystical knowledge and mystical experience.

Pantagruel, entendent l'esclandre que faisoit Panurge, dist: "Qui est ce fuyart là bas? Voyons premierement quelz gens sont. Par adventure sont ilz nostres. Encores ne voy je persone? Et si voy cent mille à l'entour. Mais entendons. J'ay leu qu'un Philosophy, nommé Petron, estoyt en ceste opinion que feussent plusieurs mondes soy touchans les uns les aultres en figure triangulaire ae-quilaterale, en la parte et centre des quelz disoit estre le manoir de Verité, et là habiter les Parolles, les Idées, les Exemplaires et protraictz de toutes choses passés et futures: autour d'icelles estre le Siecle. Et en certaines années, par longs intervalles, part d'icelles tomber sus les humains comme catarrhes, et comme tomba la rousée sus la toison de Gedéon; part là rester reservée pour l'advenir, jusques à la consommation du Siecle.

"Me souvient aussi que Aristoteles maintient les parolles de Homere estre voltigeantes, volantes, moventes, et par consequent animées.

"D'adventaige Antiphanes disoit la doctrine de Platon es parolles estre sem-blable, lesquelles en quelque contrée, on temps du fort hyver, lors que sont proferées, gelent et glassent à la froydeur de l'air, et ne sont ouyes. Semblable-ment ce que Platon enseignoyt es jeunes enfans, à peine estre d'icelux entendu lors que estoient vieulx devenuz."

On hearing Panurge make all this uproar, Pantagruel asked: "Who is that coward down there? Let's see first what people they are. They may happen to be our friends. But still I can't catch sight of anyone, though I can see a hundred miles all round. But let's listen. I have heard that a certain philosopher called Petron believed that there are several worlds touching one another, as at the

points of an equilateral triangle. The inner area of this triangle, he said was the abode of truth and there lived the names and forms, the ideas and images of all things past and future. Outside this lies the Age—the secular world. In certain years, however, at long intervals, some part of these falls on humankind like distillations, or as the dew fell on Gideon's fleece, to remain there laid up for the future, awaiting the consummation of the Age. I remember, too, that Aristotle maintains Homer's words to be bounding, flying, and moving, and consequently alive. Antiphanes, also, said that Plato's teaching was like words that congeal and freeze on the air, when uttered in the depths of winter in some distant country. That is why they are not heard. He said as well that Plato's lessons to young children were hardly understood by them till they were old."
[2.204−5; pp. 567−68]

Pantagruel, as the true Platonist and mystic, sees in the frozen and thawing words significations of eternal truths, forms, and ideas. His teaching—much of it actually taken from the *De Defectu Oraculorum* of Plutarch (*Moralia*, 422A−E)—is both rational and obscure, containing in its finite application truths that are infinite, ineffable. But he cannot allay the fears of the disbelievers—including Panurge. So the captain of their ship tries his hand (4.56).

> Le pillot feist responce: "Seigneur, de rien ne vous effrayez. Icy est le confin de la mer glaciale, sus laquelle feut, au commencement de l'hyver dernier passé, grosse en felonne bataille, entre les Arismapiens et les Nephelibates. Lors gelerent en l'air les parolles et crys des hommes et femmes, les chaplis des masses, les hurtys des harnois, des bardes, les hannissemens des chevaulx et tout aultre effroy de combat. A ceste heure la rigeur de l'hyver passée, advenente le serenité et temperie du bon temps, elles fondent et sont ouyes."

> It was the captain that answered: "My lord, don't be afraid. This is the edge of the frozen sea, and at the beginning of last winter there was a great and bloody battle here between the Arimaspians and the Cloud-riders. The shouts of the men, the cries of the women, the slashing of the battle-axes, the clashing of the armour and harnesses, the neighing of the horses and all the other frightful noises of battle became frozen on the air. But just now, the rigours of winter being over and the good season coming on with its calm and mild weather, these noises are melting, and so you can hear them." [2.206; p. 568]

The world of nature offers a variant explanation, equally sufficient, plausible, fantastic. We can, in Rabelais's world of disputations, take our choice. But we may wish, in the triangularity of a humanist poetics, to reconcile them: to see the episode of the frozen words as an exemplum of the nature of religion and the religion of nature. In examining his very own humanist rhetoric, Rabelais would argue that Plato and Hippocrates are, at root, one rather than two.

After so stunning a passage on the nature of truth, of reason, and of language, *Le Cinquième Livre* appears scattered, unfocused, and lacking in such richly woven statements and symbols. This volume completes the sea voyage, but it advances neither characterization nor idea. *Le Cinquième Livre* was first published as an entire work in 1564, a decade after Rabelais's death, and we do not know if Rabelais wrote any part of it—scholarly consensus now leans toward another author or authors for most of it, although Rabelais may well have written the opening and closing chapters.[39] The book's final prophecy *Trinch* (5.45) retains the ambiguity that drink may be either the Eucharist of salvation or the incoherence and oblivion of a drunken stupor, or both. The final word of importance in the fiction we inherit—the sole commandment of the holy bottle—is at once equivocal, prophetic, enigmatic. Like the letter E at Delphi that Plutarch's essay explores—the Senecan original for *Le Cinquième Livre,* if one is needed (*Moralia,* 384D–394C)—the mysterious word may mean everything, many things, or nothing. The priestess Bacbuc tells Panurge and his companions:

"Si avez noté ce qui est en lettres Ioniques escrit dessus la porte du temple, vous avez peu entrendre qu'en vin est verité cachée. La dive Bouteille vous y envoye, soyez vous mesmes interpretes de vostre entreprinse."

"If you have noticed what is written in Ionic characters above the gate of the temple, you may have understood that the truth lies hidden in wine. The Holy Bottle directs you to it. You must be your own interpreters in this matter." [2.454; p. 705]

Nor had any scientists, philosophers, or theologians of the New Learning come into possession of all the facts that were to be known.

"Vos philosophes qui se complaignent toutes choses estre par les anciens escriptes, rien ne leur estre laissé de nouveau à inventer, ont tort trop evident. Ce que du ciel vous apparoist, et appellez Phenomenes, ce que la terre vous exhibe, ce que la mer et autres fleuves contiennent, n'est comparable à ce qui est en terre caché."

"Your philosophers who complain that everything has been described by the ancients, and that nothing new is left for them to discover, are only too patently wrong. So much as you can see of the heavens, and which you call *Phenomena*, so much as the earth reveals to you, so much as the sea and all the rivers contain, is not to be compared with what is concealed in the earth." [2.461; p. 710]

For Bacbuc, the earth remains the home of Ceres, the fertile mother of incredible riches, the eternal Gargamelle. The means of finding those riches, in due course of time, is by the path of a Christian humanism. "Car tous Philosophes et sages antiques, à bien seurement et plaisamment parfaire le chemin de la cognoissance divine et chasse de sapience, ont estimé deux choses necessaires, guyde de Dieu et compagnie d'homme"; "For all ancient philosophers and sages have reckoned two things to be necessary for safe and pleasant travel on the road of wisdom and in the pursuit of knowledge; God's guidance and the company of men" [2.461–62; p. 710]

Other early works of Continental humanist poetics have ended inconclusively—the *Encomium Moriae* in paradox, *Il Cortegiano* and *L'Heptaméron* in an unfinished debate—and Rabelais's monumental contribution is no exception. In the last line of *Le Cinquième Livre* the boats are in the harbor once more, but it is unclear whether they have returned home or are about to set sail again. We, and they, may still be in midvoyage. Rabelais's encyclopedic complexity and imagination finally defy total analysis. They render our examination inferior to our needs for judgment, and the powers of our imagination must emend our learning. Rabelais too practices the art of methexis.

SIX

Post tenebras spero lucem: Cervantes, *El Ingenioso Hidalgo,*

and the Poetics of Imitatio

UNLIKE THE WORKS OF HIS
PREDECESSORS, CERVANTES'
MAGNIFICENT HUMANIST FICTION,
EL INGENIOSO HIDALGO DON QUIJOTE
DE LA MANCHA (1605; *SEGUNDA PARTE,* 1615) IS
THE PRODUCT OF LATE AGE—LATE IN THE LIFE
of the author and late in the age of humanism, and of a Continental humanist
poetics. Strikingly similar in certain ways to the work of Rabelais, *Don Quijote*
is a *diegesis*—in this instance, of two companions, Don Quijote and Sancho
Panza, "one the pole-star of knight errantry and the other the star of squirely
fidelity" according to the Duchess; "el uno, por norte de la andante caballería, y
el otro, por estrella de la escuderil fidelidad" [1]—that is also an act of peirastics,
a narrative that inquires after truth. Like *Gargantua* and *Pantagruel, Don Quijote*
is a rich and seemingly inexhaustible work, written, as Mark Van Doren tells
us, by a man who had "a mind both spacious and subtle, both full to overflow-
ing and free to overflow." [2] At the same time, the astonishingly variegated
world of the Don and Sancho seems at once simpler and more accessible than
that of Pantagruel and Panurge. Rather than surprise us with the unexpected
and the fabulous, *Don Quijote* insists on realizing old models anew, aligning the
prototypical with the present and so authenticating (and giving timeless value
to) the past. This emphasis on models is evident everywhere, for *Don Quijote* is
primarily a book about books, about the shapes, uses, and effects of books. As
such, it allows us at once, in this grand metafiction, to locate ourselves in the
structures and forms of the chronicle, pastoral, romance, novella, verse, debate, essay, satire, burlesque, ballad, drama, and proverb—the whole arsenal
of humanist writings—in ways that constantly solicit our attention (as they
often do with the characters of this novel) and invite our unending speculation
(which the characters too frequently forgo). As a consequence, *Don Quijote* is

profoundly humanist, despite its focus on the chivalric adventures indigenous to an earlier cultural period, because it makes the chief humanist practice of imitatio *both subject and method*. In so structuring his work, Cervantes continually shows the misapplication, inadequacy, and even irrelevancy of humanist forms of thought and expression, much as the Don and Sancho learn that the age of iron in which they live cannot sustain the golden age of chivalry now dead: *Don Quijote* recalls the folly of Erasmus and the plangency of Castiglione in its critique of humanist teaching. But, dialectically, *Don Quijote* is also a stunning late exemplar of such teaching, for in its ongoing disputation between precept and practice—between what is desirable and what is possible—the novel examines the central issues and tensions raised by a century of humanist teaching. Under such instructive and informing pressures, our own attitudes and judgments—like those of the Don and Sancho—are subject to change and transformation.

Cervantes is thus "the magician of refracted meaning," as Frederick Willey has it;[3] and Don Quijote himself wryly agrees: "My history," he says, "needs a commentary to make it understandable"; "Y asi debe de ser de mi historia, que tendrá necesidad de comento para entenderla" (2.3; 2:33; p. 490). But such a commentary is not far for us to seek, as it could not have been for Cervantes' early readers. We can begin with his own hypostatic interest in imitatio. That is, after all, where the work itself begins, when the Don sells off many acres of cornland to buy every book of chivalric adventure he can find.

> En resolucíon, él se enfrascó tanto en su lectura, que se le pasaban las noches leyendo de claro en claro, y los días de turbio en turbio; y así, del poco dormir y del mucho leer se le secó el celebro, de manera que vino a perder el juicio. Llenósele la fantasía de todo aquello que leía en los libros, así de encantamentos como de pendencias, batallas, desafios, heridas, requiebros, amores, tormentas y disparates imposibles: y asentósele de tal modo en la imaginación que era verdad toda aquella máquina de aquellas sonadas soñadas invenciones que leía, que para él no habia otra historia más cierta en el mundo.

> In short, he so buried himself in his books that he spent the nights reading from twilight till daybreak and the days from dawn till dark; and so from little sleep and much reading, his brain dried up and he lost his wits. He filled his mind with all that he read in them, with enchantments, quarrels, battles, challenges, wounds, wooings, loves, torments, and other impossible nonsense; and so deeply did he steep his imagination in the belief that all the fanciful stuff he read was true, that to his mind no history in the world was more authentic.

> [1.1; 1:24; p. 32]

Thus directed by his own antique texts, he chooses a life not in imitation of Christ but in imitation of Amadís, shaping both his and Sancho's life to a chivalric pattern, as he confesses straightforwardly to the canon at the close of his third sally:

> —Yo no sé que haya más que decir; sólo me guío por el ejemplo que me da el grande Amadís de Gaula, que hizo a su escudero conde de la Insula Firme

> "I do not know what more there is to say. I am guided solely by the example of the great Amadis of Gaul, who made his squire Count of the Firm Isle."

> [1.50; 1:335; p. 443]

But the flat statement is really the hard-won conclusion of an argument he has delivered early on to Sancho, an argument that, not coincidentally, is the fundamental definition of humanist poetics.

> Quero Sancho, que se pas que el famoso Amadís de Gaula fue uno de los más perfectos caballeros andantes. No he dicho bien *fue uno:* fue el solo, el primero, el único, el señor de todos cuantos hubo en su tiempo en el mundo. Mal año y mal mes para don Belianís y para todos aquellos que dijeren que se le igualo en algo, porque se engañan, juro cierto. Digo asimismo que, cuando algún pintor quiere salir famoso en su arte, procura imitar los originales de los más únicos pintores que sabe; y esta mesma regla corre por todos los más oficios o ejercicios de cuenta que sirven para adorno de las repúblicas, y así lo ha de hacer y hace el que quiere alcanzar nombre de prudente y sufrido, imitando a Ulises, en cuya persona y trabajos nos pinta Homero un retrato vivo de prudencia y de sufrimiento, como también nos mostró Virgilio, en persona de Eneas, el valor de un hijo piadoso y la sagacidad de un valiente y entendido capitán, no pintándolo ni describiéndolo como ellos fueron, sino como habían de ser, para quedar ejemplo a los venideros hombres de sus virtudes. Desta mesma suerte, Amadís fue el norte, el lucero, el sol de los valientes y enamorados caballeros, a quien debemos de imitar todos aquellos que debajo de la bandera de amor y de la caballería militamos. Siendo, pues, esto ansí, como lo es, hallo yo, Sancho amigo, que el caballero andante que más le imitare estará más cerca de alcanzar la perfección de la caballería.

> "So I would have you know, Sancho, that the famous Amadis of Gaul was one of the most perfect of knights errant. I was wrong to say *one;* he was the sole, the first, the unique, the prince of all there were in the world in his day. A fig for Sir Belianis and for all who claimed to be in any respect his equal. For I swear they are mistaken. What is more I say that when any painter wishes to win fame in his art, he endeavors to copy the pictures of the most excellent painters he knows;

and the same rule obtains for all professions and pursuits of importance that serve to adorn the commonwealth. So what any man who wants a reputation for prudence and patience must do, and does, is to imitate Ulysses, in whose person and labours Homer paints for us a lively picture of prudence and patience; just as Virgil shows us in the person of Aeneas the virtue of a dutiful son and the sagacity of a brave and skilful captain. They do not paint them or describe them as they were, but as they should have been, to serve as examples of their virtues for future generations. In the same way Amadis was the pole-star, the morning star, the sun of all valiant knights and lovers, and all of us who ride beneath the banner of love and chivalry should imitate him. This being the case, Sancho my friend, I conclude that the knight errant who best copies him will attain most nearly to the perfection of chivalry." [1.25; 1 : 153; p. 202]

This is a poetic we have seen often before, especially in *Il Cortegiano* where it draws with equal force on Cicero and Raphael; with Don Quijote, such imitative behavior governs every act—his name, his knighthood, his lady, his mission—and his every speech. In thus yoking precept to experience, he finds direction, purpose, solace, even *liberty;* he seems never at a loss to explain events even across a landscape altogether new to him. Indeed, when he thinks it is his duty to demonstrate his love for Dulcinea del Toboso (his perfection of the peasant girl Aldonza Lorenzo, for Don Quijote's powers of imitation lend him powers of transformation too), he adds to his resources in Amadís the pattern of Roldán's madness, a double imitation that he finds ready to copy in the story of Cardenio who transforms himself into Grisóstomo,[4] naming himself after Chrysostom, the orator "of the golden mouth" in patristic history. Thus we are not surprised when, weary on his way homeward for the last time, he finds sudden release and joy when he stumbles upon a print shop in Barcelona, the first cause of his inspiration now the final cause for joy.

> Sucedío, pues, que yendo por una calle, alzó los ojos don Quijote, y vio escrito sobre una puerta, con letras muy grandes: *Aqui se imprimen libros;* de lo que se contentó mucho, porque hasta entonces no había visto emprenta alguna, y deseaba saber cómo fuese. Entró dentro, con todo su acompañamiento, y vio tirar en una parte, corregir en otra, componer en ésta, enmendar en aquélla, y, finalmente toda aquella máquina que en las emprentas grandes se muestra. Llegábase don Quijote a un cajón y preguntaba qué era aquello que allí se hacía; dábanle cuenta los oficiales; admirábase, y pasaba adelante.

> Now, as they were going down a street, Don Quixote happened to raise his eyes, and saw written over a door in very large letters: *"Books printed here,"* which

greatly pleased him, for he had never before seen any printing and longed to know how it was done. So he went in with all his followers, and saw them drawing off the sheets in one place, correcting the proofs in another, setting up the type in a third and revising in yet another—in fact he saw all the processes of a large printing-house. Don Quixote went up to one compartment and asked what they were doing there. The workmen explained to him; and he watched in wonder and passed on. [2.62; 2:322; p. 876]

Don Quijote, whose adventures have been willful acts of transformation, now seems himself transformed.

The Don's deliberate yoking together of precept and experience is reduplicated by the increasingly faithful Sancho Panza, "the great Sancho Panza, flower and mirror of all Governors of Isles" ("del gran Sancho Panza, flor y espejo de todos los insulanos gobernadores," 2.52; 2:273; p. 810). Whereas greed first motivates Sancho to follow his mad master in Book 1, his desire to govern a realm, to advance himself and his family, slowly translates his initial skepticism into the possibility—he becomes insistent about this—of governing his own land. With him too what is conceived can be realized and, inversely, illusion can become delusion. By Book 2, the double act of imitation is his, for he imitates Don Quijote's imitation of knights-errant not only in his pursuit of adventures but in his transformation of Aldonza Lorenzo into Dulcinea—his own act of enchantment—and increasingly in his speech: in his defense of the Don (2.33), in his statement of the chivalric mission (2.49), and in his use of archaic language (2.72). He is the last in Cervantes' work to cite chivalric romances positively (2.74) and the one who, in the end, attempts to urge the Don to return to a fourth sally as shepherd-errant (2.74). Conversely, the false *Don Quijote* by the apparently pseudonymous Alonso Fernandez de Avellaneda (?September 1614), first mentioned by Cervantes in 2.59, is condemned as false and treacherous because its characters do not conform to the 1605 prototypes. This "new history" is spurious and untrustworthy, that is, precisely because it is *non*imitative, because it *refuses* to practice imitatio.

This is important, for Cervantes' burlesques of chivalric adventures—seen, for example, in the dubbing of Don Quijote in 1.3—suggest a residual skepticism on his part concerning the value of humanist imitatio, even for a writer of humanist fiction. But his attitude is not so simple as that. At the very outset, in the Prologo to Book 1, Cervantes suggests, initially at least, that Don Quijote is a self-projection, his own imitatio of himself, begun during a term of imprisonment for debts.

Desocupado lector: sin juramento me podrás creer que quisiera que este libro, como hijo del entendimiento, fuera el más hermoso, el más gallardo y más discreto que pudiera imaginarse. Pero no ne podido yo contravenir al orden de naturaleza; que en ella cada cosa engendra su semejante. Y así, ¿qué podra engendrar el estéril y mal cultivado ingenio mío sino la historia de un hijo seco, avellando, antojadizo y lleno de pensamientos varios y nunca imaginados de otro alguno, bien como quien se engendró en una cárcel, donde toda incomodidad tiene su asiento y donde todo triste ruido hace su habitación?

Idle reader, you can believe without any oath of mine that I would wish this book, as the child of my brain, to be the most beautiful, the liveliest and the cleverest imaginable. But I have been unable to transgress the order of nature, by which like gives birth to like. And so, what could my sterile and ill-cultivated genius beget but the story of a lean, shrivelled, whimsical child, full of varied fancies that no one else has ever imagined—much like one engendered in prison, where every discomfort has its seat and every dismal sound its habitation?

[Pro.; 1:11; p. 25]

Yet this too may be a parody, for he extends this underlying identity to show us that it is grounds for an antihumanist rhetoric (something he means here to associate with his rival, Lope de Vega). He tells a "lively and very intelligent friend" ("*gracioso y bien entendido*," Pro.; 1:11; p. 26) who appears unexpectedly, that his work is

una leyenda seca como un esparto, ajena de invención, menguada de estilo, pobre de concetos y falta de toda erudición y doctrina, sin acotaciones en las márgenes y sin anotaciones en el fin del libro, como veo que están otros libros, aunque sean fabulosos y profanos, tan llenos de sentencias de Aristóteles, de Platón y de toda la caterva de filósofos, que admiran a los leyentes y tienen a sus autores por hombres leídos, eruditos y elocuentes? ¡Pues qué, cuando citan la Divina Escritura, no dirán sino que son unos santos Tomases y otros Doctores de la Iglesia; guardando en esto un decoro tan ingenioso, que en un renglón han pintado un enamorado destraído y en otro hacen un sermoncico cristiano, que es un contento y un regalo olle o leelle! De todo esto ha da carecer mi libro.

a tale as dry as a rush, barren of invention, devoid of style, poor in wit and lacking in all learning and instruction, without quotations in the margins or notes at the end of the book; whereas I see other works, never mind how fabulous and profane, so full of sentences from Aristotle, Plato and the whole herd of philosophers, as to impress their readers and get their authors a reputation for wide reading, erudition and eloquence. And when they quote Holy Scripture! You will be bound to say that they are so many St. Thomases or other doctors of the church, observing such an ingenious solemnity in it all that in one line they will depict a distracted lover and in the next preach a little Christian homily, that is a treat and a pleasure to hear or read. My book will lack all this.

[Pro.; 1 : 12; p. 26]

Yet in a novel that urges us to avoid the rashness of Don Quijote in our reading of books, to exercise caution but not dismiss him entirely, this may be only an attack on extreme uses of florilegia, an advocacy of Attic over Asiatic style. The dedication, for instance, to the Duque de Béjar, talks of him as a patron because of his special disposal to "the liberal arts" ("las buenas artes," Ded.; 1 : 9; p. 23), and though the friend provides Cervantes with various traditional sources, some of them in common with Don Quijote's own—Cato, Homer, Vergil, Caesar, Cicero, Plutarch, the Bible—he advises against them:

Y, pues, esta vuestra escritura no mira a más que a deshacer la autoridad y cabida que en el mundo y en el vulgo tienen los libros de caballerías, no hay para qué andéis mendigando sentencias de filósofos, consejos de la Divina Escritura, fábulas de poetas, oraciones de retóricos, milagros de santos, sino procurar que a la llana, con palabras insignificantes, honestas y bien colocadas, salga vuestra oración y período sonoro y festivo, pintando, en todo lo que alcanzáredes y fuere posible, vuestra intención; dando a entender vuestros conceptos sin intricarlos y escurecerlos.

And since this book of yours aims at no more than destroying the authority and influence which books of chivalry have in the world and among the common people, you have no reason to go begging sentences from philosophers, counsel from Holy Writ, fables from poets, speeches from orators, or miracles from saints. You have only to see that your sentences shall come out plain, in expressive, sober and well-ordered language, harmonious and gay, expressing your purpose to the best of your ability, and setting out your ideas without intricacies and obscurities. [Pro.; 1 : 14; p. 30]

But this is a matter of style, not a matter of *imitatio* itself. About that the friend is decisive: "Sólo tiene que aprovecharse de la imitación en lo que fuere escribiendo, que cuanto ella fuere más perfecta, tanto mejor será lo que se escribiere"; "In what you are writing you have only to make use of imitation, and the more perfect the imitation the better your writing will be" (Pro.; 1 : 14; p. 30). You have *only* to make use of imitation: The prologue argues in favor of humanist imitatio as the sole means of a humanist poetics, then; what it argues *against* is imitating the wrong objects. When we recall that the knights imitated in *Don Quijote* are only previous fictions, precepts rather than realities, precepts without realities, we shall get right what Cervantes means to suggest. The knights are, throughout, simulacra: On the one hand, they are material images or representations of what is good and valuable; on the other hand, they may be unreal or specious. When Don Quijote reenacts the fictitious Amadís on the Sierra Morena, or when he observes Cardenio pretending to be Grisóstomo, he is watching imitations of imitations—the sort of poetry Plato condemns, as does Aristotle, for it is essentially *un*real, *unmimetic,* and so unrepresentative. It does not connect to life and so does not serve life; it does not, finally, cultivate good learning or properly instruct. Indeed, the very Spanish term *ficción* addresses the problem. John G. Weiger has summed it best.

> It is one thing to criticize the romances for violations of aesthetic principles; it is a different sort of criticism when works of fiction are censured because they are fabricated or because they are "feigned" or "pretended," which is what the adjective frequently used—*fingido*—means. Now this word, the past participle of *fingir,* "to pretend," comes from the Latin *fingere,* meaning "to fashion," "shape," "form," "mold"; also "to represent," "imagine," "conceive"; and as well "to feign," "fabricate," "devise." The Latin past participle—*fictus*—meaning "feigned," corresponds to the Spanish *fingido,* and, of course, words like "fiction" and "fictive" are derived therefrom. Covarrubias, in his dictionary published midway between the publication of the two parts of *Don Quixote,* defines *ficción* as a well-composed ruse or lie, done with artifice, but Cervantes invokes the basic Latin meaning of fashioning, fabricating, molding, or, as it were, creating. For Cervantes, this meaning has a pejorative connotation. The romances of chivalry are wholly "compostura y ficción de ingenios ociosos" ("composition and fabrication of idle minds." [1.32][5]

Whatever else it is about, *Don Quijote* is about the awful power and the misplaced trust in books—about their ability to inspire, mislead, or destroy—and we are told this by studying the very book before us: Don Quijote finds the greatest marvel in his authentic world in the printing press at Barcelona, and we are reminded, glancing back to 1.6—"*Del donoso y grande escrutinio que el cura y el barbero hicieron en la librería de nuestro ingenioso hidalgo*"; "*Of the great and pleasant Inquisition held by the Priest and the Barber over our ingenious gentleman's Library,*" (1:42; p. 56)—that this is the time books could be thought so dangerous, so subversive, that they could be called in, mutilated, and burned.

The power of words was immense, and it is essential to note that Cervantes makes the matter even more urgent by ridding the world of some of them at the beginning of his novel even while, in Barcelona, beginning to manufacture them once again. His insistence, then, on a poetics of imitatio—where the humanist writer needs only to make use of imitation—is his way of requiring us to tell good imitatio from bad. So *Don Quijote* also becomes a book not only of dialectic and disputation but also of irresolution. *Don Quijote* too is a work of methexis.

Within such a study of the validity and reliability of humanist belief, it is only natural that Cervantes centers in Book 1 on the central humanist debate, that of arms versus letters. It is a debate presided over by the Don himself—"un Cid en las armas y por un Cicerón en la elocuencia," we are told; "a Cid in arms and a Cicero in eloquence" (2.22; 2:121; p. 607)—since in this dialectical work in which Don Quijote is at odds with the world, a separation that imitatio, properly utilized, might heal, he is also, more importantly, at odds with himself. The barber states forthrightly that the Don is more soldier than scholar (1.26). It is the position which, sometime later, Don Quijote confirms in a wonderfully delivered oration that, as one of the centerpieces of the book, stays in our minds as an operating premise.

sino volvamos a la preeminencia de las armas contra las letras, materia que hasta ahora está por averiguar, según son las razones que cada una de su parte alega: y entre las que he dicho, dicen las letras que sin ellas no se podrian sustentar las armas, porque la guerra también tiene sus leyes y está sujeta a ellas, y que las leyes caen debajo de lo que son letras y letrados. A esto responden las armas que las leyes no se podrán sustentar sin ellas, porque con las armas se defienden las repúblicas, se conservan los reinos, se guardan las ciudades, se aseguran los caminos, se despejan los mares de cosarios, y, finalmente, si por ellas no fuese, las repúblicas, los reinos, las monarquías, las ciudades, los caminos de mar y tierra estarían sujetos al rigor y la confusión que trae consigo la guerra el tiempo que dura y tiene licencia de usar de sus privilegios y de sus fuerzas. Y es razón averiguada que aquello que más cuesta se estima y debe de estimar en más. Alcanzar alguno o ser eminente en letras le cuesta tiempo, vigilias, hambre, desnudez, vaguidos de cabeza, indigestiones de estómago, y ostras cosas a éstas adherentes, que, en parte, ya las tengo referidas; mas llegar uno por sus términos a ser buen soldado le cuesta todo lo que al estudiante, en tanto mayor grado, que no tiene comparación, porque a cada paso está a pique de perder la vida. Y ¿qué temor de necesidad y pobreza puede llegar ni fatigar al estudiante, que llegue al que tiene un soldado, que, hallándose cercado en alguna fuerza, y estando de posta, o guarda en algún rebellin o caballero, siente que los enemigos están minando hacia la parte donde él está, y no puede apartarse de allí por ningún caso, ni huir el peligro que de tan cerca la amenaza? Sólo lo que puede hacer es dar noticia a su capitán de lo que pasa, para que lo remedie con alguna contramina, y él estarse quedo, temiendo y esperando cuándo improvisamente ha de subir a las nubes sin alas, y bajar al profundo sin su voluntad.

"let us come back to the pre-eminence of Arms over Letters,—a question which remains still to be resolved, since each side puts up so many arguments on its own behalf. Besides those which I have given, the scholars say that without them arms could not survive. For war too has its laws and is subject to them, and laws fall within the province of letters and learning. But to this Arms reply that laws could not survive without them; because by Arms states are defended, kingdoms preserved, cities guarded, the roads kept safe, and the seas swept free of pirates. In short, if it were not for them, states, kingdoms, monarchies, cities, and the highways on land and sea, would be subject to the savagery and confusion which war entails, so long as it lasts and is free to exercise its privileges and powers.

"What is more, it is a well-known truth that what costs most is, and should be, the most highly valued. Now to attain eminence in the learned professions costs a man time, nights of study, hunger, nakedness, headaches, indigestion, and other such things, some of which I have mentioned already. But to reach the point of being a good soldier, requires all that it requires to be a student, but to so much greater a degree that there is no comparison; for the soldier is in peril of losing his life at every step. What fear of poverty or want that can befall or afflict a student can compare with the fear a soldier knows when he is besieged in a fortress, on watch or guard in some redoubt or strongpoint, knowing that his enemies are mining towards the spot where he is, and that he may on no account leave his post, or run away from the danger which threatens him so closely? The only thing which he can do is to inform his captain of what is happening, in the hope that he will meet the situation with a counter-mine; and he must stand calmly, though in fear and expectation of suddenly rising to the clouds without wings and sinking again to the depths against his will."

[1.38; 1:261–62; pp. 343–44]

This description of the soldier's life is the anchoring passage of Book 1; the *responsio* on learning comes in the anchoring passage in Book 2.

—Es una ciencia—replicó don Quijote—que encierra en si todas o las más ciencias del mundo, a causa que el que la profesa ha de ser jurisperito y saber las leyes de la justicia distributiva y comutativa, para dar a cada uno lo que es suyo y lo que le conviene; ha de ser teólogo, para saber dar razón de la cristiana ley que profesa, clara y distintamente, adondequiera que le fuera pedido; ha de ser médico, y principalmente herbolario, para conocer en mitad de los despoblados y desiertos las yerbas que tienen virtud de sanar las heridas; que no ha de andar el caballero andante a cada triquete buscando quien se las cure; ha de ser astrólogo, para conocer por las estrellas cuántas horas son pasadas de la noche, y en qué parte y en qué clima del mundo se halla; ha de saber las matemáticas, porque a cada paso se le ofrecerá tener necesidad dellas; y dejando aparte que ha de estar adornado de todas las virtudes teologales y cardinales, decendiendo a otras menudencias, digo que ha de saber nadar como dicen que nadaba el paje Nicolás, o Nicolao; ha de saber herrar un caballo y aderezar la silla y el freno; y volviendo a lo de arriba, ha de guardar la fe a Dios y a su dama; ha se ser casto en los pensamientos, honesto en las palabras, liberal en las obras, valiente en los hechos, sufrido en los trabajos, caritativo con los menestersos, y, finalmente, mantenedor de la verdad, aunque le cueste la vida el defenderla. De todas estas grandes y mínimas partes se compone un buen caballero andante; porque vea vuesa merced, señor don Lorenzo, si es ciencia mocosa lo que aprende el caballero que la estudia y la profesa, y si se puede igualar a las más estiradas que en los ginasios y escuelas se enseñan.

"It is a science," replied Don Quixote, "that comprises all or most of the sciences in the world, since he who professes it must be a jurist and know the laws of justice concerning persons and property, so that he may give to everyone what is his own and his due. He must be a theologian, so that he may give reasons for the Christian rule he professes, clearly and distinctly, wherever he may be asked. He must be a physician, and especially a herbalist, so that he may recognize in the midst of deserts and wildernesses those herbs which have the virtue of healing wounds, for the knight errant cannot go looking at every step for someone to cure him. He must be an astronomer, to know by the stars how many hours of the night are passed, and in what part and climate of the world he is. He must know mathematics, for any time he may find himself in need of them. Not reckoning that he must be adorned with all the virtues, theological and cardinal, I will descend to other small details and say that he must be able to swim as they say Fish Nicholas or Nicolao did. He must know how to shoe a horse and mend a saddle and bridle. Also, to return to higher matters, he must keep faith with God and his lady; he must be chaste in his thoughts, straightforward in his words, liberal in his works, valiant in his deeds, patient in his afflictions, charitable towards the needy and, in fact, a maintainer of truth, although its defence may cost him his life. Of all these parts, great and small, a good knight errant is composed. So you may see, Don Lorenzo, whether it is a snivelling science that chivalry teaches those who study and profess it, and whether the loftiest taught in colleges and schools are the equal of it."

[2.18; 2 : 101; pp. 582–83]

What strikes us most forcibly is that, however sensible the first argument is, the Don is speaking in humanist commonplaces. His description of a soldier has no bearing at all on the knight's life he intends to lead; the second passage, though centering on the knight-errant, is almost equally remote from his experiences of the first three sallies. When he is sensible, that is, he seems irrelevant. When he makes more extravagant claims—that he is all of the Twelve Peers and the Nine Worthies in one (1.5, 20)—he is much nearer to his own intentions of protecting the helpless, avenging wrongs, relieving injuries, and punishing treachery (1.17; cf. 1.19). He describes this life in some detail in Book 1 to Sancho Panza during the adventure of the barber's basin that becomes Mambrino's helmet (1.21) and in Book 2 to Don Diego de Miranda following the adventure with the lions (2.17); in the first, he projects the knight (potentially himself) commanded by the King and beloved by the gracious Princess; in the second, he sees the knight conquer parching sun and deadly frost and survive labyrinths to conquer not only lions but hobgoblins and dragons. What is more, the world of the novel seems at first to uphold such plans: His is an alien landscape in which he can nevertheless make sense (through his amending imagination) of windmills and sheep as giants and an army as well as accept (through his predisposed perceptions) the adventures in Book 2 of the fantastic horse Clavileño and the potentially dangerous Cueva de Montesinos. Cervantes' point, of course, is not that for Don Quijote arms conquer letters, as he claims, but that his literary imagination conquers his experience. It is letters that really win, as we learn in his ability to materialize, at least to his own satisfaction, Amadís himself:

> la cual verdad es tan cierta, que estoy por decir que con mis propios ojos vi a Amadís de Gaula, que era un hombre alto de cuerpo, blanco de rostro, bien puesto de barba, aunque negra, de vista entre blanda y rigurosa, corto de razones, tardo en airarse y presto a deponer la ire.

> "by supporting my argument with evidence so infallible that I might say I have seen Amadis of Gaul with my own eyes. He was a man tall of stature and fair of face, with a well-trimmed black beard. His looks were half mild and half severe. He was short of speech, slow to anger, and quickly appeased."

[2.1; 2 : 24; pp. 478–79]

The Don's fantastic aims and understanding are posited against the material-ist Sancho Panza, who is very much a part of the authentic world and whose motives are always materialistic—worldly gain and worldly power (1.7)—in Book 1.

Indeed, it is Sancho's view that squares best with their adventures, despite the Don's sense of glorious opportunities with windmills and fulling mills, for as Sancho points out repeatedly, his misapprehensions cause both of them real pain: The Don loses four teeth, half an ear, and half a helmet by Sancho's reckoning (1.18), while winning only one battle. Indeed, almost always de-feated, they are figuratively and literally stripped by the galley slaves (1.22). Such a discrepancy between precept and experience, reading and living, is one that even the Don must confront. He does so in his famous distinction between the iron age in which he and Sancho are condemned to live and the golden age he wishes forcibly to retrieve and redeem. That this is always ready to his mind is shown in another well-formulated oration, which he delivers to the goatherds when they offer him simple acorns for sustenance.

—¡Dichosa edad y siglos dichosos aquellos a quien los antiguos pusieron nombre de dorados, y no porque en ellos el oro, que en esta nuestra edad de hierro tanto se estima, se alcanzase en aquella venturosa sin fatiga alguna, sino porque entonces los que en ella vivian ignoraban estas dos palabras de *tuyo y mio!* Eran en aquella santa edad todas las cosas comunes. . . . Y agora, en estos nuestros detestables siglos, no está segura ninguna, aunque la oculte y cierre otro nuevo laberinto, como el de Creta; porque allí, por los resquicios o por el aire, con el celo de la maldita solicitud se les entra la amorosa pestilencia y les hace dar con todo su recogimiento al traste. Para cuya seguridad, andando más los tiempos y creciendo más la malicia, se instituyó la orden de los caballeros andantes, para defender las doncellas, amparar las viudas y socorrer a los huérfanos y a los menesterosos. Desta orden soy yo, hermanos cabreros, a quien agradezco el gasaje y buen acogimiento que hacéis a mi y a mi escudero.

"Happy the age and happy the times on which the ancients bestowed the name of golden, not because gold, which in this iron age of ours is rated so highly, was attainable without labour in those fortunate times, but rather be-cause the people of those days did not know those two words *thine* and *mine*. In that blessed age all things were held in common. . . .

"But now, in this detestable age of ours, no maiden is safe even though she be hidden in the centre of another Cretan labyrinth; for even there, through some chink or through the air, by dint of its accursed persistence, the plague of love gets in and brings them to ruin despite their seclusion. Therefore, as times rolled on and wickedness increased, the order of knights errant was founded for their protection, to defend maidens, relieve widows, and succour the orphans and the needy. Of this order am I, brother goatherds, whom I thank for the welcome and entertainment which you have given to me and my squire."

[1.11; 1:65–66; pp. 85–87]

The amalgam astonishes: His accurate (and classical) description of the golden age, drawn originally from the antique Hesiod, is a sharp if indirect rejoinder to Sancho's motives for accompanying the Don, replacing his materialism with a sense of compassion; but his description of his own time—which he should know far better, know at *first* hand—is unrealistic, even approaching the fantastic. Elsewhere, when he is unable to conquer his enemies or win his battles, the Don blames his ill luck not on his lack of skill, training, observation, or knowledge but on the *encantamientos,* the evil enchantments (first suggested by his unbelieving niece as an explanation [1.7]), while inventing for his own support and solace their antitype in the good necromancers. Don Diego senses and defines Don Quijote best: "él es un entreverado loco, lleno de lúcidos intervalos"; "He is mad in patches, full of lucid streaks" (2.18; 2:102; p. 583).

But both worlds come together, too, and in Don Quijote's own premise to the goatherds: It is comradeship and compassion that past and present should most hold in common. Cervantes' grand work of metafiction, of metahumanist poetics, highlights (as Marguerite does) metaphysics too. As the Don puts it, "porque de la caballeria andante se puede decir lo mesmo que del amor se dice: que todas las cosas iguala"; "for it can be said of knight errantry as of love: that it puts all things on the same level" (1.11; 1:64; p. 84). It is this sense of a *mission* of love, spreading out from Dulcinea to enclose all those he senses in need that so disturbs the Don, that so awakens in him a sense of duty, of enormous need for service, and that results in continuing beatings and sacrifice. He is not simply a knight-errant, an elderly hidalgo named Quijada or Quesada (1.1) and rechristened Don Quijote by an innkeeper, but one who is inspired to save the world from itself—a savior who would *redeem* a past before the Fall. Sancho senses this too, without knowing consciously all its implications, when he notes the disappointment constantly etched in the Don's face and so renames him Caballero de la Triste Figura, Knight of the Woeful Countenance (1.19). This suggestion of Christ may be fitting for a knight who (like those who suffered the Crusades against the infidels in the earlier age) first commends himself always to God (1.50); it is an analogy to which the Don later returns again and again—and so does Cervantes. For Don Quijote and Sancho Panza seek not fame in history but deeds that will transcend history: "los christianos, católicos y andantes cabelleros más habemos de atender a la gloria de los siglos venideros, que es eterna en las regiones etéreas y celestes, que a la vanidad de la fama que en este presente y acabable siglo se alcanza"; "Christians, Catholics and knights errant, have more to expect from future and everlasting glory enjoyed in the ethereal and celestial regions than from the vanity of fame achieved in this present transient life" (2.8; 2:53; p. 518). Sancho learns this lesson with uncharacteristic swiftness: "que nos demos a ser santos"; "that we should set about turning saints" (2.8; 2:54; p. 519), a minor premise that the Don confirms in their shared syllogism:

> —Todo eso es asi—respondió don Quijote—; pero no todos podemos ser frailes, y muchos son los caminos por donde lleva Dios a los suyos al cielo: religión es la caballería, caballeros santos hay en la gloria.
>
> "All that is so," replied Don Quixote, "but we cannot all be friars, and many are the ways by which God bears His chosen to heaven. Chivalry is a religion, and there are sainted knights in glory." [2.8; 2:55; p. 520]

As in *L'Heptaméron*, the power of words always derives from and reaches back to the Word; and, with Don Quijote, increasingly in Book 2 the stations of argument are not dissimilar to stations of the cross: His are acts of inverted kenosis, as he conceives them. This gives a higher purpose to the humanist ideas—the *Christian* humanist ideas—behind *Don Quijote* and helps to explain why Cervantes transforms the identity of his hero from that of an ingenious gentleman (ingenioso hidalgo) in Book 1 to that of an ingenious knight (ingenioso caballero) in Book 2. If the Don is born at the wrong time, as he repeatedly says, it is because he finds himself in a fallen world, one he must be prepared to redeem. This is the one way in which—throughout Cervantes' sweeping work—the Don himself redeems humanism, too, by bringing together arts and letters through his own sense of mission.

> —De todo sabian y han de saber los caballeros andantes, Sancho—dijo don Quijote—; porque caballero andante hubo en los pasados siglos que así se paraba a hacer un sermón o plática en mitad de un campo real como si fuera graduado por la Universidad de París; de donde se infiere que nunca la lanza embotó la pluma, ni la pluma la lanza.
>
> "Knights errant, Sancho, knew—and have to know—about everything," said Don Quixote; "for in the olden times a knight errant would be as ready to deliver

a sermon or make a speech in the middle of the royal camp as if he were a graduate
of the university of Paris; whence it can be inferred that the lance has never
blunted the pen, nor the pen the lance." [1.18; 1 : 108–9; p. 140]

Patches of madness in Cervantes' fiction can indeed be flashes of illumination.
Don Quijote, that is, has profound connections to Erasmian Folly—it
stretches back through Jerónimo de Mondrangón's *Censura de la locura humana y
exelencias della* (Censure and Excellencies of Madness) of 1598, where in Part 1
those who are thought sane are actually mad and, in Part 2, those who are
thought by the world to be mad are worthy of great praise, to the *Encomium
Moriae* with its elaborate oration and its inherent disputations. For "One
moment," we are told of the Don, "they thought him a man of sense, and the
next he slipped into craziness; nor could they decide what degree to assign him
between wisdom and folly" ("Aquí le tenían por discreto, y allí se les deslizaba
por mentecato, sin saber determinarse qué grado le darían entre la discreción y
la locura," 2.59; 2 : 304; p. 852). Sancho can note this too, although he can
stumble in his observation:

> yo tengo a mi señor don Quijote por loco rematado, puesto que algunas veces
> dice cosas que, a mi parecer, y aun de todos aquellos que le escuchan, son tan
> discretas y por tan buen carril encaminadas, que el mesmo Santanás no las podría
> decir mejores.
>
> "I reckon my master Don Quixote's stark crazy, although sometimes he will talk
> in a way which, to my thinking and in the opinion of all who hear him, is so wise
> and leads down so good a track that Satan himself could not speak better."
>
> [2.33; 2 : 180; p. 687]

Thus the Don who takes pity on Andrew and frees him from punishment (1.4)
can also free convicted galley slaves indiscriminately (1.22); the knight who
excessively praises a peasant girl as Dulcinea can also admit that the most
important things in life often cannot be verified (2.32). And what is true of the
Don is equally true of his squire, for his foolishness also has many sides, not all
of them equally foolish. "Sancho is in part the stupid Spanish peasant," Michael
Bell writes, but he is also "in part the cunning one. He is partly the clever fool
of literary tradition and partly the genuine fool on whom that tradition was
based. He is also on occasion the wise or holy fool of religious drama." [6] Tested
as the governor (*gobernar*) of La Insula Barataria—actually a small portion of the
lands of the Duke and Duchess—he has the good wit and common sense to
adjudicate wisely the cases of the tailor and of the herdsman and whore among

others (2.45), the ability to draw confessions and solace his people when making his rounds (2.49), and the wisdom to establish prudent ordinances (2.51). And like Erasmus's Folly, who moves from ingenuousness to a sense of the Eucharist itself, Sancho also learns to be lowly wise and to surrender the things of this world: "si vuestra señoría no me quisiere dar la ínsula por tonto, yo sabré no dárseme nada por discreto"; "if your ladyship doesn't wish to give me the isle because I'm a fool, I shall be wise enough not to care" (2.33; 2:181; p. 688). This humble peasant learns the true significance of humility as the Don learns the true wisdom of sacrifice. Both learn to govern themselves before governing others (2.33).

But there are other, more distant classical resources, too; there are other Senecan originals for *Don Quijote*. Cervantes, like Rabelais, may well have turned to the "Father of History," Herodotus, but, if so, his concerns were more general in his use of that model than the matter and manner of *Historia 2*. Herodotus is concerned not merely with the history but with the writing of history, and in his attempt to record the events of the Persian War he exaggerates his characters much as Cervantes does—the heroes are often more heroic, the villains more villainous. His narration is interrupted, as Cervantes' is, by formal debates and orations and by catalogues, such as the long and detailed one of the nations included in the Persian Empire and the amounts of tribute each had to pay; his work from the start is also, like *Don Quijote,* a work of multiple perspectives, for he starts with what the learned men of Persia say (1.1) followed by their accounts of the Greeks (1.2 ff.). It is also the job of the historian, he tells us, to incorporate προσθηκας, additions and digressions, much like the inset tales of the *Quijote;* but with such a variety of sources and subjects, not all of it is equally reliable. For this reason much of the *Historia* is recorded in the speeches and comments of others, as Cervantes' grand novel is, while from time to time Herodotus himself, like Cervantes, will express skepticism. His refusal to believe is echoed in Cervantes' dubiety over the accuracy of the Moorish Cide Hamete Benengeli. Yet throughout this series of events reported with varying accountability, Herodotus, like Cervantes, always sees them as means for moral edification.

"I wish it were possible to imitate Herodotus," Lucian writes some six centuries later,[7] but it is precisely the Lucianic tone of skepticism, grounded in his keen observations and highly developed sense of the ridiculous, that everywhere infuses the *Quijote*. Here too we find that strange and memorable mixture of committed investigation and detached amusement, the persistent interest in parody, and the use of teasing paradoxes and conundrums based on a perennial concern with epistemology that we have come to think of as especially Cervantean. Almost without exception Lucian's satires circle around problems of truth, verisimilitude, and historicity, problems he addresses at the opening of *A True Story* (1.2−4) where he discusses in particular the fantastic voyage as a means of ironically manipulating both characters and readers. In focusing on what Michael Zappala calls "the problem of the marvelous and the reader's gullibility,"[8] his attitude closely resembles that of the lively and intelligent friend in the Prologo to Book 1 of the *Quijote* and may well be its Senecan original. Many authors, Lucian writes, have by means of imitatio been guided by Homer's Odysseus in guiding and instructing readers in stories of charlatanry. "Well, on reading all these authors," he goes on,

> I did not find much fault with them for their lying, as I saw that this was already a common practice even among men who profess philosophy. I did wonder, though, that they thought that they could write untruths and not get caught at it. Therefore, as I myself, thanks to my vanity, was eager to hand something down to posterity, that I might not be the only one excluded from the privileges of poetic license, and as I had nothing true to tell, not having had any adventures of significance, I took to lying. But my lying is far more honest than theirs, for though I tell the truth in nothing else, I shall at least be truthful in saying that I am a liar. I think I can escape the censure of the world by my own admission that I am not telling a word of truth. Be it understood, then, that I am writing about things which I have neither seen nor had to do with nor learned from others— which, in fact, do not exist at all, and, in the nature of things, cannot exist. Therefore my readers should on no account believe in them.[9]

This poetics—for it is nothing less than that—will remind us of the Don's account of the Cueva de Montesinos and Sancho's report of his ride on Clavileño (and the enchantment of Dulcinea), but, more importantly, this acknowledged distinction between truth and verisimilitude—both various means of "history"—is Cervantes' distinction between the narrative of Cide Hamete (and the documents he found) and Cervantes' own. The sense of history as independently truthful *or* verisimilitudinous—or both—is a kind of oxymoronic understanding, derived from Lucian, that is the source of Cervantes' explorations of the strategies of fiction as well as the source of his irony. The novels of chivalry that constitute the Don's library, for instance, and in-form his own adventures, transhistorically instruct him in such serious lessons as service and sacrifice by a verisimilitude of conventions that are often superfluous and now even nonsensical.

Lucian illustrates just what he means in a key passage of the *Icaromenippus,* which in its narrative and in the response to the narrative clearly stands just behind the voyage on Clavileño. Menippus is telling his friend, in this parody of a Platonic dialogue, about his visit to the heavens in order to understand the cosmos better.

> MENIPPUS. . . . In the first place, imagine that the earth you see is very small, far less than the moon, I mean; so that when I suddenly peered down I was long uncertain where the big mountains and the great sea were, and if I had not spied the Colossus of Rhodes and the lighthouse on Pharos, I vow I shouldn't have known the earth at all. But as it was, the fact that they were high and prominent and that the ocean glinted in the sun showed me that what I saw was the earth. But as soon as I had concentrated my gaze fixedly, the life of man in its entirety disclosed itself to me, and not only the nations and cities but the people themselves as clear as could be, the traders, the soldiers, the farmers, the litigants, the women, the animals and, in a word, all the life that the good green earth supports.
>
> FRIEND. What you say is completely beyond belief and self-contradictory, for you told me just now that you had to look for the earth because it was diminished by the intervening distance, and that if the Colossus hadn't given you your bearings, perhaps you would have thought you were looking at something else. How is it, then, that you have suddenly turned into a Lynceus and can make out everything on earth—the men, the animals and very nearly the nests of the mosquitoes?
>
> MENIPPUS. Thanks for reminding me; somehow or other I neglected to say what I certainly should have said, [10]

and he is off once again, telling about using the eye of an eagle, just as he had flown to the heavens in the first place by attaching eagle wings to his body. It is just this interplay of truth and truth-likeness, in which the boundaries of probability and possibility are always tested and often breached, that so concerns Cervantes and is so central to *ficción* itself. Lucian senses this, too, in his *Navigium,* or *The Ship or the Wishes,* a dialogue in which Adimantus is so lost in the world of his dream of wealth that he has difficulty reestablishing contact with the authentic world around him—that is, the fictional world of the dialogue! His dream is matched in time by that of Samippus for kingship and Timolaus's for many rings with magical properties. It may not be coincidental that the first and second of these dreams resemble Sancho's and the third that of the Don; the point, however, for Lucian, is not only the easy substitution of what we would call daydreams for actuality but the interference of the two, that very interference, transcending any moment in history, containing its own true observations on human nature (as well as on the nature of make-believe). Still another Lucian dialogue, *The Dream; or, The Cock,* centers on the dream of Micyllus for the fortune of Eucrates as an alternative reality. It is in just such situations as these, in which the relativity and elusiveness of all perspectives are advanced, that Lucian repeatedly raises questions pertaining to truth and to history and so establishes the poetics for a *necessary* ficción.

There is also considerable likelihood that Cervantes drew on Heliodorus. The linear *Quijote* at first seems to have little in common with the scrambled and entangled plots and events of the *Ethiopian History,* but the high adventures, the episodic management of events, and the stunning way in which prophecy, magic, destiny, character, and human will are masterfully disposed to be correlative to fortune and to each other and, ultimately, to providence are all matters that are reflected in Cervantes' work. The *Ethiopian History* found widespread popularity in the 1587 Spanish translation by Fernando de Mena, but an earlier Spanish version, an anonymous one of 1554, also prints an enthusiastic preface for the French version by Jacques Amyot, which at least one scholar of Cervantes is almost certain he knew.[11] According to the Spanish rendering of Amyot, Heliodorus's work is an "ingenious fiction" (*ingeniosa ficción*), actually a "disguised history" (*historia disfrazada*) that means to combine both the true and the false to present a semblance of reality (*aparencia de verdad*). Amyot insists that no work can please a good intellect unless it includes verisimilitude, erudition, and edification, much as the *Quijote* does, and he especially notes that what is important is not artistic selectivity or economy—both of which are relatively lacking in Cervantes—but *admiratio,* which is central. Indeed, in his chief passage on truth, history, and fiction, he might well be providing Cervantes with still another useful poetics for *Don Quijote.*

Porque el artificio de la invención poetica, como doctamente escribe Strabón, consiste en tres cosas; primeramente en la Historia, de la que el fin es verdadero. Por lo cual no es lícito a los poetas, cuando hablan de las cosas de natura, escrebir a su voluntad de otra suerte que la verdad, porque esto les sería imputado no a licencia o artificio, mas a ignorancia. Segundamente, en orden y disposición, de lo cual el fin es la declaración y fuerza de atraer al lector. Terceramente, la ficción, de la cual el fin es admiración, y la delectación que procede de la novedad de las cosas extrañas y llenas de admiración. Por lo cual, mucho menos se delen permitir todas cosas en la ficciones que queremos disfrazar con el nombre de

Historia verdadera, antes es menester mezclar tan doctamente lo verdadero con lo falso, gueradando siempre aperancia de verdad, y refiriendo lo uno a lo otro, de suerte que no haya discordancia del principio al medio ni del medio al fin (pp. lxxix–lxxx).[12]

Because, as Strabo writes so learnedly, the art of poetic invention consists of three things: first, of history, the aim of which is truth. Consequently it is not permitted that poets, when speaking of natural things, should write as they please, contradicting truth, because this would be attributed not to their license or art, but rather to their ignorance. Secondly, of order and disposition, the aim of which is to present the subject matter and to hold the reader's attention. Thirdly, of fiction, the aim of which is to inspire wonder and to arouse that delectation which proceeds from the experience of the novelty of things which are strange and wonderful. Accordingly, unrestricted license in the inclusion of things should be all the more prohibited in fictions which we wish to disguise with the name of true history. It is necessary to mix intelligently truth and falsehood, maintaining always the appearance of truth and relating the one to the other, so that there is no discord between the beginning and the middle, and between the middle and the end.

The other Spanish critical treatise that deals at some length with Heliodorus (and the poetics of romance) and that Cervantes almost surely knew is the *Philosophía antigua poética* of López Pinciano (1596). El Pinciano puts considerable stress on verisimilitude and plausibility, even if adventures are undergone in strange and distant places, and in Epistle Eleven he praises Heliodorus especially as an example of an author who deceives with the appearance of truth. As we have seen, it is just such an *appearance* of truth that causes Don Quijote to be so frequently mistaken and his squire so baffled in Book 1; it is the appearance of truth that the Duke and Duchess rely on for their elaborate tricks in Book 2; and it is the truth *despite* appearances that, in the end, transforms the Don and Sancho.

Such grounding as this in antique humanist texts demonstrates Cervantes' use of a humanist poetics. He shares the humanists' allegiance to rhetoric too. Discourse dislocates the early adventures of the Don and threatens at times to *become* those adventures: first, when he listens to the arguments presented by Andrés and by his master Juan Haldudo and decides in favor of the former (1.4); then, in the adventure of the fulling mills, which results not in an attack but in a debate with Sancho (1.20); later, in the Don's examination of the galley slaves and his decision to free them despite the *responsio* of their sergeant (1.22);

and finally in the "adventure" of Mambrino's helmet, which is little more than sophistic pronouncements (1.10, 21, 45). For all its open claims to be a chivalric romance, in fact, *Don Quijote* is nearly always rooted in declamation and disputation. Book 1, for instance, centers on formal discourses on the golden age (1.11), on arms and letters (1.38), and on the defense of novels of chivalry (1.50), which inform Don Quijote's acts and which he consistently uses as testimonials. They correlate to three formal orations in Book 2 on the defense of poetry (2.16, 18), the defense of the profession of knight errantry (2.32), and the government of isles (2.42, 43).[13] We have already noted how even Don Quijote's formal declamations, like the one on arms and letters, can become an inherent disputation by implicitly arguing the opposite cause, and this should only sharpen our awareness—as it must have done for Cervantes' early humanist readers—so that we must study the Don's orations with special care. Mary Mackey has done just that with his speech on the golden age. She notes that the Don's *inventio* rests solely on the authority of a fable with which his audience may not agree, but which he takes no pains to support in his *propositio* or *confirmatio;* instead of dealing with questions of fact (*an sit*) or even definition (*quid sit*), he makes everything a matter of quality (*quale sit*). Although his tripartite declamation redefines the golden age by the iron age in the *negatio,* his *conclusio,* which means to be a justification of the order of chivalry, has no logical connection with either of the foregoing parts. Moreover, the Don merely declaims and describes; he does not persuade. He pays no attention, in fact, to Aristotelian pathos or ethos, the needs of his audience, or the need to establish his own authority. His gift is clearly for epideictic here as it is nearly everywhere else; he is not equipped for forensic oratory. This is because his attitude—as seen most simply in the presentation of this familiar speech—depends for its acceptance not on his reasoning powers (he is mad, after all) but on our own compatible predisposition.[14]

Don Quijote's style is Ciceronian, its syntax hypotactic. He has "a predilection for tropes," Mackey comments. "Don Quijote's entire discourse sacrifices clarity to embellishment. Pushed to excess, ornament becomes an encumbrance; sense flounders and is then obscured by style" ("Rhetoric," p. 60). His language is also heavily formulaic; in employing the classical schemes and tropes commonplace in the handbooks of Aristotle, Cicero, and Quintilian—and expanded by Erasmus in *De Copia*—Don Quijote's speeches and remarks in being commonplace are authentic and natural, but in being formulaic they are also distanced and artificial. Even in appealing to our instincts and intuitions, they are meant to invite us to question and to *dis*believe. This is all the more obvious when we note that his encrusted ideas and style tend to do his thinking and speaking for him, so that what we at first admire in Don Quijote's speeches are the nuggets of traditional wisdom the culture has already embedded rather than anything like his own unique perspective. His rhetoric locks him into celebration and certainty of the values of Christian knighthood which, juxtaposing the Don with Sancho Panza and a skeptical world, Cervantes really means us to *question*. Edwin Williamson has recently written that

> Metaphor, hyperbole, irony, burlesque, parody, all the artifice of discourse, the restless, posturing masquerade of language is reduced by the mad knight to a ritual celebration of certainty. Don Quixote seeks to restore to language a virtue which it appeared to enjoy in romance, and which the chivalric code—with its truth-seeking duels, its system of pledges and inescapable obligations—was meant to preserve against time or evil, namely, its capacity to serve as an unequivocal medium of communication which even in its figurative usages, in symbolic or allegorical discourse, could still be relied upon to denote some knowable if transcendent reality.[15]

What results, of course, is sophistry pure and simple—Lucian's chief concern is also one of Cervantes' major targets. If we look carefully, for instance, we shall see quickly enough that Andrés and his master never come to a locked argument, robbing Don Quijote of any real position as judge; in the episode with the *galeotes,* the galley slaves, the Don's sympathy is so strong for the apparently oppressed that his stubbornness in their defense becomes, as Anthony Close has it, "perverse."[16] Indeed, the Don argues precisely opposite to the case we should expect or want.

> —De todo cuanto me habéis dicho, hermanos carísmos, ha sacado en limpio que, aunque os han castigado por vuestras culpas, las penas que vais a padecer no os dan mucho gusto, y que vais a ellas muy de mala gana y muy contra vuestra voluntad: y que podría ser que el poco ánimo que aquél tuvo en el tormento, la falta de dineros déste, el poco favor del otro y, finalmente, el torcido juicio del juez, hubiese sido causa de vuestra perdición, y de no haber salido con la justicia que de vuestra parte teníades. Todo lo cual se me representa a mi ahora en la memoria, de manera que me está diciendo, persuadiendo y aun forzando, que muestre con vosotros el efeto para que el cielo me arrojó al mundo, y me hizo profesar en él la orden de caballería que profeso, y el voto que en ella hice de favorecer a los menesterosos y opresos de los mayores.

"From all that you have told me, dearest brethren, I clearly gather that, although it is for your faults they have punished you, the penalties which you are to suffer give you little pleasure. You are going to them, it seems, very reluctantly and much against your wills; and possibly it is only lack of courage under torture in one, shortage of money in another, lack of friends in another—in short, the unfair decisions of the judge—that have been the cause of your undoing and of your failure to receive the justice which was your due. All of which is now so clear in my mind that it bids me, persuades me, and even compels me, to demonstrate on you the purpose for which Heaven has sent me into the world and made me profess therein the order of chivalry which I follow, and the vow I made to succour the needy and those who are oppressed by the strong."

[1.22; 1:136; pp. 177–78]

Don Quijote's unexplored imposition of perspective on the world, that is, demands a similar imposition of conventional rhetoric, of maxims also *un*tried. Aristotle is notably concerned about such use of maxims (or enthymemes) in his *Rhetoric,* and his anticipation of Don Quijote's later use of them is bluntly put: He opposes "ending with a conclusion syllogistically expressed, although there has been no syllogistic process" (2.24.2).[17] Moreover, Aristotle lists here a number of examples we see frequently in the *Quijote:* using similar words for different things; heightening by exaggeration; omitting context (2–11). "His use of emotive moral maxims in an unsound cause," Close reminds us—as when the Don shifts ground in his definition of Mambrino's helmet (1.45) or when he defends his unnecessary attack on the lion by grand generalizations about knight-errantry (2.17)—"seems a sign of unmistakable casuistry" ("Don Quixote's Sophistry and Wisdom," p. 106). An understanding of the Don puts Sancho's proverbs—which are themselves maxims—in a proper perspective, for Sancho's apparently discrete rhetoric, characterized by paratactic brevity, is actually only the simpler equivalent of the Don's elaborate schemes and tropes, just as his use of language—more obvious, surely—is meant to *mirror* rather than to *oppose* Don Quijote's. "Sancho uses language as the ductile medium of his desires and fears," Williamson notes; "He becomes in consequence a potentially anarchic element in his master's scheme of things by unsettling words in their stable relation to meaning" (*Half-way House,* pp. 144–45). But of course Don Quijote has been doing precisely the same thing with his interchanging of maxims. Rather than working dialectically, Sancho's simpler rhetoric finally has the force of exposing Don Quijote's weakness of thought by revealing the weakness of his speeches and his arguments.

This may also help to explain why the Don and Sancho come to speak more nearly alike during the progression of the novel, and why they can even take over each other's rhetorics. Yet it should not be lost on us that the proverbial basis for much of this expression and much of this argumentation by enthymeme makes use, as Sancho's expressions repeatedly do, of actual Spanish proverbs imported from actual Arabic origins. At the heart of the speech of *both* characters, then, lies the shadowy figure of the narrator Cide Hamete Benengeli, the one not to be trusted. In thus removing any substantial basis for much of the argumentation of the Don and Sancho, Cervantes resorts once more to the art of methexis. It is an art of triangulation, moreover, that uses sophistry to insist on our participation in the novel's meaning. When Don Quijote's rhetorical sophistry begins to infect Sancho's straightforward statements in Book 1, Cervantes establishes an inherent disputation between them that we are meant to judge—like the outside-inside of the Silenus box in Erasmus and in Rabelais. In Book 2, sophistry spreads to the Duke and Duchess, whose tricks effectively victimize both the Don and Sancho so that the dialectic is posed in new terms. But it has not, as a method, essentially changed.

The fact that *Don Quijote* does not founder on the evasive perspective of Lucian and the use of sophistry against which Aristotle so decisively warned is due primarily to Cervantes' use of humanist logic to countermand misuse of humanist rhetoric. We have already seen that the novel is syllogistically organized, building up the dialectical opposition of Don Quijote and Sancho, or of the Don and his world, or of the Don and himself, which, as major and minor premises, invites us to supply through our interpretations and judgments the conclusions that are implicitly required. It is a pattern we have seen with all of Cervantes' predecessors as well in constructing a humanist poetics, particularly with Erasmus, who seems to have begun such a poetics in the Renaissance. That Cervantes means to have such a pattern operating finds further evidence in the essentially syllogistic structuring of the inset tales—the five obvious ones told by frustrated or disappointed lovers in Book 1, the five rather more subtle ones told by parents in Book 2—as Colbert I. Nepaulsingh pointed out some time ago.[18] Thus the stories of Grisóstomo, Cardenio, Anselmo, Ruy Pérez de Viedma, and Eugenio all vary slightly the tale of a man becoming obsessed, convincing another of his obsessions, and being in turn betrayed or cured by that friend, a pattern in miniature that schemes the larger one behind the whole of the *Quijote* and so makes the apparently digressive tales considerably more integral. In Book 2, Nepaulsingh writes,

Quiteria's father refuses her childhood sweetheart; the countess Trifaldi, a lady-
in-waiting with the family for many years, refers to Antonomasia as "mi niña";
Doña Rodriguez is widowed and has to marry her daughter; Ricote is sure that
his daughter "no se curaría de las solicitudes de ese señor mayorazgo"; Claudia
Jerónima dares not reveal to her father that she is in love with the son of his worst
enemy. ["Cervantes," p. 251]

Each of these stories is about a parent with an unusually beautiful daughter;
about money, or the lack of it, complicating the circumstances of the daughter's
marriage; and about the resolution—either defiance or cooperation between
parent and child.[19] Both sets of syllogistic shorter narratives and the inherent
syllogisms of the work as a whole, however, do more than merely raise questions about the proper use of rhetoric or the ways in which, as Aristotle and
Cicero taught the humanists, logic should always be allied with rhetoric; they
also raise questions of truth, verisimilitude, and history. In thus finding a
structure by which to use a chivalric romance to investigate not only romance in
general but problems of humanist thought and speech as well, *Don Quijote* (by
good fortune or good design) raises more penetrating questions about humanist
beliefs in imitatio, in the relationship of precept to experience, and in the
relationship of thought to language than any other Spanish fiction of its time.

This may seem an astonishing achievement for a man who spent much of his
time in poverty and many of his years abroad. "Of Cervantes' life, we know
even less than of Shakespeare's," the poet W. D. Snodgrass sums; "all we do
know is disheartening."[20] Cervantes was born in 1547, one of seven children of
a wandering physician, an apothecary surgeon who had no diploma, suffered
from deafness, and was jailed at least once for debt. At twenty-one he was a
student in Madrid; the next year he served the household of Cardinal Acquaviva
in Rome as chamberlain; the year after that, at twenty-three, he joined a
Spanish company stationed in Italy. At twenty-four he took part in the great
battle of Lepanto, insisting on taking his turn although he was sick with
malaria and had to be carried on deck; there he was twice wounded in the chest
and his left hand was permanently maimed. He fought elsewhere in the Mediterranean, and then, at twenty-eight, he left with his brother and with letters
of commendation from the duke of Sessa and Don John of Austria to return
home to Spain. But his ship was captured by pirates who, thinking him a
person of some importance, held him for ransom in Algiers. After five years in
prison, during which time he made several courageous attempts to escape, his
family ransomed him, at the age of thirty-four, by going deeply and irrevocably
into debt.

Back in Spain at last, he found cold comfort: His family was impoverished, and no government post, however minor, was offered him. He tried his luck at writing—thirty plays, for instance, in the shadow of the prolific, arrogant, and popular Lope de Vega—but not one of them was ever performed. He wrote a pastoral romance, the *Galatea,* but it received little notice. In 1584, at the age of thirty-eight, he married a peasant girl of nineteen and spent much of the rest of his life scrabbling together enough money to support her, an illegitimate daughter, two sisters, a niece, and a servant. He took on minor government duties now—he was roving commissioner for the royal fleet first, requisitioning supplies for the Invincible Armada; then, for a decade and a half, he was tax collector, spending much of his time on the road haggling with the poor folk in the countryside of Andalusia and La Mancha until in time they demonstrated against him. He was excommunicated for, it was said, appropriating church supplies, and two times—perhaps three times—he was arrested for debt and for faulty accounts.

All of these facts are well known, and most of them are well documented. What is less well known is his schooling. He may have studied with a kinsman, a choirmaster who opened a school in Córdoba to teach boys reading, writing, and music; in Madrid, at the Estudio de la Villa, he studied with the well-known Erasmian Juan Lopez de Hoyos, who singled him out for high praise, at the age of twenty-one, for one of his poems; he may also have found further resources in the household of Cardinal Acquaviva. And at least from the age of thirty-three on, he seems to have spent every spare moment writing, perhaps training himself, since most of those works that have come down to us are, as we might guess from the *Quijote,* imitative of other works in a variety of genres.

Many of these extant works bear resemblances to *Don Quijote.* Several of the *Novelas Ejemplares* (*Exemplary Novels*), for example, are cast more or less in dialogue form. The best known is *The Colloquy of Dogs,* in which two dogs, surprised at their power of speech, proceed to use it principally to expose the ills of human nature. They are as unlike as the Don and Sancho at the start: Berganza is impetuous, voluble, and given to gossip and digressions; Cipión is intellectual. As the colloquy proceeds, Cipión becomes the critic of society, Berganza the critic of rhetoric and of Cipión. This dialectic—and any hope for resolution—is further complicated by joining to it *The Deceitful Marriage,* an Italian narrative by Campuzano, an unreliable syphilitic who gives his friend Peralta a transcript of the dogs' discussion. Another of these tales, *Master Glass,* is the story of Tomás Rodaja, who is well educated at the university and on a Grand Tour to Palermo, Messina, Naples, Rome, and Venice before a frustrated lover, seeking poison from a Moor, causes him to spend much of his life

262 · Post tenebras spero lucem

thinking he is made of glass and that he will break should anyone come near him. Like Don Quijote, others think him mad; and when, in the end, he is cured and attempts a career as a lawyer, no one will believe him.

Cervantes' *Entremeses* (*Interludes*) also combine this interest in colloquy with lives of illusion and delusion. *El Juez de los Divorcios* (*The Divorce-Court Judge*) puts on trial a May–December marriage in which the elderly husband accuses the young wife of hounding him to his grave and she accuses him of constantly annoying her with his aches and pains; the trial ends irresolutely in a truce, as both opponents—like the other two couples on trial—need to preserve their own fixed sense of themselves at any cost. *El Retablo de las Maravillas* (*The Wonder Show*) tells how the wily Chanfalla dupes an entire town by showing his audience an empty stage but announcing that only those who are bastards or heretics would fail to see the performance; when the quartermaster enters and claims to see nothing, he is shouted down by the crowd, of whom not one is willing to expose the hoax. In *El Viejo Celoso* (*The Jealous Old Husband*), old Cañizares is so certain he will not be cuckolded that his wife Lorenza's young lover easily sneaks past him behind a tapestry; the husband further refuses to accept his wife's detailed description of her matchmaking, for he finds the trick too bold to be believed. In all of these works, as in the *Quijote,* cherished illusions tend to transform the authentic world of the characters and give them new and precious ways to view themselves. Their lives, it would seem, rest on safeguarding such indispensable illusions.

Yet, of all his works, it is *El Ingenioso Hidalgo Don Quijote de la Mancha* that, when he was fifty-eight and within ten years of the end of his life, won Cervantes instant (and lasting) acclaim. Six editions appeared the first year; Cervantes signed rights to print the book in Portugal, Aragon, Valencia, and Catalonia. Within a few weeks, it found its way into palaces, roadside inns, and modest cottages. It is not hard to see why: Choosing to explore the humanist concern of the perfectibility of man, he ignored the earlier Spanish tradition of humanist fiction—which, as with Fernando de Rojas's *Celestina,* featured largely the exercise of base passions through hatred, revenge, violence, and sexuality— and used as his Senecan originals the far more popular chivalric romances, in which "the essence . . . is the imitation of the ideal hero," as J. Huizinga puts it.[21] Such works, at least as early as the *Erec et Enide* and *Lancelot* of Chrétien de Troyes, had argued that men should strive to speak well and teach the right; from nearly the beginning, too, such chivalric works had been decisively influenced by the Church, which had harmonized the knight's quest for glory with the Christian search for salvation, and by courtly love, which provided motivation for the knight in service and adoration of a lady whose beauty and need invited his aid. From nearly the start, then, chivalric romances had defined glory both as personal courage and bravery and as service and salvation. Knights could safeguard themselves against unwarranted pride and foolish courage by tempering their thoughts and actions with those ennobling traits that fair women inspired: selflessness, courtesy, humility, and loyalty. In protecting or assisting women there were of course physical dangers, through trial, journey, and close combat but also through rivalry, rashness, violence, vengeance, failure, and defeat. As the romances developed over time, knights often faced perils of distant and exotic lands and of strange and unexpected enchantments and enchanters. Nor was this simply a matter of escapist fiction.[22] Even for Chrétien, chivalric adventuring derives its deeper logic from the need to defend an order of existence against the encroachments of time, a tarnished and decaying present.

A number of these romances, written across Europe in various genres, have been suggested as partial originals for Cervantes' magnificent gesture of imitatio. Ramon Menendez Pidal chooses a novel by the Italian Sacchetti in which Agnolo di Ser Gherardo, obsessed with thoughts of the chivalric life at the age of seventy, mounts a lean nag and goes off to fight in the jousts at a town near Florence; a ballad by Juan del Encina (which circulated widely in cancioneros and broadsides) about a knight who forsakes his steed to mourn on cliffs and in forests, much like Cardenio; and the oldest known Spanish book of chivalry, *El Caballero Cifer*, with its rustic squire who is an "inexhaustible sayer of proverbs."[23] Closer in time to Cervantes are other works whose incidents may be the Senecan originals for parts of the *Quijote*. The *Palmerén de Ingalaterra* of Francisco de Moraes Cabral has an enchanted boat like the one the Don and Sancho find (2.29), a visionary meadow like the one the Don sees in the Cueva de Montesinos (2.23), and a funeral procession like the one the Don and Sancho witness (1.19). The *Orlando Furioso* of Ludovico Ariosto, twice mentioned in *Don Quijote*, may be a source for Mambrino's helmet, the madness in the Sierra Morena (1.25), and the ride on Clavileño (2.41). "The Ballad Farce," written late in the sixteenth century, concerns a man who goes mad reading too many books about Christian and Saracen knights and leaves home to imitate their lives.

But the most important Senecan original, as both Cervantes and the Don make clear, was a Spanish variant on the Arthurian romance, the *Amadís de Gaula* as rewritten by Garci Rodríguez de Montalvo and first published in 1508. Modeled clearly on French romances, the *Amadís*, like the later *Don*

Quijote, was widely popular. Amadís is the natural son of King Perion of Wales and the lovely Elisena; cast adrift in a boat carrying only a ring and a sword, he grows up in the home of Gandales of Scotland. As a young man he meets Oriana, daughter of Lisuarte, king of Brittany, and through her help he is, despite his lowly birth, made a knight; his subsequent adventures are meant to earn him the right to marry her. In his attempt he is aided by a good fairy, Urganda the Unknown (descended from either Morgan Le Fay or the Lady of the Lake), and hindered by the evil enchanter Arcalaus (derived from Merlin). But it is not only the similarities between Montalvo and Cervantes but, as with all works of imitatio, the divergences that matter in this extended description of the knightly code and life. Amadís is young, strong, and handsome whereas the Don is old, weak, and plain; Amadís's love makes him strong in battle whereas the Don fumbles with women as well as with his many opponents; Amadís is always protected by a good witch whereas the Don is forever hounded by anonymous evil enchanters. Most importantly, Amadís consummates his love early and has an illegitimate child, which further prompts his attempt to secure Oriana in marriage; the Don's loves are always platonic, never physical.[24] This last discrepancy has also prompted some scholars, beginning with Herbert J. Grierson,[25] to propose that Cervantes modeled his novel on saints' lives, such as that of the sixteenth-century Spanish Saint Teresa of Avila, whose autobiography tells us that she was first inspired by books she also imitated, and by the work of San Juan de la Cruz, Saint John of the Cross, whose life has resemblances to Cervantes' own and whose sixteenth-century account of the dark night of the soul and of his flights to visionary heights—

> Por una estraña manera
> mil buelos passe de un buelo
> porque esperança de çielo
> tanto alcança quanto espera
> esperè solo este lançe
> y en espere no fui falto

> Then—marvelous!—I made
> a thousand flights in one,
> for hope of heaven will see
> all it can wish, be done.
> I hoped for this alone;
> I hoped; was not downcast[26]

—has both haunting and ridiculous resonances in the Don's downward search in the cave and his upward flight on the wooden horse.

Such authorial practices of imitatio as these resources suggest lead to a novel about imitatio in which the humanists' chief means of learning is put to the severest of tests in the most exoteric way. Don Quijote first openly addresses the subject and merits of chivalric romance with the priest and barber in various symposia (1.1), but the point of the opening of Cervantes' work is the Don's gradual evolvement *into* them. The slow elision of verbal forms and meanings shows us how the elusive perspective of Lucian is brought to bear in the *Quijote:*

> Decía mucho bien del gigante Morgante, porque, con ser de aquella generación gigantea, que todos son soberbios y descomedidos, él solo era afable y bien criado. Pero, sobre todos, estaba bien con Reinaldos de Montalbán, y más cuando le véia salir de su castillo y robar cuantos topaba, y cuando en allende robó aquel ídolo de Mahoma que era todo de oro, según dice su historia. Diera él por dar una mano de coces al traidor de Galalón, al alma que tenía y aun a su sobrina de añadidura.

> He spoke very well of the giant Morgante; for, though one of that giant brood who are all proud and insolent, he alone was affable and well-mannered. But he admired most of all Reynald of Montalban, particularly when he saw him sally forth from his castle and rob everyone he met, and when in heathen lands overseas he stole that idol of Mahomet, which history says was of pure gold. But he would have given his housekeeper and his niece into the bargain, to deal the traitor Galalon a good kicking. [1.1; 1:24; p. 33]

The Don's initially unique ability to enter *into* the adventures and *become part of them*—others will follow him shortly—is verified by Cide Hamete Benengeli, who tells us (at the outset of 1.28) that events in this "authentic history" will be authentic because of their being a part of it ("no son menos agradables y artificiosos y verdaderos que la misma historia," 1.181; p. 236). Indeed, the Don's involvement is captured symbolically at the very beginning, when he enters into his ancestral history (of the past) by making it part of his own history (or life) through his pasteboard addition:

> Y lo primero que hizo fue limpiar unas armas que habían sido de sus bisabuelos, que, tomadas de orín y llenas de moho, luengos siglos había que

estaban puestas y olvidadas en un rincón. Limpiólas y aderezólas lo mejor que pudo; pero vio que tenían una gran falta, y era que no tenían celada de encaje, sino morrion simple; mas a esto suplió su industria, porque de cartones hizo un modo de media celada, que, encajada con el morrión, hacían una apariencia de celada entera. Es verdad que para probar si era fuerte y podía estar al riesgo de una cuchillada, sacó su espada y le dio dos golpes, y con el primero y en un punto deshizo lo que había hecho en una semana; y no dejó de parecerle mal la facilidad con que la había hecho pedazos, y, por asegurarse deste peligro, la tornó a hacer de neuvo, poniéndole unas barras de hierro por de dentro, de tal manera, que él quedó satisfecho de su fortaleza y, sin querer hacer nueva experiencia della, la diputó y tuvo por celada finísima de encaje.

The first thing that he did was to clean some armour which had belonged to his ancestors, and had lain for ages forgotten in a corner, eaten with rust and covered with mould. But when he had cleaned and repaired it as best he could, he found that there was one great defect: the helmet was a simple head-piece without a visor. So he ingeniously made good this deficiency by fashioning out of pieces of pasteboard a kind of half-visor which, fitted to the helmet, gave the appearance of a complete head-piece. However, to see if it was strong enough to stand up to the risk of a sword-cut, he took out his sword and gave it two strokes, the first of which demolished in a moment what had taken him a week to make. He was not too pleased at the ease with which he had destroyed it, and to safeguard himself against this danger, reconstructed the visor, putting some strips of iron inside, in such a way as to satisfy himself of his protection; and, not caring to make another trial of it, he accepted it as a fine jointed headpiece and put it into commission. [1.1; 1:25; pp. 33–34]

Fiction and truth become one—and both become history—through the mediation of verisimilitude, as Lucian argued.

But an even stranger transformation has already, more subtly, occurred. The narrator—who seems here to be Cervantes—has begun the novel in this way:

Frisaba la edad de nuestro hidalgo con los cincuenta años; era de complexión recia, seco de carnes, enjuto de rostro, gran madrugador y amigo de la caza. Quieren decir que tenía el sobrenombre de Quijada, o Quesada, que en esto hay alguna differencia en los autores que deste caso escriben; aunque por conjeturas verosímiles se deja entender que se llamba Quejana. Pero esto importa poco a nuestro cuento; basta que en la narración del no se salga un punto de la verdad.

Our gentleman was verging on fifty, of rough constitution, lean-bodied, thin-faced, a great early riser and a lover of hunting. They say that his surname was Quixada or Quesada—for there is some difference of opinion amongst authors on this point. However, by very reasonable conjecture we may take it that he was called Quexana. But this does not much concern our story; enough that we do not depart by so much as an inch from the truth in the telling of it.

[1.1; 1:23; p. 31]

In acknowledging his ignorance Cervantes conjectures what might be true, and then by making it true (and making it work) he ignores his ignorance and makes ignorance truth—just as Don Quijote will do when he begins realizing a life of knight-errantry. With only an occasional reference to further sources, Cervantes continues in the next few pages to *observe* Don Quijote rather than *tell about* him, so that his perspective and the Don's coalesce. All this is a necessary preliminary, of course, to what ensues when the innkeeper joins the Don to perpetuate the view that his inn is a castle (1.3), when Sancho Panza accepts the knight and agrees to become his squire (1.7), and even when the carrier becomes an evil enchanter and Maritornes becomes Dulcinea (1.17; 1:16). The historical and authentic world of the novel (and of its narration) conforms to the Don's fictional imposition, so that as readers we are left no alterity, no *opposing* view such as we found in the image of the Silenus in Erasmus and Rabelais. Indeed, the matter is complicated still further when the Don sees himself projected and doubled in the person of Cardenio (1.23) and refracted infinitely when he faces (as he will later in 2.12) the Knight of the Mirrors. Nor is this simply a matter of acquiescence. In time, when the troopers come to arrest Don Quijote on behalf of the Holy Brotherhood, the barber comes to demand from the Don his stolen basin, and the innkeeper comes to collect what is owed him for board and damages, the priest *conspires* (by paying the barber) to *preserve* the Don's view of truth and history (1.46). Even the narrator, in his simple act of telling the story of Don Quijote, shares a complicity in a series of historical acts that together verify and promulgate the Don's view of the present. Since that view has, by now, meant also the transformation of Aldonza Lorenzo and the admission of evil enchanters, the narrator (or author) has subscribed to his *ficción* both as an authentic history drawing on records and documents and a marvelous tale of magic and improbable events. Cervantes means to employ the fullest possible spectrum of narrative art so as to supply the fullest possible examination of the way men learn and the way written works instruct. At the same time, however, the narrator, in a peculiar, limited, but essential way, has become at times complicit with his protagonist, so that early on the dispensation and disposition of ideas and events no longer seem open to his dispassionate judgment but are instead up to us.

The problem of reading Cervantes, then, is nearly identical with the problem we face in reading Erasmus; the elusive and coalescing perspective of Folly, which reaches out to incorporate everything good and bad in the *Encomium Moriae*, is very much like the all-embracing perspective in *Don Quijote*. To imply the sort of bifocalism, then, that can help to distance us from a work that always invites us to join in with it completely, Cervantes (like Erasmus) allows for a kind of triangulation among two opposing views and the reader by incorporating debates within the fiction. These alert our enabling judgments and remind us to distance ourselves from what is, after all, a novel. One of the clearest and simplest examples of this is Don Quijote's inner debate in the Sierra Morena on whether it is better to imitate Roldán or Amadís de Gaula.

—Si Roldán fue tan buen caballero y tan valiente como todos dicen, ¿qué maravilla, pues, al fin era encantado, y no le podía mater nadie si no era metiéndole un alfiler de a blanca por la punta de pie, y él traía siempre los zapatos con siete suelas de herro? Aunque no le valieron tretas contra Bernardo del Carpio, que se las entendió, y le ahogó entre los brazos, en Roncesvalles. Pero, dejando en él lo de la valentia a una parte, vengamos a lo de perder el juicio, que es cierto que le perdió, por las señales que halló en la Fortuna y por las nuevas que le dio el pastor de que Angélica había dormido más de dos siestas con Medoro, un morillo de cabellos enrizados y paje de Agramante; y si él ententió que esto era verdad y que su dama la había cometido desaguisado, no hizo mucho en volverse loco; pero yo, ¿como puedo imitalle en las locuras, si no le imito en la ocasión dellas? Porque mi Dulcinea del Toboso osaré yo jurar que no ha visto en todos los días de su vida moro alguno, ansí como él es, en su mismo traje, y que se está hoy como la madre que la parió; y haríale agravio manifesto si, imaginando otra cosa della, me volviese loco de aquel género de locura de Roldán el furioso. Por otra parte, veo que Amadís de Gaula, sin perfer el juicio y sin hacer locuras, alcanzó tanta fama de enamorado como el que más; porque lo que hizo, según su historia, no fue más de que, por verse desdeñado de su señora Oriana, que le había mandado que no pareciese ante su presencia hasta que fuese su voluntad, de que se retiró a la Peña Pobre en compañia de un ermitaño, y allí se hartó de llorar y de encomendarse a Dios, hasta que el cielo le acorrió, en medio de su mayor cuita y necesidad.

Y si eso es verdad, como lo es, ¿para qué quiero yo tomar trabajo agora de desnudarme del todo, ni dar pesadumbre a estos árboles, que no me han hecho mal alguno? Ni tengo para qué enturbiar el agua clara destos arroyos, los cuales me han de dar de beber cuando tenga gana. Viva la memoria de Amadís, y sea imitado de don Quijote de la Mancha en todo lo que pudiere; del cual se dirá lo que del otro se dijo: que si no acabó grandes cosas, murió por acometellas; y si yo no soy desechado de Dulcinea del Toboso, básteme, como ya he dicho, estar ausente della. Ea, pues, manos a la obra: venid a mi memoria cosas de Amadís, y enseñadme por dónde tengo de comenzar a imitaros. Mas ya sé que lo que más que él hizo fue rezar y encomendarse a Dios; pero, ¿qué hare de rosario, que no le tengo?

"If Roland was as good a knight and as valiant as they all say, where is the wonder? since, after all, he was enchanted, and no one could kill him except by stabbing a long pin into the sole of his foot, which was the reason why he always wore shoes with seven iron soles. But these contrivances were of no avail against Bernardo del Carpio, who understood them, and throttled him with his bare hands at Roncesvalles. But, setting his bravery on one side, let us consider his madness, which certainly arose from the evidence he found beside the spring and the news which the shepherd gave him that Angelica had slept more than two afternoons with Medoro, a little curly-haired Moor and page to Agramante. Now if he believed that this was true, and that his lady had done him this foul wrong, it is not surprising that he went mad. But how can I imitate him in his madness without a similar cause? For I dare swear that my Dulcinea del Toboso has never seen a real Moor in his real Moorish dress in all her life, and that she is to-day as her mother bore her; and I should do her a grave injury were I to imagine otherwise and go mad, after the fashion of Roland the Furious.

"On the other hand, I know that Amadis of Gaul achieved an unrivalled reputation as a lover without ever losing his wits or having raving fits. For, as the history tells, on finding himself scorned by his lady Oriana, who had commanded him to appear no more in her presence until it was her pleasure, what he did was merely to retire to the Bare Rock in the company of a hermit; and there he wept his fill and commended himself to God so earnestly that Heaven succoured him in the midst of his greatest tribulation. Now if this is true—and it is—why do I now take pains to strip myself stark naked and give pain to these trees which have done me no harm, and disturb the clear water of these streams, which must give me drink when I am thirsty? All honour then to the memory of

Amadis, and let him be the model, so far as it is possible, for Don Quixote de la Mancha, of whom it shall be said, as it was said of that other, that if he did not achieve great things he died attempting them. If I am not cast off and despised by Dulcinea del Toboso, let it suffice, as I have said, that I am absent from her. So now to work! Come into my mind, deeds of Amadis, and teach me where to begin to imitate you. I remember now that most of the time he prayed and commended his soul to God. But what shall I do for a rosary, for I have none?"

[1.26; 1 : 162–63; pp. 214–15]

Yet this apparently simple choice of action becomes restless and takes on numerous levels of significance, as words and events in Cervantes always do. Don Quijote knows well enough that Roldán's madness has no authentic purpose for him, and he can see how madness functions in Roldán's case; at the same time, imposing on himself the role of Amadís would cause him to violate nature with an art robbed of any authentic function. His imitation, then, must be governed by his own status, by his own circumstances, and by his own best sense of purpose—and it is here that he moves to bridge his reading with his actions. That religion itself plays a part for Amadís, however, does not deter the Don from distinguishing between the fact that he is not immune to divine aid and the fact that he may bring that part of fictional history into his own truthful history. Thus this debate has the same function of juggling truth, history, and fiction to a proper deployment as the Don's conversational remarks frequently do—such as his warning to Maritornes that he is unable to help her because of chivalric rules but that he has compassion for her plight (1.44)—and that his conversations with Sancho or with the barber and priest always do.

The Don can also impose and withdraw fiction from history when there is cause to do so. Even Dulcinea is not exempt from this practice of his. In another startling opposition—a kind of warning disputation to the reader, in effect—he does just that in conversation with an anonymous traveler.

Aquí dio un gran suspiro don Quijote, y dijo:
—Yo no podré afirmar si la dulce mi enemiga gusta, o no, de que el mundo sepa que yo la sirvo; sólo sé decir, respondiendo a lo que con tanto comedimiento se me pide, que su nombre es Dulcinea; su patria, el Toboso, un lugar de la Mancha; su calidad, por lo menos, ha de ser de princesa, pues es reina y señora mía; su hermosura, sobrehumana, pues en ella se vienen a hacer verdaderos todos los imposibles y quiméricos atributos de belleza que los poetas dan a sus damas; que sus cabellos son oro, su frente campos elíseos, sus cejas arcos del cielo, sus ojos soles, su mejillas rosas, sus labios corales, perlas sus dientes, alabastro su

cuello, mármol su pecho, marfil sus manos, su blancura nieve, y las partes que a la vista humana encubrió la honestidad son tales, según yo pienso y entiendo, que sólo la discreta consideración puede encarecerlas, y no compararlas.

—El linaje, prosapia y alcurnia querríamos saber—replicó Vivaldo.

A lo cual respondió don Quijote:

—No es de los antiguos Curcios, Gayos y Cipiones romanos, ni de los modernos Colonas y Ursinos, ni de los Moncadas y Requesenes de Cataluña, ni menos de los Rebellas y Villanovas de Valencia, Palafoxes, Nuzas, Rocabertís, Corellas, Lunas, Alagones, Urreas, Foces y Gurreas de Aragón, Cerdas, Manriques, Mendozas y Guzmanes de Castilla, Alencastros, Pallas y Meneses de Portugal; pero es de los del Toboso de la Mancha, linaje, aunque moderno, tal, que puede dar generoso principio a las más ilustres familias de los venideros siglos.

Here Don Quixote heaved a deep sigh and said: "I cannot affirm whether my sweet enemy is pleased or not at the whole world's knowing that I serve her. I can only say, in reply to your very polite question, that her name is Dulcinea; her country El Toboso, a village in La Mancha; her degree at least that of Princess, for she is my Queen and mistress; her beauty superhuman, for in her are realized all the impossible and chimerical attributes of beauty which poets give to their ladies; that her hair is gold; her forehead the Elysian fields; her eyebrows rainbows; her eyes suns; her cheeks roses; her lips coral; her teeth pearls; her neck alabaster; her breast marble; her hands ivory; she is white as snow; and those parts which modesty has veiled from human sight are such, I think and believe, that discreet reflection can extol them, but make no comparison."

"We should like to know her lineage, race, and family," said Vivaldo.

And Don Quixote replied: "She is not of the ancient Curtii, Caii, or Scipios of Rome; nor of the modern Colonnas and Orsinis; nor of the Moncadas and Requesenes of Catalonia; nor yet of the Rebellas and Villanovas of Valencia; of the Palafoxes, Nuzas, Rocabertis, Corellas, Lunas, Alagones, Urreas, Fozes, and Gurreas of Aragon; of the Cerdas, Manriques, Mendozas, and Guzmans of Castile; nor of the Alencastres, Pallas, and Meneses of Portugal; but of El Toboso of La Mancha, a lineage which, though modern, may yet give noble birth to the most illustrious families of future ages." [1.13; 1:76–77; pp. 100–101]

This allocution of the Don's is perfectly reasoned within itself and perfectly ordered: It manages to idealize Dulcinea without threatening to destroy that vision with contrary facts; it also manages to authenticate her by the traditional terms of defining fair ladies. What holds its various perspectives and elements

of history and fiction together is the Don's willful act of the imagination—
something he freely admits to Sancho: "in my imagination I draw her as I would
have her be" ("y pintola en mi imaginación como la deseo," 1.25; 1 : 159;
p. 210). Debates, that is, can cease to be debates when subjected to the
imaginative constructs that preserve a sense of illusion *and identity* (the theme
that Cervantes pursues in his brief *Entremeses*). It is this that not only allows the
Don to transcend history in order to rewrite history in terms of beautiful
women and chivalric missions, but also allows him to explain (and even explain
away) defeat by imagining (or importing from fictive histories) evil enchanters.
Sancho learns this lesson of self-preservation, too: When frightened by the
fulling mills he ties Rocinante's legs together and blames it on the *encantamientos* (1.20), and when he makes up a story about his trip to see Dulcinea he makes
over Dulcinea herself (1.25). This allows for an intricate inner disputation for
Cervantes but one that is representative of the dialectical way in which the
Quijote is forever functioning: When Sancho *lies* about Dulcinea on returning to
the Don in the Sierra Morena, he describes her in *truthful* terms—right down
to her foul smell—and the Don in response *lies* about her perfection while
asking Sancho to tell him the whole *truth* (1.31). Such moments of dialogue or
colloquy—inherent disputations, really—push the imagination aside for us,
as Folly manages to do in the *Encomium Moriae,* so that we as readers are forced
to subvert the characters, the actions, the story, and the narrator and face our
own best judgments.

Another means of inherent disputation, which Cervantes employs so as to
distance the reader, is the use of inset stories of adventure and inset narratives or
tales. We have already looked at the story of Andrés (1.4) as the Don sees him,
with compassion—and we note somewhat later his reversal of fortune because
of the Don (1.31); we have noted too the inherent discrepancies in the adventure of the galley slaves (1.22). As for the inset tales, the first of them, that of
the goatherd, centers on a debate between the young lover Grisóstomo, who
dies for his unfulfilled romance, and his beloved, Marcela, who defends herself
(1.13–14). But what appears to be a relatively separate story—despite its
calling attention to the issues of frustrated love and its essentially syllogistic
structuring—is further blended into the main narrative when we realize (although it must be *our* realization) that Grisóstomo is, in many ways, a me-
tonymy of Don Quijote, as his dying lament means partly to show:

> *Mata un desdén, atierra la paciencia,* . . .
> *mas yo, ¡milagro nunca visto!, vivo*

celoso, ausente, desdeñado y cierto
de las sospechas que me tienen muerto,
y en el olvido en quien mi fuego avivo,
y, entre tantos tormentos, nunca alcanza
mi vista a ver en sombra a la esperanza,
ni yo, desesperado, la procuro;
antes, por estremarme en mi querella,
estar sin ella eternamente juro.

Disdain doth kill; and whether false or sound . . .
But I—amazing miracle!—still live,
Jealous, absent, disdained, and certain too
Of the suspicion that my life undo,
Drowned in oblivion, I my fire revive,
And amongst all those pains have never scope
Once to behold the shadow of a hope,
Nor, thus despairing, will I hope allow;
But rather, to exacerbate my wrong,
To live for ever hopeless here I vow. [1.14; 1:80; p. 105]

For only moments earlier, the Don has told Vivaldo the traveler about a knight-errant's total dependence on his lady for inspiration, direction, and comfort (1.13). That we are to see the similarities between the Don and Grisóstomo (as well as the differences; the Don is not capable of giving up his life as the sentimental Grisóstomo does) is given further testimony in Marcela's response when her self-description seems identical to the descriptions the Don gives us of Dulcinea (1.14) and is verified still further when the Don directly defends her in those terms (1.14).

Whether or not the Don senses himself in Grisóstomo, he surely does see himself mirrored in Cardenio. The first description the Don hears startles him, because Cardenio has anticipated the mad acts the Don had just been planning himself when he imitated Roldán in the mountains. Seeing Cardenio confirms his sense that they are little more than alter egos—in effect, the same person.

En llegando el mancebo a ellos, los saludó con una voz desentonada y bronca, pero con mucha cortesía. Don Quijote le volvió las saludes con no menos comedimiento, y, apeándose de Rocinante, con gentil continente y donaire, le fue a abrazar, y le tuvo un buen espacio estrechamente entre sus brazos, como si de luengos tiempos le hubiera conocido. El otro, a quien podemos llamar *el Roto de la mala Figura,* como a don Quijote *el de la Triste,* después de haberse dejado abrazar, le apartó un poco de si, y, puestas sus manos en los hombros de don Quijote, le estuvo mirando, como que quería ver si le conocía; no menos admirado quizá de ver la figura, talle y armas de don Quijote, que don Quijote lo estaba de verle a él.

When the youth came up he greeted them in a rough and toneless voice, but very courteously. Don Quixote returned his greetings no less politely and, charmingly and graciously dismounting from Rocinante, advanced to embrace him, and held him for some time clasped in his arms, as if he had known him for a long while. The other, whom we may call the Ragged Knight of the Sorry—as Don Quixote was of the Sad—Countenance, after allowing himself to be embraced drew back a little and, placing his hands on Don Quixote's shoulders, stood gazing at him, as if to see whether he knew him, being no less surprised, perhaps, to see Don Quixote's face, figure, and armour than Don Quixote was to see him.

[1.23; 1 : 145; p. 191]

It is an astonishing moment, and astonishing for the narrator, too, who is the putative author here of a title for Cardenio that makes him the alter ego to the Don—"for anyone who was there to see it," as he implies. It is a significant point of transference, for from here on the Don must also be viewed as Cardenio. Yet, almost as soon as this happens, Cardenio divorces himself from the Don with his own story of his love for Lucinda—for in his youth, in his actual courtship, and in his actual mission to serve the court of the Duke, he realizes what the Don only imagines for himself; the "history" of Cardenio becomes the Don's cherished projection of his own life, his best autobiographical "fiction." This seems certain to him when Cardenio announces his great respect for *Amadís de Gaula* (1.24), and the Don enthusiastically, despite his pledge, enters into the narrative by trying to amend Cardenio's story. At this point the accumulating *divergences* between them also surface, and their shared reflections break into debate and fighting.

En tanto que don Quijote estaba diciendo lo que queda dicho, se la había caído a Cardenio la cabeza sobre el pecho, dando muestras de estar profundamente pensativo. Y, puesto que dos veces le dijo don Quijote que prosiguiese su historia, ni alzaba la cabeza ni respondia palabra: pero al cabo de un buen espacio le levantó y dijo:

—No se me puede quitar del pensamiento, ni habrá quien me lo quite en el mundo, ni quien me dé a entender otra cosa, y sería un majadero el que lo contrario entendiese o creyese, sino que aquel bellaconazo del maestro Elisabat estaba amancebado con la reina Madásima.

—Eso no, ¡voto a tal!—respondió con mucha cólera don Quijote, y arrójole, como tenía de costumbre—; y ésa es una muy gran malicia, o bellaqueria, por mejor decir: la reina Madásima fue muy principal señora, y no se ha de presumir que tan alta princesa se había de amancebar con ùn sacapotras; y quien lo contrario entendiere, miente como muy gran bellaco. Y yo se lo daré a entender, a pie o caballo, armado o desarmado, de noche o de día, o como más gusto le diere.

Estábale mirando Cardenio muy atentamente, al cual ya había venido el accidente de su locura y no estaba para proseguir su historia; ni tampoco don Quijote se la oyera, según le había disgustado lo que de Madásima le había oído. ¡Estrano caso; que así volvió por ella como si verdaderamente fuera su verdadera y natural señora; tal le tenían sus decomulgados libros! Digo, pues que, como ya Cardenio estaba loco, y se oyó tratar de mentis y de bellaco, con otros denuestos semejantes, parecióle mal la burla, y alzó un guijarro que hallo junto a sí, y dio con él en los pechos tal golpe a don Quijote, que le hizo caer de espaldas. Sancho Panza, que de tal modo vio parar a su señor, arremetió al loco con el puño cerrado, y el Roto le recibió de tal suerte, que con una puñada dio con él a sus pies, y luego se subió sobre él y le brumó las costillas muy a su sabor. El cabereo, que le quiso defender, corrió el mesmo peligro. Y después que los tuvo a todos rendidos y molidos, los dejó, y se fue, con gentil sosiego a emboscarse en la montaña.

Whilst Don Quixote was saying all this, Cardenio let his head fall on his breast, seemingly plunged in deep thought; and although the knight twice asked him to go on with his story, he neither raised his head nor answered a word. But at the end of a good while he looked up and said: "One thing I cannot get out of my mind, and no one in the world can persuade me or convince me otherwise—indeed, anyone holding the contrary opinion would be an idiot. That arch-scoundrel Master Elisabat was Queen Madasima's lover."

"That is false, I swear," replied Don Quixote in great wrath, bursting out in his usual fashion, "and a most malicious, or rather villainous calumny. Queen Madasima was a very noble lady, and it is not to be supposed that so great a princess would take a quack for a lover. Whoever says otherwise lies like an arrant scoundrel, and I will make him acknowledge it, on foot or horse, armed or unarmed, by night or day, or however he will."

Cardenio sat staring at him very attentively. For a fit of madness had come on him and he was in no state to continue his tale; nor would Don Quixote have listened if he had, so disgusted was he by what he had heard concerning Madasima. It was extraordinary to see him take her part as though she were in fact his real and natural mistress; such was the power his unholy books had over him.

But, as I said, Cardenio was now mad, and when he heard himself called a liar and a scoundrel and other such names, he took the joke in bad part. In fact he picked up a stone from beside him, and hit Don Quixote so hard on the chest that he knocked him backwards. When Sancho Panza saw his master thus treated, he attacked the madman with clenched fists. But the Ragged Knight gave him such a reception that he had him stretched at his feet at the first blow, after which he got on top of him and trampled his ribs to his heart's content. The goatherd, who tried to defend him, met with the same fate, and after Cardenio had threshed and bruised them all, he left them and retired quietly to his mountain ambush.

[1.24; 1:150–51; p. 198]

It is important that, once the Don perceives the *differences* between Cardenio and himself, Cardenio's "history" becomes madness and the chivalric romances unholy books, although the first battle they join is over their *shared* belief *in,* and realization of, those very books. The point of all this, of course, is that Don Quijote here (as with Grisóstomo and Marcela earlier) moves in and out of the inset tales with complete freedom. It follows, then, that when Cardenio's "true" history, corroborated independently by Dorotea, has been concluded, Dorotea's fictitious "history" as the Princess Micomicona can also involve the Don—indeed, depends for its very existence on the Don's participation. And another inset story, which *must* be a *story* because it is found on eight manuscript leaves in an abandoned trunk at the inn ("The Tale of Foolish Curiosity," "la novela del Curioso impertinente") about the suspicious husband Anselmo and his insistence on testing his wife Camilla's fidelity by proposing the advances of his friend Lotario [1.33–35], is interrupted by the Don's actions in the Battle of the Wine-Skins, which the innkeeper discovers.

Y con esto, entró en el aposento, y todos tras él, y hallaron a don Quijote en el más estraño traje de mundo. Estaba en camisa, la cual no era tan cumplida, que por delante le acabase de cubrir los muslos, y por detrás tenia seis dedos menos; las piernas eran muy largas y flacas, llenas de vello y no nada limpias; tenía en la cabeza un bonetillo colorado, grasiento, que era del ventero; en el brazo izquierdo tenía revuelta la manta de la cama, con quien tenía ojeriza Sancho, y él se sabía bien el porqué; y en la derecha, desenvainada la espada, con la cual daba cuchilladas a todas partes, diciendo palabras como si verdaderamente estuviera peleando con algún gigante. Y es lo bueno que no tenía los ojos abiertos, porque estaba durmiendo y soñando que estaba en batalla con el gigante; que fue tan intensa la imaginación de la ventura, que iba a fenecer, que la hizo soñar que ya había llegado al reino de Micomicón, y que ya estaba en la pelea con su enemigo. Y había dado tantas cuchilladas en los cueros, creyendo que las daba en el gigante, que todo el aposento estaba lleno de vino.

With that he ran into the room, and the others after him. They found Don Quixote in the strangest outfit in the world. He was in his shirt, which was not long enough in front to cover his thighs completely, and was six inches shorter behind. His legs were very long and thin, covered with hair, and not over-clean. On his head he wore a little greasy red cap which belonged to the innkeeper, and round his left arm he had wound the blanket of the bed—against which Sancho bore a grudge, and very well he knew why. In his right hand was his naked sword, with which he was lamming out in all directions, shouting all the time as if he were really fighting with a giant. The cream of the joke was that his eyes were not open, because he was asleep, and dreaming that he was battling with the giant. For his imagination was so bent on the adventure which he was going to achieve, that it made him dream he had got to the kingdom of Micomicon and was already at grips with his enemy.

What is more, he had slashed the wine-skins so many times, in the belief that he was getting at the giant, that the whole room was flooded with wine.

[1.35; 1:242; p. 317]

This absurd battle attesting to the Don's mission for the "Princess" is less absurd when we note its exact parallel with the tale it interrupts, for the Don now replicates Anselmo in wishing into existence what he both fears and hopes for—and the world in which he lives collaborates with him in providing the occasion. The judgment we are meant to give Anselmo's foolish curiosity and the judgment we are meant to give the Don's are, therefore, reciprocal.

The inset stories—especially the tale of foolish curiosity—are all heightened fictions, but as they tangle with and invade the Don's "history," preserved in documents discovered by Cervantes and translated by him, recorded by Cide Hamete Benengeli before him, and soon to be authenticated once more and popularized in a book and its imitation by an independent hand, they eliminate the normal boundaries we place between such fictions and such histories. Either all of these narratives are equally authentic, or none of them is authentic. The histories have no more claim on our credibility—but no less claim either—than the most fabulous and marvelous of adventures. What is happening in *El Ingenioso Hidalgo,* then, is that the inherent disputation of the Don's adventures and the inset tales collapses into a composite plane of narration, just as the inherent debates coalesced through the willful act of the imagination. The inside-outside dichotomies that have allowed us to read and understand all of Cervantes' chief Continental predecessors are here rendered illusory. Nothing—or everything—is rendered either stable or verifiable, depending on the value we are willing to place on fiction.

In thus testing the humanists' priority given to precepts and their confirmation in experience, Cervantes carries to a final outcome for humanist poetics the issue first raised by such antique writers as Lucian and first promulgated in the Renaissance by Folly: the interpenetration of truth and fiction (and history). That truth and fiction interpenetrate and that this is the foundation of the *Quijote*—and that this compound is unstable and in flux, aleatory, even vertiginous—are shown us nearly at the start: Don Quijote sees only giants when he looks at windmills (1.8), but when he sees fulling mills by daylight they remain fulling mills (1.20). Truth and fiction interpenetrate with Sancho too in time: His *story* of Lope Ruiz depends alternately on what he *saw* and what he was *told* to *say* (1.20). This instability of perception reaches out in the novel to embrace those we wish to see as the most "realistic" and unimaginative when the barber and priest are willing to put on costumes and become a squire and damsel in distress to woo the Don back home: The world of the novel capitulates to the mad knight-errant's vision, at once releasing the imagination and imprisoning it by subjecting it to a single model. Leo Lowenthal has argued that this instability finds its origins in the unsettled life of Cervantes himself and in the rigidly hierarchical social system of late Renaissance Spain—of its golden age—in which there are no class, no position, and no *place* for someone like Don Quijote who wishes to challenge his present and to change it radically.[27] In such a reading, Sancho Panza's capitalist motivation—looking ahead as it does to the commercial world of trade and competition that was already threatening the world of the humanists—is directly opposed to the structured, backward-looking world of Don Quijote. But the instability of this period in Western cultural history and the uncertainty of Don Quijote's position in the society of La Mancha are both subjected finally in this novel to the instability of the *text,* the chief humanist means of preserving the past in ways that would instruct, civilize, and cultivate the present and future.

This instability of the text is frequently apparent in the guesses, inferences, propositions, conjectures, and tests that the characters of the *Quijote* are continually making about themselves or others. The *Quijote* is, when we read it this way, a remarkably *speculative* and inquiring novel; again and again, we are reminded how much it matters for the characters to understand themselves and their place, and how difficult it is for them to interpret, or even define, the circumstances in which they find themselves. And what is difficult for *them* singly is in the aggregate far more difficult for *us*. The very language makes this transparent. Ruth El Saffar sees this too: "Cervantes' play with words, along with his introduction of so many levels of discourse and so many literary styles," she writes, "tends to break down whatever assumptions the reader might harbor about the fixed nature of literary language and the power of the word to assign meaning."[28]

Indeed, even the traditional humanist form of narrative—found in all the basic handbooks of rhetoric and practiced in all the humanist schoolrooms—is questioned and rendered unstable by Cervantes. Where, for instance, does this novel begin? With Chapter 1 or with the Prologo? This matters a great deal, for our understanding and our response to the novel will be very different, depending on our answer to that question. And what is the whole story? The lacuna that breaks the story abruptly in 1.9 is only the first of the interrupted stories—as if stories are by nature not organic but episodic and so subject to composition (and, presumably, recomposition). Who, in fact, is the narrator? We have seen how Cervantes proposes himself on the first page of the novel but then disappears. What appears in his place—but first as a *story* within the story—is the Arab Cide Hamete Benengeli. And this is a strange account indeed, for it makes of this discovery of an authentic "history" both a commodity—something to be bargained for on the open market—and an instructive story, reliable as history, perhaps reliable in *translation,* and perhaps unreliable because of the background of the historian who recorded it (1.9). This key passage concludes with a strong affirmation of the humanist premium on history, in precisely humanist terms (truth, "cuya madre es la historia, émula del tiempo, depósito de las acciones, testigo de lo pasado, ejemplo y aviso de lo presente, advertencia de lo por venir"; "whose mother is history, rival of time, storehouse of great deeds, witness of the past, example and lesson to the present, warning to the future"), and on classical notions of the characteristics of history—in precisely Lucianic, or satiric, terms ("habiendo y debiendo ser los historiadores puntuales, verdaderos y no nada apasionadas, y que ni el interés ni el miedo, el rencor ni la afición, no les hagan torcer del camino de la verdad"; "historians are bound by right to be exact, truthful, and absolutely unprejudiced, so that neither interest nor fear, dislike nor affection, should make them turn from the path of truth," 1.59; p. 78). Which are we to believe? And there are more troubling questions earlier in the passage that these clichés may mean to mask but only oppose: How does Cervantes know Don Quijote's name unless this "story" is truly "history"? If it is true, then Don Quijote's Dulcinea is not a salter of pork; she is a refined lady (if there is such a person at all as Dulcinea; this authentic history says that Don Quijote made her up). Finally, if we cannot trust an Arab historian, why then should we trust any more an Arab translator of an Arab historian? That Cervantes' chief means in openly discussing the stability of the text is that of equivocation is apparent frequently in the novel, but nowhere more so than when he returns to describe Benengeli at some length.

> Real y verdaderamente, todos los que gustan de semejantes historias como ésta deben de mostrarse agradecidos a Cide Hamete, su autor primero, por la curiosidad que tuvo en contarnos las semínimas della, sin dejar, cosa, por menuda que fuese, que no la sacase a luz disintamente. Pinta los pensamientos, descubre las imaginaciones, responde a las tácitas, aclara las dudas, resuelve los argumentos; finalmente, los átomos del más curioso deseo manifiesta. ¡Oh autor celebérimo! ¡Oh don Quijote dichoso! ¡Oh Dulcinea famosa! ¡Oh Sancho Panza gracioso! Todos juntos y cada uno de por sí viváis siglos infinitos, para gusto y general pasatiempo de los vivientes.

> In very truth, all who enjoy stories like this should show their gratitude to Cide Hamete, its first author, for his meticulousness in recording its minutest details, leaving nothing, however trivial, which he does not bring clearly to light. He depicts thoughts, reveals intentions, answers unspoken questions, clears up doubts, resolves objections; in fact elucidates the slightest points the most captious critic could raise. O most renowned author! O fortunate Don Quixote! O famous Dulcinea! O droll Sancho Panza! May you live, jointly and separately, for infinite ages, to the delight and general amusement of mankind!

> [2.40; 2:206; p. 721]

Such vacillation pervades the *Quijote:* Benengeli is the most meticulous investigator of every detail (2.50) and the flower of historians (2.61), but he is also deceitful, like any Moor (1.40) whose interpreter or translator made further errors (2.44), an equivocation perhaps grounded in Cervantes' own knowledge of the actual marabouts or holy men of Algiers who, called "Cide," could be both scholars and necromancers. But who is making these judgments? Cervantes himself? If so, does this mean that he gives some credence at least to the overall usefulness (and entertainment) of recording as *accurately* as possible this "true" "history" of Don Quijote? And if "truth" is a main issue, why does Cervantes include a chapter (2.5) declared apocryphal? Why does Benengeli admit to reliance on other reports, resort frequently to conjecture, and even narrate incidents at which he was not present and could not in any way know? (For that matter, how did he come to "know" what he knows?) Richard L. Predmore may have part of the answer when he argues that, whatever else is true of Benengeli, he clearly *cares* about Don Quijote and his task as the historian of the Don's adventures as he keeps checking his facts and making observations.[29] In this sense of compassion, which weds Benengeli to his story as it mediates the "history" for us, we do have a bridge that somehow over-comes and transcends troubling questions about the veracity and validity of history and the instability of the text. In fact, in the very concentration on Cide Hamete—the narrator equivalent to Don Quijote as a bridge between precept and act, between truth and history—Cervantes demonstrates conclusively the Lucianic poetic that both thought and life rest solely on the *necessary* belief, on *necessary* ficción. This alone can accommodate the historical documents in Arabic and Castilian, the stories they tell, and the conjectures they make so that in the *Quijote* we have not only the strongest possible test of humanist fiction but what appears to be its strongest tribute as well.

For Cervantes clearly sees the healing and amending powers of fiction; the self-dividing knowledge of the *Quijote* and its apparent instability finally result not in sophistry (as with Erasmus) or in eternal debate (as with Castiglione) but in a mind searching for unity (as in Marguerite and Rabelais). A number of instances could be cited, but a major and representative one—on which Cervantes lavishes much attention—is the case of Mambrino's helmet. In many ways, it serves as a synecdoche for much of the *Quijote*. The helmet is first mentioned in passing by Don Quijote, who clearly knows of its independent "existence" in romance before he encounters it in his "history" (1.10). He is therefore prepared to recognize its appearance and through his enabling imagi-nation transform it from past fiction to current history so as to make it function in *his* world.

> —Dime, ¿no ves aquel caballero que hacia nosotros viene, sobre un caballo rucio rodado, que trae puesto en la cabeza un yelmo de oro?
> —Lo que yo veo y columbro—respondió Sancho—no es sino un hombre

sobre un asno, pardo como el mío, que trae sobre la cabeza una cosa que relumbra.

—Pues ése es el yemo de Mambrino—dijo don Quijote—. Apártate a una parte y déjame con él a solas; verás cuán sin hablar palabra, por ahorrar el tiempo, concluyo esta aventura, y queda por mío el yelmo que tanto he deseado. . . .

Es, pues, el caso que el yelmo, y el caballo y caballero que don Quijote veía, era esto: que en aquel contorno había dos lugares, el uno tan pequeño, que ni tenía botica ni barbero, y el otro, que estaba junto, sí; y así, el barbero del mayor servía al menor, en el cual tuvo necesidad un enfermo de sangrarse, y otro de hacerse la barba, para lo cual venía el barbero, y traía una bacía de azófar; y quiso la suerte que, al tiempo que venía, comenzó a llover, y porque no se le manchase el sombrero, que debía de ser nuevo, se puso la bacía sobre la cabeza; y, como estaba limpia, desde media legua relumbraba. Venía sobre un asno pardo, como Sancho dijo, y ésta fue la ocasíon que a don Quijote le pareció caballo rucio rodado, y caballero, y yelmo de oro; que todas las cosas que veía con mucha facilidad las acomodaba a sus desvariadas caballerías y malandantes pensamientos. Y cuando él vio que el pobre caballero llegaba cerca, sin ponerse con él en razones, a todo correr de Rocinante le enristró con el lanzón bajo, llevando intención de pasarle de parte a parte; mas cuando a él llegaba, sin detener la furia de su carrera, le dijo:

—¡Defiéndete, cautiva criatura, o entriégame de tu voluntad lo que con tanta razon se me debe!

El barbero, que, tan sin pensarlo ni temerlo, vio venir aquella fantasma sobre si, no tuvo otro remedio, para poder guardarse del golpe de la lanza, sino fue el dejarse caer del asno abajo; y no hubo tocado al suelo, cuando se levantó más ligero que un gamo, y comenzó a correr por aquel llano, que no le alcanzara el viento. Dejóse la bacía en el suelo, con la cual se contentó don Quijote, y dijo que el pagano había andado discreto, y que había imitado al castor, el cual, viéndose acosado de los cazadores, se taraza y harpa con los dientes aquello por lo que él, por distinto natural, sabe que es perseguido. Mandó a Sancho que alzase el yelmo, el cual, tomándola en las manos, dijo:

—Por Dios que la bacía es buena, y que vale un real de a ocho como un maravedi.

Y dandosela a su amo, se la puso luego en la cabeza, rodeándola a una parte y a otra, buscándole el encaje; y como no se le hallaba, dijo:

—Sin duda que el pagano a cuya medida se forjó primero esta famosa celada, debia tener grandísma cabeza; y lo peor dello es que le falta la mitad.

Cuando Sancho oyó llamar a la bacía celada, no pudo tener la risa; mas vínosele a las mientes la cólera de su amo, y calló en la mitad della.

—¿De qué te riés, Sancho?—dijo don Quijote.

—Riome—respondió él—de considerar la gran cabeza que tenía el pagano dueño deste almete, que no semeja sino una bacía de barbero pintiparada.

—¿Sabes qué imagino, Sancho? Que esta famosa pieza deste encantado yelmo, por algún estraño acidente debió de venir a manos de quien no supo conocer ni estimar su valor, y, sin saber lo que hacía, viéndola de oro purísimo, debió de fundir la otra mitad para aprovecharse del precio, y de la ostra mitad hizo ésta, que parece bacía de barbero, como tú dices. Pero, sea lo que fuere; que para mi que la conozco no hace al caso su trasmutación; que yo la aderezaré en el primer lugar donde haya herrero, y de suerte que no le haga ventaja, ni aun le llegue, la que hizo y forjó el dios de las herrerías para el dios de las batallas; y en este entretanto, la traeré como pudiere, que más vale algo que no nada; cuanto más que bien será bastante para defenderme de alguna pedrada.

"Tell me, can you not see that knight coming towards us on a dapple-grey steed with a gold helmet on his head?"

"What I see and perceive," replied Sancho, "is nothing but a man on a grey ass like mine with something glittering on his head."

"Why, that is Mambrino's helmet," said Don Quixote. "Stand aside and leave me to deal with him. You will see how, so as to save time, I shall complete this adventure without uttering a word, and the helmet I have so much desired will be mine." . . .

Now the truth of this matter of the helmet, the horse, and the horseman that Don Quixote saw is this. There were in that district two villages, one so small that it had neither an apothecary's shop nor a barber, while the other, near-by, had both. So the barber of the bigger place served the smaller, in which there was a sick man who needed bleeding and another fellow who wanted to be shaved; which was why the barber was now on the road carrying a brass basin. Now fate would have it that, as he came along, it began to rain. So, fearing that his hat, which was no doubt a new one, might get spoiled, he put the basin on his head; and, as it was clean, it shone from more than a mile away. He rode, as Sancho said, on a grey ass, and that is the reason why Don Quixote took them for a dapple-grey steed, a knight, and a golden helmet. For everything which he saw he adapted with great facility to his wild, chivalrous and errant fancies. So, when he saw the luckless horseman draw near, without entering into any parley with him, he urged Rocinante into a canter and attacked him with lance couched, intending to run him through and through; and as he got up to him without checking the fury of his career, he cried out: "Defend yourself, base caitiff creature, or surrender of your own free will what is so rightfully mine."

The barber, seeing this apparition descending on him so unexpectedly and without warning, had no other means of avoiding his lance but by sliding down from his ass. But, once on the ground, he leapt up lighter than a deer, and began to run across the plain faster than the wind. The basin he left on the ground, and the delighted Don Quixote observed that the pagan had acted most prudently in imitation of the beaver, who, when hard pressed by the hunters, with his own teeth bites off what he knows by his natural instinct to be the object of the chase. So he bade Sancho pick up the helmet. And when he had it in his hands, the squire exclaimed: "By God, it's a good basin, and worth a *real* if it's worth a farthing."

He then gave it to his master, who placed it on his head, turning it round and round to find the vizor. But, unable to discover it, he remarked: "Certainly the pagan to whose measure this famous headpiece was first shaped must have had an enormous head; and the worst of it is that one half of it is missing."

When Sancho heard the basin called a headpiece he could not restrain his laughter; but suddenly he remembered his master's anger, and stopped short.

"What are you laughing at?" asked Don Quixote.

"It makes me laugh," he replied, "to think what a big head that pagan must have had, who owned that headpiece. It's like nothing so much as a barber's basin. Just like it, it is."

"Do you know what I think, Sancho? This famous piece, this enchanted helmet, must have fallen by some strange accident into the hands of someone who did not esteem it at its true value. So, not knowing what he was doing, and seeing that it was pure gold, he must have melted down the other half for the sake of the metal, and made from this half what looks like a barber's basin, as you say. But, however that may be, its metamorphosis is of no consequence to me, who know what it really is. For I will have it set right in the first village where there is a smith, and so well that it will not be surpassed or even equalled by the helmet which the god of smithies forged and made for the god of battles. In the meantime, however, I will wear it as best I can, for something is better than nothing; and, besides, it will do very well to defend me from a stoning."

[1.21; 1 : 124–25; pp. 161–63]

The passage opens in a way that, as we have come to learn, character-izes humanist writing at least from Erasmus on: Two opposing views (a gold helmet versus something glittering) are resolved by a third view ("Now the truth . . ."), although we are not told precisely who interrupts or the source of his knowledge. The Don has long wanted Mambrino's helmet for himself, and his imagination now wills the helmet into being, as well as an adventure in which the Don can secure ownership. He is able to admit it is incomplete, but he is unable to tell its brass from the gold that he wishes it to be (and for him it is); and he is realistic enough to know that, whatever is thought of it, it will indeed protect his head from a stoning. It can *function* as a helmet even if it is a basin; even the barber knew that. So does the third view ("the truth") really take into account its true usefulness, as the barber and the Don have made it out to be? The next time the subject is raised, Don Quijote comes closer yet to the truth by widening the possibilities to incorporate all three propositions— "y así, eso que a ti te parece bacía de barbero, me parece a mí el yelmo de Mambrino, y a otro le parecerá otra cosa"; "what seems to you to be a barber's basin appears to me to be Mambrino's helmet, and to another as something else" (1.25; 1:155; p. 204)—without giving preference to any of them. There is no "truth" now except in the eyes of the beholder; and if we accept that, as this speech wishes us to do, then "the truth" (singular) of the adjudicating narrator was incomplete and therefore wrong. This seems confirmed when the helmet is brought up for the last time and the decision is made that, since it is used as a helmet, it must *be* a helmet. On this the priest, Cardenio, Don Ferdinand, and his followers all agree, and by paying the barber for his basin they turn the supposition into fact. Even the barber seems to agree, though he is perplexed, since his "basin had been turned into Mambrino's helmet before his eyes" ("el barbero, cuya bacía allí delante de sus ojos se le había vuelto en yelmo de Mambrino," 1.45; 1:307; p. 405). The imagination, that is, not only *transforms* experience but *amends* it; it also *enfranchises* experience, and life.

What the humanist Cervantes seems to be proposing, then, is also an amendment to the Aristotelian understanding of art as simple mimesis (1.47) and Cicero's restatement of art as that which holds the mirror up to nature (1.48), unless that mirror does not merely reflect but *perfects*. Such, at any rate, seems to be Don Quijote's understanding when he tells the canon, in defending the possibility (and therefore the fact) of knight-errantry, that art, imitating nature, seems to surpass itself (*and* nature); that is the *purpose* of art (1.50). So long as art can transform, then, nature will continue to be the basis of our understanding; but it remains the basis only, since the means, by our perceptions, is always an amending and perhaps a transforming (a renaming, a recrediting, a reestablishing) act.

So we learn by the close of Book 1 of the *Quijote* that, like earlier humanist fictions, this work too has no closure. Yet throughout Book 1 the *Quijote* has left verisimilitudinous matters to our artful imaginations (perhaps even more than to our judgments) by its narrative incompletion, conjecture, and multiple perspective. The "author" of this "history" does not finish the story of the battle with the Basque (1.8); Sancho does not complete his story of Lope Ruiz (1.20). Documentation is likewise incomplete, as with Don Quijote's poems composed in the Sierra Morena (1.26). Even Don Quijote's own faith in his accomplishments (licensing the imagination although continually opposed by Sancho) falters in the instance of the Battle of the Wine-Skins: "I prefer to be silent, in case I may be accused of falsehood" ("quiero callar, porque no me digan que miento," 1.37; 1:255; p. 335). At such times even Cervantes' deployment of humanist rhetoric becomes conditional. The concluding extracts of Book 1 make this certain. They attempt to be marmoreal passages, epitaphs carved in marble or stone that fix for all time a judgment on Don Quijote—except that they are written by an academician named "Mumbo Jumbo" ("monicongo," 1.52; 1:347; p. 458). The actual "history" concludes just previously, and that announces another expedition as yet unrecorded—like the boats left to sail once more at the closing of *Le Cinquième Livre* of Rabelais. In Cervantes' world, too, controlled by the imagination and always wanting to be perfected by art, *Don Quijote* shows us, before Don Quijote later tells us, that "Everything is possible" ("Todo podría ser," 2.25; 2:142; p. 637).

Book 1 of the *Quijote,* that is, ends in paradox, for the healing element of the imagination leads to an infinite diversity of perspectives by which any kind (or no kind), of unity may be achieved. It is hinted at by the canon, who tells the priest that fiction cannot deal with impossibilities—with the land of Prester John—but, at the same time, it can be astonishing and entertaining: It need not hold strictly to mimesis in order to achieve imitatio.

Y si a esto se me respondiese que los que tales libros componen los escriben como cosas de mentira, y que así, no están obligados a mirar en delicadezas ni verdades, responderlas hía yo que tanto la mentira es mejor cuanto más parece verdadera, y tanto más agrada cuanto tiene más de lo dudoso y posible. Hanse de casar las fábulas mentirosas con el entendimiento de los que las leyeren, escribiéndose de suerte que, facilitando los imposibles, allanando las grandezas, suspendiendo los ánimos, admiren, suspendan, alborocen y entretengan, de modo que anden a un mismo paso la admiración y la alegría juntas; y todas estas cosas no podrá hacer el que huyere de la verisimilitud y de la imitación, en quien consiste la perfección de lo que se escribe.

If you reply that the men who compose such books write them as fiction, and so are not obliged to look into fine points or truths, I should reply that the more it resembles the truth the better the fiction, and the more probable and possible it is, the better it pleases. Fictions have to match the minds of their readers, and to be written in such a way that, by tempering the impossibilities, moderating excesses, and keeping judgement in the balance, they may so astonish, hold, excite, and entertain, that wonder and pleasure go hand in hand. None of this can be achieved by anyone departing from verisimilitude or from that imitation of nature in which lies the perfection of all that is written. [1.47; 1 : 322; p. 425]

This wonderfully synthetic poetic fuses Aristotle's prescriptions and Don Quijote's practices through the Lucianic means of verisimilitude—allowing the kind of imitatio practiced by the Don, by Sancho, and by the other characters of the *Quijote*. But it is not unique in Cervantes' time. It is anticipated by Minturno, who finds the chief source of the marvelous in the unexpected turn of events (*peripeteia*) in the development of an initially Aristotelian plot.[30]

But the full-scale development of such a moderating poetics is to be found in Tasso's *Discorsi del Poema Eroico,* well known and rather widely accepted by the time of the *Quijote*. Tasso does not counter Aristotle, but he relaxes "Aristotelian" rules. Tasso sets out his syncretic definition in Libro Primo.

> Ma 'l poeta epico non ha altro fine, e all'incontro muove compassione per muover maraviglia; pero la muove molto maggiore e più spesso. Diremo dunque che 'l poema eroico sia imitazione d'azione illustre, grand e perfetta, fatta narrando con altissimo verso, affine di muovere gli animi con la maraviglia e di giovare in questa guisa.

> But the epic poet has no other purpose, moves compassion in order to move wonder, and in fact moves it much more powerfully and more often. We shall then say that the epic poem is an imitation of a noble action, great and perfect, narrated in the loftiest verse, with the purpose of moving the mind to wonder and thus being useful.[31]

His theory is openly derived in Libro Secondo of the *Discorsi del Poema Eroico* from a standard resource for the humanists, Plato's *Sophist* (235B–236C).

> Scrive il Mazzone, ne l'introduzione della *Difesa di Dante,* che l'imitazione è [di] due maniere, l'una icastica, l'altra fantastica, seguendo in çiò la dottrina insegnataci da Platone nel *Soffista;* e chiama icastica quella ch'imita le cose che si trovano o si sono trovate, fantastica l'altra specie, ch'è imitatrice de le cose che non sono; e questa vuol che sia la perfetta poesia, la qual ripone sotto la facoltà sofistica, di cui è soggetto il falso e quel che non è. Ma per consolare i poeti, e me

con gli altri, a cui fa più d'aiuto e di consolazione mestieri, fa due o tre specie d'arte sofistica, e ripone la poesia sotto la prima specie, ch'è la più antica; e questra, s'io non m'inganno, è quella medesima ch'è in tanti luoghi rifutata da Socrate e da Platone. Però io non posso concedere né che la poesia si metta sotto l'arte de' sofisti, né che la perfettissima specie di poesia sia la fantastica. Quantunque io le concedessi che la poesia fosse facitrice degli idoli, come la sofistica, e non solamente degli idoli, ma degli iddii (poich'a la sovrana lode de' poeti si conviene il deificare e il riporre i principi giusti e valorosi nel numero degli immortali, e agli immortali secoli consecrar la lor memoria), non gli concederei nondimeno che fosse la medesima l'arte de' sofisti e quella de' poeti. Dico adunque che senza dubbio la poesia è collocata in ordine sotto la dialettica insieme con la retorica, la qual, come dice Aristotele, è l'altro rampollo de la dialettica facultà, a cui s'appertiene di considerare non il falso, ma il probabile; laonde tratta del falso, non in quanto egli è falso, ma in quanto è probabile. . . . Nondimeno la perfettissima imitazione, o la propissima specie de la poesia, non si ripone sotto la sofistica, o nuova o antica ch'ella sia, ma sotto la dialettica.

Mazzoni writes, in the Introduction to his *Difesa della Comedia di Dante,* that imitation is of two kinds, the one icastic, the other phantastic, here following Plato's doctrine in the *Sophist.* He calls the kind that imitates things present or past icastic and the kind that imitates non-existent things phantastic. And this latter he chooses to call perfect poetry, which he places under the sophistic faculty, whose subject is the false and the non-existent. But to console the poets, and among them myself, who especially need help and consolation, he distinguishes two or three kinds of sophistic art, and places poetry under the first kind, which is the most ancient. Yet this, if I am not mistaken, is the very kind Socrates and Plato in so many passages argued against. I cannot therefore concede either that poetry is to be placed under the sophist's art or that the phantastic is the most perfect kind of poetry. And even if I did concede that poetry like the sophistic art creates idols, and not merely idols but gods (since the highest praise of poets is properly that they deify just and valorous princes and set them among the immortals, consecrating their memory to eternity), I still would not concede that the sophist's art and the poet's are the same. I say, therefore, that poetry surely belongs under dialectic along with rhetoric, which, as Aristotle says, is the other child of the dialectical faculty, its function being to consider not the false but the probable. . . . All the same, the most perfect imitation, or the most proper kind of poetry, is not to be placed under the sophistic art, whether new or old, but under dialectic. [Pp. 86–88; pp. 28–30]

This draws securely on Plato, to be sure, but it remains a bold, imaginative act, at once fusing the imaginative powers of poetry and its ability to expand what may be traditionally verisimilitudinous with classical rhetoric and logic. Poetry can share features with sophistry but is not necessarily itself sophistic—at least not in ways that prevent it from also coming under dialectic (that is, logic). Poetry thus maintains the power to persuade—and to convince. Whether or not Cervantes knew Tasso's poetics, it is clear that he was working out something very similar indeed in the *Quijote*. Just how similar is strikingly clear in a slightly later passage of Libro Secondo in which Tasso takes up the legitimate marvelous.

Attribuisca il poeta alcune operazioni, che di gran lunga eccedono il poter de gli uomini, a Dio, a gli angioli suoi, a' demoni o a coloro a' quali da Dio o da' demoni è conceduta potestà, quali sono i santi, i magi e le fate. Queste opere, se per se stesse saranno considerate, meravigliose parranno, anzi miracoli sono chiamati nel commune uso id parlare. Queste medesime, se si averà riguardo alla virtù e alla, potenza di chi l'ha operate, versimili saranno giudicate, perché, avendo gli uomini nostri bevuta nelle fasce insieme col latte questa opinione, ed essendo poi in loro confermata da i maestri della nostra santa fede (cioè che Dio e i suoi ministri e i demoni e i magi, permettendolo Lui, possano far cose sovra le forze della natura meravigliose), e leggendo e sentendo ogni di ricordar[n]e nuovi essempi, non parrà loro fuori del verisimile quello che credono non solo esser possibile, ma stimano spesse fiate esser avvenuto e poter di nuovo molte volte avvenire. Si come anco a quegli antichi, che vivevano ne gli errori della lor vana religione, non deveano parer impossibili que' miracoli che de' lor dei favoleggiavano non solo i poeti, ma l'istorie; perché, se pur gli uomini scienzati gli prestavano picciola credenza, basta al poeta in questo, com' in molte altre cose, la opinion della moltitudine, alla quale molte volte, lasciando l'essatta verità delle cose, e suole e dee attenersi. Puo esser dunque una medesima azione e meravigliosa e versimile: meravigliosa riguardandola in se stessa e circonscritta dentro a i termini, naturali, verisimile considerandola divisa da questi termini, nella sua cagione, la quale è una virtù sopranaturale, possente e usata a far simili meraviglie.

The poet ought to attribute actions that far exceed human power to God, to his angels, to demons, or to those granted power by God or by demons, for example, saints, wizards, and fairies. Such actions, if considered in themselves, will seem marvellous; nay, they are commonly called miracles. But if regarded in terms of their agent's efficacy and power, they will seem verisimilar. For men, having drunk in this notion along with their milk from the time they were in swaddling clothes, and having been confirmed in it by the teachers of our holy faith (that is, that God and his ministers, and by his permission demons and magicians, can do marvellous things beyond the force of nature), and reading and hearing of new examples daily, will not think unlikely what they believe not only is possible but has often occurred and can occur often again. So too the ancients, who lived in the errors of their false religion, must not have thought impossible the miracles recounted of their gods not merely by poets but in histories. Even if learned men gave them little credit, in this respect as in many others the poet is content with the view of the masses, which, often departing from the exact truth of things, he follows and should follow.

One same action can then be both marvellous and verisimilar: marvellous when regarded in itself and confined within natural limits, verisimilar when considered apart from these limits in terms of its cause, which is a powerful supernatural force accustomed to performing such marvels.

[Pp. 96–97; pp. 38–39]

History, then, should admit religion—and would be incomplete without it. What may appear marvelous to us, if credible in the eyes of God, is not only a compatible but a desirable part of the necessary ficción. This understanding of poetry transfigures its basis in rhetoric and dialectic, in both sophistry and logic, into something like inspired knowledge. It likewise transforms the imagination by admitting to it—and even stressing for it—matters of belief. This poetic may be a striking amalgam even for the Christian humanist, but it goes far to explain Book 2 of the *Quijote,* the story of the *Ingenioso Caballero.* "History is like a sacred writing," the Don tells us now, "for it has to be truthful; and where the truth is, in so far as it is the truth, there God is" ("La historia es como cosa sagrada; porque ha de ser verdadera, y donde está la verdad, está Dios, en cuanto a verdad," 2.3; 2:33; p. 490).

At first, much seems familiar about Book 2 rather than distinct. Once again Cervantes begins with Don Quijote arguing the cause of knight-errantry, this time with his niece and housekeeper.

Dos caminos hay, hijas, por donde pueden ir los hombres a llegar a ser ricos y honrados: el uno es el de las latras; otro, el de las armas. Yo tengo más armas que letras, y nací, según me inclino a las armas, debajo de la influencia del plenta Marte; así, que casi me es forzoso seguir por su camino, y por él tengo de ir a pesar de todo el mundo, y será en balde cansaros en persuadirme a que no quiera yo lo que los cielos quieren, la fortuna ordena y la razón pide, y, sobre todo, mi voluntad desea.

"There are two roads, my daughters, by which men can come to honour and riches. One is the way of Letters; the other the way of Arms. For myself I have more arms than learning, and my inclination is to Arms, for I was born under the influence of the planet Mars. So I am almost compelled to follow that road, and must pursue it despite the whole world; and it will be vain for you to weary yourselves in persuading me to go counter to the heavens' wishes, Fortune's decrees, reason's demands and, more than that, against my heart's desires."

[2.6; 2:45; p. 506]

We still find the customary declamations and disputations. There are the Don's speech on the ape (2.25) and his argument to urge the braying villagers to pursue peace (2.27), and there are the predictable debates between the Don and his family and friends (2.1–6). Sancho Panza has a colloquy with himself about his mission to Dulcinea (2.10) and debates with the Doña Rodríguez on waiting women and virtue (2.37); he also delivers a number of brief judicial speeches as *gobernador* of Barataria (2.45, 49). Despite all this, however, the overwhelming sense we have reading Book 2 after Book 1 is one of change, of difference. Whereas Book 1 has an expansive geographical setting, Book 2 has a confining, repressive, essentially social setting. Whereas Book 1 is character-ized by plenitude and progression, Book 2 seems to emphasize loss, even regression. This may be in part because in Book 1 Don Quijote and Sancho Panza are faced with a real world, which the Don continually fictionalizes; in Book 2 they confront a distorted, unnatural world, which they are repeatedly invited to make real. It is a disturbing change for us as readers, too: Whereas Book 1 asks us to trust appearances (and confirms them when windmills remain windmills), Book 2 forces us to *dis*trust appearances (Clavileño is in no way a horse). Beginning with the Knight of the Mirrors (2.12), the Knight of the Wood (2.13–15), and the heightened, theatrical wedding of Comacho and Quiteria interrupted by Basilio's "death" (2.21) through the puppet show of Maese Pedro (2.26) and the various tricks of the Duke and the Duchess (2.30 ff.), we grow suspicious and the threads of illusion we maintain through Book 1 wear thin. Whereas Don Quijote was the subject of Book 1, in the foreground of the action and our imagination, he is made into an object by others in Book 2; and it is they and their machinations that take up our attention and disturb us. "[L]ess active, more victim than aggressor," as El Saffar puts it,[32] the Don no longer makes false starts but seems almost passively to await what is coming to him: He grows more introspective; his need for belief grows deeper; and so his narrator grows more concerned for him, as we do. Issues of religion come more frequently to the Don's mind, too; just as in Book 1 his imagination opened the way to wizards, to magic, and to the marvelous, as Tasso says good epics should, so Book 2 opens us more and more to God and the miraculous. We see this both in the oration on the ape—

—No me entiendes, Sancho: no quiero decir sino que debe de tener hecho algún concierto con el demonino, de que infunda esa habilidad en el mono, con que gane de comer, y después que esté rico le dará su alma, que es lo que este universal enemigo pretende. Y háceme creer esto el ver que el mono no responde sino a las cosas pasadas o presentes, y la sabiduria del diablo no se puede estender a más; que las por venir no las sabe si no es por conjeturas, y no todas veces; que a solo Dios está reservado conocer los tiempos y los momentos, y para Él no hay pasado ni porvenir; que todo es presente. Y siendo esto así, como lo es, está claro que este mono habla con el estilo del diablo.

"You do not understand, Sancho. I only mean to say that he must have made some bargain with the Devil, who has infused this talent into the ape so that he can gain his living by it; and when he is rich, he will give him his soul; for that is what the universal enemy is after. This I conclude from the fact that the ape only answers questions concerning things past or present, for the Devil's knowledge extends no further; he only knows the future by guesswork, and not always then. For to know the times and the seasons is reserved to God alone; for Him there is no past or future, for all is present. And that being so, as it is, it is clear that this ape speaks in the style of the Devil." [2.25; 2 : 142; p. 636]

—and in the speech to the braying villagers where the Don claims that defense of the Catholic faith is the primary cause to take up arms. Moreover,

cuanto más que el tomar venganza injusta, que justa no puede haber alguna que lo sea, va derechamente contra la santa ley que profesamos, en la cual se nos manda que hagamos bien a nuestros enemigos y que amemos a los que nos aborrecen; mandamiento que, aunque parece algo dificultoso de cumplir, no lo es sino para aquellos que tienen menos de Dios que del mundo, y más de carne que de espíritu; porque Jesucristo, Dios y hombre verdadero, que nunca mintió, ni pudo ni puede mentir, siendo legislador nuestro dijo que su yugo era suave y su carga liviana; y así, no nos había de mandar cosa que fuese imposible el cumplirla. Así que, mis señores, vuesas mercedes están obligados por leyes divinas y humanas a sosegarse.

"the taking of unjust vengeance—and no vengeance can be just—goes directly against the sacred law we profess, by which we are commanded to do good to our enemies and to love those who hate us, a commandment which may seem rather difficult to obey, but which is only so for those who partake less of God than of the world, and more of the flesh than of the spirit. For Jesus Christ—God and true man—who never lied, nor could, nor can lie, being our law-giver, said that His yoke was gentle and His burden light, and therefore He could not have commanded us to do anything impossible to perform. So, my dear sirs, you are bound to keep the peace by law divine and human." [2.27; 2 : 152; p. 650]

Whereas Don Quijote in Book 1 called on wicked enchanters to explain evil, now the Caballero de la Triste Figura calls on God and the Devil. So this "authentic history" is in Book 2 transformed.

This conspicuous new emphasis on belief rather than on "story" is more noticeable because the Don who is chastened, instructed, and disciplined in Book 1 now also becomes more *skeptical*. Rather than standing in the pathway challenging those who come toward him, Don Quijote is now more apt to inquire of those whom he meets: "he was rather curious and always possessed by the desire to learn something new" ("y como él era algo curioso y siempre le fatigaban deseos de saber cosas nuevas," 2.24; 2 : 135; p. 626). He has, in fact, learned something about the right means of governance, as he tells the Duke and Duchess: "el toque está en que tengan buena intención y deseen acertar en todo"; "The whole point is to have good intentions and to desire to do right in everything" (2.32; 2 : 177; p. 683). And he is now capable, at times, of trusting in Dulcinea not as a person but as an *idea*:

Dios sabe si hay Dulcinea o no en el mundo, o si es fantástica, o no es fantástica; y éstas no son de las cosas cuya averiguación se ha de llevar hasta el cabo. Ni yo engendré ni parí a mi señora, puesto que la contemplo como conviene que sea una dama que contenga en sí las partes que puedan hacerla famosa en todas las del mundo.

"God knows whether Dulcinea exists on earth or no, or whether she is fantastic or not fantastic. These are not matters whose verification can be carried out to the full. I neither engendered nor bore my lady, though I contemplate her in her ideal form, as a lady with all the qualities needed to win her fame in all quarters of the world." [2.32; 2 : 175; p. 680]

Don Quijote does not speak this way exclusively in Book 2; and there has been a slight anticipation of it even in Book 1 when, early on his first sally, he meets some merchants on the road. One of them asks to see Dulcinea.

—Si os la mostrara—replicó don Quijote—, ¿que hiciérades vosotros en confesar una verdad tan notoria? La importancia está en que sin verla lo habéis de creer, confesar, afirmar, jurar y defender.

"If I were to show her to you," replied Don Quixote, "what merit would there be in your confessing so obvious a truth? The essence of the matter is that you must believe, confess, affirm, swear and maintain it without seeing her."

[1.4; 1:37–38; p. 51]

But at this early juncture we see it only as the way the Don preserves illusion— withholds challenges to his imagination—and even the wonderfully providential ending to Book 1, where all the characters seem to return to the inn to straighten out their various affairs, is not in a major key.

After the publication of Book 1 and during the composition of Book 2, in 1613, Cervantes received the habit of the Third Order of Saint Francis, the Franciscan Tertiaries, at Alcalà de Henares. Perhaps this accounts for the marked change. For it is surely there. From the outset, when the Don first visits his lady for a blessing regardless of her appearance or reaction (2.8), his faith mounts, if sporadically. Others, including Cide Hamete, falter (2.10). Confronted with other equally difficult challenges, the Don does not hesitate. When he finds Dulcinea transformed into a peasant who is only annoyed that he and Sancho stop her, he does not lose his faith in her or grow angry; instead, he suffers regret and despair (2.10). He is even able to defend the Christian values of knight-errantry to a priest in the face of his *listener's* dis*belief* (2.32). Moreover, his deeds collate. He attacks the puppets in Pedro's show because they are Moorish invaders (2.26); he can mount Clavileño "with a strong and resolute heart" ("de muy buen grado y de mejor talante," 2.41; 2:210; p. 727). And Sancho follows faithfully in his master's footsteps. The Duke offers him proper clothes as he departs for Barataria, but he refuses them; he even refuses arms and letters because they are not necessary—he has something better: "pero bástame tener el *Cristus* en la memoria para ser buen gobernador"; "I have the big Christ-cross in my memory, and that's enough to make me a good governor" (2.42; 2:217; p. 737). His statutes of rule that follow are pointedly derived from Ecclesiastes (2.51) and respect for the Sabbath (2.53). His judgments, moreover, follow the stricture the Don had laid down for him: "mercy is more precious and resplendent in our sight than justice" ("más resplandece . . . el de la misericordia que el de la justicia," 2.42; 2:219; p. 740). (Sancho has become lowly wise, confirmed and parodied when he later falls into the pit, a satiric counterpoint, but a no less valuable lesson, to the Cueva de Montesino, 2.55.)

Such beliefs as these—it is the Don's premise in Book 2, and a splendid vision—might even renew the age of gold (2.2). Thus Sancho's somewhat later comment that "we should set about turning saints" ("que nos demos a ser santos," 2.8; 2:54; p. 519), which may at first sound so naive, may in the end be not so far from the mark. "Chivalry is a religion," Don Quijote replies, "and there are sainted knights in glory" ("religión es la caballería; caballeros santos hay en la gloria," 2.8; 2:55; p. 520). We see this, however tentatively, in the Don's comment on the Robin Hood life of Roque Guinart:

> —Señor Roque, el principio de la salud está en conocer la enfermedad y en querer tomar el enfermo las medicinas que el medico le ordena; vuestra merced está enfermo, conoce su dolencia, y el cielo, o Dios, por mejor decir, que es nuestro médico, le aplicará medicinas que le sanen, las cuales suelen sanar poco a poco y no de repente y por milagro; y más, que los pecadores discretos están más cerca de enmendarse que los simples; y pues vuestra merced ha mostrado en sus razones su prudencia, no hay sino tener buen ánimo y esperar mejoría de la enfermedad de su conciencia; y si vuestra merced quiere ahorrar camino y ponerse con facilidad en el de su salvación, véngase commigo, que yo le enseñare a ser caballero andante, donde se pasas tantos trabajos y desventuras, que, tomándolas por penítencia, en dos paletas le pondrán en el cielo.

> "Sir Roque," he replied, "the beginning of health lies in the knowledge of the disease, and in the sick man's willingness to take the medicines the doctor prescribes. You are sick; you know your complaint, and Heaven, or rather God, who is our doctor, will apply medicines to cure you, medicines which generally cure slowly, not suddenly and by a miracle. What is more, wise sinners are nearer to a cure than foolish ones, and since you have shown your good sense in your speech, you have only to keep up your courage, and hope for an improvement in the sickness of your conscience. But if you would shorten the journey and set yourself easily on the path of your salvation, come with me, and I will teach you to be a knight errant, a calling beset with such toils and misfortunes as, taken as a penance, will carry you to Heaven in a twinkling."

[2.60; 2:312; pp. 862–63]

Imitatio is not now merely a matter of Roldán or Amadís but also a matter of the divine, as this *comedia* is. Occasionally this allows the Don to pursue a mistrust of faith, but it also leads him to deeper and higher thoughts, as in his speech on ingratitude (2.28) or his speech on liberty.

> —La libertad, Sancho, es uno de los más preciosos dones que a los hombres dieron los cielos; con ella no pueden igualarse los tesoros que encierra la tierra ni

el mar encubre; por la libertad, así como por la honra, se puede y debe aventurar la vida, y, por el contrario, el cautiverio es el mayor mal que puede venir a los hombres. Digo esto, Sancho, porque bien has visto el regalo, la abundancia que en este castillo que dejamos hemos tenido; pues en metad de aquellos banquetes sazonados y de aquellas bebidas de nieve, me parecía a mi que estaba metido entre las estrechezas de la hambre, porque no lo gozaba con la libertad que lo gazara si fueran míos; que las obligaciones de las recompensas de los beneficios y mercedes recebidas son ataduras que no dejan campear al ánimo libre. ¡Venturoso aquel a quien el cielo dio un pedazo de pan, sin que le quede obligación de agradecerlo a otro que al mismo cielo!

"Liberty, Sancho, is one of the most precious gifts Heaven has bestowed upon man. No treasures the earth contains or the sea conceals can be compared to it. For liberty, as for honour, one can rightfully risk one's life; and, on the other hand, captivity is the worst evil that can befall men. I say this, Sancho, because you have witnessed the luxury and abundance that we have enjoyed in this castle which we are now leaving. Yet in the midst of those highly-spiced banquets and snow-cooled drinks I seemed to be confined within the straits of hunger, since I did not enjoy them with the same liberty as if they had been my own; for obligations to return benefits and favours received are bonds that curb a free spirit. Happy is he to whom Heaven has given a crust of bread, without the obligation of offering thanks for it to any but Heaven itself!"

[2.58; 2:293; p. 837]

This is a wiser, more subdued sense of *admiratio* than anything we have seen in Book 1, and it is connected to the Don's second, and richer, defense of poetry.

Pero vuestro hijo, a lo que yo, señor, me imagino, no debe de estar mal con la poesía de romance, sino con los poetas que son meros romancistas, sin saber otras lenguas ni otras ciencias que adornen y despierten y ayuden a su natural impulso, y aun en esto puede haber yerro; porque, según es opinión, verdadera, el poeta nace: quieren decir que del vientre de su madre el poeta natural sale poeta; y con aquella inclinación que le dio el cielo, sin más estudio ni artificio, compone cosas, que hace verdadero al que dijo; *est Deus in nobis.* . . , etcétera.

"But your son, sir, as I imagine, does not dislike vernacular poetry, but poets who are merely vernacular and know no other tongues nor sciences to adorn, stimulate and help out their natural inspiration. Yet even in this he may be in error. For, according to true belief, the poet is born—I mean the natural poet comes out of his mother's womb a poet and, with that impulse which Heaven has given him, without further study, or art, composes things which prove the truth of the saying: 'There is a god in us . . .' etcetera." [2.16; 2:91; p. 569]

Heroic poetry, Tasso had said, ought to attribute suprahuman actions to God, but surely the inverse premise of his notion of the marvelous-credible is that God speaks through the heroic poet. It seems to happen in Book 2 of the *Quijote:* although Cide Hamete Benengeli invokes Allah early on (2.8), even he comes in time to swear as a Catholic Christian—and to be taken seriously for it (2.27). Indeed, the matter of belief becomes so strong and so secure in Book 2 that it can even be parodied, as when the Don tells Sancho that he will believe what his squire saw from Clavileño so long as the squire accepts the report of the Don's vision in the Cueva de Montesinos (2.41). The second book of *Don Quijote*, we are told quite forthrightly, is a book we must read with "renewed attention and fresh powers of belief" ("nueva atención y nuevo crédito," 2.9; 2:58; p. 524).

Consequently, Book 2 is also, more frequently, more openly, and more powerfully, a book of love. "The servant sleeps and the master watches," Don Quijote says, looking down on a slumbering Sancho, "reflecting on means of sustaining, bettering and favouring him" ("Duerme el criado, y está velando el señor, pensando cómo la ha de sustentar, mejorar y hacer mercedes," 2.20; 2:110–11; p. 594). He is replying in kind to Sancho's earlier defense of the Don, when he was not present, to the Squire of the Wood, the Basque who called the Don foolish.

> —Eso no es el mío—respondió Sancho—: digo, que no tiene nada de bellaco; antes tiene una alma como un cántaro: no sabe hacer mal a nadie, sino bien a todos, ni tience malicia alguna: un niño le hará entender que es de noche en la mitad del día, y por esta sencillez le quiero como a las telas de mi corazón, y no me amaño a dejarle, por más disparates que haga.

> "That my master isn't," replied Sancho. "I mean there's nothing of the rogue in him. His soul is as clean as a pitcher. He can do no harm to anyone, only good to everybody. There's no malice in him. A child might make him believe it's night at noonday. And for that simplicity I love him as dearly as my heart-strings, and can't take to the idea of leaving him for all his wild tricks." [2.13; 2:75; p. 547]

Such love is necessary in the present, fallen age, as the Don implies to Don Lorenzo, in yet another plea in defense of *faith* in knight-errantry.

> —la mayor parte de la gente del mundo está de parecer de que no ha habido en él caballeros andantes; y por parecerme a mí que si el cielo milagrosamente no les da

a entender la verdad de que los hubo y de que los hay, cualquier trabajo que se tome ha de ser en vano, como muchas veces me lo ha mostrado la experiencia, no quiero detenerme agora en sacar a vuesa merced del error que con los muchos tiene; lo que pienso hacer es el rogar al cielo le saque dél, y le dé a entender cuán provechosos y cuán necessarios fueron al mundo los caballeros andantes en los pasados siglos, y cuán útiles fueran en el presente si se usaran; pero triufan ahora, por pecados de las gentes, la pereza, la ociosidad, la gula y el regalo.

"The majority of people in this world are of the opinion that knights errant have never existed; and I hold that unless Heaven miraculously convinces them to the contrary, any labour undertaken for that purpose must be in vain, as experience has many times shown me. So I will not stop now to deliver your worship from the error you hold in common with the multitude. What I mean to do is to pray Heaven to deliver you from it, and make you see how beneficial and necessary knights errant were to the world in past ages, and how useful they would be in the present, if they were in fashion. But now, for the peoples' sins, sloth, idleness, gluttony and luxury triumph." [2.18; 2:102; p. 583]

Yet this speech, like those of the Don and Sancho for each other, has a certain *proleptic* quality about it; and as Book 2 develops, we find that a number of these statements of hope and belief are also propaedeutic to despair.

It is in this frame of mind that, almost without warning, Don Quijote meets another alter ego, succeeding Grisóstomo and Cardenio. But this time it is death. "The first figure which presented itself before Don Quixote's eyes was Death himself with a human face" ("La primera figura que se ofreció a los ojos de don Quijote fue la de la misma Muerte, con rosto humaño," 2.11; 2:65; p. 534). He soon learns that it is a whole Cortes de la Muerte dressed in costume for a Corpus Christi play, and he tries to pass off his alarm with a kind of blessing:

—y ahora digo que es menester tocar las apariencias con la mano para dar lugar al desengaño. Andad con Dios, buena gente, y haced vuestra fiesta.

"appearances are not always to be trusted. Go, in God's name, good people, and hold your festival." [2.11; 2:66; p. 535]

It is clear, however, that he is haunted by this sight and broods on it.

—Pues lo mesmo—dijo don Quijote—acontece en la comedia y trato deste mundo, donde unos hacen los emperadores, otros los pontífices, y, finalmente, todas cuantas figuras se pueden introducir en una comedia; pero en llegando al fin, que es cuando se acaba la via, a todos les quita la muerte las ropas que los diferenciaban, y quedan iguales en la sepultura.

"Now the same thing," said Don Quixote, "happens in the comedy and traffic of this world, where some play Emperors, others Popes and, in fact, every part that can be introduced into a play. But when we come to the end, which is when life is over, Death strips them of all the robes that distinguished them, and they are all equals in the grave." [2.12; 2:69; p. 539]

This is a new view of the divine comedy of life.

But Cervantes means it to be a central view here, for this new dialectic between hope and despair is the subject of the visit to the Cueva de Montesinos, a prolonged episode that Juan Bautista Avalle-Arce has rightly called "the narrative epicenter" of Book 2.[33] The Don himself sees this as an essential but terrifying test of faith.

Y luego se hincó de rodillas y hizo una oración en voz baja al cielo, pidiendo a Dios le ayudase y le diese buen suceso en aquella, al parecer, peligrosa y nueva aventura. . . .—Yo voy a despeñarme, a empozarme y a hundirme en el abismo que aquí se me representa, sólo porque conozca el mundo que si tú me favoreces, no habrá imposible a quien yo no acometa y acabe.

Then he knelt down and said a prayer to Heaven in a low voice, begging God to aid him and give him good fortune in this seemingly novel and perilous adventure. . . . "I am about to cast myself, to plunge and bury myself, in the abyss which opens here before me, solely that the world may know that with your favour there is nothing so impossible that I cannot undertake and accomplish it." [2.22; 2:124; pp. 612–13]

It is vital to recognize that the Don is no longer addressing Dulcinea but addressing God. The others about him kneel in prayer while Sancho shouts out to him directly.

y al entrar, echandole Sancho su benedicion y haciendo sobre el mil cruces, dijo:
—¡Dios te guíe y la Peña de Francis, junto con la Trindad de Gaeta, flor, nata y espuma de los caballeros andantes! ¡Allá vas, valentón del mundo, corazón de acero, brazos de bronce! ¡Dios te guíe, otra vez, y te vuelva libre, sano y sin cautela a la luz desta vida, que dejas, por enterrarte en esta escuridad que buscas!

Sancho threw him his blessing and made countless signs of the cross over him, saying:
"May God guide you, and the Rock of France, together with the Trinity of

Gaeta, O flower, cream, and skimming of knights errant! There you go, brag-gart of the world, heart of steel, and arm of brass! Once more, God guide you and bring you back, safe, sound and unharmed to the light of this world which you have forsaken to bury yourself in that darkness you're seeking."

[2.22; 2:125; p. 613]

What the Don sees when he descends we have only by his report. He tells Sancho and the scholar who accompanied them to the cave's edge and held the rope that when he awoke he saw a crystal palace or castle; the warden, Mon-tesinos himself, came to greet him. At a lower level he discovered the famous knight Durandarte, his very body lying in place of the normal effigy on his tomb, while his lady, the famed Belerma, grief-stricken, walked about with his heart in her hands. There he also finds other knights, squires, and fine ladies from Nordic epic and from the Breton and Carolingian cycles of medieval ballads; unexpectedly, he also finds Dulcinea, still dressed as a peasant. She flees from him, then sends him a message telling him she is in great need and requesting a small loan against the security of a petticoat. He also learns from Montesinos that Merlín the magician has transformed Guadiana, Durandarte's squire, into a river that runs through Castile, and the Ruidera ladies into a lagoon beside it.

In a work that is stressing belief—including our belief as readers—what are we to make of this strange and singular concatenation? "On a predominantly literal plane," Helena Percas de Ponseti contends,

> the episode may be read as a dream, a nightmare, or an hallucination, reflecting
> Don Quixote's obsession with his ideal world. Several descriptive details, pos-
> sible but extraordinary or grotesque in nature, prompt this interpretation. For
> instance: Montesinos keeps passing between his fingers an enormous rosary with
> beads "larger than medium sized nuts," each tenth bead being the size of "an
> ostrich egg." His attire, a strange assortment of pieces of clothing, is inappropri-
> ate for the warden of a castle. Belerma, Durandarte's lady, wears an equally
> inappropriate Turkish turban on her Christian head. She is called beautiful, but
> she is quite ugly, with uneven teeth, circles under her eyes, and a sallow com-
> plexion, a result—Montesinos explains—of her bad nights and worse days in
> the enchanted cave. On Durandarte's tomb, in place of his effigy lies the knight
> himself. Dulcinea's messenger leaps two yards into the air instead of making a
> curtsey as she departs. The mummified heart that Belerma carries about is
> preserved with salt, so that it will not stink.[34]

Had Don Quijote been delivering a "story" or an "authentic history" of his voyage into the depths, his reading would hardly have produced so many doubtful and critical responses, including Durandarte's single comment— "patience and shuffle the cards" ("paciencia y barajar," 2.23; 2 : 129; p. 618)— unless, of course, it is the Don's last, somewhat wild and grief-stricken dismissal of a firm belief in the past of knight-errantry for a new and most direct self-confrontation. Ponseti senses this too: "The descent into a cave reminds us of Saint John (of the Cross's), Saint Theresa's, or Saint Ignatius Loyola's descent into a cave for the purpose of shutting out the world and confronting the self. . . . In literary works, such as the *Song of Songs* and Saint John's *Living Flame of Love,* the cave is the image chosen to convey depth of concentration" ("Cave of Montesinos," p. 984). As suggestive as they are, however, these remain extratextual conjectures. Don Quijote himself provides his interpretation: He awakened "in the middle of the most beautiful, pleasant and delightful meadow nature could create or the liveliest human imagination conceive" ("ameno y deleitoso prado que puede criar la naturaleza ni imaginar la más discreta imaginación humana," 2.23; 2 : 126; p. 615). But which? It is just possible, of course, that this is a vision from God in which, in Tasso's terms, the marvelous-credible is the meetingplace of God's acts and man's conceptions, here gone a little awry. But, in a passage where Don Quijote has been terrified to see what is at the depths of the cave, we may feel that he is deliberately evading or obscuring what happened there. Sancho Panza, for one, stoutly refuses to believe him (2.23), and even Cide Hamete, now grown affectionate toward the Don, cannot accept it, calling it apocryphal and writing in the margin of his manuscript,

> "Tú, letor, pues eres prudente, juzga lo que te pareciere, que yo no debo ni puedo más; puesto que se tiene por cierto que al tiempo de su fin a muerte dicen que se retrató della, y dijo que él la había inventado, por parecerle que convenía y cuadraba bien con las aventuras que había leído en sus historias."

> "You, judicious reader, must judge for yourself, for I cannot and should not do more. One thing, however, is certain, that finally he retracted it on his deathbed and confessed that he had invented it, since it seemed to him to fit in with the adventures he had read of in his histories." [2.24; 2 : 133; p. 624]

But that cannot be altogether true, for the Don's vision *subverts* those histories, caricatures them, including Don Quijote's own history of Dulcinea del Toboso. *Something* happened down there.

If we as judicious readers are to determine what that something was, the terms Cervantes presents to us, displacing those of "story" and "history" in Book 1, are the increasing despair of the Don and man's increasing need for belief. The need for illusion has darkened considerably. Earlier, when he was in the Sierra Morena, Don Quijote sent Dulcinea a letter intending to mark his passage from *fenhedor* to *precador*—from one who dissembles to one who entreats.[35] But now he perceives a very different world, one in which encantadores have multiplied, perhaps to infinity, and hound him beyond life itself: He tells the Duke and Duchess, "Enchanters are persecuting me, and enchanters will persecute me till they sink me and my high chivalries into the profound abyss of oblivion" ("Perseguido me han encantadores, encantadores me persiguen, y encantadores me persiguirán hasta dar conmigo y con mis altas caballerías en el profundo abismo del olvido," 2.32; 2:175; p. 680). Indeed, the presence of death, first projected into his life by the acting company, seems to have injected him with a growing melancholy. He is defeated in combat by the Knight of the White Moon, but his easy and swift surrender may make us think that his loss is not due to his opponent alone.

> Don Quijote, molido y aturdido, sin alzarse la visera, como si hablara dentro de una tumba, con voz debilitada y enferma, dijo:
>
> —Dulcinea del Toboso es la más hermosa mujer del mundo, y yo el más desdichado caballero de la tierra, y no es bien que mi flaqueza defraude esta verdad. Aprieta, caballero, la lanza, y quítame la vida, pues me has quitado la honra.

> Then, battered and stunned, without lifting his vizor Don Quixote proclaimed in a low and feeble voice, as if he were speaking from inside a tomb: "Dulcinea del Toboso is the most beautiful woman in the world, and I am the most unfortunate knight on earth; nor is it just that my weakness should discredit that truth. Drive your lance home, knight, and rid me of life, since you have robbed me of honour." [2.64; 2:332–33; p. 890]

Earlier he had developed this morbidity at greater length, after he and Sancho had been chased by bulls and shortly before they will be just as ignominiously trampled by hogs.

> —Come, Sancho amigo—dijo don Quijote—, sustenta la vida, que más que a mí te importa, y déjame morir a mí a manos de mis pensamientos y a fuerzas de mis degracias. Yo, Sancho, nací para vivir muriendo, y tú para morir comiendo; y porque veas que te digo verdad en esto, considérame impreso en historias,

famoso en las armas, comedido en mis acciones, respetado de príncipes, solicitado de doncellas; al cabo al cabo, cuando esperaba palmas, triunfos y coronas, granjedas y merecidas por mis valerosas hazañas, me he visto esta mañana pisado y acoceado y molido, de los pies de animales immundos y soeces. Esta consideración me embota los dientes, entorpece las muelas, y entomece las manos, y quita de todo en todo la gana del comer, de manera que pienso dejarme morir de hambre, muerte la más cruel de las muertes.

"Eat, Sancho, my friend," said Don Quixote. "Sustain life, for you have more need than I; and let me die a victim of my thoughts and of the force of my misfortunes. I was born, Sancho, to live dying, and you to die eating; and to prove the truth of my words gaze upon me. Printed in histories, famous in arms, courteous in my actions, respected by Princes, courted by maidens; yet after all, when I expected palms, triumphs and crowns, earned and merited by my valorous exploits, I have seen myself this morning trampled, kicked and pounded by the feet of unclean and filthy animals. This reflection blunts my teeth, dulls my grinders, numbs my hands, and completely robs me of appetite, so that I think I may let myself die of hunger, the most cruel of all deaths."

[2.59; 2:301; p. 847]

Instead, he has been treated to ignominy when visiting Don Antonio Moreno, a scene that reminds us of nothing so much as the King of the Jews.

Aquella tarde sacaron a pasear a don Quijote, no armado, sino de rúa, vestido un balandrán de paño leonado, que pudiera hacer sudar en aquel tiempo al mismo yelo. Ordenaron con sus criados que entretuviesen a Sancho, de modo que no le dejasen salir de casa. Iba don Quijote, no sobre Rocinante, sino sobre un gran macho de paso llano, y muy bien aderezado. Pusiéronle el balandrán, y en las espaldas, sin que lo viese, le cosieron un pargamino, donde le escribieron con letras grandes: *Éste es don Quijote de la Mancha.*

That afternoon they took Don Quixote through the city, clad not in armour but in street dress, a long overcoat of tawny cloth which would have made the very ice sweat at that season. They gave their servants orders to keep Sancho entertained, and not to let him leave the house. Don Quixote rode, not on Rocinante but on a big, easy-paced mule with every fine trappings, and when they put on him his overcoat they stitched a parchment to his back, without his noticing it, on which they had written in large letters: *"This is Don Quixote de la Mancha."*

[2.62; 2:318; p. 870]

For six days, the Don lies bedridden (2.65); briefly, he flirts with the alien ideal of the pastoral life (2.67). But at the close he comes quite clearly to see the world as one full of false appearances—*including himself*—and he retreats (or ascends) to his orignial name, to his "authentic self." He asks for his friends the priest, the scholar, and the barber.

> Apenas los vio don Quijote, cuando dijo:
> —Dadme albricias, buenos señores, de que ya yo no soy don Quijote de la Mancha, sino Alonso Quijano, a quien mis costumbres, me dieron renombre de *Bueno*. Ya soy enemigo de Amadís de Gaula y de toda la infinita caterva de su linaje; y me son odiosas todas las historias profanas del andante cabálleria; ya conozco mi necedad y el peligro en que me pusieron haberlas leido; ya, por misericordia de Dios, escarmentando en cabeza propia, las abomino.

> And the moment Don Quixote saw them he exclaimed: "Congratulate me, good sirs, for I am Don Quixote de la Mancha no longer, but Alonso Quixano, called for my way of the Good. Now I am the enemy of Amadis of Gaul and of all the infinite brood of his progeny. Now all profane histories of knight errantry are odious to me. I know my folly now, and the peril I have incurred from the reading of them. Now, by God's mercy, I have learnt from my own bitter experience and I abominate them." [2.74; 2:366–67; p. 936]

"Of all tales," writes Lord Byron in *Don Juan*, "'tis the saddest" (12.9.1).

But that is not at all clear—not in Book 2 where belief is held out against despair. Don Quijote dies willingly, gladly, and, it would seem, at peace with himself and with his life at long last. The dialectic of Book 2 forces us to ask whether this is an act of defeat or an act of victory. It is a question on which the Don's close friend, Sampson Carrasco, as if true to the end to the humanist poetics that refuses closure, noticeably hedges in his epitaph.

> *Tuvo a todo el mundo en poco;*
> *fue el espantajo y el coco*
> *del mundo, en tal coyuntura,*
> *que acreditó su ventura*
> *morir cuerdo y vivir loco.*

> The world as nothing he did prize,
> For a scarecrow in men's eyes,
> He lived, and was their bugbear too;
> And had the luck, with much ado,
> To live a fool, and yet die wise.

> [2.74; 2:369; p. 939]

At the end of his life, Don Quijote—or Alonso Quijano—knows that "profane histories" lead to folly: perhaps because they are profane, perhaps because they are human histories; perhaps both. But, in the course of following them, his amending imagination gave way to an enabling belief, belief in selflessness and sacrifice, purity of love, loyalty in friendship, peace. These are not the characteristics so often shared by those who are at his bedside. They remain in this world of what Sebastian Juan Arbó has called "their terrible common sense,"[36] with the need to judge. The real completion of *Don Quijote* lies, if it lies anywhere, in *them,* and in us.

In the center of the title page of the first edition of *El Ingenioso Hidalgo* was an emblem of the publishing house, an armorial shield with the motto *Post tenebras spero lucem* ("After the darkness I hope for the light"). If we apply that to the trajectory of *Don Quijote* we will find that it is suggestive, as the *Encomium Moriae* and Rabelais's great untitled work are. It resembles an uncompleted arc in which those who can still be trained and disciplined by what they read and by how they think will still find a place. Perhaps many people did, and do: There have been to date 2,300 editions of the *Quijote* in sixty-eight dialects and languages, making it, after the Bible, the world's most widely translated book.[37] In attempting to account for this, Cervantes' recent biographer William Byron writes,

> Quixote refuses to face what Cervantes saw as the basic contradiction of human effort: man may not be God. To presume to try is madness. Yet he is impelled to usurp God's function by the God within him. Only God can administer justice justly. Art is vanity, imagination idle, vision a delusion; God is the only perfect artist, the great creator. But to resign himself to this leaves man no choice but death; the vision must still be sought in life, for it is the act of striving that confirms his divinity. Without such a vision and, more important, without its active prosecution, existence is sterile, man a stone.
>
> It is the knight's gradual perception of this paradox that holds the story together. And it is his obstinacy almost until the very end in refusing to accept the paradox that so appeals to us.[38]

The Caballero de la Triste Figura, the Knight of the Woeful Countenance, is a joke when Sancho first fashions the name because it is literal and limited; but the burden of the *Quijote* is to take that concept to its farthest, and most various, reaches: Like everything else in this novel, it is simultaneously comic and serious, indivisibly so. It asks us whether, as humanists, we should attempt to celebrate the past—the classical past of Plato, Aristotle, Lucian, Herodotus, and Heliodorus; the medieval past of chivalric romance—to help us civilize ourselves in the present, to redeem the present by redeeming the past. At the same time, it does not blink a world undergoing revolutionary change in which every peasant wishes to become rich and every aging nobleman sees his inheritance in danger of disappearing. In a way, Cervantes, like Demosthenes looking back on the Hellenizing of the Mediterranean or Brutus on the eve of Roman imperialization, composes an elegy over a falling and a fallen state. It is a fallen state of civilizations once rediscovered but not actually existent; it is a fallen state of man. Perhaps, in some ways, these are indivisible too. "His lifetime," Melveena McKendrick has recently said of Cervantes, "spans the apogee of Spanish power and influence in Europe and the New World and the beginnings of its decline. The transition from greatness to incipient decay, from supreme confidence to insecurity and despair, was registered by Cervantes and is echoed in the changing mood and tone of his writing." [39] The elegiac tone that so infuses the end of Book 2 of the *Quijote* has its significance for the dying age of humanism too.

But that is not the whole story. Lionel Trilling has said that "In any genre it may happen that the first great example contains the whole potentiality of the genre. It has been said that all philosophy is a footnote to Plato. It can be said that all prose fiction is a variation on the theme of *Don Quixote*." [40] Dialectically, then, such a haunting, sad book as the *Quijote* may be—such an elegy—is in turn an aubade for the novel. Coming as it does at the close of the humanist tradition and the tradition of a humanist poetics, it manages through its examination of truth, history, and fiction and through its exploration of exemplary, dialectical, and open-ended literary exercise to realize a new form—that *new* necessary *ficción*—towards which humanist poetics had been slowly working since the time of Erasmus. In anatomizing humanist precepts concerning the nature of man and the nature of a Christian humanism, it establishes firmly a new genre for a new age.

SEVEN

La maladie naturelle de leur esprit: Contestation,

Subversion, and the Decline of Continental

Humanist Poetics

 DON QUIJOTE'S IDEAS AND
DEEDS REQUIRE A LARGER
WORLD THAN THAT OF HIS OWN RE-
FLECTIONS AND IMAGINATION TO
GENERATE THEM AND RESPOND TO THEM; *EL
INGENIOSO HIDALGO* KEEPS REQUIRING THAT
we as readers adjudicate debates between the Don and Sancho, between the
knight-errant and his fallen world, between his own lucid and mad interpretations and our own. The art of methexis Cervantes practices is complicit, but it
is one that he shares with all those who practice a humanist poetics; there is only
a superficial distinction between the Don and Folly, or Bembo, Oisille, or
Panurge. One reason humanist poetics produces such striking and enduring
works of art is that it insists on raising fundamental questions (and fundamental
doubts) about human nature and human achievement; another reason is that it
stoutly refuses to answer the questions it raises. Humanist poetics is pronoun-
cedly a poetics that denies closure to its works of art. In the images and
constructs of its dialectically situated narratives, it is—sometimes directly,
sometimes insinuatingly—always in the interrogative mode.

Victoria Kahn has recently pointed out the similarities between humanist
poetics and our own current habits of reading.

> Historical knowledge of the humanist emphasis on the activity of reading and
> judging suggests an analogy with modern critical interest in "reader response"—
> if by this we understand the assumption that the meaning of a work does not
> exist as a timeless object, but is produced in the reader's interaction with the
> text, that is, in the act of reading. It also makes clear that reader-response

criticism could only be seen as new and fashionable when the assumptions of the humanist rhetorical tradition had been forgotten.[1]

Just as we judge the competence of a text by its significance to us in our own time as well as its significance for the time in which it was composed and of which it is constituent, so our own competence as readers depends fundamentally on our comprehension of that text in its own time as well as in ours. And that comprehension, according to Edward W. Said, rests on understanding and distinguishing between filiation, the relationship of a text to its ancestry, and affiliation, the relationship of a text to its environment. Humanist thinkers, writers, and educators were centrally concerned with their inherited exemplary texts from earlier Greek and especially Roman civilizations, drawing from them a basic understanding of the nature of man, of right human conduct, of ethics, and of speech; here they found patterns for daily thought and behavior as well as patterns for their own critical and imaginative writing. At the same time that they imitated their past, however, they adjusted its lessons to suit their own times and needs, and their texts everywhere display this need, or what Said calls affiliation, which "enables a text to maintain itself as a text." Affiliation, he tells us, "is covered by a range of circumstances: status of the author, historical moment, conditions of publication, diffusion and reception, values drawn upon, values and ideas assumed, a framework of consensually held tacit assumptions, presumed background, and so on and on."[2] This Janus-view of texts and of what they embody is a primary cause of the dialectic that the humanists enact; their joy of discovery sooner or later is transformed into a joy of performance. Inherited texts and ideas are important only when they are reborn, revived, made to function once more. Thus education for the humanists led out of the past into the ongoing present, and their many treatises on cultivating their readers and students were meant to transplant old seeds in new soil. Their acts of discovery, and of recovery, lead directly to acts of experimentation and testing. Humanist poetics is therefore a dynamic poetics because it is forever mediating past and present, filiation and affiliation. Such mediation adds yet a further conative dimension, and a deeper purpose, to humanist poetics as a poetics of exploration and collusion.

We can trace this dialectic of filiation and affiliation to the very beginnings of the Continental Renaissance, to Guarino's arrival at Ferrara in the Quattrocento.

Pudendum erat quam parumper litterarum sciebant nostri (Ferrarienses) homines ante Guarini adventum. Nemo erat, non dicam qui oratoriam facultatem nosceret, qui rhetoricum profiteretur, qui graviter et ornate diceret et in publico aliquo conventu verba facere auderet, sed qui veram grammaticae rationem cognosceret, qui vocabulorum proprietatem vimque intelligeret, qui poetas interpretari posset. Iacebat Priscianus, ignorabatur Servius, incognita erant opera Ciceronis, miraculi loco habebatur, si quis Crispum Sallustium, si quis C. Caesarem, si quis T. Livium nominaret, si quis ad veterum scriptorum intelligentiam aspiraret. Quadragesimus fere annus cives nostros in ludo puerili occupatos inveniebat in iisdem elementis semper laborantes, semper convolutos. Usque adeo bonarum litterarum ruina facta erat. Postea vero quam divinus hic vir dextro sidere Ferrariam ingressus est, secuta est mirabilis quaedam ingeniorum commutatio. . . . Currebatur undique ad vocem iucundissimam, ut alterum Theophrastum diceres, ad quem audiendum legimus perrexisse discipulos ad duo milia. Nemo putabatur ingenuus, nemo in lauta vitae parte, nisi Guarini esset auditor. Unde brevi de obscurissimis tenebris educti sunt nostri homines in veram et clarissimam lucem, omnes repente diserti, omnes eruditi, omnes limati, omnes in dicendo suaves extiterunt.

It was shameful how little the men of Ferrara knew of letters before the arrival of Guarino. There was no one who even understood the basic principles of grammar, who understood the propriety and impact of words, who was able to interpret the poets, let alone who was learned in the art of oratory, who professed rhetoric, who was competent to speak gravely and elegantly and dared to do so in public. Priscian was lost in oblivion, Servius was unheard of, the works of Cicero were unknown, and it was considered miraculous if someone mentioned Sallust, or Caesar, or Livy, or if anyone aspired to understand the ancient authors. At forty our citizens were still occupied with childish studies, still struggling and embroiled with the rudiments, until the liberal arts had been reduced entirely to ruins. But after a propitious star had brought this divine individual to Ferrara, there followed an extraordinary transformation in competence. . . . From all quarters they came to listen to that most felicitous voice, so that one might call him another Theophrastus (of whom it is said that his teaching attracted at least two thousand scholars). No one was considered noble, no one as leading a blameless life, unless he had followed Guarino's courses. So that in a short space of time our citizens were led out of the deepest shadows into a true and brilliant light, and all suddenly became eloquent, learned, elegant and felicitous of speech.[3]

There is here all the excitement of newly found texts, of suddenly relieved hunger for learning; yet in understanding the ancients these humanists learn to

understand *the propriety and impact of words*. Guarino's eager students are not
simply introduced to Caesar and Livy but learn to *interpret the poets* and *speak*
effectively *in public*. Texts are at once put to use, are prudential, as Kahn's study
conclusively demonstrates. Anthony Grafton and Lisa Jardine, in their account
of humanist teaching based on lecture notes and student commentaries, show
how subsequent teachers, such as the Byzantine scholar Georgius Trapezuntius, taught through such dazzling rhetoric that they served as their own best
examples of the power and importance of language. Still others, such as
Lorenzo Valla, imitating Quintilian, systematized the New Learning so as to
make it at once more comprehensible and more practical.[4] It is this fundamental aim to mediate filiation and affiliation that causes Thomas More to address
the Reverend Fathers, vice-chancellor, proctors, and other members of the
Masters' Guild at Oxford, urging them to retain the study of Greek in their
curriculum. His remarks revealingly merge the prudential with the vocational.

> Nemo saltem dubitat, literas unam prope, atque unicam esse rem, propter
> quam frequentatur Oxonia: quandoquidem rudem illam et illiteratam virtutem
> quaeuis bona mulier liberos suos ipsa docere non pessime posset domi: praeterea
> non quisquis ad vos venit, protinus ad perdiscendam theologiam venit: oportet
> sint qui et leges perdiscant. Noscenda est et rerum humanarum prudentia, res
> adeo non inutilis theologo ut absque hac sibi fortassis intus non insuauiter possit
> canere, at certe ad populum inepte sit cantaturus: Quae peritia haud scio an
> alicunde uberius, quam e poetis, oratoribus atque historijs hauriatur.

> Certainly no one disputes that learning is virtually the one and only incentive
> that draws people to Oxford, inasmuch as that rude and illiterate virtue is
> something which any good woman can teach well enough to her children at
> home. Furthermore, not everyone who comes to Oxford comes just to learn
> theology; some must also learn law. They must also learn prudence in human
> affairs, something which is so far from being useless to a theologian that without
> it he may be able to sing well enough for his own pleasure, but his singing will
> certainly be ill suited for the people. And I doubt that any study contributes as
> richly to this practical skill as the study of poets, orators, and histories.[5]

Such practical purpose, too, is what helps Erasmus choose the "strings of
classical authors," as J. K. Sowards has it,[6] that inform and punctuate his
commentaries and prefaces, his letters and apologias, and his various sets of
instruction, including the influential *De Ratione Studii,* for St. Paul's School in
London. This is because the humanists perceived learning communally; it was

communally taught and communally enacted. "The humanist model of reading is not that of isolate reader confronting an isolate text" as we might do
today, Nancy Struever cautions, "but of a continuity of acts of interpretation on
the part of a later society confronting an earlier one: learning is in structure
social, and historical, and ethical."[7] If filiation was the source of the humanist
movement, as it traced its textual heritage, the consequence of affiliation was
unavoidable. The practical end of studying even the basic trivium of grammar,
rhetoric, and logic was its chief interest. "The central assumption," Kahn tells
us of the humanist training, "is that reading is a form of prudence or of
deliberative rhetoric and that a text is valuable insofar as it engages the reader in
an activity of discrimination and thereby educates the faculty of practical reason
or prudential judgment which is essential to the active life" (*Rhetoric,* p. 11).

Humanist poetics is thus a poetics of palimpsests—of meaning that is
located in a new text as it resituates itself on those that have gone before. The
triumph of humanism and of humanist poetics is what Thomas M. Greene sees
as the triumph of the text which, uncovered, discovered, and recovered from
the past, helps to reshape both past and present. "The triumph of the text," he
writes, "lies in its power to discover or uncover the density of the signifier and
the sedimented substance of a tradition that does not merely erode or debase."[8]
Such new texts rely, then, on a transforming imitatio; and Roger Ascham,
representing all humanists, proposes in *The Scholemaster* (1570) that each student of the past keep for himself (or herself) "A booke thus wholie filled with
examples of Imitation, first out of *Tullie,* compared with *Plato, Xenophon,
Isocrates, Demosthenes,* and *Aristotle,* then out of *Virgil* and *Horace,* with *Homer*
and *Pindar,* next out of *Seneca* with *Sophocles* and *Euripides,* lastlie out of *Liuie,*
with *Thucydides, Polibius,* and *Halicarnassaeus.*"[9]

Such homemade texts were meant as reservoirs for discursive inquiry and for
examples of rhetorical organization; in addition, they were storehouses for, as
Kahn puts it, "cognitive strategy" and "argumentative tactic" (*Rhetoric,*
p. 11). The common element in the ongoing dialectic between past and
present, between imitatio as copying and as creating, was the most efficient and
effective use of language, the employment of rhetorical power, which was
learned, as we have seen, in the structuring of speeches and debates and won in
the mastery of arguing both sides of the same question, *in utramque partem,*
implying that the same situation or text can be variously interpreted and
reinterpreted. It is this *practical* sense of *arguing in both parts,* in fact, that Cicero
says makes the ideal orator—and this alone.

Sin aliquis exstiterit aliquando qui Aristotelio more de omnibus rebus in utramque sententiam possit dicere et in omni causa duas contrarias orationes praeceptis
illius cognitis explicare, aut hoc Arcesilae modo et Carneadis contra omne quod
propositum sit disserat, quique ad eam rationem adiungat hunc usum exercita-
tionemque dicendi, is sit verus, is perfectus, is solus orator.

If there has really been a person who was able in Aristotelian fashion to speak on
both sides about every subject and by means of knowing Aristotle's rules to reel
off two speeches on opposite sides of every case, or in the manner of Arcesilas and
Carneades argue against every statement put forward, and who to that method
adds the experience and practice in speaking indicated, he would be the one and
only true and perfect orator. (3.21.80)[10]

Nor should we think of such matters as limited to those at grammar school and
university; in a homely illustration in Thomas More's *Confutation of Tyndale's
Answer,* we can see how pervasive the dialectical way of thinking had become
and how it draws on argumentative strategies, concrete images, and practical
examples to converse: how (as we saw in *Il Libro del Cortegiano) conversazione*
becomes—is indistinguishable from—*controversiae.*

Now whyle he was tellynge her thys tale, she notyng wente about to consyder
hys wordes / but as she was wont in all other thynges, studyed all the whyle
nothynge ellys, but what she myghte saye to the contrary. And whan he hadde
wyth myche worke and ofte interruptynge, brought at laste hys tale to an ende,
well quod she to hym as Tyndale sayth to me, I wyll argue lyke and make you a
lyke sample. My mayde hath yender a spynnynge whele / or els bycause all your
reason resteth in the roundenes of the world, come hyther thou gyrle, take out
the spyndle and brynge me hyther the wharle. Lo syr ye make ymagynacyons I
can not tell you what. But here is a wharle and it is rounde as the worlde is / and
we shall not nede to ymagyn an hole bored thorow, for it hath an hole bored
thorow in dede. But yet bycause ye go by ymagynacyons / I wyll ymagyne
wyth you.[11]

At least from the time of the Silenus box in the *Encomium Moriae* onward,
images were often used as counters to arguments (as here) or as indicative of
double meanings (as in the apothecary box in Rabelais) or as an outward
signifier of an inward meaning (as the falsely glittering gold and the implied
biblical references to silver and lead indicate to Shakespeare's Bassanio the
contents of Portia's three caskets).[12] As we have seen earlier, such bifocalism,
such widespread *double-mindedness* allowed humanist writers to indicate mean-

ing by the *divergences* of their texts from their models. It also allows fiction to parade as fact because it is meant to reveal a higher truth than mere authentic experience was capable of doing—a technique that Michael O'Connell has traced back, in an important essay, to Petrarch's deliberate fictionalizing of his ascent of Mount Ventoux despite his claim to its autobiographical importance. For if he did not climb the mountain as he says he did, or write the letter about the adventure when he said he did, his purpose—to recall his Senecan original in Augustine's *Confessions* even as he departs from it—helps him to drive home his point about the need for individual and inward conversion of spirit as a part of the New Learning. "Only in this way can he 'save' his sense of the validity of his own experience and at the same time yield to the spiritual authority Augustine has for him." As O'Connell explains, Petrarch

follows the two essential elements of Augustine's story, the chance opening of a book and the reading of a sentence that applies uncannily to oneself. But he does not follow two other elements of Augustine's story. He does not adapt from the *Confessions* the direction from outside to open the book. Augustine had heard a child chanting "Tolle, lege" outside the garden where he was sitting in his distress. Petrarch says that his reading came of his own impulse to lift his spirit as he had lifted his body in the climb. This alteration is small and perhaps insignificant, but it does suggest Petrarch's desire to appropriate the event and make it his own. For the real voice telling him to take up and read is Augustine's own in the book he carries. The other element he does not follow is the sharing with his companion of his encounter with the text. Augustine, upon reading the passage in St. Paul, had shown the book to his companion Alypius, who read the next verse and applied it to himself. St. Anthony had been accompanied by his sister, who also applied the directive of the Gospel to herself. But Petrarch does not show the book to Gherardo, and instead closes it and asks not to be disturbed. The reason for this can be seen in the earlier allegory of the climb; Gherardo does not need to share in the experience of conversion, for his own subsequent conversion suggests that implicitly he was already advanced beyond his older brother in spiritual maturity. But the effect of this change is also to isolate the self in the experience of conversion. Petrarch's experience of the passage of the *Confessions* remains entirely his own. The impulse to read it comes to him from within, and the experience of the chastening sentence does not go beyond him. The episode in the *Confessions* is the only thing without which Petrarch could not have written the letter. He needn't really have climbed the mountain, needn't really have opened the book at random, but without Augustine's story of conversion, with its implicit call for the reader's conversion, Petrarch would have had no motive or center for his own story. The displacement of the external voice can be seen as an attempt to refashion the conversion experience and make it come from the self. And the limitation of the experience to himself appears to place the entire relevance and responsibility for it on the individual self.[13]

This divergent fiction, which argues truth by the first of the Continental humanists, is quite likely the first humanist fiction, the first important work of humanist poetics, and it too mediates between its source and the audience to whom it is addressed: It too is grounded in filiation and affiliation.

Such a creative use of dialectic as Petrarch employs in his inventive "Ascent of Mount Ventoux" would seem to blur decisively and fatally the Schoolmen's (and the humanists') cherished distinction between rhetoric, or the art of persuasion, and logic, based on syllogistic reasoning. But in actual fact Aristotle had blurred the boundaries between such strategies of language in his *Topics* when he announced that the dialectical syllogism differs from the epideictic syllogism in dealing with contingency rather than necessity and that it takes the probable as its point of departure, thereby achieving a lesser degree of certainty in its conclusions. And the probable is defined in terms simply of common opinion (100b20).[14] Given this more fanciful base for a major premise (or for a propositional enthymeme), Aristotle himself permits the beginnings of a more creative use of dialectic, which the humanists will use for argumentation and for fiction, often (as with Erasmus, Castiglione, and Rabelais) indiscriminately. For these artists have come to realize, as we have just seen in considerable detail, how the essentially syllogistic deep structure of humanist fiction, placing the new work against a Senecan original as a minor premise against a major premise, is a rhetorically effective way of creating new works that enliven older ones by renewing them through recontextualization. Even so late a humanist as the dedicated, self-taught Ben Jonson is aware of this, writing his own Roman plays by putting "rhetorical effectiveness" ahead of "logical rigor," as Katharine Eisaman Maus had amply demonstrated.[15]

In a recent study on rhetorical stance examining the *Phaedrus* and the *Gorgias,* Lynette Hunter has shown how Aristotle's relaxation of logical rigor in the case of dialectical syllogisms is extended when he further distinguishes logic, as the use of deductive reasoning, from rhetoric, which exists "to deal with things about which we deliberate, but for which we have no systematic rules."[16] This essentially boundless province for rhetoric—while still keeping to the ordered and classified kinds of orations outlined in his *Rhetoric*—allows Aristotle to admit an endless variety of matter as places within argumentation, and allows the process of constructing an argument to come surprisingly close to the dialectical search for truth we find in Plato's dialogues, with what Patrick Grant calls their "brilliant expression of the mind's kaleidoscopic energies in search of truth." [17] Like Plato, Aristotle, followed by Cicero and Quintilian, would use rhetoric to—in Wolfgang Iser's memorable phrase—broaden the audience's "horizon of expectations." [18] We can see what prompts Erasmus's *De Copia* and his essentially copious encomium for Moria and what so energizes the imagination and rhetoric of Rabelais. Both were anticipated and surrounded, as Anthony Grafton and Lisa Jardine have charted so carefully, by humanist scholars and teachers who were themselves copious and *performative,* at times openly competing, as Trapezuntius and Valla did, for crowded classrooms of students eager for and appreciative of their own rhetorical means of teaching rhetoric. And the generation of Roman teachers succeeding the generations of Guarino and Valla—Calderini, Filetico, Leto—became more ingenious yet, decoding obscure antique allusions and delighting in chasing tricky bits of syntax. They also became creative, like Petrarch. "Some of them," Grafton and Jardine tell us, "fabricated evidence to give their lectures more spice: Pomponio Leto pretended to have a full text of the long-lost *Annales* of Ennius, and Calderini invented an ancient biographer of Suetonius" (*Humanism to Humanities.* p. 86). Such fabrication transformed the simulation of classical rhetoric into dissimulation, and in time this seems to have become increasingly the fashion.

Just such dissimulation, or fabrication, as this also became the basis of the literary theories of the sixteenth century, promulgated by Girolamo Fracastoro and Torquato Tasso. Fracastoro's dialogue between Andrea Navagero and Giambattista dello Torre, *Navagero; or, A Dialogue on the Art of Poetry* (*Navagerius sive de Poetica Dialogvs*), finds its Senecan original for such creativity in Plato's definitions of icastic and fantastic art. Navagero begins his theory of poetry with reference to faculty psychology and an emphasis on prudence.

> nam cū duae partes sint in homine, voluntas & intellectus, & voluntatis pruden-
> tia sit finis, intellectus finis cognitio & ītellectio, si poeta imitetur & naturalia,
> non tantum personas, videbitur quidem omnem finem & omne institutum
> adimplesse, in imitatione quidem personarum prudētiam faciendo, in illa vero,
> quae est naturalium & similium, faciendo cognitionem: imitabitur enim & in
> hoc perfectiones, & excellentias rerum.

"For there are two faculties in man, the will and the intellect, and practical knowledge is the aim of the will, and perception and understanding the aim of the intellect. If the poet imitates nature as well as people, it will seem indeed that his whole purpose and design has been made complete, by producing practical knowledge through the imitation of people, and perceptive knowledge through the imitation of natural objects, in which he will imitate what is perfect and excellent in things." [19]

Such a theory aligns the poet with the painter because of their common interest in the universal and the beautiful, a comparison that may also stem from *The Sophist*.

poeta vero illi assimiletur qui nō hunc, non illum vult imitari, non uti forte sunt, & defectus multos sustinent, sed uniuersalem, & pulcherrimam ideā artificis sui cōtemplatus res facit, quales esse deceret. . . . poeta vero non hoc, sed simplicem ideam pulchritudinibus suis vestitam, quod uniuersale Aristoteles vocat.

"the poet is like the painter who does not wish to represent this or that particular man as he is with many defects, but who, having contemplated the universal and supremely beautiful idea of his creator, makes things as they ought to be. . . . The poet imitates not the particular but the simple idea clothed in its own beauties, which Aristotle calls the universal." [Sigs. RR2–RR2v; p. 60]

But Fracastoro is also aware of the association of art, in Plato's time and his own, with sophistry and of the ongoing debate concerning the value of art. He too speaks in an age in which simulation and dissimulation have become entangled. Navagero defends art:

quam perfectionē & decorem soli magni artifices norunt: quae si à rebus auferas, profecto anima quodā modo propriá ijs abstulisti, quare quae & pictores & poetae rebus addunt ad perfectione, non extra rem sunt, si rem consideres non nudam (ut plebei artifices, aut qui fine aliquo coerciti & astricti sunt, faciunt) sed perfectam & animatam: qualem cōsiderant summi artifices, praecipue autem ex omnibus poeta, qui admirandus in omnibus esse uult.

What perfection and beauty are, only the great artists know. And if you take them away from the subject, assuredly you have somehow taken away life itself. Therefore what the painters and the poets add to things for perfection is not extraneous, if we mean by "thing" not the bare object such as common artificers, or those who are controlled and restricted by some purpose, make, but the object perfected and given life. Such an interpretation the greatest artists make,— most of all the poet who wishes to arouse admiration in all. [Sig. SS2v; p. 69]

But Giambattista notes that, rather than heighten and enhance truth, humanist poetics *undermines* it:

Equidē non satis scio, Naugeri, an ita facile tibi concedā pulchriora esse, que poeta imitatur & sumit: [quia] illa quae tu pulchra vocas, precipue illa sunt, [quia] poetis superadduntur, que & fabule dicuntur. [Omnia] quidem partim efficta, partim ēt falsa, & supra veritatē. nà [quia] multa effingant poete, [qua] nullo pacto sūt, tute ēt dixisti! [quia] vero & aperte falsa, & impudenter quidē assumant, manifestū esse potest in ijs que de Aenea, & Didone Virg. scribit: quos constat multo tɟe discretos suisse. quae oīa cum falsa sint, ego quidē non video, qūo pulchra esse possunt. falsum [nam]. omne turpe est, cum ex ijs constet, que non sunt: quare & nulla utilitas esse videtur in addiscēdo falsa.

"Indeed, I am not satisfied, Navagero, nor will I so easily grant that what the poet imitates and sets forth is more beautiful. For the things that you call beautiful are just those things that are added by poets and are called fictitious. Everything, then, is partly invented and partly untrue and exaggerated. You have just said rightly that poets portray many things that do not exist in reality. That they present open and shameless falsehoods can be seen in what Virgil writes of Aeneas and Dido, who, it is known, lived in widely separated periods. Since all these things are false, truly I do not see how they can be beautiful, for everything false is ugly, since it consists of things that are not real. So I see no usefulness in adding [learning] untruth." [Sig. SS2v; p. 69]

Fracastoro's treatise on poetry therefore turns into an inconclusive dialectic.

Tasso at first seems to escape these problems by tying fiction closely to history. Even the marvelous and incredible, for him, must have something of the credible about it: Fantasy is rooted in verisimilitude. Moreover, poetry's aim is moral betterment; it therefore gives a particular place and premium to poetry. But his mature *Discorsi del Poema Eroico* reveals a surprising uneasiness and a frankness, which also seems—at least potentially—to be sharply at odds with his other testimony on behalf of the poet:

Cerca nondimeno il poeta di persuadere che le cose da lui trattate siano degne di fede e d'autorità, e si sforza di guadagnarsi ne gli animi questa opinione e questa credenza con l'autorità dell'istoria e con la fama de' nomi illustri, e d'acquistarsi bene volenza con la lode della virtù e de gli uomini valorosi, avenga che sia pericoloso l'essere odiato, come dice Platone (parlo di quelli ch'imitatori, l'azioni illustri, quali sono il tragico e l'epico). E ciò si potrebbe confermare con l'autorità Aristotele, perchè, si i poeti sono imitatori, conviene che siano imitatori del vero, perchè il falso non è; e quel che non è, non si può imitare; pero

quelli che scrivono cose in tutto false, se non sono imitatori, non sono poeti, e i
suol componimenti non sono poesie, ma finzioni più tosto; laonde non meritano
il nome di poeta, o non tanto.

None the less the poet seeks to persuade us that what he treats deserves belief and
credit; he makes an effort to gain such belief and credit through the authority of
history and renowned names and to win good will by praising virtue and
valorous men, since, as Plato says, it is dangerous to be hated. (I mean those who
imitate illustrious deeds, the tragic and the epic poet.) And Aristotle's authority
confirms this: if poets are imitators, it is fitting that they imitate truth, since the
false does not exist, and what does not exist cannot be imitated. Those who write
what is wholly false, then, not being imitators, are not poets, and their compositions are not poems but rather fictions; hence they either do not deserve, or
deserve far less, the name of poet.[20]

It will not do, of course, to label as *fiction* that which is composed of lies and
poetry that which is true, because Tasso, again reminiscent of Plato in the
Republic, and of Pindar, has admitted earlier that poets are often by nature liars
because they *deceive the reader with the semblance of truth.* Verisimilitude itself
misleads. The poet's defense, that all that is true may not yet be known so that
he must *make an effort to gain such belief and credit as he can,* in turn questions
Tasso's idea of the *marvelous* and suggests sharper boundaries for the *marvelous-
credible.* And if we recall from Fracastoro that history itself may be erroneously
presented when so great a poet as Vergil tells *fictions* about Aeneas and Dido,
there seem few grounds left on which to defend the wholly imaginative work.
The needs of truth by and for the reader—the pressures of affiliation—begin to
limit and circumscribe the poet's resources, including the texts constituting
filiation. Tasso returns to these troubling matters of Libro Secondo, and precisely in terms of the difficulties of resolving matter with audience, the imagination of a humanist poetics with the known (as opposed to the unknown)
world, in his dedication to Libro Terzo.

Credono molti, illustrissimo Signore, che delle scienze e dell'arte più nobili
sia avenuto come de' popoli e delle provincie e delle terre e de' mari, molti de'
quali non erano ben conosciuti da gli antichi, ma di nuovo son ritrovati oltre le
Colonne d'Ercole verso occidente, o vero di là da gli altari che pose Alessandro
nell'oriente; e rassimigliano costoro gli ammaestramenti dell'arte poetica e della
retorica alle mete e a' segni i quali son posti per termini a' timidi naviganti. Ma sì
come io non biasimo l'ardire guidato dalla ragione, così non lodo l'audacia senza

consiglio, parendomi pazzia ch'altri voglia fare arte del caso, virtù del vizio e prudenza della temerità, e tutto concedere alla fortuna, la qual ha minor parte nell'operazioni dell'ingegno che nelle fatiche del corpo; tutta volta in quelle medesime che si fanno con la parte men nobile, cerchiamo di moderare i fortunosi avenimenti e di restringerli quasi sotto alcuna legge. Laonde molto piu debbiamo considerare l'operazioni dell'intelletto, a cui sempre è proposto a guisa di segno un obietto medesimo nel quale ei rimira: e questo è il vero, il quale non si muta giamai ne sparisce a gli occhi della mente. Ma l'Orse or celano a coloro ch'avendo passato Abila e Calpe, navigano nell'ampissimo Oceano; nondimeno altre stelle sono in quello emisfero con le quali essi devono reggere il corso (altrimente non avrebbono arte alcuna del navigare), e possono in qualche modo schifare l'incostanza delle maritime cose con la constanza delle celesti. Ma quanto sono più stabili, quanto più vere, quanto più certe le cose intellettuali, alle quali drizziamo l'intelletto! E se pur tal volta consideriamo le cose verisimili, non possiamo aver altra notizia di loro se non quella che ci dà la cognizione del vero. Però andiamo formando l'idee delle cose artificiali: nella quale operazione ci pare d'esser quasi divini e d'imitare il primo Artefice. Ma qualunque sia questo nostro artificio, da niuno altro può esser meglio estimato. Legga dunque V. S. illustrissima quel ch'io discorro con lei quasi in un ragionamento, perchè s'egli è gran difficoltà il ritrovare il vero fra le cose verisimili, il giudicarlo non è minor lode, o alla filosofia men conveniente.

Many people think, my illustrious lord, that the same thing has happened with the noblest arts and sciences as with peoples, provinces, lands, and oceans, a number of which were not well known to the ancients, but have recently been discovered beyond the Pillars of Hercules to the west, or indeed beyond the altars Alexander set up in the east. They compare the achievements of the poetic and rhetorical arts to the goals and other marks placed as boundaries to timid navigators. But just as I do not blame a daring that is guided by reason, so I do not praise a boldness without reflection, for I think it an insanity that anyone should want to create an art from chance, virtue from vice, and prudence from temerity, and leave everything to luck, which plays a still smaller role in the workings of intellectual talent than in the efforts of the body. Even in the efforts that we make with the less noble part of ourselves we try to moderate the chances of fortune and keep them under some kind of law. Still more then ought we to reflect on the workings of the intellect, which always has before it the object itself as the mark it regards: and this is the truth, which never changes or disappears from the mind's eye. But the sign of the Bear disappears to those who, having left behind Abyla and Calpe, sail into the full ocean, although other stars appear in that hemisphere, by which they ought to steer (otherwise they would lack the art of seamanship); and they can somehow manage to elude the sea's inconstancy by the constancy of things celestial. But how much more stable, true, and sure are things intellectual to which we direct the intellect! And even if sometimes we look to things verisimilar, the only notion we can have of them is what our knowledge of truth gives. That is how we go about forming ideas of artificial things, a work almost godlike that seems to imitate the First Maker. But whatever this art of ours may be, no one can judge better than your lordship. May your lordship, then, read what I shall discuss with you, as it were speculatively, for, if to find the truth among verisimilar things is highly difficult, to judge it is no less praiseworthy or proper to philosophy. [Pp. 116–17; p. 57]

To be successful, poetry must mediate its truth from the poet's discovery to the reader's recovery, and such a shared task is like a voyage into the unknown parts of the world, the inconstant and uncertain seas where only the intellect— the poet's *claim* to truth—has any hope of authority. Humanist poetics is no longer the joyful art of imitatio fostering wordplay, eloquence, and instructive copia and debate. Forced past the limits of what is known (from antique texts and from the geography of the present, now itself always shifting), it has become risky business.

Once such troubling doubts are raised in the Continental Renaissance, even the revered antique texts contribute to them. As emphasis on Cicero's *Brutus, Orator,* and *De Oratore* receded, more and more attention was paid to his *Academica,* where in Book 2, in his own person, Cicero puts forth what were by the sixteenth century already growing shibboleths of a New Skepticism. Cicero begins by citing instances of our biological shortcomings. From where he is standing, Cicero claims, he can see Catulus's place at Cumae but not his villa at Pompeii, although there is nothing to obstruct his view, and this despite other men who have been said to see as far as twenty-five miles and some birds that see even farther (2.25.80). Moreover, even our recording senses are often unreliable. A distant ship appears to be at anchor but is actually moving (2.25.81). There may be nothing larger than the sun, yet it appears to be merely a foot in diameter, and Epicurus has argued it may even be somewhat smaller than it looks (2.26.82). It is not simply that man's senses are untrustworthy and that therefore his judgment may be faulty, but that *man is no longer even the measure:* Cicero's skepticism strikes at the roots of humanist thought. He moves on from the unreliability of man's senses to the invalidity of logic or dialectic, thus directly challenging the fundamental practices of the Continental Renaissance.

Nempe fundamentum dialecticae est quidquid enuntiatur (id autem appellant ἀξίωμα, quod est quasi effatum) aut verum esse aut falsum; quid igitur? haec vera an falsa sunt: "Si te mentiri dicis idque verum dicis, mentiris?" Haec scilicet inexplicabilia esse dictis, quod est odiosius quam illa quae nos non comprehensa et non percepta dicimus.

Clearly it is a fundamental principle of dialectic that every statement (termed by them *axiōma,* that is, a "proposition") is either true or false; what then? is this a true proposition or a false one—"If you say that you are lying and say it truly, you lie?" Your school of course says that these problems are "insoluble," which is more vexatious than the things termed by us "not grasped" and "not perceived." [2.29.95][21]

Not content thus to challenge the Old Academy of Socrates and Plato, Cicero goes on to challenge Aristotelian thought by arranging his argument along the three main divisions advocated by the Peripatetics—physics and ethics follow hard on this examination of logic. The sea now looks purple under the west wind, he notes, but the wise man will not assent to this perception, for he will know it has previously appeared blue, may tomorrow appear gray, and under sunlight becomes a shimmering white (2.33.105). We do not know our universe because we do not know our selves; ethics has also been a matter of disputed perception and judgment. Aristo proved in practice what Zeno argued in theory, that nothing is good except virtue; others hold that the end of goodness is pleasure; Carneades insisted the chief good was that recommended by nature; and the Stoics, claiming that all sins are equal, aroused violent disagreement from Antiochus (2.42.130–43, 133). In light of such various but comparably demonstrable theories, in the study of morality as in the study of dialectic and biology, the best that man can honestly advance is what is probable, for *nothing* remains clear and nothing remains certain. Nothing is even *preferential.*

Cicero also registers doubts by the Academic skeptic Cotta in the *De Natura Deorum,* where he examines the reliability and validity of human reason itself.

Sentit domus unius cuiusque, sentit forum, sentit curia campus socii provinciae, ut quem ad modum ratione recte fiat sic ratione peccetur, alterumque et a paucis et raro, alterum et saepe et a plurimis, ut satius fuerit nullam omnino nobis a dis inmortalibus datam esse rationem quam tanta cum pernicie datam.

Our private homes; the law-courts, the senate, the hustings; our allies, our provinces—all have cause to know that just as right actions may be guided by reason, so also may wrong ones, and that whereas few men do the former, and on rare occasions so very many do the latter, and frequently; so that it would have been better if the immortal gods had not bestowed upon us any reasoning faculty at all than that they should have bestowed it with such mischievous results. [3.27.69][22]

Worse yet, Cotta notes, these gods have allowed unaccountable events—the exiling of Publius Rutilius, for instance, a man of impeccable honor and of consummate learning, and the death of the beloved Socrates—while permitting evil men such as the brigand Harpalus, who praises the gods, to live (3.32.80–34.83).

The Continental Renaissance draws on *De Natura Deorum* as a storehouse of allusions to the gods, as do the authors of Continental and Tudor emblem books, but they blink the radical attack on the possibilities of man and his learning; they do not disturb the foundation of humanist thought and humanist poetics—at least at the beginning. When Erasmus comes to tackle the implications of these matters in the *Encomium Moriae,* for instance, in his abbreviated but celebrated comments on the philosophers of his day, he submits such attacks to his own rhetorical strategies.

Quam vero suaviter delirant, cum innumerabiles aedificant mundos, dum Solem, dum Lunam, Stellas, Orbes, tanquam pollice filove metiuntur, dum Fulminum, Ventorum, Eclipsium ac caeterarum inexplicabilium rerum causus reddunt, nihil usquam haesitantes, perinde quasi naturae rerum architectrici fuerint a secretis, quasive e Deorum consilio nobis advenerint: quos interim Natura cum suis conjecturis, magnifice ridet. Nam nihil apud illos esse comperti, vel illud satis magnum est argumentum, quod singulis de rebus inexplicabilis inter ipsos est digladiatio. Ii cum nihil omnino sciant, tamen omnia se scire profitentur.

how sweetely doe they raue in theyr owne opinion: whan constauntly they affirme there be worlds innumerable? Or whan they take vpon theim to measure the sonne, the moone, the planets and theyr compasses, as it were by *vnchemease, or drawne with a sine:* Or whan they expounde the causes of thunder, of wyndes, of eclipses, and suche other inexplicable thyngs, nothyng doubtyng, as if they had crepte into natures bosome, or were of counsaile with the Godds. And yet dooeth nature lowdely laughe theim to scorne, with all theyr coniectures: coniectures I saie, and no certaine knowlage, whiche appereth by this, that one secte of theim agreeth not with an other, but rather contendeth together vpon euery little thing. And yet these men, who in deede know nothing, wil take vpon them to know all thyngs.[23]

Erasmus implies that the errors arise in the derivative and shallow wranglings of the Scholastics who intervened between the ancients and the men of the Renaissance New Learning. Moreover, he places such dyslogistic opinion at a distinct remove, in the mouth of Folly. But such willed ignorance could not persist; by 1543 Copernicus is writing to Pope Paul III in his dedication to *De Revolvtionibvs Orbium coelestium* that it was precisely Cicero's *Academica,* followed by readings in Plutarch—"Ac repperi quidem apud Ciceronem primum, Nicetum sensisse terram moueri. Postea & apud Plutarchum inueni quosdam alios in ea fuisse opinione, cuius uerba, ut sint omnibus obuia" (sig. iiii)[24]—that alerted him to the possibility that the earth itself was in orbit. It was this antique learning that inaugurated his heliocentric theory of the universe, eventually heralding for the later Continental Renaissance a world sharply opposed to that propagated by the philosophic faith and deductive logic of humanism.

The *Hypotyposes* of Sextus Empiricus had an even more profound effect on later Continental humanists. This comprehensive and authoritative outline of Pyrrhonistic thought—still "the best and most complete presentation of ancient Scepticism that has been preserved to modern times," as Mary Mills Patrick once put it[25]—was translated into Latin in 1562 and again with the whole corpus of Sextus in Paris in 1569. It influenced Montaigne and his distant cousin Francisco Sanchez. If the earlier Rabelais could mock the Pyrrhonist Trouillogan (3.15–16), the later Tudor writer Thomas Nashe actually paraphrases Sextus.[26] Beginning with the principle of *akatalepsia,* or the lack of certain knowledge concerning the inner nature of things, Sextus proposes the withholding of assent or dissent (*epoche*), preserving instead *isostheneia,* or equipollence, a balancing of arguments on both sides of the question. This, he tells us, leads not only to an openness to further discovery and understanding but also to a quietude of mind. What at first seems to be a version of *in utramque partem,* however, is not: There is no sense of a better, or more persuasive or successful, argument, and the mind is *temporarily* resolute. But beyond that, the *idea of resolution,* with the Skeptics such as Sextus, is *withheld.* For him, the consequent formulas are two: "Omnia sunt incomprēsibilia" and "Nihil defino" (sig. ii4); "All things are non-apprehensible" and "I determine nothing" (1.29.211). Sextus's work follows closely the outline and presentation of Cicero's *Academica,* but his virtue is systematic detail; he is the greater codifier of classical Skepticism. Thus Book 1 classifies examples of the unreliability of the senses into ten tropes of *epoche:* those based on differences in animals; in men; among the five senses; circumstances; position, distance, and place;

mixtures; the quantity and constitution of objects; relations; frequency or rarity of occurrence; and cultural relativity in systems, customs, laws, mythical beliefs, and dogmatic opinions (1.14.47–152). In addition, every matter of inquiry admits to an additional five modes developed by later Skeptics and examined in chapter 15; these are based on discrepancy, or regression ad infinitum, on relativity, on hypothesis, and on circular reasoning, or what became for the New Academy of the sixteenth century fallacious methods of reasoning. As a consequence, whereas Cicero sought the proper and arguable boundaries for rhetoric, Sextus came to hate and dismiss rhetoric altogether.

To give due credit to the Continental humanists, they tried to offset such potential shortcomings (taking their cue from Aristotelian logic rather than Sextus's skepticism) by enlarging the sphere of argumentation to include such conceptualizations as analogy and deduction could provide them. But Sextus had already faced that challenge: From the outset, logic is his chief concern, the detailed attack on Aristotelian dialectic the very heart of his *Outline*. A disjunctive proposition, he claims, denies the validity of signs in syllogisms, for they are either apparent and therefore unnecessary or nonevident and therefore unworkable (2.11.127–28). Sextus further demonstrates—and quite rightly—that the deductive logic of the Aristotelian syllogism "proves" nothing, since the conclusion is already embedded in one or both of the premises (2.14): "Coagmentatio itaque ex sumptionibus & conclusione, non est demonstratio" (sig. oo2); "the argument which deduces what is non-evident by means of pre-evident premises is indiscoverable" (2.13.169).[27] Conversely, induction is a faulty method because the possibility of a single exception in any definable group requires that every instance be examined in the category being analyzed, and such scrutiny renders the induction redundant (2.14.195–96). Further, a full review of particulars is impossible, because particulars are by nature infinite and indefinite (sig. pp1; 2.15.204). Certain knowledge is as undiscoverable for Sextus in physics as it is through dialectic, as his further disjunctive arguments show (3.5.12). His treatment of ethics is abbreviated (3.23), but this may be due to the fact that cultural relativity, which denies the absolute truth of any single ethical proposition (his basic argument), was previously discussed and illustrated as the tenth trope in Book 1 (the skeptical belief advanced in our own day by Clifford Geertz).

By thus eliminating any precise and ascertainable body of knowledge, Sextus removes the possibility for those absolute premises—such as the centrality and perfectibility of man, his educability and his transformation—upon which Continental humanists erected an entire philosophy. It removes as well any possibility for exemplary models upon which humanists had constructed an entire system of education by means of imitation—and a humanist poetics for fiction. Sextus anticipates just this latter situation. In 3.28 he argues that there is no matter to be taught, for falsehood should not be taught and truth, as the entire Skeptic philosophy demonstrates, is unobtainable and unknowable. He further argues, in 3.29, that there can be no such thing as a teacher and a learner; it is absurd, he says, for an expert to teach an expert or a nonexpert to teach a nonexpert, or a nonexpert an expert, and, seeing that teaching one truth does not make a nonexpert expert, there is no means by which a nonexpert can be made expert (259–63).[28] Whereas indeterminacy had previously led humanists to develop fictional possibilities, an increasing sense of skepticism leads to strategies for deferral, from Marguerite's increasing faith in God's later providence to Rabelais's ship about to set sail (perhaps) and Cervantes' necessary ficción, necessary imagination, to offset a world shattered by doubt.

Balachandra Rajan has recently argued that two means of poetic—for which we can substitute rhetoric—are contestation and subversion. "Contestation," he writes, "interrogates a proposition by confronting the mind with an alternative," such as the humanists practiced by means of *in utramque partem*. "In fundamental contestations," he continues, "the proposition can be only apprehended in relation to the alternative. Subversion undermines a proposition without putting an alternative before us," such as Sextus's challenges to any verbal constructs to signify potential meaning. "A contested understanding is advanced by its interrogation. A subverted understanding is overthrown or frustrated by being subversively questioned."[29] Sextus's doubts in the classical period are conveyed to the Renaissance in Henrie Cornelius Agrippa's *Of the vanitie of artes and sciences*, Englished by James Sanford in 1569, but Agrippa goes to the original humanist texts as his chief targets. Of rhetoric, he writes that

> *Socrates* in *Plato* dothe proue with very strong reasons, that it is neither Arte, neither Science, but a certaine subtiltie and sharpnesse of witte, and that it is neither commendable, nor honest, but rather a dishonest, and seruile flatterie. [Sig. F1]

> To knowe how to speake perfectly, eloquently, grauely, and plentifully, is alwaies a goodly, delectable, and a profitable thinge, sometimes for al that dishonest, and vnconuenient, and very often daungerous, and alwaies suspected. [Sig. F2v]

> *Rhetorike* is nothing els, but an Arte of perswadinge and mouinge the affections, with subtile Eloquence, with exquisite colouringe of woordes, and with a false

likelihoode of the truth doth allure the mindes of the simple, and leadeth them into the prison of erroure, seekinge to subuerte the sence of the truth. [Sigs. F3–F3v]

Nor is poetry exempt; his words, in fact, resonate when placed alongside those of Tasso: "as for poetry, her lies are fained with so greate skill, that oftentimes they hinder true histories, euen as the mater is manifest" (sig. D4). Agrippa pointedly, if reductively, shows how "The easy alliance of rhetoric and Academic skepticism" that Cicero had managed "begins to be undermined" in the Renaissance, "by the arguments of Pyrrhonism," Victoria Kahn writes. "The exchange of contradictory opinion is no longer subordinate to a belief in practical certainty; contradiction becomes paradoxical and resistant to a prudent interpretation or practical resolution. Skepticism, in short, is no longer compatible with rhetorical persuasion; instead, it takes the possibility of persuasion itself as its object" (Rhetoric, p. 20). Simulation, poetic prosopopoeia like Folly or Gaspare, Pantagruel or Sancho Panza, is displaced by *dis*simulation. On the one hand, there is the rise of anamorphic art, such as the "cunningly contrived" room in Urbino where, Ronald Levao reports, "The walls are decorated with wood inlays that, when viewed from the center of the room, create the illusion of statuettes, shelves stacked with books, and tables displaying musical instruments. Should the observer leave the center, however, all turn into flat, distorted shapes, those strange, misshapen forms characteristic of anamorphic art."[30] Rhetorical manuals of dissimulation had indeed invaded the painterly art. In a more homely way, Shakespeare's Audrey inquires of Touchstone, in *As You Like It,* "I do not know what 'poetical' is: is it honest in deed and word? is it a true thing?" No is the reply: "No, truly, for the truest poetry is the most feigning" (3.3.17–20).

Lucien Febvre's account of Thomas Platter, with which this study began, is matched in his work on *Life in Renaissance France* with another kind of student, a kind more numerous and (perhaps consequently) more anonymous. These persons "were consumed by a feverish desire to know, to understand, which encompassed not only the geographical and physical world but also that other world within man. In Montpellier around 1540 students went to the cemetery every night to steal freshly buried corpses, risking death twenty times over. They spent the night dissecting, trying to penetrate the secrets of the construction of the human body, revealed to the world by Vesalius."[31] The real world crowds out the world of fancy, of imagination, of rhetoric, of words. Such purely empirical learning was given its best-known philosophical underpinning by Francis Bacon whose "fecund mind and manual dexterity," as A. Wigfall Green has it, "had already produced, during the spring and early summer of 1603, the proem of two prose handmaidens: *Experientia Literata* and *Interpretatio Naturae*."[32] Here Bacon argues three ways to advance learning: without plan, groping by trial and error; proceeding from experiment to experiment; following the light itself. He advocates moving from axiom through experiment to the penetration of truth, of light, of the mysteries of nature. If we are prevented from achieving truth, he adds in *The Advancement of Learning* (1605), it is not because our senses are deceived but because our intellect is weak and is unable to design or govern our collection of data properly. Bacon therefore rejects the belief of Skeptics that certainty is not possible, but for him certainty is never a matter of humanist belief, rhetoric, or argumentation.

Thus, whereas Aristotle's *Organon,* the antique storehouse of scientific knowledge, works deductively, Bacon's *Novum Organon,* the new systematic treatment of learning, works inductively. This is heralded by Bacon in the very first aphorism of *De Interpretatione Naturae et Regno Hominis*—"Homo, Naturae minister et interpres, tantum facit et intelligit quantum de Naturae ordine re vel mente observaverit, nec amplius scit aut potest"; "Man, being the servant and interpreter of Nature, can do and understand so much and so much only as he has observed in fact or in thought of the course of nature: beyond this he neither knows anything nor can do anything"[33]—which in turn reiterates his earlier essay "Of Studies": "Crafty men contemn studies, simple men admire them, and wise men use them; for they teach not their own use; but that is a wisdom without them, and above them, won by observation" (12.252). *Won by observation:* Such means of discovery far surpasses even Aristotelian logic. Later aphorisms in the *Novum Organon* make this plain enough:

X. Subtilitas naturae subtilitatem sensus et intellectus multis partibus superat; ut pulchrae illae meditationes et speculationes humanae et causationes res male-sania sint, nisi quod non adsit qui advertat. . . .

XII. Logica quae in usu est ad errores (qui in notionibus vulgaribus fundantur) stabiliendos et figendos valet, potius quam ad inquisitionem veritatis; ut magis damnosa sit quam utilis.

XIII. Syllogismus ad principia scientiarum non adhibetur, ad media axiomata frustra adhibetur, cum sit subtilitati naturae longe impar. Assensum itaque constringit, non res.

XIV. Syllogismus ex propositionibus constat, propositiones ex verbis, verba notionum tesserae sunt. Itaque si notiones ipsae (id quod basis rei est) confusae sint et temere a rebus abstractae, nihil in iis quae superstruuntur est firmitudinis. Itaque spes est una in *inductione* vera. . . .

XXIV. Nullo modo fieri potest, ut axiomata per argumentationem constituta ad inventionem novorum operum valeant; quia subtilitas naturae subtilitatem argumentandi multis partibus superat. Sed axiomata a particularibus rite et ordine abstracta nova particularia rurus facile indicant et designant; itaque scientias reddunt activas. [1.243–47]

X. The subtlety of nature is greater many times over than the subtlety of the senses and understanding; so that all those specious meditations, speculations, and glosses in which men indulge are quite from the purpose, only there is no one by to observe it. . . .

XII. The logic now in use serves rather to fix and give stability to the errors which have their foundation in commonly received notions than to help the search after truth. So it does more harm than good.

XIII. The syllogism is not applied to the first principles of sciences, and is applied in vain to intermediate axioms; being no match for the subtlety of nature. It commands assent therefore to the proposition, but does not take hold of the thing.

XIV. The syllogism consists of propositions, propositions consist of words, words are symbols of notions. Therefore if the notions themselves (which is the root of the matter) are confused and over-hastily abstracted from the facts, there can be no firmness in the superstructure. Our only hope therefore lies in a true induction. . . .

XXIV. It cannot be that axioms established by argumentation should avail for the discovery of new works; since the subtlety of nature is greater many times over than the subtlety of argument. [8.69–72]

In *The Advancement of Learning,* Bacon extends his charge against humanist learning by finding it subject to three distempers: It is fantastical, contentious, and vain (6.117). He spells out such charges.

Here therefore [is] the first distemper of learning, when men study words and not matter: whereof though I have represented an example of late times, yet it hath been and will be *secundum majus et minus* in all time. And how is it possible but this should have an operation to discredit learning, even with vulgar capacities, when they see learned men's works like the first letter of a patent or limned book; which though it hath large flourishes, yet it is but a letter? It seems to me that Pygmalion's frenzy is a good emblem or portraiture of this vanity: for words are but the images of matter; and except they have life of reason and invention, to fall in love with them is all one as to fall in love with a picture. . . . Hercules, when he saw the image of Adonis, Venus' minion, in a temple, said in disdain, *Nil sacri es,* [you are no divinity;] so there is none of Hercules' followers in learning, that is, the more severe and laborious sort of inquirers into truth, but will despise those delicacies and affectations, as indeed capable of no divineness. And thus much of the first disease or distemper of learning. [6.120–21]

Of the second kind, contentious learning, he writes of the medieval Aristotelians, the scholastics:

This kind of degenerate learning did chiefly reign amongst the schoolmen; who having sharp and strong wits, and abundance of leisure, and small variety of reading; but their wits being shut up in the cells of a few authors (chiefly Aristotle their dictator) as their persons were shut up in the cells of monasteries and colleges; and knowing little history, either of nature or time; did out of no great quantity of matter, and infinite agitation of wit, spin out unto us those laborious webs of learning which are extant in their books. For the wit and mind of man, if it work upon matter, which is the contemplation of the creatures of God, worketh according to the stuff, and is limited thereby; but if it work upon itself, as the spider worketh his web, then it is endless, and brings forth indeed cobwebs of learning, admirable for the fineness of thread and work, but of no substance or profit. [6.122]

The humanist image of the bee that signaled for humanist poetics the wide and creative search for matter for humanist fiction is here displaced by the spider, spewing forth what is already within and thus not so much creating, or nurturing, as relieving itself. The third distemper of learning comes closest to what we have seen previously as charges against poetics: "the third vice or disease of learning, which concerneth deceit or untruth, it is of all the rest the foulest. . . . This vice . . . brancheth itself into two sorts; delight in deceiving, and aptness to be deceived; imposture and credulity; which, although they appear to be of a diverse nature, the one seeming to proceed of cunning, and the other of simplicity, yet certainly they do for the most part concur" (6.125). So strong is Bacon's attack on language divorced from direct observation of actual nature that he has the least use of all for poetry, as we would expect. The attack here—and precisely on those grounds anticipated by Fracastoro and Tasso—comes most pointedly in *De Augmentis Scientiarum,* Book 2. Poetry, he says,

ad Phantasiam refertur, quae iniqua et illicita prorsus rerum conjugia et divortia comminisci et machinari solet. . . . videtur Poesis haec humanae naturae

330 · *La maladie naturelle de leur esprit*

largiri, quae historia denegat; atque animo umbris rerum utcunque satisfacere, cum solida haberi non possint.

is referred to the Imagination, which may at pleasure make unlawful matches and divorces of things. . . . Poesy seems to bestow upon human nature those things which history denies to it; and to satisfy the mind with the shadows of things when the substance cannot be obtained. [2.220–21; p. 439–40]

Once all imagined objects, all inspired beliefs, become merely shadows, there is no province left for Don Quijote to address the world, and Sancho Panza remains forever condemned to what is factious. Cervantes' whole dialectical art, which can both instruct and inspire us, collapses like a house of cards; filiation and affiliation both are subverted.

The *creative* response to the challenges of Skepticism and Baconian reason is the doubtful form of writing (*forme d'escrire douteuse*) practiced by Montaigne.[34] Though he anticipates Bacon in seeing rhetoric as a lying and deceitful art (*un'art piperesse et mensongere*, 1.51) and disparages Cicero's eloquence (2.10), he nevertheless transforms abstract philosophical issues into a successfully new, wholly Renaissance self-fashioning of persona: He creates a mental autobiography, built on a character known by his provisionary doubt (*doute provisoire*) or misgiving, doubt that is grounded entirely in the character of language and man's customary speech, his humanist rhetoric.

Nostre parler a ses foiblesses et ses defauts, comme tout le reste. La plus part des occasions des troubles du monde sont Grammairiennes. Nos procez ne naissent que du debat de l'interpretation des loix; et la plus part des guerres, de cette impuissance de n'avoir sçeu clairement exprimer les conventions et traictez d'accord des princes. Combien de querelles et combien importantes a produit au monde le doubte du sens de cette syllabe: *hoc!* Prenons la clause que la logique mesmes nous presentera pour la plus claire. Si vous dictes: Il faict beau temps, et que vous dissiez verité, il fait donc beau temps. Voylà pas une forme de parler certaine? Encore nous trompera elle. Qu'il soit ainsi, suyvons l'exemple. Si vous dictes: Je ments, et que vous dissiez vray, vous mentez donc. L'art, la raison, la force de la conclusion de cette cy sont pareilles à l'autre; toutes fois nous voylà embourbez. Je voy les philosophes Pyrrhoniens qui ne peuvent exprimer leur generale conception en aucune maniere de parler; car il leur faudrait un nouveau langage. [1.587]

Our speech hath his infirmites and defects, as all things else have. Most of the occasions of this worlds troubles are Grammaticall. Our suits and processes proceed but from the canvasing and debating the interpretation of the Lawes, and most of our warres, from the want of knowledge in State-counsellors, that could not cleerely distinguish and fully expresse the Covenants, and Conditions of accords betweene Prince and Prince. How many weighty strifes, and important quarels, hath the doubt of this one sillable, *hoc,* brought forth in the world? examine the plainest sentence that Logike it selfe can present unto us. If you say, it is faire weather, and in so saying, say true; it is faire weather then. Is not this a certaine forme of speech? Yet will it deceive us: That it is so; Let us follow the example: If you say, I lye, and that you should say true, you lye then. The Art, the reason, the force of the conclusion of this last, are like unto the other; notwithstanding we are entangled. I see the Pyrhonian Phylosophers, who can by no manner of speech expresse their Generall conceit: for, they had need of a new language.

But language is not all that makes things relative: for Montaigne, *unlike Bacon,* senses are also open to question.

Nostre fantasie ne s'applique pas aux choses estrangeres, ains elle est conceue par l'entremise des sens; et les sens ne comprennent pas le subject estranger, ains seulement leurs propres passions; et par ainsi la fantasie et apparence n'est pas du subject, ains seulement de la passion et souffrance du sens, laquelle passion et subject sont choses diverses; parquoy qui juge par les apparences, juge par chose autre que le subject. Et de dire que les passions des sens rapportent à l'ame la qualité des subjects estrangers par ressemblance, comment se peut l'ame et l'entendement asseurer de cette resemblance, n'ayant de soy nul commerce avec les subjects estrangers? Tout ainsi comme, qui ne cognoit pas Socrates, voyant son pourtraict, ne peut dire qu'il luy ressemble. Or qui voudroit toutefois juger par les apparences: si c'est par toutes, il est impossible, car elles s'entr'empeschent par leurs contrarietez et discrepances, comme nous voyons par experience; sera ce qu'aucunes apparences choisies reglent les autres? Il faudra verifier cette choisie par une autre choisie, la seconde par la tierce; et par ainsi ce ne sera jamais faict.

Finalement, il n'y a aucune constante existence, ny de nostre estre, ny de celuy des objects. [1.677−78]

Our phantasie doth not apply it selfe to strange things, but is rather conceived by the interposition of senses; and senses cannot comprehend a strange subject; Nay not so much as their owne passions; and so, nor the phantasie, nor the apparence is the subjects, but rather the passions only, and sufferance of the sense: which passion and subject are divers things: Therefore *who judgeth by apparences, judgeth by a thing different from the subject.* And to say, that the senses passions referre the qualitie of strange subjects by resemblance unto the soule: How can the soule and the understanding rest assured of that resemblance, having of it selfe no commerce with forraigne subjects? Even as he that knowes not *Socrates,* seeing his picture, cannot say that it resembleth him. And would a man judge by apparences, be it by all, it is impossible; for by their (contrarieties) and differences they hinder one another, as we see by experience. May it be that some choice apparences rule and direct the others? This choice must be verified by another choice, the second by a third: and so shal we never make an end. In few, *there is no constant existence, neither of our being, nor of the objects.* [2.399]

Since all things are in flux, nothing can be certain: Senses, like the imagination, are deceived when they attempt to give priority, or permanence, to symbol and episode. Montaigne calls this *la maladie naturelle de leur esprit;* "the naturall infirmity of their minde" (2.519; 3.405). And it is not simply this world that is forever changing; it is our perception of past texts that were themselves written in quite other times: filiation, like affiliation, is being subverted by Montaigne too. We can, in fact, measure this rather precisely. Where we saw, from Hesiod onward, the antique and humanist use of the bee as one who recombines what is old to produce something that is new, to *create,* Montaigne deliberately transforms that idea too by redeploying the image.

> Les abeilles pillotent deçà delà les fleurs, mais elles en font après le miel, qui est tout leur; ce n'est plus thin ny marjolaine: ainsi les pieces empruntées d'autruy, il les transformera et confondera, pour en faire un ouvrage tout sien, à sçavoit son jugement. [1.162]

> The Bees doe here and there sucke this, and cull that flower, but afterward they produce the hony, which is peculiarly their owne, then is it no more Thyme or Majoram. So of peeces borrowed of others, he may lawfully alter, transforme, and confound them, to shape out of them a perfect peece of worke, altogether his owne; alwaies provided, his judgement, his travell, studies, and institution tend to nothing, but to frame the same perfect. [1.178–79]

What results is *not* a new composition but a series of unending *judgments* in which reason, not the imagination, is invoked, and closure for the artist (rather than the reader) is what is emphasized.

But the problem is still further compounded for the skeptical Montaigne, for like the humanists he also saw doubt as the condition of readers when they confronted texts where they could also recognize the impossibility of closure.

Les hommes mescognoissent la maladie naturelle de leur esprit: il ne faict que fureter et quester, et va sans cesse tournoiant, bastissant et s'empestrant en sa besongne, comme nos vers de soye, et s'y estouffe. *"Mus in pice."* Il pense remarquer de loing je ne sçay quelle apparence de clarté et verité imaginaire; mais, pendant qu'il ycourt, tant de difficultez luy traversent la voye, d'em-peschemens et de nouvelles questes, qu'elle l'esgarent en l'enyvrent. Non guiere autrement qu'il advint aux chiens d'Esope, lesquels, descouvrant quelque appar-ence de corps mort floter en mer, et ne le pouvant approcher, entre prindrent de boire cette eau, d'assecher le passage, et s'y estouffarent. A quoy se rencontre ce qu'un Crates disoit des ecrits de Heraclitus, "qu'ils avoient besoin d'un lecteur bon nageur," afin que la profondeur et pois de un doctrine ne l'engloutist et suffocast. [2.519−20]

Men misacknowledge the naturall infirmity of their minde. She doth but quest and firret, and uncessantly goeth turning, winding, building and entangling her selfe in hir owne worke; as doe our silke-wormes, and therein stifleth hir selfe. *Mus in pice. A Mouse in pitch.* He supposeth to note a farre-off I wot not what apparence of cleerenesse and imaginary truth; but whilest he runneth unto it, so many lets and difficulties crosse his way, so many impeachments and new quest-ings start up, that they stray loose and besot him. Not much otherwise than it fortuned to *Æsops* Dogs, who farre-off discovering some shew of a dead body to flote upon the Sea, and being unable to approach the same, undertooke to drinke up all the Water, so that they might drie-up the passage; and were all stifeled. To which answereth that, which *Crates* said of *Heraclitus* his compositions, that they needed a Reader, who should bee a cunning swimmer, lest the depth and weight of his learning should drowne and swallow him up. [It is nothing but a particular weakenesse, that makes us [contented] with that which others or we our selves have found in this pursuite of knowledge. A more sufficient man will not be pleased therewith.] [3.405−6]

Such *fundamental doubts* thus ally Montaigne with the Pyrrhonian skeptics, like Sextus, whose radical questioning came to undermine the imagination alto-gether, rather than with the more exploratory skepticism of a Cicero who means to preserve rhetoric and poetic. Montaigne is forced to withdraw to a position that likewise not only questions but denies general validity to the imagination—and thus to a work, questioning as *it* is, such as *Don Quijote*.

What Montaigne creates instead by his essaying is actually a new mimesis, a *mimesis of the human and individual mind*. No longer is the world *out there* the subject, but the recording of the world inwardly. The individual mind is not only what is recorded but what is doing the recording: Subject and process become one. This new mimesis must then record observations alongside passions, fluctuations, disturbances, and idiosyncrasies that are always subject to change. And just as all observations, however concrete, or all ideas, however specific, are made abstract by such a process, all language is at once figural—and then by turn *metaleptical*—denying in any useful way the authentic or the verisimilar world, which had been the necessary referential coordinates for the necessary ficcíon of the humanists from Erasmus to Cervantes. This is not, then, simply a matter of contestation but truly a matter of subversion. Rabelais's copia of language now becomes a copia of fragmentation, a copia of revision that can be traced back to no beginning—can find no Senecan original—just as it can find no end or even settle into a dialectic, *in utramque partem*. The world of phenomena advanced by the New Science and the world of skepticism, even at its most creative, force out the imagination, and humanist fiction is driven into retreat. What the new age brings is the new mimesis of the mind in search—in Descartes, Browne, and Bunyan.

But fiction is, of course, only driven into *retreat*. There is no more amorphous, no more flexible form of the literary imagination than that of fiction and no more durable need, creatively, than the need for storytelling, for narrative. The survival power of fiction in Western culture is unlimited (and unmatched). When fiction resurfaces in a continuing, visible tradition, it has absorbed the phenomenal world of the scientist and the rationalizing world of the essayist, much as the Don learned to accommodate Sancho, with the realistic novels of Balzac or Zola—different as they are—or the fiction of Chekhov. The sense of ritual in Marguerite and the sense of romance in Cervantes, along with the interest in wordplay in Erasmus and the form of the voyage in Rabelais, will all contribute in their ways to the fiction of later centuries. Humanist poetics on the Continent provided Europe with a Renaissance work of art grounded in debate and dialectic (in time captured in dialogue) and posited a reader who was continually asked to interpret and judge the world of the novel. Those fundamental principles, drawing on the antique rhetoric the humanists preserved and practiced, critically and creatively, are still the fundamental forces in prose narrative in our own time. When we understand how our own fiction can still trace its ancestry back through the humanists to antique rhetoric, demonstrating the power of fiction to survive fundamental shifts in culture and cultural history, we can not only understand how it functions *dramatically and rhetorically* but realize anew its power of endurance and its power to prevail.

NOTES

CHAPTER I

1 · A. J. Krailsheimer, ed., *The Continental Renaissance, 1500–1600* (Sussex, 1978), p. 21. Because of this very fact, I have found it unavoidable to launch this study, as I introduced *Humanist Poetics,* with Erasmus's *Encomium Moriae.* I have reworked and enlarged here on the critical reading first presented there.

2 · Lucien Febvre, *Life in Renaissance France,* ed. and trans. Marian Rothstein (Cambridge, Mass., 1977), pp. 34–37.

3 · Sears Jayne, *John Colet and Marsilio Ficino* (Oxford, 1963), p. 5 et passim.

4 · Paul Oskar Kristeller, *Renaissance Thought and Its Sources,* ed. Michael Mooney (New York, 1979), pp. 174–75.

5 · Pomponazzi, *Tractatus de immortalitate animae,* ed. Gianfranco Morra (Bologna, 1954), pp. 184–204; cf. Ernst Cassirer et al., eds., *The Renaissance Philosophy of Man* (Chicago, 1948), pp. 353–63.

6 · The letter is translated by Morris Bishop, *Letters from Petrarch* (Bloomington, Ind., 1966), pp. 292 ff.

7 · *Lettere di Francesco Petrarca,* ed. Giuseppe Fracassetti (Florence, 1892), 4:422; Bishop, *Letters,* pp. 182–83.

8 · Barbara C. Bowen, "Renaissance Collections of *facetiae,* 1499–1528: A New Listing," *Renaissance Quarterly* 39, 1 (1986): 1–15; 39, 2 (1986): 263–75.

9 · Seneca, *Epistulae Morales* 73, trans. Richard M. Gummere, Loeb Classical Library (London, 1970).

10 · Cicero, *De Oratore* 1.34.157–59, trans. E. W. Sutton and H. Rackham, Loeb Classical Library (London, 1948, 1959).

11 · J. E. Spingarn, *A History of Literary Criticism in the Renaissance* (New York, 1899, 1938), p. 24.

12 · Pliny, *Letters,* trans. William Melmoth, rev. W. M. L. Hutchinson, Loeb Classical Library (London, 1915).

13 · Pliny, *Letters,* trans. William Melmoth, rev. W. M. L. Hutchinson, Loeb Classical Library (London, 1923).

14 · Cicero, *De Inventione* 2.2.4–6, trans. H. M. Hubbell, Loeb Classical Library (London, 1918, 1968).

15 · Macrobius, *Saturnalia,* ed. Franciscus Eyssenhardt (Leipzig, 1893), pp. 2–3; trans. Percival Vaughan Davies (New York, 1969), p. 27.

16 · Cicero, *Orator*, trans. H. M. Hubbell, Loeb Classical Library (London, 1939, 1962).

17 · Quintilian, *Institutio Oratoria* 8.4.1–3, trans. H. E. Butler, Loeb Classical Library (London, 1921, 1966).

18 · Victoria Kahn, *Rhetoric, Prudence, and Skepticism in the Renaissance* (Ithaca, N.Y., 1985), p. 22.

19 · Jonathan Culler, "Prolegomena to a Theory of Reading," in *The Reader in the Text*, ed. Susan R. Suleiman and Inge Crosman (Princeton, N.J., 1980), p. 65.

20 · James J. Murphy, "The Origins and Early Development of Rhetoric," in *A Synoptic History of Classical Rhetoric*, ed. Murphy (Davis, Calif., 1983), p. 7.

21 · *Ad Herennium* 1.11.18–19, 14.24, trans. Harry Caplan, Loeb Classical Library (London, 1954, 1968).

22 · Walter J. Ong, *Rhetoric, Romance, and Technology* (Ithaca, N.Y., 1971), pp. 65, 66.

23 · *Opvs Epistolarvm Des. Erasmi Roterodami*, ed. P. S. Allen (Oxford, 1910), 1:545; see also William Ringler, Introduction to John Rainolds, *Oratio in Laudem Artis Poeticae* (Princeton, N.J., 1940), p. 20.

24 · Plato, *Phaedrus*, trans. Harold North Fowler, Loeb Classical Library (London, 1914, 1977), 272D–273A.

25 · Kathy Eden, *Poetic and Legal Fiction in the Aristotelian Tradition* (Princeton, N.J., 1986), pp. 25–26.

26 · Sextus Empiricus, *Outlines of Pyrrhonism*, trans. R. G. Bury, Loeb Classical Library (Cambridge, Mass., 1933), 3.110–11. Plutarch also often expresses impatience with the Sophists. See *Praecepta gerendae reipublicae* 802E, 815B; *Life of Lucullus* 3.4; *Life of Cicero* 51.1; *Life of Lycurgus* 9.5; and *Life of Pompeius* 77.3.

27 · Plato, *Sophist*, trans. Harold North Fowler, Loeb Classical Library (Cambridge, Mass., 1921, 1952).

28 · Richard McKeon, "Literary Criticism and the Concept of Imitation in Antiquity," *Modern Philology* 34, 1 (1936): 19.

29 · Seneca, *Epistulae Morales* 65, trans. Gummere, Loeb Classical Library (Cambridge, Mass., 1925).

30 · Wesley Trimpi, "The Ancient Hypothesis of Fiction: An Essay on the Origins of Literary Theory," *Traditio* 27 (1970): 12; reprinted in *Muses of One Mind* (Princeton, N.J., 1983).

31 · Quoted and trans. in Bernard Weinberg, *A History of Literary Criticism in the Italian Renaissance* (Chicago, 1961), p. 726.

32 · Quoted and trans. in Weinberg, *History*, pp. 744, 748.

33 · Quoted and trans. in Weinberg, *History*, pp. 784–85. This paragraph is derived from Weinberg, *History*, and Spingarn, *History*, as is the one that follows.

34 · Thomas M. Greene, *The Light in Troy: Imitation and Discovery in Renais-*

sance Poetry (New Haven, 1982), chap. 3; "dialectical" imitation is discussed on pp. 45-47.

CHAPTER 2

1 · A. J. Krailsheimer, ed., *The Continental Renaissance, 1500-1600* (Sussex, 1971), p. 361.

2 · *The Letters of Aretino,* trans. George Bull (Harmondsworth, 1976), p. 175.

3 · Johan Huizinga, *Erasmus of Rotterdam,* trans. F. Hopman (London, 1952), p. 70.

4 · Introduction to *Twentieth Century Interpretations of "The Praise of Folly,"* ed. Kathleen Williams (Englewood Cliffs, N.J., 1969), p. 1.

5 · Philip Sidney, *Defence of Poesie* (1595 Ponsonby Quarto) sigs. F3-F3v; *Miscellaneous Prose of Sir Philip Sidney,* ed. Katherine Duncan-Jones and Jan Van Dorsten (Oxford, 1973), p. 100.

6 · *The Works of John Milton,* ed. Frank A. Patterson (New York, 1936), p. 220.

7 · Margaret Mann Phillips, *Erasmus and the Northern Renaissance* (London, 1949), p. 13.

8 · Huizinga, *Erasmus,* p. 4.

9 · These works and others are discussed by Genevieve Stenger in *"The Praise of Folly* and Its *Parerga,"* *Medievalia et Humanistica,* n.s. 2 (1971):97-117.

10 · For the influence of the *Imitatio,* see esp. vol. 1, chaps. 3, 12, 14, 15, 22; vol. 2, chap. 1; vol. 3, chaps. 37, 45, 46, 53, 54; vol. 4, chaps. 4, 7, 18, of *Encomium Moriae.*

11 · *Desiderii Erasmi Roterodami Opera Omnia* (Lugduni Batavorum; London, 1703); hereafter cited as *LB.*

12 · Marjorie O'Rourke Boyle, *Christening Pagan Mysteries* (Toronto, 1981), p. 8.

13 · *Opus Epistolarvm des. Erasmi Roterdami,* ed. P. S. Allen (Oxford, 1906-58), 1:439; trans. F. M. Nichols (London, 1901-18), Ep. 205; hereafter cited as *EE.*

14 · *EE* 1:545; trans. Nichols, 2:107.

15 · *LB* 1:526C; trans. William Harrison Woodward, *Desiderius Erasmus concerning the Aim and Method of Education* (New York, 1964), p. 172.

16 · *LB* 1:526C; Woodward, p. 173.

17 · *LB* 1:572F-573A; trans. R. A. B. Mynors, in *Collected Works of Erasmus* (Toronto, 1978), 23:xxiv.

18 · Brant's work catalogues a series of fools by having them talk openly about themselves; there is heavy moral satire but little real irony. The *Narrenschiff* was an unusually popular work, Englished in 1508 by Alexander Barclay as *Shyp of Folys.*

19 · *LB* 4:406C-D; trans. Thomas Chaloner (1549), sig. A1v.

20 · Folly understands logic, however, for she later claims to argue "Docebo autem non Crocodilitis, aut Sortis ceratinis, aut aliis id genus Dialecticorum argutiis" (*LB*

4:420A); "neither with *Barbara,* nor *Celarent,* nor any suche *Dialectical* quaynt subtilties" (sig. C4v).

21 · "She is a woman with a woman's varying moods, now confidential, now aloof, sometimes amused, often furious, ready to break her ironic vein to coax or plead, or to pursue some tangential thought" (Sr. Geraldine Thompson, *Under Pretext of Praise: Satiric Mode in Erasmus' Fiction* [Toronto, 1973], p. 54).

22 · This is further confounded by the Girardus Listrius commentary to the *Encomium Moriae,* a standard addition from the 1515 Basel edition onward, which is also partly Erasmus's own work. See J. Austin Gavin and Thomas M. Walsh, "The *Praise of Folly* in Context: The Commentary of Girardus Listrius," *Renaissance Quarterly* 24 (1971): 193-209.

23 · *The Panegyric* for Philip, archbishop of Austria and duke of Burgundy, declaimed at the royal castle in Brussels on 5 January 1504; George Faludy, *Erasmus* (New York, 1970), cites Erasmus's complaint about doing it (p. 97).

24 · Hoyt Hopewell Hudson, *The "Praise of Folly" by Desiderius Erasmus* (Princeton, N.J., 1941), pp. 129-42; Walter Kaiser, *Praisers of Folly* (Cambridge, Mass., 1963), pp. 35-50. See also Ephraim Emerton, *Desiderius Erasmus of Rotterdam* (New York, 1900), p. 159; Huizinga, *Erasmus,* p. 69; and Thompson, *Pretext of Praise,* pp. 53, 57, 57n., who advances a new tripartite structural arrangement (pp. 57-83).

25 · J. A. K. Thomson, *Irony: An Historical Interpretation* (London, 1929), p. 253.

26 · See Wayne A. Rebhorn, "The Metamorphoses of Moria: Structure and Meaning in *The Praise of Folly,*" *PMLA* 89 (1974): 463-76; cf. Richard Sylvester, "The Problem of Unity in *The Praise of Folly,*" *ELR* 6 (1976): 125-39.

27 · More later appears as a character in *Encomium Moriae;* see Sylvester, "Problem of Unity," p. 133n.

28 · This combination of foolery and satire is common to the period's "fool literature," such as Barclay's translation of Brant (1508) and French "Sottie" plays. See P. S. Allen, Introduction to *The Praise of Folly* (Oxford, 1913).

29 · See Phillips, *Erasmus,* p. 94.

30 · Paul Oskar Kristeller maintains that this genealogy is patterned (at least in part) after that of love in Plato's *Symposium.* See "Erasmus from an Italian Perspective," *Renaissance Quarterly* 23 (1970): 11. His view of further borrowing in the Platonic ecstasy at the close of the *Encomium* (p. 11) is correctly modified by Clarence A. Miller, "Some Medieval Elements and Structural Unity in Erasmus' *The Praise of Folly,*" *Renaissance Quarterly* 27 (1974): 510.

31 · Other companions are Self-love, Adulation, and Delicacy and her nurses Drunkenness and Rudeness.

32 · Love as the *vinculum Mundi,* the binding force of the universe, is from Plotinus; Panurge will parody this in *Le Tiers Livre* of Rabelais by making debt the binding force (3.3).

33 · Craig R. Thompson, Introduction to *Translations of Lucian*, in *The Complete Works of Thomas More* (New Haven, Conn., 1974), 3.1, p. xxxv.

34 · Plato, *Symposium* 215A−B. The Silenus of Alcibiades is also the subject of one of Erasmus's *Adagia* of 1515. See Margaret Mann Phillips, *The Adages of Erasmus* (Cambridge, 1964), pp. 269−96; Scriptures are likened to the Silenus in the *Enchiridion*. Lynda Gregorian Christian sees the Silenus as the sole thematic and structural principle of the *Encomium* in "The Metamorphoses of Erasmus' 'Folly'," *Journal of the History of Ideas* 32 (1971): 289−94.

35 · This is the same technique Erasmus used with his critics, including Dorp, to vary between accepting Folly as his spokesperson and denying her as true folly.

36 · Huizinga (*Erasmus*, pp. 74−75) finds two intertwined themes, and, later in the oration, he finds Folly dancing the tightrope of sophistry.

37 · But James D. Tracy notes that the criticism of rhetoric is "weak . . . in comparison [to that] aimed at dialectic or even grammar" (*Erasmus: The Growth of a Mind* [Geneva, 1972], p. 121).

38 · It is no accident that "Good lorde" (sig. N2v et passim) is Folly's favorite expletive.

39 · Ernst Curtius, *European Literature and the Latin Middle Ages*, trans. Willard R. Trask (New York, 1953), pp. 138 ff. Curtius argues that Erasmus's source may be Lucian, *Menippus or Necyomantia*, in *Lucian*, trans. A. M. Harmon, Loeb Classical Library (Cambridge, Mass., 1925), 4:99−101. Here, Leonard Dean finds, "The debunking is so thorough that there is no positive ground left to stand on" (in Williams, *Interpretations*, p. 52).

40 · The fictional Folly's simplistic judgment is otherwise, of course. "It was thei that raued, and had more nede than thou of *Elleborus* to purge theim, who toke in hand to driue and expell out of the, so pleasaunt, and happie a madnesse, in stede of a great disease, as thei toke it" (sig. G4v).

41 · This may be a fictional reference to the bullfights in Siena and the Vatican courtyard, which so offended Erasmus during his Italian journey in 1506−9, as the attack on Church institutions may result from his research at that time in Roman libraries. See Tracy, *Erasmus*, p. 116.

42 · Folly also refers to "my friends," Erasmus's *Adagia*, on sigs. P4v, Q4v.

43 · James D. Tracy develops a similar theory concerning Erasmus's critique of medieval religion and of contemporary education; see "Erasmus the Humanist," in *Erasmus of Rotterdam: A Quincentennial Symposium*, ed. Richard De Molen (New York, 1971), p. 44.

44 · Rosalie Colie, *Paradoxica Epidemica* (Princeton, N.J., 1966), pp. 17−21; my italics.

45 · The practice was classical in origin: "Thucydides used paired speeches to create historical distance: to set forth two points of view permits a third point of view to

be derived from the conflict of the two motives. The reader of history transcends, goes beyond, the *agon;* the historian creates a distance in the lapsed time between political debate and historical judgment" (Nancy S. Struever, *The Language of History in the Renaissance* [Princeton, N.J., 1970], pp. 18−19). The method is endemic to Platonic dialogue as well, and in the sixteenth century it became a distinguishing characteristic of much humanist writing.

46 · *EE,* Ep. 193, 1:149; trans. Nichols, pp. 425−26.

47 · Quoted in Hudson, "The Folly of Erasmus: An Essay," *Praise of Folly,* p. xviii.

48 · Lucian, *Icaromenippus,* trans. A. M. Harmon, Loeb Classical Library (Cambridge, Mass., 1915), 2:297−99.

49 · Introduction to Clarence H. Miller's translation of *Desiderius Erasmus: The Praise of Folly* (New Haven, Conn., 1979), p. xix.

50 · Phillips, *"Adages" of Erasmus,* pp. 61−62.

51 · Erasmus, *Julius Exclusus,* trans. Paul Pascal (Bloomington, Ind., 1968), p. 48. Albert Hyma, in *The Life of Desiderius Erasmus* (Assen, 1972), maintains that the *Julius Exclusus,* published anonymously because of the scurrilous attacks on the pope, is not by Erasmus.

52 · Rebhorn, "Metamorphoses," p. 463.

53 · Miller, "Medieval Elements," pp. 499−511.

54 · *EE* 1:273−74; trans. Nichols, 1:226.

55 · Boyle suggests that Erasmus had earlier borrowed the setting of the *Phaedrus* for his *Antibarbari* (*Pagan Mysteries,* p. 23).

56 · Plato, *Phaedrus,* trans. Harold North Fowler, Loeb Classical Library (Cambridge, Mass., 1914, 1977); for θειδς γ' εἰ περ νοδς λόγομς, ω φαιορε κθιατεχνιὶς θαυρατιος, Fowler has "simply a superhuman wonder as regards discourses" (p. 459), but the translation of Walter Hamilton for the Penguin Classics text (Harmondsworth, 1973), is perhaps closer in spirit to Chaloner: "Your passion for rhetoric, Phaedrus, is superhuman, simply amazing" (p. 43). Subsequent references are therefore to both translations.

57 · That is, Erasmus here Christianizes a text, as he urges the *rhetor* to do in the *Antibarbari* (and the later *Ciceronianus*) and manages to do so well himself in the *Enchiridion.*

58 · Boyle also argues (*Pagan Mysteries,* chap. 2) the importance of the *Republic* to the *Encomium Moriae.*

59 · W. David Kay, "Erasmus' Learned Joking: The Ironic Use of Classical Wisdom in *The Praise of Folly*," *Texas Studies in Language and Literature* 19 (1978−79): 247−67.

60 · Cicero, *Paradoxa Stoicorum,* trans. Newton, in *Fovvre Seuerall Treatises of M. Tvllivs Cicero* (1577), sig. M6v, Loeb Classical Library (Cambridge, Mass., 1942), proem 5.

61 · From the selection in the Introduction by Larue Van Hook to the Loeb Classical Library text of Isocrates (Cambridge, Mass., 1955), 3:56–57.

62 · The listing is taken from Henry Knight Miller, "The Paradoxical Encomium with Special Reference to Its Vogue in England, 1600–1800," *Modern Philology* 53 (1955): 152.

63 · A. E. Malloch, "The Techniques and Function of the Renaissance Paradox," *Studies in Philology*, 55 (1955): 193.

64 · Quoted in Evelyn M. Simpson, *A Study of the Prose Works of John Donne* (Oxford, 1948), p. 316.

65 · The references to Valla are from an unpublished essay, which Lisa Jardine has shared with me; the translations are hers.

66 · *LB* 1:527A–B; trans. Brian McGregor, *Collected Works of Erasmus* (Toronto, 1978), 24:683.

67 · William J. Kennedy, *Rhetorical Norms in Renaissance Literature* (New Haven, Conn., 1978), pp. 84–85.

68 · Trans. Van Hook.

69 · Joel B. Altman, *The Tudor Play of Mind: Rhetorical Inquiry and the Development of Elizabethan Drama* (Berkeley, Calif., 1978), pp. 58, 64.

70 · Thomas à Kempis, *Imitatione Christi* 1:24, trans. Leo Sherley-Price (Harmondsworth, 1952, 1976), p. 61.

CHAPTER 3

1 · Wayne A. Rebhorn, *Courtly Performances: Masking and Festivity in Castiglione's "Book of the Courtier"* (Detroit, 1978), p. 20.

2 · The edition of Vittorio Cian (Florence, 1894 et seq.) and the translation by Leonard Eckstein Opdycke (New York, 1901) cite Castiglione's borrowings in detail and with his Senecan patternings, making additional discussion here needless. In Book 4 Castiglione also leans on Bembo's *Asolani* and, in Bembo's speech and its aftermath, on the Bible (Exod. 3; Acts 2; 2 Kings 2; 2 Cor. 12; and Luke 7).

3 · Ralph Roeder, *The Man of the Renaissance* (Cleveland, 1933, 1968), p. 214.

4 · Leonard Mades, *The Armor and the Brocade* (New York, 1968), p. 67.

5 · George Bull, Introduction to the Penguin text (Harmondsworth, 1967), p. 13.

6 · The work is entitled *The School of Athens;* Lawrence V. Ryan is representative of modern scholars in calling Castiglione primarily the disciple of these two philosophers. See "Book Four of Castiglione's *Courtier:* Climax or Afterthought?" *Studies in the Renaissance* 19 (1972): 169.

7 · *LB* 1:850; trans. Craig R. Thompson, *The Colloquies of Erasmus* (Chicago, 1965), pp. 460–61.

8 · This is apparent, for example, in a 1598 imitation of Castiglione, which

mingles the light and the serious: Haniball Romei, *The Courtiers Academie: Comprehending seuen seuerall dayes discourses: wherein be discussed, seuen noble and important arguments, worthy by all Gentlemen to be perused.* They include Of Beauty, Of Human Love, Of Honor, Of Combat and single fight, Of Nobility, Of Riches, and Of precedence of Letters of Arms.

9 · Ghino Ghinassi, "L'ultimo revisiore del 'Cortegiano,'" *Studi di filologia italiana,* 22:217–64; "Fasi dell'elaborazione del 'Cortegiano,'" *Studi di filologia italiana,* 25:155–96; and his edition of *La seconda redazione del 'Cortegiano' di Baldassare Castiglione* (Florence, 1968). In the next to last redaction, Gaspare Pallavicino first appears, replacing Ottaviano as the chief critic of women; Ottaviano is then made to advocate political and social service in Book 4, and Bembo's discussion of love may be the last addition of all (in 1528). For most of this period, 1514–26, *Il Libro* consisted of only three books.

10 · Jakob Burckhardt, *The Civilization of the Renaissance in Italy,* trans. S. Middlemore (New York, 1960), p. 30; W. B. Yeats, *Collected Poems* (New York, 1941), p. 120.

11 · I am indebted for this observation to Rebhorn, *Courtly Performances,* p. 49.

12 · P. 24; pp. 9–10; citations are from the original 1528 text and the edition by Ettore Bonora (Milan, 1972), which follows closely—this supersedes the text by Cian, which misrepresents the original at several points, for which see Bruno Maier, *Giornale Storico della Letteratura Italiana* 130 (1960): 226 ff. Reliable modern English translations are by George Bull and by Charles S. Singleton (Garden City, N.Y., 1959). Citations in this chapter are to Hoby's 1561 text (rep., London, 1975). General references are by book and chapter.

13 · These further examples are cited by J. H. Whitfield in his Introduction to the modern printing of Hoby's translation (see n. 12), pp. xi–xii.

14 · Joseph Anthony Mazzeo, *Renaissance and Revolution: The Remaking of European Thought* (New York, 1965), p. 135.

15 · Kenneth Burke, *A Rhetoric of Motives* (rep., Cleveland and New York, 1962), p. 746.

16 · William J. Kennedy, *Rhetorical Norms in Renaissance Literature* (New Haven, Conn., 1978), p. 5.

17 · Quoted in James Richard McNally, *"Rector et Dux Populi:* Italian Humanists and the Relationship between Rhetoric and Logic," *Modern Philology* 76 (1978); 172.

18 · Aretino's work is summarized in some detail in Hiram Haydn, *The Counter-Renaissance* (New York, 1950), pp. 567 ff. Thomas Sackville commends Hoby's translation, remarking that *"No proude no golden Court doth he set forth, / But what in Court a Courtier ought to be"* (Hoby's trans., sig. A2v), and Gabriel Harvey in a letter circa 1578 and John Florio in his *Second Fruites* of 1591 speak of *Il Cortegiano* as a means of quickly picking up some Italian. Daniel Javitch chronicles contemporary references in "Rival Arts of Conduct in Elizabethan England: Guazzo's *Civile Conversation* and Castiglione's *Courtier,*" *Yearbook of Italian Studies* 1 (1971): 180–81. Ben Jonson praises Castiglione

in *Timber* (1640) and uses him in *Every Man in His Humour* (1601), as do John Marston in his *Satires* (1598) and *The Malcontent* (1604), John Webster and Thomas Dekker in *Westward Hoe* (1607), and Henry Peacham, Thomas Nashe, John Taylor the Water Poet, Joseph Hall, and Shakespeare. Some of these borrowings are discussed by Mary Augusta Scott, "The Book of the Courtyer: A Possible Source of Benedick and Beatrice," *PMLA* 16 (1901): 488–89.

19 · Cicero, *Brutus* 12.45; trans. G. L. Hendrickson, Loeb Classical Library (Cambridge, Mass., 1939, 1962).

20 · Pico makes this distinction to Barbaro in a letter of June 1455 in which he "distinguishes between the subject-matter of rhetoric and philosophy. The former deals with words, the latter with things (*res*). . . . The orator affects verbal ornaments; he must persuade, and to succeed in it he must stoop to deception. The philosopher's sole business is in knowing (*cognoscenda*) and demonstration of truth (Quirinus Breen, "Giovanni Pico della Mirandola on the Conflict of Philosophy and Rhetoric," *Journal of the History of Ideas* 24 [1963]: 498).

21 · J. R. Woodhouse, *Baldesar Castiglione: A Reassessment of "The Courtier"* (Edinburgh, 1978), p. 55: "The complexity of new political alignments and the internal problems of court diplomacy, required the subtlety of chess rather than the brusqueness of a duel or a tourney (now reduced largely to a ceremonial role)."

22 · The most considered view of this dark side of *Il Cortegiano* can be found in Lauro Martines, "The Gentleman in Renaissance Italy: Strains of Isolation in the Body Politic," in *The Darker Vision of the Renaissance: Beyond the Fields of Reason*, ed. Robert S. Kinsman (Berkeley, Calif., 1974), pp. 77–93.

23 · Robert Grudin, "Renaissance Laughter: The Jests in Castiglione's *Il Cortegiano*," *Neophilologus* 58 (1974): 201.

24 · Cf. Dain A. Trafton, "Politics and the Praise of Women: Political Doctrine in *The Courtier*'s Third Book," an unpublished essay shared with me by the author (pp. 13–14): "The Magnifico assembles an impressive collection of women who benefitted their countries because they understood—often better than their men—the need for martial virtue. Persian women who shamed a routed Persian army into returning to battle (III.32); Spartan women 'who rejoiced in the glorious death of their sons . . . who disowned or even slew their sons when they saw them act like cowards' (III.33); women of Saguntum who fought against Hannibal (III.33); Pisan women 'who in the defense of their city against the Florentines showed that generous courage, without any fear whatever of death, which the most unconquerable spirits that ever lived on earth might have shown' (III.36); Queen Isabella of Spain, to whom 'alone is the honor of the glorious conquest of the kingdom of Granada to be attributed' (III.35)."

25 · Quoted in Rebhorn, *Courtly Performances*, p. 62; the quotation from Raphael is taken from Vicenzo Golzio, ed., *Raffaello nei documenti, nelle testimonianze dei contemporanei e nella letteratura del suo secolo* (Vatican City, 1936), p. 31.

26 · I am indebted for some of these observations to Rebhorn, *Courtly Performances*, p. 96.

27 · See Mazzeo, *Renaissance and Revolution*, p. 133.

28 · This deliberately reverses the scene in Book 1, which concluded with a dance displacing debate. In *Il Cortegiano*, the importance of the mind is shown in the way it surrounds and subordinates physical activity.

29 · Ryan, "Book Four."

30 · One slight measure of the effectiveness of this conclusion to *Il Cortegiano* is Romei's imitation, Englished by one I.K. in 1598. This too moves toward the metaphysical: "Out of question the man learned, in bountie and dignitie will be superiour to the soulder; in that hee learned, is endewed with that vertue, which maketh a man like to things diuine. For science and sapience which be incident to the learned, by meane of contemplation, make a man companion with God, vniteth him with chiefe good, and true felicitie" (sig. 2N3v).

31 · Ficino's Basel, 1561, text as ed. and trans. Sears Reynolds Jayne, *Marsilio Ficino's Commentary on Plato's "Symposium": The Text and a Translation with an Introduction*, University of Missouri Studies (Columbia, 1944), pp. 45–46, 137.

32 · Cicero, *De Oratore* 1.20.85, trans. E. W. Sutton and H. Rackham, Loeb Classical Library (Cambridge, Mass., 1942, 1969). The following discussion of Cicero and Aristotle was first advanced in *Humanist Poetics*, pp. 123–29.

33 · Quoted and translated in Daniel Javitch, *Poetry and Courtliness in Renaissance England* (Princeton, N.J., 1978), p. 22n. Remensis's comments come in his preface to Francis I, in *In Omnes De Arte Rhetorica M. Tul. Ciceronis Libros Doctissimorum Virorum Commentaria*.

34 · Cicero, *Orator*, 2.7–8, trans. H. M. Hubbell, Loeb Classical Library (Cambridge, Mass., 1939, 1962).

35 · Quintilian, *Institutio Oratoria* 12.10.78; the translation is a paraphrase of H. E. Butler's text (Loeb Classical Library [Cambridge, Mass., 1922, 1968]).

36 · For a detailed study of the manuscript changes and their import, see Ryan, "Book Four." Woodhouse, *Castiglione*, chap. 6, makes a number of applications of Aristotelian doctrine to *Cortegiano 4*; see also Alfred D. Menut, "Castiglione and the *Nicomachean Ethics*," *PMLA* 58 (1943): 309–21.

37 · Aristotle, *Politics*, trans. H. Rackham, Loeb Classical Library (Cambridge, Mass., 1932, 1977).

38 · Aristotle, *Ethics*, trans. H. Rackham, Loeb Classical Library (Cambridge, Mass., 1926, 1975).

39 · See Javitch, *Poetry and Courtliness*, pp. 30–31, where he develops the point in related ways.

40 · Rebhorn makes a number of other connections (*Courtly Performances*), pp. 161–68.

41 · Cicero may be another source for Castiglione's understanding of the form of

the symposium, especially the *Tusculan Disputations*, where the participants are isolated from the practical and routine affairs of reality at Tusculum, much as the courtiers are at Urbino: "in qua disputationem habitam non quasi narrantes exponimus, sed eisdem fere verbis, ut actum disputatumque est"; "there a discussion took place which I do not present in narrative form, but as nearly as I can in the exact words of our actual discussion" (2.4.10)—trans. J. E. King, Loeb Classical Library (Cambridge, Mass., 1927, 1971). Richard A. Lanham further notes how this form allows Castiglione "to prohibit any single-orchestration coziness. He leads us in several directions at once" (*The Motives of Eloquence: Literary Rhetoric in the Renaissance* [New Haven, Conn., 1976], p. 144).

42 · This material has been conveniently gathered by William Harrison Woodward in *Vittorino da Feltre and Other Humanist Educators* (Cambridge, 1897; rep., New York, 1963). Vittorino taught Duke Federico at Urbino; Woodward sketches his portrait (pp. 20–21) and his curriculum (p. 38) and provides an extensive discussion of ideas and his influence. Woodward also translates the texts cited here. Readers of *Il Cortegiano* will find in Vergerius apposite discussions of the function of arts and letters (pp. 103–4); the Greek curriculum, which resembles that of *Cortegiano 2* (p. 107); the use of emulation (pp. 87, 98); and cautions about the misuse of rhetoric (p. 99). Bruni's treatise is for women, but he gives his chief praise to oratory—and to eloquence (p. 128). Piccolomini, too, praises the study of letters (p. 141), grammar and rhetoric (p. 154), and style (p. 143) and stresses the need for a good disposition in the student himself (p. 136)—that is, he sees education as a matter of nature and art.

43 · *Opere Volgari di Leon Batt. Alberti* (Florence, 1849), 5:11–12; trans. Renée Neu Watkins (Columbia, S.C., 1969).

44 · The text and translation are from Michael J. B. Allen, ed. and trans., *Marsilio Ficino: The "Philebus" Commentary* (Los Angeles, Calif., 1975), pp. 143, 142.

45 · The problem is further complicated by the historical Bembo, who once answered a friend who inquired about life at the authentic Urbino, "What do we do here? There is little to tell: we laugh, we jest, we play games, we invent new tricks and practical jokes, we study and sup, and now and then write verses" (quoted in Roeder, *Man of the Renaissance*, p. 232).

46 · Tasso: "Mentre dureranno le Corti, mentre dureranno i Principi, le donne e i Cavalieri insieme si raccoglieranno; mentre valore e cortesia avranno albergo negli animi nostri, sarà in pregio il nome del Castiglione"; "While Courts shall last, while Princes shall endure, and ladies and knights shall meet together; while valour and courtesay shall have an abode in our souls, the name of Castiglione shall remain precious to us."

CHAPTER 4

1 · A. Mary F. Robinson, *Margaret of Angoulême, Queen of Navarre* (London, 1896), p. 91.

2 · L. Cazamian, *A History of French Literature* (Oxford, 1955), p. 66.

3 · Hugh M. Richmond, *Puritans and Libertines: Anglo-French Literary Relations in the Reformation* (Berkeley, Calif., 1981), p. 73.

4 · Marcel Tetel, *Marguerite de Navarre's "Heptameron": Themes, Language, and Structure* (Durham, N.C., 1973), p. 3.

5 · Jules Gelernt, *World of Many Loves: The Heptameron of Marguerite de Navarre* (Chapel Hill, N.C., 1966), p. 12.

6 · Michelet quoted in Percy W. Ames, Introduction to Elizabeth I's translation of *The Mirror of the Sinful Soul* (London, 1897), p. 36.

7 · Maurice Valency, *In Praise of Love* (New York, 1958).

8 · Citations to *L'Heptaméron* are to the definitive and accessible French edition by Michel François (Paris: Éditions Garnier, 1967) and to the recent translation by P. A. Chilton for Penguin Classics (Harmondsworth, 1984).

9 · Plato, *Theaetetus*, trans. Harold North Fowler, Loeb Classical Library (Cambridge, Mass., 1921, 1961).

10 · Plato, *Sophist*, trans. Harold North Fowler, Loeb Classical Library (Cambridge, Mass., 1921, 1961).

11 · Plato, *Symposium*, trans. W. R. M. Lamb, Loeb Classical Library (Cambridge, Mass., 1925, 1961).

12 · Plotinus, *Enneads*, trans. Stephen McKenna (New York, n.d.), pp. 191–92.

13 · Augustine, *Confessions*, trans. William Watts, Loeb Classical Library (Cambridge, Mass., 1912, 1960).

14 · Thomas O. Sloane, *Donne, Milton, and the End of Humanist Rhetoric* (Berkeley, Calif., 1985), p. 102.

15 · Citations are to the Editions Garnier, p. 1., and to the Chilton trans., p. 60. Interpolations are from De Thou's 1559 text.

16 · Chilton discusses this in his Introduction, pp. 7–8.

17 · Donald Stone, Jr., "Observations on the Text of the *Histoires des omans fortunez*," *Renaissance Quarterly* 32, 2 (1980): 201–13.

18 · Tetel makes this same point (*Marguerite's "Heptameron,"* pp. 141 ff.), as have others.

19 · In the foregoing discussion, I am following Gelernt, *World of Many Loves*, pp. 18–24.

20 · In these descriptions, I am indebted to the detailed analysis of Betty J. Davis, *The Storytellers in Marguerite de Navarre's "Heptaméron"* (Lexington, Ky., 1978), and to discussions with Professor Davis.

21 · A. J. Krailsheimer, "The *Heptameron* Reconsidered," in *The French Renaissance and Its Heritage: Essays presented to Alan M. Boase by Colleagues, Pupils, and Friends* (London, 1968), p. 78.

22 · Chilton, *Introduction*, p. 21.

23 · Pierre de Bourdeille (Abbé de Brantôme), *The Lives of Gallant Ladies*, trans. Alec Brown (London, 1961), pp. v–vi.

24 · Quoted in Tetel, *Marguerite's "Heptameron,"* p. 10.

CHAPTER 5

1 · Quoted in J. M. Cohen, Translator's Introduction to *The Histories of Gargantua and Pantagruel* (Harmondsworth, 1955), p. 17.

2 · Mary E. Raglund, "A New Look at Panurge," *Hartford Studies in Literature* 8:61.

3 · Alice Fiola Berry, "Rabelais: Homo Logos," *Journal of Medieval and Renaissance Studies* 3:51.

4 · This felicitous phrase is from Samuel Putnam's Introduction to *The Portable Rabelais* (New York, 1946, 1960), p. 39.

5 · Quoted in Donald M. Frame, *François Rabelais: A Study* (New York, 1977), pp. 11–12; the original is from Rabelais, *Oeuvres complètes*, ed. P. Jourda (Paris, 1962), 2:499–500.

6 · Quoted in C. S. Lewis, *English Literature in the Sixteenth Century Excluding Drama* (Oxford, 1954), p. 52.

7 · See Mikhail Bakhtin, *Rabelais and His World*, trans. Helene Iswolsky (Cambridge, Mass., 1965), pp. 452–53.

8 · Quoted in Putnam, Introduction, p. 4.

9 · A. J. Krailsheimer, *Rabelais and the Franciscans* (Oxford, 1963), p. 209.

10 · 1.232; p. 177. References are to the modern publication of the 1542 text by P. Jourda, and the modern Penguin translation by Cohen.

11 · Quintilian, *Institutio Oratoria*, trans. H. E. Butler, Loeb Classical Library (London, 1921,1966), pp. 319–23.

12 · So an annotation in a 1588 copy of *Pantagruel* cited in Lewis, *English Literature*, p. 125.

13 · A. J. Krailsheimer, ed., *The Continental Renaissance, 1500–1600* (Sussex, 1971), p. 304.

14 · Floyd Gray, "Ambiguity and Point of View in the Prologue to Gargantua," *Romantic Review* 56:16.

15 · Thomas M. Greene, *Rabelais: A Study in Comic Courage* (Englewood Cliffs, N.J., 1970), p. 24.

16 · Walter Kaiser, in *Praisers of Folly* (Cambridge, Mass., 1963), p. 104, notes that the abbey's motto is a translation of a sentence Erasmus wrote against Luther.

17 · Numerous other references, often made in passing, keep the possible connections between both worlds before us. Thus we find, in a work with allusions to contemporary Frenchmen and his father's own feud with a neighbor, references in Rabelais to

Tunstall (1.23) and to Peter Giles (5.31) as well as to Nowhere Island (4.2) and Raphael (3.16); Gargantua, we are reminded (1.8) is king of Utopia. Here too the Amaurots are seen as the major force (1.28–31). Other resonances occur because of the common use of Plato, Plutarch, and Lucian.

18 · Richard A. Lanham, *The Motives of Eloquence: Literary Rhetoric in the Renaissance* (New Haven, Conn., 1976), p. 176.

19 · Lucian, *How to Write History,* trans. W. Kilburn, Loeb Classical Library (Cambridge, Mass., 1959).

20 · M. A. Screech, *Rabelais* (London, 1979), pp. 224–25.

21 · Plutarch, *Moralia,* trans. Harold North Fowler, Loeb Classical Library (Cambridge, Mass., 1936, 1960).

22 · Cicero, *De Officiis* 2.24.84, trans. Walter Miller, Loeb Classical Library (Cambridge, Mass., 1913, 1975).

23 · This subject is treated at length by Screech in "Aspects of Rabelais's Comedy," his inaugural lecture at the University of London (1968), p. 12, and in *Rabelais,* pp. 270 ff.

24 · Screech, *Rabelais,* p. 266.

25 · Cf. Greene, *Rabelais,* pp. 5, 6.

26 · Krailsheimer, *Rabelais and the Franciscans,* p. 283. This is the best concentrated survey of Rabelais's indebtedness to classical writing.

27 · Screech also makes this observation in *Rabelais,* p. 7.

28 · Herodotus, *Historia* 2.35, trans. A. D. Godley, Loeb Classical Library (Cambridge, Mass., 1920, 1966).

29 · Dorothy Gabe Coleman makes many acute remarks on Rabelais and Lucian throughout *Rabelais: A Critical Study in Prose Fiction* (Cambridge, 1971); see esp. chap. 4.

30 · Hippocrates, *Aphorisms,* trans. W. H. S. Jones, Loeb Classical Library (Cambridge, Mass., 1923).

31 · Galen, *The Diagnosis and Cure of the Soul's Errors,* chap. 1, trans. Paul W. Harkins (Columbus, Ohio, 1963).

32 · See *Galen on Language and Ambiguity,* trans. Robert Blair Edlow (Leiden, 1977).

33 · Screech, *Rabelais,* p. 322.

34 · Lucian, *True Story,* trans. A. M. Harmon, Loeb Classical Library (Cambridge, Mass., 1913, 1929), p. 275.

35 · Noted in Screech, *Rabelais,* p. 323.

36 · Cicero, *De Finibus* 3.6–7.21–26, trans. H. Rackham, Loeb Classical Library (Cambridge, Mass., 1914, 1971).

37 · Screech discusses sources, precedents, and analogues in *Rabelais,* pp. 411 ff.

38 · Plato, *Cratylus,* 383A–384D, trans. H. N. Fowler, Loeb Classical Library (Cambridge, Mass., 1926, 1977).

39 · The most recent and most detailed argument collecting "les innombrables faiblesses et incongruitès que le Ve livre prèsente" (p. 179) is Alfred Glauser, La Faux Rabelais (Paris, 1975). Screech doubts its authenticity; Greene would award Rabelais chaps. 1–8, 11–15, 45, 47.

CHAPTER 6

1 · The editions of Cervantes cited throughout are the authoritative reprints of the first editions of 1605 and 1615 for Biblioteca Breve de Bolsillo (Barcelona, 1968) and the translation by J. M. Cohen for Penguin Classics (Harmondsworth, 1950, 1984). This passage is in Book 2, chap. 32; 2:179; p. 685.

2 · Mark Van Doren, Don Quixote's Profession (New York, 1958), p. 69.

3 · Frederick Willey, "Don Quixote and the Theatre of Life and Art," Georgia Review 31 (1977): 913.

4 · Harold C. Jones, "Grisóstomo and Don Quixote: Death and Imitation," Revista Canadiense de Estudios Hispánicos 4, 1 (1979): 87–89, develops this at some length.

5 · John G. Weiger, The Substance of Cervantes (Cambridge, 1985), p. 221.

6 · Michael Bell, Cervantes (Norman, Okla., 1947), p. 327.

7 · "Herodotus or Aëtion," in the works of Lucian, trans. K. Kilburn, Loeb Classical Library (London, 1959), 6.143.

8 · Michael Zappala, "Cervantes and Lucian," Symposium 33 (1979): 66; he also relates A True Story to the Prologo (p. 65).

9 · Lucian, True Story, trans. A. M. Harmon, Loeb Classical Library (Cambridge, Mass., 1913, 1929), 1:251–53.

10 · Lucian, Icaromeniopus, trans. A. M. Harmon, Loeb Classical Library (Cambridge, Mass., 1915), 2:287–89.

11 · Alban K. Forcione, Cervantes, Aristotle, and the "Persiles" (Princeton, N.J., 1970); the remarks in this paragraph are derived from chap. 2, "Heliodorus and Literary Theory."

12 · Quoted in Forcione, Cervantes, pp. 57–58, n. 21; the translation is also his (p. 57).

13 · This was first pointed out by Colbert I. Nepaulsingh, "Cervantes, Don Quijote: The Unity of the Action," Revista Canadiens de Estudios Hispánicos 3 (1978): 252.

14 · Mary Mackey, "Rhetoric and Characterization in Don Quijote," Hispanic Review 42 (1974): 51–54.

15 · Edwin Williamson, The Half-way House of Fiction: "Don Quixote" and Arthurian Romance (Oxford, 1984), p. 138.

16 · Anthony Close, "Don Quixote's sophistry and wisdom," Bulletin of Hispanic Studies 55 (1978): 104.

17 · Aristotle, The "Art" of Rhetoric, trans. John Henry Freese, Loeb Classical Library (London, 1925).

18 · Nepaulsingh, "Cervantes," pp. 239–57.

19 · See ibid., p. 251.

20 · W. D. Snodgrass, "Glorying in Failure: Cervantes and Don Quixote," *Malahat Review* 28 (1973): 18.

21 · J. Huizinga, *The Waning of the Middle Ages,* trans. F. Hopman (Garden City, N.Y., 1954), p. 39.

22 · Most of these comments on chivalric life and fiction are drawn from Williamson, *Half-way House,* chap. 1, esp. pp. 6–15.

23 · Ramon Menendez Pidal, "The Genesis," trans. George I. Dale, in *The Anatomy of Don Quixote: A Symposium,* ed. M. J. Bernardete and Angel Flores (Ithaca, N.Y., 1932), p. 19; the other works cited here are discussed by Pidal on pp. 8–9, 22–23.

24 · For those unfamiliar with the work, there is a good discussion of *Amadís de Gaula* in Manuel Durán, *Cervantes* (New York, 1974), pp. 114 ff.

25 · "The first great quality of Don Quixote, natural and admirable, is his impeccable courage. . . . But Don Quixote's courage has in it a finer element than that of the adventurer for El Dorado. It is also the courage of the Spanish saint and martyr, like St. Teresa, the courage of one who follows a spiritual vision through every peril and perplexity. But a saint could not well be the hero of a comedy; and Cervantes had to make him what the saint sometimes verges on, or appears to the world to be, a madman, the victim of a fixed idea, yet no less fundamentally sane than the great saints from St. Paul ('I am not mad, most noble Festus!') to St. Francis" (Herbert J. Grierson, *"Don Quixote": Some War-time Reflections on Its Character and Influence,* English Association Pamphlet no. 48 [London, 1921], pp. 7–8).

26 · The Spanish text and translation are from *The Poems of St. John of the Cross,* 3rd ed., ed. and trans. John Frederick Nims (Chicago, 1979), pp. 38–39.

27 · Leo Lowenthal, *Literature and the Image of Man: Studies of the European Drama and Novel, 1600–1900* (Boston, n.d.), p. 21.

28 · Ruth S. El Saffar, *Beyond Fiction: The Recovery of the Feminine in the Novels of Cervantes* (Berkeley, Calif., 1984), p. 49.

29 · "Benengeli tells much of the story unobtrusively, but there are times when he steps out from behind the scenes and plays the role of intruding narrator. Let us glance at the kind of things he says on these occasions, most of which occur in Part II. He may complain about the self-imposed restriction of writing only on Don Quixote and Sancho (II.44). A run in Don Quixote's stocking may inspire him to cry out against poverty (II.44). He may confirm his characters' interpretation of the name 'Countess Trifaldi' (II.38). Most often he is concerned with his characters themselves: He thinks Don Quixote might have laughed on seeing Sancho tossed in a blanket if he hadn't been so angry (I.17). He debates the authenticity of Don Quixote's report of his descent into the cave of Montesinos (II.24). Reflecting on the conduct of the Duke and Duchess, he concludes that the mockers are as mad as the mocked (II.70). He confirms the notion that Sancho was a charitable soul (II.54). He exclaims that he would have given his best

mantle for the chance to have witnessed the scene in which Don Quixote leads the distressed Doña Rodríguez into his bedroom (II.48). He is tremendously proud that his writing proved equal to the task of reporting Don Quixote's deeds (II.74)" (Richard L. Predmore, *The World of Don Quixote* [Cambridge, Mass., 1967], p. 5).

30 · "Meraviglianoci di quelle cose, che oltre alla nostra openione accadeno, massimamente doue elle sì attamente sien congiunte, che l'una paia dopo l'altra ragionevolmente seguire", "We marvel at those things which occur contrary to our expectation, particularly when they are so aptly joined that the one seems to follow the other by reason" (Antonio Sebastiano Minturno, *L'arte poetica* [Venice, 1564], p. 40, as quoted in Forcione, *Cervantes,* p. 33, n. 43, and trans., p. 33).

31 · Citations to Tasso are from Torquato Tasso, *Discorsi dell'Arte Poetica e del Poema Eroico,* Scrittori d'Italia n. 228 (Bari, 1964), p. 74, and from *Discourses on the Heroic Poem,* trans. Mariella Cavalchini and Irene Samuel (Oxford, 1973), p. 1.

32 · Ruth S. El Saffar, *Novel to Romance: A Study of Cervantes's "Novelas ejemplares"* (Baltimore, 1974), p. 6.

33 · Juan Bautista Avalle-Arce, "Background Material on *Don Quixote,*" in *Approaches to Teaching Cervantes' "Don Quixote,"* ed. Richard Bjornson (New York, 1984), p. 131.

34 · Helena Percas de Ponseti, "The Cave of Montesinos: Cervantes' Art of Fiction," in *Don Quixote,* Norton Critical Edition, ed. Joseph R. Jones and Kenneth Douglas (New York, 1981), p. 983.

35 · Otis H. Green makes this point in *Spain and the Western Tradition* (Madison, Wisc., 1968), 1:196.

36 · Sebastian Juan Arbó, *Cervantes: Adventurer, Idealist, and Destiny's Fool,* trans. Ilsa Barea (London, 1955), p. 252.

37 · Statistics are from William Byron, *Cervantes: A Biography* (London, 1978), p. 442.

38 · Ibid., p. 425.

39 · Melveena McKendrick, *Cervantes* (Boston, 1980), p. 11.

40 · Lionel Trilling, "Manners, Morals, and the Novel," in *The Liberal Imagination: Essays on Literature and Society* (New York, 1957), pp. 202–3.

CHAPTER 7

1 · Victoria Kahn, *Rhetoric, Prudence, and Skepticism in the Renaissance* (Ithaca, N.Y., 1985), pp. 19–20. She cites Rosemond Tuve, *Elizabethan and Metaphysical Imagery* (Chicago, 1947), p. 180 et passim; Robert Jauss, "Literary History as Challenge," in *Toward an Aesthetic of Reception,* trans. Timothy Bahti (Minneapolis, 1982), pp. 21, 22.

2 · Edward W. Said, *The World, the Text, and the Critic* (Cambridge, Mass., 1983), pp. 174–75.

3 · *Prosatori latini del quattrocento,* ed. E. Garin (Milan and Naples, 1952),

pp. 390–92, quoted in Anthony Grafton and Lisa Jardine, *From Humanism to the Humanities: Education and the Liberal Arts in Fifteenth- and Sixteenth-Century Europe* (Cambridge, Mass., 1986), p. 34.

4 · Grafton and Jardine, *Humanism to Humanities*, pp. 66–80 et passim.

5 · "Letter to the University of Oxford," in *The Complete Works of St. Thomas More*, ed. and trans. Daniel Kinney (New Haven, Conn., 1986), 15:138–39.

6 · See J. K. Sowards, Introduction to *Collected Works of Erasmus* (Toronto, 1985), 25:xiv.

7 · Nancy Struever, "Lorenzo Valla: Humanist Rhetoric and the Critique of the Classical Languages of Morality," in *Renaissance Eloquence: Studies in the Theory and Practice of Renaissance Rhetoric*, ed. James J. Murphy (Berkeley, Calif., 1983), p. 206.

8 · Thomas M. Greene, *The Vulnerable Text: Essays on Renaissance Literature* (New York, 1986), p. xii.

9 · Roger Ascham, *The Scholemaster*, in *Elizabethan Critical Essays*, ed. G. Gregory Smith (Oxford, 1904), 1:20.

10 · Cicero, *De Oratore*, trans. E. W. Sutton and H. Rackham, Loeb Classical Library (Cambridge, Mass., 1942, 1969).

11 · *The Confutation of Tyndale's Answer*, in *The Complete Works of St. Thomas More*, ed. Louis A. Schuster, Richard C. Marius, James P. Lusardi, and Richard J. Schoeck (New Haven, Conn., 1981), 8:605.

12 · Cf. Matt. 23:27; Psalm 12; Matt. 6:19–20.

13 · Michael O'Connell, "Authority and the Truth of Experience in Petrarch's 'Ascent of Mount Ventoux,'" *Philological Quarterly* 69 (1983): 516–17.

14 · This observation is indebted to Klaus Oehler, "Der Consensus omnium als Kriterium der Wahrheit in der antiken Philosophie und der Patristik," *Antike und Abendland* 10 (1961): 103–10, via Kahn, *Rhetoric*, p. 32.

15 · Katharine Eisaman Maus, *Ben Jonson and the Roman Frame of Mind* (Princeton, N.J., 1984), p. 6.

16 · Lynette Hunter, *Rhetorical Stance in Modern Literature: Allegories of Love and Death* (London, 1984), p. 74.

17 · Patrick Grant, *Literature and the Discovery of Method in the English Renaissance* (Athens, Ga., 1985), p. 3.

18 · Quoted in Howard Felperin, *Beyond Deconstruction: The Uses and Abuses of Literary Theory* (Oxford, 1985), p. 209.

19 · Girolamo Fracastoro, *Navagero; or, A Dialogue on the Art of Poetry*, trans. Ruth Kelso, University of Illinois Studies in Language and Literature, 9:3 (1924), sigs. RRI–RRIv; p. 58. Later citations are to this edition.

20 · Tasso, *Discorsi dell'Arte Poetica e del Poema Eroico* (Bari, 1964), p. 85; *Discourses on the Heroic Poem*, trans. Mariella Cavalchini and Irene Samuel (Oxford, 1973), pp. 26–27.

21 · Cicero, *Academica,* trans. H. Rackham, Loeb Classical Library (London, 1933, 1979).

22 · Cicero, *De Natura Deorum,* trans. H. Rackham, Loeb Classical Library (London, 1933, 1979). I have noted the effects of Cicero and Sextus previously in *Humanist Poetics;* see pp. 436−37, 439−41.

23 · *LB* 4:462A−C; trans. Chaloner, sigs. L3v−L4.

24 · Copernicus refers to *Academica* 2.39.122 and cites specifically 2.39.123.

25 · Mary Mills Patrick, *The Greek Skeptics* (New York, 1929), p. 270.

26 · Nashe adapts Sextus's praise of dogs in a passage of a hundred lines in *Summers last will,* sigs. D4v−E1 (*The Works of Thomas Nashe,* ed. Ronald B. McKerrow, rev. F. P. Wilson [Oxford, 1958], 3:254−56), although he is at least acquainted with his position as early as his prefatory remarks to Sidney's *Astrophil and Stella,* sig. A4v; 3:332. See also *Pierce Penilesse,* sigs. B3v, C3v, D1v−D2, F1; 1:173, 185, 188−89, 206. Nashe presumably cites a 1591 translation of Sextus no longer extant. See *Works,* 5.120, 122; Richard H. Popkin, *The History of Scepticism from Erasmus to Descartes* (Assen, 1960), p. 18, n. 5.

27 · *Sexti Empirici* (Paris, 1569), sig. ee3v; trans. R. G. Bury, *Outlines of Pyrrhonism,* Loeb Classical Library (London, 1933, 1976).

28 · He also undermines humanist rhetoric in much the same way (3.30.267−69).

29 · Balachandra Rajan, *The Form of the Unfinished* (Princeton, N.J., 1985), pp. 19−20.

30 · Ronald Levao, *Renaissance Minds and Their Fictions* (Berkeley, Calif., 1985), p. 332.

31 · Lucien Febvre, *Life in Renaissance France,* ed. and trans. Marian Rothstein (Cambridge, Mass., 1977), p. 41.

32 · A. Wigfall Green, *Sir Francis Bacon* (New York, 1966), p. 106.

33 · *The Works of Francis Bacon,* ed. James Spedding, Robert Leslie Ellis, and Douglas Denon Heath (New York, 1864 et seq.), 1:16, 8:241.

34 · Montaigne, *Essays,* 2:12. The textual references are to *Oeuvres completès,* ed. Albert Thibaudet and Maurice Rat (Paris, 1962), and the English translation of John Florio (1603; rep., London, 1908).

INDEX

Dante Alighieri, 137, 184
Davis, Betty J., 346
Dean, Leonard, 339
declamation, 13–14, 48–51, 53, 55–56,
58, 61–62, 65, 75–76, 81, 85–87,
96, 104, 106, 110, 115–16, 119–20,
122, 131, 133, 188, 202–3, 229, 256,
291, 311; deliberative, 49, 194, 311;
epideictic, 49, 53, 76, 256; judicial, 49,
256, 291. See also orations; suasoria
deduction, 84, 108, 314, 323–24, 327
Dekker, Thomas, 343
Demetrius, 10. Works: De Elocutione, 10;
Olynthiacs, 10; Philippics, 10
demonstration, 39
Demosthenes, 5, 15, 47, 306, 311. Work:
Philippics, 10
Descartes, René, 334
Desperriers, Bonaventure, 139
Devotio Moderna, 48
dialectic, xiii, 28, 45, 64, 66–67, 70, 94,
97, 105, 132, 134–36, 140–43, 151,
155, 159–63 passim, 179, 197, 204,
223, 236, 243, 258–59, 261, 272,
288–90, 299, 304, 306–8, 311–12,
314–15, 317, 320–21, 324, 334
Dickenson, John, 79. Work: Greene in conceipt, 79
diegesis, 235
dilemma, 80–81, 156, 161, 185–86
Dio Cassius, 10
Diogenes the Cynic, 203–6, 209, 222
Dionysius of Halicarnassus, 10, 311
Dionysius the Areopagite, 138. Work:
Opuscula, 183
Diotima, 108, 128, 141–42, 148–49, 156
dispositio, 66, 79–80, 125, 128, 134,
254–55, 268
disputation, 13, 24–28, 41, 48, 55–62,
74, 81, 83–84, 87, 91, 97, 99–101,
104, 106–7, 109, 119, 130–31, 135,
143, 152, 158, 186, 188–89, 208–9,
229, 232, 236, 243, 250–51, 255–56,
259, 268, 270–72, 274–76, 278, 291,
311, 320, 327, 330–31, 334. See also
controversia
dissimulation, 104, 106–8, 124, 133–34,
137, 160, 169–71, 315–16, 326
Dive Bouteille (Divine Bottle) (Rabelais),
183, 214, 222, 228

Dolce, Lodovico, 19
dolce stil, 141
Don Quijote (Cervantes), 38, 58, 235–307,
330, 334, 350–51
Donne, John, 75
Dorotea (Princess Micomicona) (Cervantes),
276–77
Dorp, Martin, 47, 65, 78, 339
Dousa, James, 75. Work: In Laudem Um-
brae, 75
Dovizi, Bernardo ("Bibbiena") (Cas-
tiglione), 95–96, 105, 128
Duchess (Cervantes), 250, 255, 259, 291,
293, 302, 350
Duke (Cervantes), 250, 255, 259, 274,
291, 293, 302, 350
Dulcinea del Toboso (Aldonza Lorenzo)
(Cervantes), 238–39, 248, 250, 252,
267–73, 280, 291, 293–94, 299,
301–2
Durán, Manuel, 350
Dyer, Edward, 76. Work: Prayse of
Nothing, 76

Eden, Kathy, 31, 38, 336
Elean Stranger (Plato), 145–48, 153, 156
Elizabeth I, 72, 89
ellipsis, 49
elocutio, 80
Emerton, Ephraim, 338
Encina, Juan del, 263
encomium, xiii, 14, 18, 22, 45–48,
50–89, 97, 106, 208; encomium moriae (as classification), 91, 207, 216
Ennasuite (Marguerite), 157, 164
Ennius, 205
enthymeme, 39, 258–59, 263, 314
epic, xiv, 42, 110, 292
Epicurus, 320
Epistemon (Rabelais), 186, 191, 215, 222,
226
epoche, 323
Equicola, Mario, 19
Erasmus, Desiderius, xiii–xiv, 4–5, 13–
14, 22, 24, 28–29, 40, 43, 45–88, 91,
97, 99, 112, 134–35, 137–38, 140–
42, 162, 178, 181–84, 191, 196–97,
201, 203, 210, 221, 226, 229, 236,
250, 256, 259, 261, 267–68, 281,
284, 306, 310, 314, 322–23, 334,

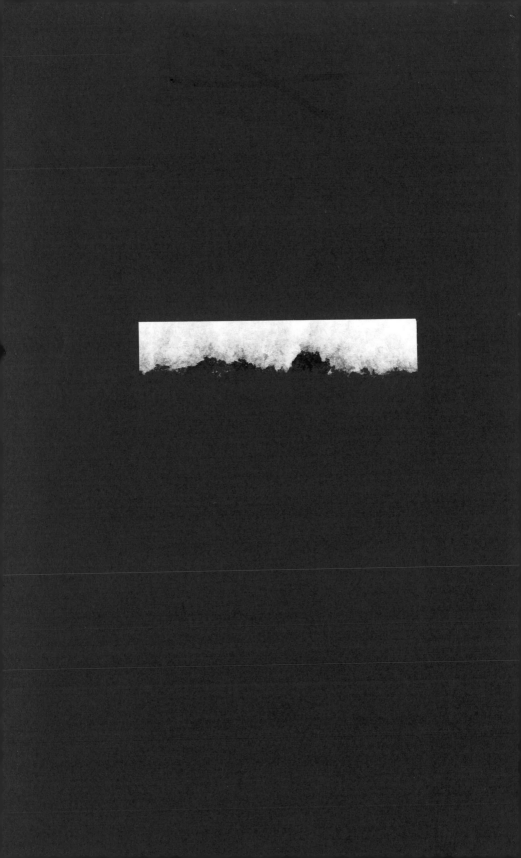